Solving Cold Cases

Solving Cold Cases

Investigation Techniques and Protocol

JOE D. KENNEDY
with HOGAN HILLING

Exposit
Jefferson, North Carolina

ISBN (print) 978-1-4766-8765-0
ISBN (ebook) 978-1-4766-4531-5

LIBRARY OF CONGRESS AND BRITISH LIBRARY
CATALOGUING DATA ARE AVAILABLE

LIBRARY OF CONGRESS CONTROL NUMBER 2022055519

© 2023 Joe D. Kennedy and Hogan Hilling. All rights reserved

No part of this book may be reproduced or transmitted in any form or by any means, electronic or mechanical, including photocopying or recording, or by any information storage and retrieval system, without permission in writing from the publisher.

Front cover images © Shutterstock/Photographee.eu

Printed in the United States of America

Exposit is an imprint of McFarland & Company, Inc., Publishers

Exposit
Box 611, Jefferson, North Carolina 28640
www.expositbooks.com

To the families and friends
of murdered victims
where the case remains unsolved.
Continue to cherish those precious memories
of your murdered loved one and cling to the hope
that their case will one day be solved.
I pray that the peace and blessings
of our Lord will always be upon you!

Acknowledgments

From Joe:
I would like to thank my wife, Janet Kennedy, and coauthor, Hogan Hilling, for their untiring support to finish this book. It simply would not have happened without you!

From Hogan:
I would like to thank Joe Kennedy for giving me this opportunity and also for his confidence, faith, and trust to help him write this book.

Table of Contents

Acknowledgments — vi
Note by Joe D. Kennedy — ix
Preface — 1
Introduction — 9

1. Evolution and Popularity of Solving Cold Cases — 39
2. Empathy for the Victims, Their Families, and Detectives — 61
3. The Biology and Physics of Cold Case Investigation — 81
4. The Difference Between a Cold and Fresh Homicide Case — 102
5. Gumshoe Work Precedes DNA Evidence — 130
6. My Gumshoe Methodology and Cold Case Checklist of Investigative Steps — 162
7. Legal and Proper Ways to Collect Evidence and Intelligence — 194
8. Meeting of the Minds with Witnesses and Suspects — 218
9. Forensic Genealogy's Role in Law Enforcement — 243
10. Lessons Learned — 272
11. Unsolved Cold Cases — 280
12. More Cold Case Success Stories — 293

Appendix A: Resources and Support Services — 311
Appendix B: List of Cases in Order of Appearance in This Book — 318
Chapter Notes — 321
Bibliography — 339
Index — 355

Note by Joe D. Kennedy

With regards to the cold cases I did not solve that are included in this book, the information provided is based on facts that were published in newspaper articles. Therefore, I consider all the information written by the reporter to be correct.

As with every homicide case, human error occurs, and sometimes detectives miss a crucial step during the initial investigation that impedes their ability to identify the murderer. Often, these missteps are unintentional and a result of legal or social issues beyond a detective's control.

In some cases, detectives have circumstantial evidence that identifies the killer but not enough physical evidence to warrant probable cause for further investigation. In other cases, detectives identified the killer but were unable to arrest him or her because there was not sufficient evidence.

The purpose of sharing these cold case stories is not to criticize or scrutinize the detectives but rather to applaud them for their diligent work to identify the killer, solve the case, and bring resolution to the victims and their families.

Preface

While I was growing up in High Point, North Carolina, baseball consumed much of my time. I had the good fortune of living in a city in which the local businesses and community religiously sponsored and supported youth sports. I had great Little League coaches who instilled hard work, competitive spirit, and a great love for the game of baseball; they helped hone my skills to have the opportunity to play baseball in high school and college.

During my junior year at Pfeiffer College, I realized that I did not have the talent to play baseball beyond college and needed to find another vocation. Baseball offered me an opportunity to prove I was good at something. Now I had to prove to myself that I could be good at something other than baseball.

I dreaded school but understood how important it was to attain a college degree. After enrolling in a law enforcement class, I was hooked and felt as though God was telling me that this was my calling and that I would be good at it. Giving up my dream to play professional baseball was not easy. However, the game of baseball laid the foundation for me to pursue another profession I have grown to love and enjoy—a career as a detective!

Baseball is a sport that reflects real life, and although the rules and challenges are different, my work as a detective has many similarities to baseball.

The crime of murder is also a reality in life. As a detective and a public servant, I bear the responsibility of identifying the criminal and solving the case. There is no time limit. There is an end game, but I don't know exactly when, and I work the extra innings I need until I solve the case.

The rules of baseball provide players with many opportunities to succeed at the plate. Yet batters only succeed in hitting the ball less than 30 percent of the time. As in life, we fail more than we succeed. Those failures make us better and stronger, helping us to be better competitors the next day.

A baseball player may take one for the team with a sacrifice bunt or fly; detectives also make sacrifices for the good of the community as they seek justice for victims and resolution for victims' families.

Baseball is a game of inches. One inch determines whether you hit a ball fair or foul; whether you hit a single, double, triple, or home run; whether you throw a strike or ball; whether you catch or drop a fly ball. This is also true in life and detective work. In a murder case, one inch is all it takes to profoundly alter a person's life. And one inch or one small mistake can be the difference between solving and not solving a murder case.

During a baseball game, unlike basketball or football, there is a lot of tedious downtime, like in between pitches and innings. This is also true of detective work: stakeouts, surveillance, writing reports, and trial appearances.

Detectives deal with curveballs in every investigation. There are times when a witness's testimony or incorrect information temporarily diverts me from identifying the suspect or leads me on a wild goose chase. This creates a lot of missed opportunities to solve the case sooner. Nevertheless, eventually, I succeed at identifying the killer(s).

Law enforcement is a team sport. Although I excel individually, it requires a team to solve a murder case.

Lastly, baseball umpires police the game. Sometimes they miss a call, and sometimes they make the correct call. As a detective, sometimes I solve a case and sometimes I do not.

Life is baseball and baseball is life. Detective work is my life and one that I love and enjoy.

Before I share how I began my career as a detective, I would like to briefly reveal how the opportunity to write this book came across my desk.

In June of 2018, I received an email from Hogan Hilling. He had watched the debut of *Wrong Man*, a documentary series I participated in as a core team expert. It chronicles the criminal convictions of three men who claim their innocence. Hilling shared a story about his visit with an incarcerated dad, Darius Walker, whom he featured in one of his fatherhood books. Walker was serving a life sentence for a murder conviction. During the visit, Walker claimed his innocence. Several weeks later Darius mailed Hilling copies of his court transcripts. Hilling reviewed them and felt that there was merit to his claim.

As Hilling watched *Wrong Man*, he noticed that the evidentiary and witness testimony problems in Walker's case were like those of the three inmates' cases on the show. Hilling asked if I'd review Walker's case; I agreed and scheduled a telephone call.

After a lengthy review of the information Hilling sent me, I determined that there was merit to Walker's claim of innocence and pitched Walker's case to director Joe Berlinger and the *Wrong Man* producers for their second show in 2019. They all agreed to consider Walker's case for the next show. Then, I called Hilling to share the good news.

During our telephone conversation, I mentioned that people in my network suggested I write a book and that I had written a rough draft of a manuscript that had been collecting dust for 20 years. Hilling, who had authored 10 books, offered to review my manuscript and also help me write my book and pitch it to a publisher. I accepted his invitation with open arms and have enjoyed the journey of writing this book with him.

My career as a detective began in 1986, after the Naval Criminal Investigative Service (NCIS) hired me as a nonmilitary special agent. NCIS is a federal law enforcement agency that employs special agents to protect the U.S. Navy and Marine Corps. NCIS agents are stationed in every state and in countries throughout the world. NCIS's primary function is to investigate criminal activities that involve the U.S. Navy and U.S. Marine Corps. NCIS's broad mandate also includes national security, counterintelligence, counterterrorism, cyberwarfare, and the protection of U.S. Naval assets worldwide.

My primary responsibility was initially drug enforcement and operating undercover, but I also handled felony crimes and homicide cases. Although I enjoyed working narcotics and being undercover, which took up most of my time, I felt the need for more challenging work and took an interest in tackling more homicide cases. Eventually, NCIS assigned me to work homicides and set up the first federal cold case homicide unit.

In my early years with NCIS I developed a reputation as a good interviewer and interrogator with an unorthodox style of investigating. My approach was quite different from those of other detectives. I approached working a murder case from an "undercover perspective." Detectives often attack a case like a great white shark during interviews and interrogations. I used a different tactic like a wolf in sheep's clothing but for the purpose of good instead of evil.

My unorthodox approach was a direct result of how my parents raised me. My mom and dad taught me to never judge anyone regardless of race, ethnicity, socioeconomic status or what accomplishments or failures a person had in their past. They taught me to treat all people with dignity and respect, so that is what I did with all the criminals I encountered. I feel this is why I have been successful.

I subsequently entered the management ranks of NCIS and quickly developed a desire and passion to solve cold cases. In 1995 I solved my first cold case, the homicide of Dana Bartlett, a U.S. Navy Lieutenant. Lieutenant Bartlett was brutally murdered by three individuals in St. Thomas, U.S. Virgin Islands, in June of 1993. His case remained unsolved for 18 months. In February of 1995, I led a special NCIS task force to join the local and federal officers in the search for the person responsible for Bartlett's murder. It took us 33 days to solve this cold case. After we identified Nefta Petersen as one of Lieutenant Bartlett's killers, we took him into custody. During the interview he confessed to the robbery and the murder, implicating Ansel Eli Cielto and a minor. I'll share more information about how I solved this case in Chapter 1 as well as about other cold cases in subsequent chapters.

Solving my first cold case gave me a sense of satisfaction and purpose like I had not experienced since playing baseball. The sense of purpose was extreme since our investigation team was able to solve a case that other investigators, including the local FBI office, had been unable to solve. I am never satisfied and consider myself a perfectionist, so the case opened the door for more challenges and re-instilled a sense of purpose that was perhaps missing in my life since graduating from college. My true motivation for becoming a police officer and detective, however, is that I'm a fact finder and truth seeker. I enjoy searching for facts that will lead me to the truth. Wherever the truth is, that's the road I follow because I'm passionate about the truth and would like it to prevail.

During my years as a cold case investigator I also developed empathy and compassion for the victims and their families. And these have become driving forces that fuel my continued passion to solve cold cases.

Jim Adcock, PhD, is the founder of Mid–South Cold Case Initiative (now called The Homicide Project), a nonprofit whose purpose is to aid departments looking to improve their cold case units. He has been raising concerns to police leadership and anyone else who will listen about the cold case crisis he claims is taking place in America's big city police departments. The data tells a grim story of thousands of murders for which no one has been held accountable. "If we don't address it, the issue is just going to get worse," according to Adcock. "The hole we're in is just going to get deeper and deeper."[1]

Because of the increasing number of unsolved homicides, I agreed to accept an invitation I received from John Wiggins to assist with operations of a company he founded called BlueLine Training Group. BlueLine provides professional and tailored training programs to meet the challenging needs of law enforcement officers, departments, and the community. John named the company based on the term "thin blue line," a figure of speech for any thinly spread military unit holding firm against attack. The phrase has also taken on the metaphorical meaning of the barrier the relatively limited armed forces of a country present to potential attackers.

"The thin blue line" is a phrase that refers figuratively to the position of law enforcement, in which a police officer is a rock between chaos and crimes and the law-abiding citizens. But "the thin blue line" means more to me. I feel it is also the difference between good and evil. Good cops have to think like criminals and anticipate what they will do next without crossing the line from good to evil. The "thin blue line" is a cop's choice of selecting to serve good over evil, and it is truly a "thin blue line."

The "thin blue line" is also about the special brotherhood, relationship, love, respect, and admiration police officers have for their profession and one another, which is evident in my professional relationship with John.

John and I met through the North Carolina Homicide Investigators Association annual conferences. John lived and worked in eastern

North Carolina. He and I connected on a personal level because of similar upbringing and a strong belief in Jesus Christ and the teachings of the Bible. However, no one would ever say we were "religious." John was also a perfectionist, like me, so we naturally got along well.

As our relationship grew, we learned from each other and shared our passion for solving cases and making sure investigations were conducted thoroughly and in the proper fashion. John is a natural leader, and one of the biggest reasons is because he truly cares about people. He leads by example and has taught me the many qualities it takes to be a leader.

I truly believe a career in law enforcement was my calling. A scene from a *Columbo* episode, "The Bye-Bye Sky High IQ Murder Case," explains it best. Columbo engages in another psychological battle with a murderer, Oliver Brandt, who has one of the highest IQs in the world. He kills his business partner, who threatened to expose the killer for stealing money from his clients. Brandt uses all his intelligence to plan what he believes is the perfect murder. Of course, Columbo solves the murder.

After Columbo exposes Brandt's mistake and proves he committed the murder, Brandt concedes that Columbo outwitted him. Brandt is so impressed that he invites Columbo to answer a difficult IQ question. Columbo answers it correctly, which prompts Brandt to ask, "Have you ever considered a different line of work?"

"Never, I couldn't do that," Columbo answers.

While there are many books that delve into the mind of criminals who commit murder, you will get an opportunity to learn how my mind as a cold case investigator works and why I've been successful in solving such cases. This book will share an in-depth, behind-the-scenes look into how a cold case is reopened and investigated as well as how I have solved cold cases and how other detectives and law enforcement agencies have used my methodology to solve them.

I hope this book will inspire investigators to solve cold cases and encourage people to assist police in their respective communities in their efforts to identify and convict killers. But more importantly, I hope it will provide families of the victims of unsolved murders with hope and resources in pursuing justice and resolution for the loss of their loved ones.

I also hope this book will enhance appreciation for all the men and women who work in law enforcement, especially the detectives, who exemplify the true meaning of "the thin blue line" and sincerely work hard to serve and protect the citizens in their communities.

—J.D.K.

Introduction

Like every good idea, the creation of my cold case methodology didn't happen overnight, and I did not do it alone. It developed over time and with the help of a long list of exceptional people I met during my career that included detectives, DNA experts, medical examiners, prosecutors, forensic scientists, genealogists, and other crime experts.

In 1988 I teamed up with Naval Criminal Investigative Service (NCIS) Special Agent Eddie Hemphill. Special Agent Hemphill was a master at interrogation techniques. He told me, "You just got to get the person talking. It does not matter what subject or topic. Just encourage him to keep talking." Eddie's approach was to talk to the suspect until the suspect finally asked, "Aren't we here to talk about the murder?" Eddie's technique taught me not to force the information you seek from a suspect, to take it easy and slow, and that it is easier to collect information if the suspect feels he or she is in control of the conversation.

In 1990 at NCIS Resident Agency in Charleston, South Carolina, I worked with Elaine Kelly. Kelly was a feisty officer manager who kept a tight rein over her team, which completed administrative tasks for all the NCIS agents and investigators in the office. Elaine paid me a huge compliment. She said, "I think you are one of the best investigators in the office. I have a cold case I would like you to review. The victim's name is Kimberly Shawn Vaught." Elaine handed me a crumpled cardboard box full of old investigative files, coffee-stained notes, and photographs. That is how I was introduced to my first cold case. I had never read one before.

I spent several days reviewing Vaught's case, but because of my caseload I had to set it aside and work on other, fresh homicide cases that needed immediate attention. Although I never had an opportunity to fully investigate and solve Vaught's case, it jumpstarted my career as a cold case detective.

In 1991 I partnered with Detective C. W. "Butch" Henerey of the North Charleston Police Department. He was one of the best detectives I worked with and a great mentor. I gained a tremendous amount of knowledge from him, especially during my time with the Low Country Serial Rapist and Missy McLauchlin Homicide Task Forces. Both focused on catching street-smart offenders.

From Detective Henerey I learned how to prepare for an investigation and network with people and confidential informants as well as that whom you know is more important than what you know. Butch was a master at persuading other people to help him solve a case. He placed great emphasis on teamwork and taught me the importance of doubt.

In February of 1995, NCIS assigned me to lead a cold case task force with local and federal officers in the United States Virgin Islands. The case involved the 1993 murder of U.S. Navy Lieutenant Dana Bartlett. I share the details of the investigation in Chapter 1.

When I reached out to other law enforcement agencies and detectives for help, I was surprised to discover that nobody had an official list of standard procedures or guidelines to investigate or solve a cold case. And none of the detectives I talked with who worked cold cases had a specific methodology for them. I felt I had the passion, confidence, and skill to investigate a cold case but no road map or set of instructions. Nevertheless, I marched on.

After my team and I spent countless hours and worked 33 days straight, we found the killer and officially solved my first cold case that led to a conviction.

The closing of Lieutenant Bartlett's cold case inspired me not only to gain more knowledge on how to investigate a cold case but also, more importantly, to possibly develop a methodology to help other detectives and agencies improve their chances of solving cold cases.

For the next few months I traveled the United States to learn how other law enforcement agencies worked cold cases. I worked 16-hour days and visited 15 agencies, including the Metro Dade-Miami Cold Case Unit, the Boston Cold Case Squad, and the North Carolina State Bureau of Investigation Murders Unsolved Team. I met exceptional

Introduction 11

detectives, like Sergeant David Rivers from Metro-Dade Miami and Tim Murray and Stephen Murphy from the Boston Police Department. They all eagerly shared their knowledge and experiences with me, and I documented everything I learned from them. After I returned to my home office in Washington, D.C., I spent two months racking my brain and developed a methodology that led to creating a standard guideline that included a checklist of chronological steps for detectives to follow when investigating a cold case. I feature the list in Chapter 6.

Not only did the long hours and hard work pay off, but I also had the good fortune of timing on my side. Prior to 1990, law enforcement agencies did not place a high priority on solving cold cases due to a lack of manpower and funding. In the early 1990s, political and public pressure led law enforcement officials to reform their operation policies, which included creating cold case units and reactivating cold cases. In 1991 and 1992 two grassroots organizations, the Vidocq Society and the Innocence Project, jumpstarted the crusade to solve cold cases.

In September of 1995, after I presented a weeklong training course for the Federal Law Enforcement Training in Glynco, Georgia, NCIS officially adopted the methodology I compiled for cold cases.

By 1996 news of my methodology had spread quickly, and the International Association of Chiefs of Police recognized it as a semifinalist for the prestigious Webber Seavey Award. Later that year I met Special Agent Jon Perry of the Virginia State Police Department, who had over 40 years of law enforcement experience.

Perry played an instrumental part in refining my methodology. He placed great emphasis on determining motive, means, and opportunity when evaluating the photos of a cold case murder scene. He taught how to read behavioral clues in crime scene photos in order to learn more about the victim and killer, how the killer committed the crime, and what was going through the killer's mind during the murder.

In 1997, after I presented the methodology to the National Sheriffs' Association, other domestic and international law enforcement agencies invited me to create a training course for cold case detectives. Some of the agencies included the Utrecht Police Department in the Netherlands, Japan National Police, and Philippine National Police.

In 2002, during a cold case training session in the Philippines,

I met Detective Dennis Baldonado of the Philippine National Police Department. I joined him in the investigation of the terrorist murder case of Sergeant First Class Mark Jackson. Sergeant Jackson died on October 2, 2002, when a nail bomb carried by a terrorist on a motor scooter exploded outside a restaurant near Jackson's base camp in Zamboanga, Philippines. The bomb also wounded a U.S. colleague and 23 Filipinos.[1]

During the investigation, I learned a valuable lesson from Detective Baldonado. He taught me how to roam around, talk to people, and ask the right questions. His support and assistance played a valuable role in identifying Abu Sayyaf, a Filipino terrorist group linked to al-Qaeda, as the group responsible for the bombing and a known Abu Sayyaf bomb maker, Alhabsy Misaya, as the main suspect.[2]

Over the next two decades, as the demand for my cold case training course grew, I refined my methodology and the list of investigative steps. Some of the improvements included how to reconstruct a crime scene from photos, work with the victim's family, solicit public support and assistance, conduct interviews and interrogations, and review 911 calls, as well as updated information about inventions of new technologies like the M-Vac and sciences like forensic genealogy. Since 1995 my methodology has led to the successful resolution of various cold cases.

Investigating and solving a murder is a daunting task. Cases can be complex and complicated and require patience and expertise developed through years of experience in responding to middle-of-the-night death scenes. The smallest misapprehension of facts can sidetrack investigators and derail the investigation, resulting in a cold case. Solving a cold case murder is much more complicated and challenging for investigators. A murder case is typically designated as a cold case if one year or more has passed and the case remains unsolved and/or the original detective is no longer working the case. Essentially every cold case contains clues that were ignored, misinterpreted, or overlooked. Cold cases involve uncompleted investigative leads. The majority of cold cases have multiple potential suspects, no suspects, or one person who has always been the suspect but has never been charged. Investigators must reconstruct the facts of the case to find overlooked clues and develop proactive investigative strategies to identify the correct perpetrator.

Cold case investigations must be conducted in a proactive, not reactive, fashion. Responding to a contemporaneous murder and crime scene enables investigators to use the five senses of smell, sight, sound, touch (feel), and taste as they carry out investigative activities. Investigators get a "feel" for the case as they examine the crime scene and interview witnesses. Images of dead bodies and evidentiary items littered throughout crime scenes are stored in their memories. However, cold case investigators must rely on old investigative files, photographs, previous witness statements, and faded memories to put the puzzle pieces together. Cold cases are labor-intensive and time-consuming. It can be difficult to locate old witnesses, references, and points of origin. Language can change significantly in older cases. Reconstructing the original investigation requires patience and attention to detail.

Investigating and solving a cold case will challenge even the most seasoned investigator. Cold cases require investigators to be patient tacticians. Many excellent investigators and homicide detectives lack the wherewithal to work cold cases. The typical frustrations (e.g., uncooperative witnesses, lack of physical evidence, failure to obtain a confession from the suspect, risk-averse prosecutors, etc,) are magnified with a cold case. A cold case is similar to the game of chess, as investigators evaluate and re-investigate leads in a strategic fashion. Otherwise, the case will likely remain cold.

> According to the FBI, the national "clearance rate" for homicide today is 64.1 percent. Fifty years ago, it was more than 90 percent. And that's worse than it sounds, because "clearance" doesn't equal conviction: It's just the term that police use to describe cases that end with an arrest, or in which a culprit is otherwise identified without the possibility of arrest—if the suspect has died, for example. Criminologists estimate that at least 200,000 murders have gone unsolved since the 1960s, leaving family and friends to wait and wonder.[3]

As cold case investigators reactivate old cases, it is important to remember that in only one of every five cold cases will a "conclusively identified" suspect be found in the investigative file. There is a cold case crisis in the United States. "In 1965, approximately 80% of homicide cases were cleared, according to the FBI's Uniform Crime Reports, but in 2017 only about 60% of homicide cases were resolved and more than 100,000 have accumulated in the past 20 years alone."[4]

Criminal investigations and homicide cases conducted by law enforcement agencies, especially those that turn cold, are routinely scrutinized. Details in an investigation are important. And to ensure that all the pertinent facts are recorded, every fresh homicide investigation is comprised of four phases. The first is *analysis*, in which a detective determines whether the case has merit, if it falls within the jurisdiction of the responsible law enforcement agencies, and if the information is valid regardless of the motive(s). Next is *programming*, which outlines the legal steps a detective must follow to obtain information and essential elements that prove the commitment of a crime. The third phase is *fact-finding*. A detective must establish whether elements exist or don't exist in a homicide case from the evidence he collects through interviews; observations; the testimony of witnesses; and examination of records, documents, and physical evidence. The last phase is *verification and evaluation*, in which a detective must establish the accuracy and authenticity of a witness's testimony, records, and physical evidence collected during the fact-finding phase. Throughout the investigation, information obtained should be checked against the outline or programming. Detectives must also resolve conflicting testimony or information and take into account witnesses' interests, biases, prejudices, integrity, reputations, sense deficiencies, and the manner in which they acquired the information.[5]

Although fresh homicide detectives do their best to abide by the four phases of an investigation, the proper evaluation of prior witnesses' testimony and statements is often lacking in many cold cases. The inconsistencies found in the information documented by the original investigators must be thoroughly analyzed and are of great importance for reactivated cold cases. When evaluating a cold case, these four phases of the investigative process are conducted in a backward fashion, and investigators must pay close attention to them. The following questions must be asked: (a) Was a proper analysis done at the onset of the original investigation, and did the crime happen the way original investigators believed or reported that it happened? (b) Was the programming phase of the investigation strategic or tactical, and what investigative leads were overlooked, ignored, misinterpreted, or not completed? (c) What facts are accurate, misleading, or missing, and what potential suspects were not fully evaluated and pursued? and (d)

Was proper verification and evaluation conducted, and was alibi information confirmed and/or refuted during the original investigation? In addition to these questions, cold case investigators must determine if the suspect pursued in the original investigation is the correct suspect. Just like with a hot murder, the verification and evaluation phase is critical as the four phases of the investigative process are essentially worked in a backward order with cold cases.

While incorporating these four phases of the investigative process into a homicide investigation, there are three key components needed for developing the probable cause, identifying the suspect(s), and solving the murder(s). These include (1) identifying and locating witnesses who have pertinent knowledge about the person(s) responsible for the crime; (2) gathering physical evidence that will link a suspect to the crime; and (3) obtaining a confession from the suspect(s). Few murders are solved by having all three of these components. Many are solved from witness testimony provided by a credible witness or confessions from suspects. Of course, witness statements and confessions from suspects must be corroborated. A smaller percentage of murders are solved solely with physical evidence. The best-case scenario is to secure all three components (i.e., witness testimony, physical evidence, and suspect confession) before an arrest warrant is obtained. However, in many instances, investigators secure only one or two of these three key components. These same three components are what solve cold cases. However, many cold cases can only be solved with a confession from the suspect. Experienced cold case detectives understand that success relies heavily upon their ability to create rapport and trust with suspects. The case will hinge on the investigator's interview and interrogation skills. Cold case investigators often must obtain a confession from the suspect before formal criminal charges can be filed. Discovering DNA, fingerprints, or other physical evidence is unlikely in the majority of cold cases.

Few murders are planned, and many murders happen during the commission of other crimes. Most murders are committed by a single perpetrator and involve a single victim. Altercation murder is the most common type of murder, and most victims are killed with firearms. The next most common murder weapons are sharp instruments. When sharp instruments are used, younger perpetrators use them with a higher degree of frequency than older offenders. When there is a significant amount of slashing and stabbing to the victim coupled with a sloppy crime scene (e.g., blood transfer, signs of a physical struggle, overturned furniture, misplaced objects, etc.) suspicion should first be placed on younger potential suspects.

Approximately two-thirds of murders are committed outdoors, while the other third are committed indoors. If the victim was found in a private residence, the case is more likely to be solved. If the victim found in the private residence is a female, the case is more likely to be solved than if the victim was a male. If the victim was found indoors rather than outdoors, there is a better chance the case will be solved. These percentages and case resolution trends apply to cold cases as well. The more recent the cold case the more likely it will be solved. Cold cases that are between eight and fourteen years old provide investigators with the best chance of a successful resolution. Cold cases not involving illegal drugs or drug users are more likely to be solved. Murders involving homosexual victims can be very difficult cold cases to solve. Murders of prostitutes are likewise difficult to investigate and solve as cold cases. Individuals who murder prostitutes often have prior arrests for solicitation or solicitation-of-a-prostitute charges in their criminal backgrounds. Cold case investigators should pay attention to individuals with these past criminal charges/convictions when narrowing down lists of potential suspects for cold case prostitute murders. Old missing person cases present the biggest challenge for cold case investigators. Unless there is a specific investigative angle to pursue with the reactivated investigation, these cases should be last in priority. Experience has shown that they are difficult to solve. Unidentified bodies and skeletal remains cases are likewise difficult to pursue as a cold case unless DNA and forensic genealogy can identify the victim. It is important to use solvability factors when deciding which cold case to reactivate. Solvability factors will help identify those cases that have the best chance of being solved. This book includes a solvability factors worksheet to assist cold case investigators with prioritizing cases.

There is most often a relationship, however slight, between the suspect and victim prior to the murder. In the majority of murders, victims are killed by people who know them or had a prior relationship with them. A smaller percentage of murders in the United States are committed by strangers. When evaluating cold cases, keep the focus on the suspect(s) who had some type of relationship (e.g., intimate, temporary, long-term, short-term, indirect, causal, brief, contentious, etc.) with the victim. The length of the relationship or association doesn't matter, just that there was one. Suspects with close ties to the victim or the victim's family and/or interfamilial relationships often hold the key to solving cold cases that have no apparent motive or prevailing theory as to why the victim was murdered. Be careful and do not assume there is a close personal relationship between the suspect and victim based on evidence of overkill (e.g., excessive stab wounds, extensive blunt force trauma, etc.) at the crime scene. If ligatures and restraining devices are present, there was likely a sexual component to the murder. This should be considered before exploring other motives unless it was obviously another crime gone bad (e.g., robbery, burglary, home invasion) or the victim was restrained so the primary crime could be completed.

Cold cases present many investigative challenges. There is no "perfect" investigation, regardless of the jurisdiction or law enforcement entity conducting the investigation. A *suspect-based investigation*, which tends to be the norm in American law enforcement agencies, concentrates on eliminating suspects until a viable or "most likely" suspect is identified. Investigative focus is then placed on that individual. On the other hand, *evidence-based investigations* are more precise and rely on evaluating all information and evidence for all potential suspects to determine who is responsible for the crime. Do not try to make a theory fit the crime. What is the crime scene telling? Read the crime scene for behavioral clues. Investigators must consider all potential suspects when following the evidence. Following the evidence and not "your theory" will solve cold cases, but following suspects will likely result in frustration, disappointment, and an unsolved case. A large majority of cold cases were suspect-based investigations when conducted originally. Investigators should pay attention to the crime scene clues, witnesses' recollections of events, and inconsistencies, not the suspects listed in the investigative file. Accurately reading the behavioral clues at the scene, correctly interpreting the smallest details of witness statements, and finding the inconsistencies will help narrow the pool of suspects. At that point, investigators can concentrate investigative activities on a particular suspect. Once a viable suspect has been identified, the investigative focus is then placed on that person. Cold case investigators must be aware of tunnel vision, confirmation bias, and groupthink as the case is reactivated. Remember what the crime scene is showing. For example, if wound pattern analysis of the injuries sustained by the victim was on the right side of the victim's head and body, this could suggest the killer was perhaps left-handed. Therefore, the reactivated cold case might initially focus on the suspects in the original investigation that were left-handed.

The following murder case from North Charleston, South Carolina, illustrates how behavioral clues left at a crime scene must be evaluated so the "correct" suspect is pursued. In June of 1990, I was assigned to Naval Criminal Investigative Service (NCIS) Resident Agency Charleston, South Carolina, working a joint homicide investigation with the North Charleston Police Department (NCPD). The case involved Ronald L. Parham, a U.S. Navy member assigned to the Naval Weapons Station in Goose Creek, South Carolina, who killed his wife, Deborah Parham, by repeatedly stabbing her in the chest and abdomen with a steak knife. The murder took place in the corner room on the second floor of the Super 8 Motel on Ashley Phosphate Road off Interstate 26 in North Charleston. Before fleeing the scene, Ronald Parham placed a bed pillow over his wife's face.[6] While at the crime scene and prior to developing Ronald Parham as a viable suspect, NCPD Sergeant Roger Pierce and I talked about the significance of the bed pillow being placed over the victim's face. It told us that there was likely an interpersonal relationship between them. The act of covering the face indicates the suspect likely knew the victim and was potentially remorseful for his actions. The suspect would not have placed the pillow over Deborah Parham's face had there not been a relationship between him and the victim. We subsequently captured Ronald Parham after a high-speed chase on Interstate I-95 in North Carolina. Ronald Parham lost his left leg after being hit by a car as he ran into the highway to avoid capture. He later pled guilty to killing his wife.

I worked on many joint investigations with NCPD and learned a tremendous amount from their investigators about how to investigate and solve cases. What I learned most from NCPD detectives was the importance of investigating rather than documenting. Many investigators merely document information as it is related to them by witnesses and persons of interest. Investigating requires doing little things that solve cases, like a thorough neighborhood canvass at a crime scene, detailed witness statements, informant recruitment and development, and quality interrogations of the suspect(s). NCPD Detective C. W. "Butch" Henerey was perhaps the best investigator I have ever encountered. He mentored me on numerous occasions as I worked alongside him. He was a humble servant and legendary investigator. I gained a tremendous amount of knowledge while working with him, especially on the Low Country Serial Rapist Task Force and the Missy McLauchlin Homicide Task Force. Butch taught me dozens of little tips about how to be a successful investigator. However, being prepared and having as much knowledge as possible about murder investigations were the two greatest things Butch taught me. He taught me that being prepared was important for solving murders. Preparation included having as many sources of information, professional contacts, networks of individuals, and informants as possible. Butch further taught me that whether someone is a good investigator depends on whom they know and not what they know. He was a master at allowing others to help him solve a case and taught me that most cases are not solved by a single person but a team of professionals working toward a common goal. He taught me about the importance of doubt. Doubt everything because doubt leads to inquiry and inquiry leads to the truth. To this day, North Charleston remains a very violent city with no shortage of homicides or violent crimes.

Shortly after the Deborah Parham murder case, I was introduced to the aforementioned Kimberly Shawn Vaught cold case by Elaine Kelly. This was the first time that I looked at an old or cold case. I was curious looking back in time at the crime scene photos and investigative reports. They challenged my investigative instincts.

On New Year's Day, 1980, Kimberly Shawn Vaught's lifeless body was found in a grassy area near the enlisted club aboard the naval base in Charleston, South Carolina. Witnesses placed Kimberly in the enlisted club the evening before his body was discovered.[7] The killer used a piece of metal wire twine removed from anchoring a tree nearby to strangle Kimberly. I started to ask why the case had not been solved and then looked at victimology and potential suspects listed in the file.

I spent several days going over the file trying to determine the focus of the original investigation. Unfortunately, time, the enemy in hot homicide cases but an ally in cold cases, was not on my side. I had a significant caseload and other investigations that needed immediate attention. Unfortunately, the Kimberly Shawn Vaught case had to be set aside for more urgent cases.

I never forgot about the Kimberly Shawn Vaught case and would go back to Elaine Kelly from time to time between 1990 and 1992 and ask her if I could study the crime scene photographs. She would pull out the old cardboard box, hand it me, and ask, "When are you going to solve it?" I spent the next several years in Charleston, South Carolina, investigating other murders and working undercover operations with NCPD as part of the United States Department of Justice Weed and Seed Task Force. I would not formally reactivate the Kimberly Shawn Vaught case until 1996 after becoming the Primary Architect and first Program Manager for the NCIS Cold Case Homicide Unit. Unfortunately, after more than 40 years, the case remains unsolved today.

I would not think about cold cases again until the fall of 1994 after I was transferred to the Special Operations Division at NCIS headquarters in Washington, D.C. My family and I moved to Washington, D.C., over the Christmas holidays in late December 1993, and I started work at NCIS headquarters in early January 1994 monitoring and coordinating various undercover operations throughout the world for the Criminal Investigations Division (Code 23). In November of 1994, Jeanmarie Sentell, a forensic consultant at NCIS headquarters, walked over to my cubicle and asked me if I would review a murder case that had happened on June 15, 1993, and had not been solved. Jeanmarie and I had worked together and shared an office in Charleston, South Carolina. She had recently completed her master's in forensic science at George Washington University in Washington, D.C., and was the "death desk" reviewer in the Criminal Investigations Division (Code 23) at NCIS headquarters.

The case that Jeanmarie handed me was the murder of U.S. Navy Lieutenant Robert Dana Bartlett. On the morning of June 15, 1993, the USS *Yorktown* (CG-48) made a port visit in St. Thomas, U.S. Virgin Islands. After Bartlett left the ship to use a public telephone at the end of the pier, he was beaten with a nail-spiked baseball bat, shot in the head, and killed by three unidentified men. Detectives concluded it was a robbery homicide.[8] The case was worked for 18 months with no success before we solved it. The case was somewhat similar to the Missy McLauchlin case from North Charleston, South Carolina, in that multiple suspects brutally killed a random victim. Cold cases involving random victims can be the most difficult to solve. The fact that there is not a previous relationship between the suspect(s) and victim causes the most difficulty in a random victim case. It can be difficult to generate viable investigative leads with these types of cases. Linking suspects and victims together at a specific time or times is necessary for every cold case. After reviewing the case, it was apparent that the original focus of the investigation was not accurate. It was a suspect-based investigation and not an evidence-based investigation. Investigators had focused on following the suspects and ignored the crime scene clues and what the witnesses initially reported. Essentially, there were three groups of potential suspects, and the case had gotten off track as the assigned investigators and supervisor pursued the wrong group of suspects. Our team was able to solve this case, which had languished for over 18 months, in just 33 days. This led to the formation of the Virgin Islands Homicide Task Force and the first successful cold case for both me and NCIS. After the success with the Virgin Islands Homicide Task Force, I returned to NCIS headquarters and was tasked by Division Chief for the Criminal Investigations Division Alan Carballo, Deputy Assistant Director (DAD) for Criminal Investigations Gerald Nance, and NCIS Director Roy Nedrow to formally establish a Cold Case Unit for NCIS. These gentlemen were visionary and truly great leaders. I would not have successfully created the NCIS Cold Case Unit without their encouragement and leadership. It shaped what has become an internationally acclaimed cold case unit.

As mentioned before, I spent the next several months traveling around the United States reviewing how other cold case units worked cold cases. I wanted to develop a solid methodology and protocol before launching the NCIS Cold Case Unit. I visited 15 law enforcement agencies, including the Metro Dade-Miami Cold Case Unit, the Boston Cold Case Squad, and the North Carolina State Bureau of Investigation Murders Unsolved Team (MUST). I met exceptional detectives working cold cases including Sergeant David Rivers from Metro-Dade

Miami and Tim Murray and Stephen Murphy from the Boston Police Department. These three gentlemen were consummate professionals with mounds of cold case investigative experience that they eagerly shared with me. What I determined from these gentlemen and various other detectives was that cold case investigation was not a new concept for law enforcement, but one that was fast emerging and becoming more popular. I realized that although many agencies were working cold cases, no one had taken the time to record the specific methods for doing so. There were no methodology and protocols in place for cold cases. I spent the next couple of months working 16-hour days compiling all of the information I gathered from these gentlemen and other law enforcement agencies into a field guide for cold case investigations. I put together a weeklong cold case training conference at the Federal Law Enforcement Training (FLETC) in Glynco, Georgia, for two dozen NCIS special agents and support personnel from various NCIS offices around the world. In addition to the methodology and protocol, DNA and other cold case topics were covered. NCIS has used this methodology and protocol to solve many cold cases over the past 25 years. It has been adopted by countless law enforcement agencies around the world resulting in the successful resolution of hundreds of cold cases. The methodology and protocol were recognized by the International Association of Chiefs of Police (IACP) as a semifinalist for the prestigious Webber Seavey Award in 1996. I presented the methodology and protocol to the National Sheriffs' Association (NSA) in 1997 and have taught it to thousands of investigators throughout the world. Rob Boon and Marshal Thieus from the Utrecht Police Department in the Netherlands have used the methodology and protocol with good success. I provided them and various other members with hands-on training in May 2001. The Japan National Police and Philippines National Police were trained in July and September of 2002 and have used the protocol with success, as have other countries that have adopted it.

As previously noted, investigators must be able to read crime scenes and understand the behaviors exhibited by offenders during the commission of a violent crime. Jon Perry, a former Kansas City, Missouri, homicide detective and special agent with the Virginia State Police, taught me the importance of reading crime scenes. Jon's over 45 years in law enforcement were an invaluable resource. He taught me the importance of reading behavioral clues at the crime scene. Investigators must understand the manner in which the crime was committed. This includes reading the crime scene to learn about the victim and suspect, while trying to determine what the suspect was thinking and how he/she likely committed the crime. Determining motive, means, and opportunity is important when evaluating a murder. During the course of a murder investigation, means and opportunity are often easily determined. The motive for murder is more elusive, and true motive is rarely determined in many murders.[9]

The best way for cold case detectives to approach the investigation of an unsolved case is to read the crime scene like a Hollywood television show or movie. Every crime scene tells a story that includes characters, a plot, and a narrative that ends in the murder. What will increase the chances of solving a cold case will be the investigators' ability to analyze human behavior and the crime scene. This involves determining who, what, why, and how the crime scene story unfolds, as well as understanding speech patterns, writing styles, verbal and non-verbal gestures, and other traits and patterns that give shape to human behavior. These individual characteristics work to cause each person to act, react, function, or perform in a unique and specific way.[10]

Criminals, however, think differently from most people. They commit crimes to fulfill their needs and fantasies. In many cases, the crime scene reflects the criminal's personality. Understanding and recognizing these behavior patterns will provide insight into the offender and assist in linking crimes committed by the same offender. It is also a means by which investigators can distinguish between different offenders committing the same type of offense. Three manifestations of crime scene behavior are *modus operandi*, *signature*, and *staging*.[11] Cold case investigators must become familiar with these concepts and the importance they play in evaluating cold cases.

A small number of homicide scenes are or could have been staged by the perpetrator. Cases involving staged murder scenes provide cold case investigators with a solid chance of solving the case. When there is a staged scene there is almost always an interpersonal relationship between the victim and perpetrator. This will help investigators narrow the pool of suspects and focus on the correct suspect.

Crime is both geographic and intentional.[12] For example, if a victim was killed in the victim's house, investigators must ask the question, "What events caused the suspect to be at the victim's house?" Investigative focus is placed on suspects who live, work, or conduct recreation near the victim's house. Cold case investigators must determine what caused the victim and suspect to cross paths or be together on the day of the murder. Was it work? Was it where one of them lived? Was it part of recreation or another activity? Who had access to and placement near the victim?

In addition to the methodology and protocol developed for cold cases, the following tips should be followed when investigating cold cases:

Investigators must focus on the three foundational building blocks of cold case investigation to successfully solve cold cases. These three building blocks include the concepts of *time, technology,* and *tenacity.*

Investigators must turn the liability of time into an asset. The enemy that worked so hard against the original investigation must become an ally. The normal passage of time causes relationships and associations to change. Investigators should focus on how "relationships change" and the "changes in relationships." People mature, become better citizens, find religion, need some help, do not mind getting involved now, or they were simply not asked the right questions during the original investigation. Murderers confide in people and new witnesses can be identified. In the majority of cases successfully closed by cold case investigators, the suspect, for any number of reasons, told at least one person about his/her involvement in the murder. Investigators must find these individuals in whom the murderers have confided. Remember that the suspects may have confided in ex-wives, ex-husbands, ex-girlfriends, ex-boyfriends, family, friends, co-workers, neighbors, associates, and acquaintances that they murdered the victim. It may seem strange, but it happens with many cold cases. Cold case investigators must be persistent and tenacious as they track down old girlfriends and ex-wives. A proper approach with these individuals can result in them disclosing those secrets from the past.

Unlike a fresh homicide case, time is an asset in a cold case. One major reason is that relationships between the perpetrator(s), relatives, friends, and witnesses change. Perpetrators often confide in people, which now makes these people new witnesses. What I've discovered is that over time some of these relationships turn sour. When one does, a person who once resisted providing information about the case will suddenly have a change of heart and volunteer information that will lead a detective to identify the killer.[13]

Technology—or the police detective's toolbox, as it is better known—has gained some valuable weapons in the past several years. Criminology and forensics are not stagnant sciences. CODIS,[14] DNA,[15] NIBIN,[16] IAFIS,[17] the Next Generation Identification (NGI) Fingerprint System,[18] forensic genealogy,[19] alternate light sources, lasers, and computer databases can aid in solving cases. Investigators must be familiar with advances in technology and appropriately apply the technology to cold cases. Self-education and self-awareness of new technological advances are critical for cold case investigators. For example, I have spent the past 24 months learning all I can about forensic genealogy. It is an excellent new tool for solving cold cases that I have used. In fact, it is the best new tool for solving cold cases in the last 25 years. I think it will become an even bigger game changer for cold cases in the years to come. In Chapter 9, I will share information about forensic genealogy's role in law enforcement.

Tenacity and the relentless gumshoe detective work from years ago is a must for anyone investigating an old, unsolved homicide. Investigators must pursue cold cases from a proactive and not reactive approach. Creative methods and investigative techniques should be continuously applied to every cold case.[20]

Investigators have to create their own breaks to solve cases. An investigator in the Republic of the Philippines, Dennis Baldonado, always told me that good investigators "just roam around" and talk to people. No a truer statement can be made for cold case investigators. The only way to get answers is to ask questions. I will be forever indebted to Dennis for the investigative support and assistance he provided to me during the terrorist bombing and murder of U.S. Army Green Beret Mark Jackson in Zamboanga City, the Republic of the Philippines on October 2, 2002. Dennis was a tremendous resource for the group of American investigators assisting the Philippine National Police with this terrorist bombing carried out by the militant group Abu Sayyaf. Ironically, I was in the Philippines teaching cold case investigation to the Philippines National Police when Mark Jackson was murdered. Persistent and tenacious investigators are the backbone for many successful cold case units. These investigators are typically skilled interviewers with experience in handling informants and a strong familiarity with statement analysis. Creative investigative approaches and "pounding the pavement" often make the difference in whether or not a cold case is successfully resolved.

Before conducting any investigative tasks, investigators must conduct a complete and thorough review of the original investigative file to determine if all the reports, field notes, photographs, videos, and related documentation are available. Do not be surprised if investigative files, official documentation, and evidence are missing when starting to review a cold case. Reconstructing the files of the original investigation can be a challenging task. It is important to review the original investigator's field notes for clues and information that were not translated into official reports and documentation. Are the main characters still alive? Can they be located? Is there a complete autopsy file and investigative file? What evidentiary items were still maintained by the law enforcement agency? What new technological advances can be applied to the investigation? These questions must be addressed.

Investigators reactivating a cold case must get over the "Why didn't they do this?" syndrome. Since cold case investigators were not on the original scene and do not know what happened, proceed with what is in the file. Investigators must determine if the case has a "pulse." Some old files will literally speak in terms of which suspect is likely responsible for the murder, while others read like a true whodunit. Investigators should read the investigative files in a quiet place with minimal interruptions so they can "learn" the case. Victimology is important, and investigators must understand the victim's history and background. Many questions must be asked, including: How and why was the victim murdered? Was the victim a high- or low-risk victim? What level of control was required by the offender to control the victim (e.g., presence, verbal commands, retraining devices, the weapon of opportunity, blunt force, ruse, con, trick, or surprise)? Why was the victim the person who was killed and what is the importance of the location where the victim was killed? Who is familiar with the location where the victim's body was discovered? Cold case investigators should keep in mind that bodies are dumped, concealed, and displayed in areas known by the offender. Each location (i.e., where a body was dumped, concealed, or displayed) can reveal different clues about the suspect. Concealed bodies typically indicate a closer relationship or interpersonal relationship between victim and suspect. Dumped bodies can suggest a lesser association between the suspect and victim. A displayed body can suggest the suspect was trying to humiliate the victim. Fire or an accelerant used to destroy the body can suggest a closer relationship between the victim and suspect. Answering these questions will help direct focus towards the correct suspect and narrow the pool of suspects.

When reviewing the file, remember that the "correct" suspect surfaces early in the investigation. Pay close attention to the first 10 to 15 percent of the case file. Often, the individual responsible for the murder is listed somewhere in the file (e.g., investigative documents, neighborhood canvass, field notes, etc.). Focusing on the first 30 days of the original investigation will often lead to the identification of the "correct" suspect.

As you review the initial investigation, reorganize all the old investigative files, crime scene photographs, evidence custody documents, forensic laboratory reports of analysis, autopsy report, and investigator's notes chronologically into three-ring binders. The binders should include documentation from any law enforcement agencies that participated in the original investigation.

Try to determine if Crime Stoppers tips hijacked the original investigation. Be careful with Crime Stoppers tips. Irrelevant tips often hijack the case, whether a hot case or a cold case. Tips called into Crime Stoppers or similar programs shortly after the murder tend to be more accurate and fruitful as follow-up investigative leads are completed than those that trickle in weeks and months after the murder. Many older Crime Stoppers tips are the result of hearsay information and recycled rumors.

Once it is established that there is a statutory case, the very next step should be to visually observe the evidence. As the lists of evidentiary items, evidence custody documents, and chain of custody forms are reviewed, remember to contact the evidence custodian or property room manager and personally view the evidence to confirm it is still maintained and available for new forensic testing and technological advancements. Re-submit the evidence to forensic laboratories and request contemporaneous examinations and evaluations of these items. An alternate light source (ALS) should be used when re-evaluating old evidentiary items. An ALS was likely never used on many cold cases to locate blood, seminal stains, or trace evidence, and the evidentiary items containing these pieces of physical evidence were never examined by a forensic laboratory.

Perhaps one of the most important steps before reactivating the cold case is to involve a prosecutor as soon as possible. Discussions about the degree of murder, statute of limitations concerns, Supreme Court decisions, privileged conversations, and spousal relationships are just a few of the topics a competent prosecutor will be able to assist with on the cold case. Re-approaching the suspect is another area where their guidance will be needed.

During the analytical review, as investigators ensure the investigative file and all related materials are chronologically organized into three-ring binders, digitizing old cases is important. The CaseMap computer program by LexisNexis is excellent for digitizing and electronically storing old cases. Background checks, including National Crime Information Center (NCIC) indices and social media reviews (e.g., Facebook, Instagram, Twitter, Snapchat, etc.), will help determine which individuals listed within the case file are still in contact and communication with each other. This is a very important step to help maintain the element of surprise for the interrogation of the suspect. What relationships are still intact all these years later? What relationships are strained or have been terminated since the murder?

Remember, the suspect is almost always listed somewhere in the investigative file. The so-called "ghost suspect"[21] is the exception and not the rule. A ghost suspect is a person ultimately found responsible for the murder whose name was not listed or recorded anywhere in the original investigative file. Few cold cases that are successfully resolved involve a ghost suspect. The one technological advance that is solving cold cases via a ghost suspect is forensic genealogy.

When reviewing the crime scene photographs and videos, go slow, use a magnifying glass, and start from the corners and work inward as there are often clues that were overlooked during the initial investigation. Crime scene photographs and video recordings contain valuable information that is often overlooked. Look for the clues in these photographs and video recordings. Paying attention to the minute details can solve old cases. For example, there was a case where the suspect discarded a cigarette butt (twisted in a circle manner) at the crime scene. At first glance, the cigarette butt looked like it had been dropped at the scene by the perpetrator. However, close examination of the crime scene photo with a magnifying glass revealed the twisted manner of the cigarette butt. A review of the old cigarette butt confirmed it was twisted. There were three suspects in the original case that smoked but only one that twisted his cigarette butt in a circle manner. Needless to say, he was the correct suspect.

While studying the photographs and videos, reconstruct the crime. Determine if the crime could have happened in the manner it was documented in the original investigation. Closely evaluating crime scenes to determine how the murder unfolded requires patience and repetition. It may take several times reviewing the old crime scene photos before overlooked clues are noticed. Investigators must focus on the blood at the crime scene, in particular passive blood flow and vertical blood droplets. The passive blood will help determine if a body was moved at the scene while the vertical blood droplets help determine the path the victim and/or suspect took after being shot or stabbed, etc. When reviewing blood evidence, concentrate on the voids. Where is blood not found that it should be and why is it not there? Was the perpetrator standing in a particular position as the bloodletting commenced? Forced entry or lack thereof is also important for evaluating cold case crime scenes. Signs of a physical struggle are important. Was the crime an organized or disorganized event? Reconstructing the crime will help verify statements of witnesses and suspects. It is important to review the original investigator's field notes when reconstructing the crime. Often limited or no attention was placed on the crime scene by investigators. Revisit the crime scene to conduct scientific experiments and re-enactments. Visit the crime scene at different times, both in the daytime and at night. Make sure there was only one crime scene and that a secondary crime scene was not overlooked during the original investigation. Secondary crime scenes are important. Investigators will have an initial crime theory after reviewing the original investigation; that should lead to an updated theory after completing cold case investigative tasks and ultimately result in a final crime theory before any cold case interrogation or re-interrogation of the suspect. The crime scene should be reconstructed by the new investigator to ensure the crime could have happened the way it was reported to have happened. All factors of the initial investigation, including the crime scene, autopsy, interviews, interrogations, and related documentation, should be considered when attempting to reconstruct the crime. It is very important that the new investigator get a "feeling" for the case. If possible, original investigators and crime scene technicians should accompany the new investigator to the crime scene and explain their observations and actions during the original investigation.

There are three groups of people investigators evaluate and interview during the course of a murder investigation. These include (1) family and friends, (2) neighbors and co-workers, and (3) associates and acquaintances. The facts of the case and the suspect's prior relationship with these respective individuals will dictate the order of the interviews. Cold case investigators must determine the focus of the original investigation. What new, additional, or clarifying information can be obtained from these individuals? As with a regular homicide investigation, cold case investigators must establish rapport with witnesses and suspects. Investigators must develop trust with the witnesses to obtain critical pieces of information that were not divulged during the original investigation. This requires detectives to be friendly and open with the witnesses. Investigators must display genuine empathy that is embraced by witnesses before long-held critical information is shared. Remember it is a process of "cat and mouse." Cold case investigators will have to develop interview methods and creative approaches for obtaining information from witnesses who were unwilling to disclose this information during the initial interview. Establishing a good rapport with the witnesses will result in trust and hopefully allow the witnesses to speak candidly with cold case investigators. Investigators must use open-ended questions and cognitive interviewing techniques when talking with witnesses. This allows the witnesses to fully answer questions and demonstrates to them that the interviewer is interested in what they have said or think about a question.

When interrogating cold case suspects, investigators should complete the interviews in nontraditional locations (e.g., parks, fellowship halls of churches, hotel rooms, park benches, local libraries, the suspect's carport or back porch, etc.). Suspects must be given a false sense of security and, as with witnesses, building rapport and trust is the only way the suspect will confess and discuss their involvement in the murder. Successful interrogators display empathy for the suspects, building that bridge of trust. Listening is the least developed skill in interrogations, and investigators must be prepared and ready to listen. Many cold case confessions are secured after multiple interactions and interviews with the suspect. Interrogators must be able to persuade murder suspects that they are individuals the suspects can trust, who feel empathy for them, and who understand what they went through that led them to commit the crime. The importance of multiple interviews with the suspects cannot be overstated. Theme development during the interviews is critically important. Blaming the victim and always referring to the murder as an accident normally resonates with suspects, providing them with rationalizations for confessing or admitting involvement in the murder. At the same time, successful interrogators must be able to sell suspects on the idea that confessing to the crime and telling the police all about it is in their best interest. Former NCIS Special Agent Eddie Hemphill was an excellent interrogator. Eddie always said, "You just got to get the person talking" in an interview or interrogation. It does not matter what is talked about, but just get the suspect talking. Eddie's approach was to talk to the suspect until the suspect finally asked, "Aren't we here to talk about the murder?" Forcing the suspect to bring up the murder is critical for cold cases. When they do, they are ready to discuss it. The interview process cannot be forced when conducting cold case interviews. Slow and methodical interviews are the key to success.

When reviewing the neighborhood canvasses of the original investigation, it is important to determine if all the occupants of a particular location were identified and interviewed. Look closely at individuals who were interviewed more than once in the original investigation. Look for names recorded in the original neighborhood canvasses for which there is no documentation of interviews in the file. Before interviewing individuals identified in the original neighborhood canvass or as part of the initial investigation, complete a background check on these individuals. What relationships changed after the murder? What friends and family members are no longer associating with a particular person or group of individuals? Murderers do not tend to break up long-term friendships and associations unless there are underlying suspicions. Try and determine pre-murder and post-murder relationships and changes within the victim's family dynamics (friends, associates, etc.). Focus on individuals listed in filed notes who were not interviewed or whose interview was not documented in the investigative file. Investigators should focus on individuals who "inserted" or "interjected" themselves into the investigation. Murderers make 911 calls, appear in neighborhood canvasses, and show up at the police station unannounced to make inquiries about the progress of the investigation. These are but just a few of the examples of how the "correct" suspect will try to insert him- or herself into the investigation and why the investigative focus must be placed on these individuals. Analyzing the 911 calls to identify indicators of guilt or innocence for the caller is of vital importance. It will sometimes reveal clues that were not initially thought to be significant. This is good for cases that were originally thought to be a suicide but where there are indications it was possibly a murder. Murders staged to look like suicides are one of the most overlooked types of cold case in America.

Pay very close attention to individuals who did not belong at the crime scene before or after the murder. There may be a neighbor who always visited the victim in the evening. However, there were reports this neighbor was observed at the victim's house in the morning shortly before the murder. There is no question of whether the neighbor belonged at the victim's house (known relationship); the question is whether the neighbor truly belonged at the victim's house at that time (morning). Who did not belong at the crime scene and who should not have been in the neighborhood canvass? Those individuals who should have been in the neighborhood canvass but were not equally important avenues to follow.

Investigators should pay very close attention to "post offense behavior." Look for major shifts in behavior. Determine which suspect's life has deteriorated since the murder as well as those occasions when the suspect straightens his life out for the better. Both are potential indicators of guilt. Suspects often move some distance after committing a murder. This move could be as simple as two blocks down the street or 2,000 miles across the country. Comments recorded in the field notes or original investigative file that a particular follow-up interview was never completed because the witness had moved across town or to another state or county should be fully evaluated. Murder suspects move and leave the immediate area after the murder to avoid suspicion and further contact with law enforcement. They can move immediately or weeks after the murder. Anyone in the file that moved should not be eliminated as a viable suspect; in fact, any person that moved after the murder should be a person of interest. Of course, this would not apply if that person was scheduled to move before the murder. Suspects who are normally on time will be late and those suspects normally late will be on time the day after the murder. Look for changes or reports of behavior changes in the way a suspect normally interacts with others. It is important to identify these changes in behavior and determine if the changes are a result of their participation and/or knowledge of the murder. Everyone has a pattern of life. Find the person whose pattern of life changed after the murder. Investigators need to look for patterns of life changes.

Investigators must remember that suspects responsible for the murder could have passed a polygraph during the original investigation. Do not take investigative focus off a particular individual just because they passed a polygraph during the original investigation. Polygraph examinations are only as good as the examiners administering them. Remember that polygraphs are an investigative tool that have sidetracked many murder investigations and caused them to go cold.

Many people who commit a murder that turns into a cold case will never murder again. However, the murder itself will have a profound effect on their life. They are unable to maintain stable or regular employment, and they often move from residence to residence. The opposite can also be found; the original suspect may never leave the physical address where they live after murdering the victim and never change jobs. Cold case suspects can turn to alcohol and drugs after murdering the victim. Look for DUI/DWI, open containers, etc. This can be a strong clue they are responsible for the murder and are using the alcohol and drugs to try and cope, especially if there were no prior DUI/DWI arrests before the murder.

Statement analysis is a critical component for identifying inconsistencies with witness statements. Statement analysis should be conducted on all witness interviews, results of interviews, and investigative reports. It will disclose clues to identify the right offender and sort out which case facts are correct and which are false. Look for missing facts and blocks of time in original witness statements and investigative documents. Remember, look for information that was omitted or omissions on the part of the suspect, as bald-faced lies are not normally recorded in written documents by suspects.

Developing a list of inconsistencies is one of the most important steps for investigators as they re-investigate an old murder, and this process complements statement analysis. Be suspicious of coincidences and make sure to write down all the inconsistencies as they are discovered. Example: A witness told the original investigators they were not with the victim on the night of the murder, but a neighbor of the victim later told police that the witness in question told them they did see the victim on the night of the murder. This would be an example of inconsistency. A list of inconsistencies is critical to visualize all the circumstantial pieces of information and evidence that point to a particular suspect or individual. They are excellent for weeding out large groups of suspects so that the cold case effort can focus on the correct suspect.

Ensure the original investigator is contacted to determine the focus of the original investigation. Contacting the original investigator can be a tricky proposition in some cases. Many old homicide detectives can be thin-skinned when discussing their old unsolved cases. Others can become too involved in a renewed investigation. Many former and retired detectives keep copies of their old investigative files, so do not ask them *if* they have copies of the old file but rather *where* the copies of the old file are. In addition to contacting original investigators, anyone listed in original files (e.g., first responders, morgue personnel, police, fire, rescue squad, EMTs, etc.) should all be located and interviewed to determine what they can remember about the original investigation. These interviews are important and can help support what the prevailing theories were during the original investigation. These individuals can also provide other valuable insights about the initial investigative activities.

The medical examiner should be contacted to determine what information or evidence (e.g., swabs with DNA, etc.) might still be maintained in the medical examiner's old files. They have proven to be a treasure trove with several old cases and yielded viable DNA samples on glass slides that original investigators ignored or were unaware of. Do not forget that suspects like the Golden State Killer were ultimately identified from a glass slide containing DNA that was recovered from a victim during an autopsy and had been sitting on the shelf of a medical examiner's office for years.

Much like contacting the original investigators, contacting the victim's family can be difficult. Be sure not to unjustly raise their hopes. Do not contact the family if a member of the family is considered to be a suspect or complicit in the victim's murder.

If possible, conduct proactive law enforcement strategies and undercover evaluations whether to solicit information from suspects or the surreptitious collection of DNA. Chance meetings with associates of the suspect can produce invaluable information and set the stage for a successful interrogation. The first case in which NCIS was able to operationalize this concept was that of Pamela Kimbrue, which I will feature in Chapter 3. This was the first case that was met with success. From that point, most NCIS cold cases were pursued from an undercover angle with a focus on the surreptitious collection of DNA and forcing the suspect to relive the case before the interrogation. The element of surprise is important for cold cases. The suspect should not be aware that the cold case has been reactivated until the knock on their door. Creative methods and investigative techniques should continuously be applied to every cold case. The surreptitious collection of DNA and other physical evidence should be the norm for all cold case investigations. Undercover scenarios and ruses are effective tools for securing confessions from suspects.

Before conducting any interviews with individuals listed in the old investigative files, make sure to identify those "changing relationships." Fully explore social media and other avenues to determine if particular individuals are still in regular communication with each other. The strategic interviews of these individuals are critical. Remember family, friends, co-workers, neighbors, associates, and acquaintances of the victim should be a significant focus of the cold case investigation. Collect solid background information on individuals listed in the original investigative file from social media, trash pulls, mail covers, surveillance, subpoenas, credit histories, informants, court orders, wiretaps, passive listening posts, prison staff, jailhouse informants, ministry and civic outreach officials, computer databases, public information, open-source materials, wills, lawsuits, arrests, booking reports, and judgments. NCIC off-line checks are important. Identify the "changing relationships" so strategic interviews can be accomplished. NCIC off-line checks can put people in places and locations that they possibly lied about during the murder and original investigation. For example, NCIC off-line may show that a suspect was stopped for a traffic violation with the victim before the murder when the suspect claimed not to have been with the victim on the day of the murder.

Determining who benefited most, financially, from the death of the victim can get the investigation going in a completely different direction. Do not ignore this investigative step.

Begin the interviews with peripheral witnesses. Otherwise, the "grapevine effect" can hinder the productivity of the re-interviews with original witnesses and others listed in the investigative file. "To hear something through the grapevine or on the grapevine is to learn about something via an informal source or hearsay, from another person; it may refer to an overheard conversation or anonymous sources of information."[22]

Again, make sure to use "changing relationships" as an advantage. Once previous suspects or major witnesses begin to be interviewed, the interviews must be completed in a strategic and orderly fashion. Simultaneous interviews of many witnesses typically yield the best results, restricting witnesses from talking with one another about what questions were asked or the focus of investigators reinvestigating the cold case. Demonstrate your concern for the victim and family. Any lack of concern and respect for the victim can make witnesses uncooperative. Do not rush the interviews, and be prepared to spend hours, days, and weeks with critical witnesses and potential suspects.

Introduction

Cold cases can be like working gang homicides. Many initial interviews result in false statements and half-truths. Do not forget that half-truths can lead to a fairly accurate story. Use the half-truths to challenge witnesses so that a more truthful recollection of events is obtained. The second and third interviews of key witnesses and potential suspects will help expose more of the truth. Attempt to interview the suspect in a non-custodial environment if possible. Remember that individuals, especially potential suspects, should be interviewed in nontraditional locations (e.g., state park, hotel room, fellowship hall at a church, the suspect's carport) and props (e.g., photos of the crime scene, photos of the victim, maps, Google street views, etc.) should be utilized to force the suspects or key witnesses to "relive" the murder as they are being interviewed. The key to many successful cold case interviews and interrogations is not acting like the police (e.g., no badges, guns, logos, etc.). Indirect assessments of suspects must be completed before efforts are made to interrogate them. Learn all you can about the suspect and what they like or dislike. Use their language in the interrogation, dress like them, and provide them with drinks and snacks that they like. Theme development and control of the interview process are critical for its success. Cognitive interviewing is the key. Cold case suspects will confess; however, investigators must be prepared and methodical before re-approaching old suspects. The element of surprise coupled with multiple interrogation themes and approaches will be required for success. Conduct these interrogations in nontraditional locations where the suspect feels at ease and is not threatened by the presence of investigators. Many suspects have carried the burden of having killed someone and are always looking over their shoulder waiting to be arrested. Interviewing cold case suspects at their residences has proven to be a very successful interrogation tool for the cold case process.

During interrogations, always display photos of the victim and the crime scene to make interviewees relive the crime during the interview process. When conducting the re-investigation of the murder, focus on incriminating statements, alibi information, inconsistent statements, third-party conversations, corpus delicti facts, documents, records, diaries, journals, digital media, electronic mail, and computers.

Do not stop investigating after a suspect has been arrested.

Experience has shown that cold case suspects are vulnerable after they have been arrested. They cannot stop talking about their involvement in the murder and further admitting their actions. Interview those people the suspect talked to after being arrested to determine what admissions were made by the suspect. Document those jail calls.

There will be cases that forensic genealogy solves, and there will be cases in which DNA will be discovered in an old piece of evidence. There will be circumstantial cases where witnesses are located that the suspect has confessed to over the years, but the reality is that many cold cases are going to come down to the investigator's ability to build rapport with the suspect and get them to confess. Forensic genealogy will solve only a limited number of cases. In fact, it has solved fewer than 700 of the 250,000 unsolved homicides in the past two years.

It is a myth that a victim's family gets "closure" when a cold case is solved. This is an inaccurate statement as the victim's family never receives closure. At best, they will have some resolution by knowing who was ultimately responsible for their loved one's death, but they never get "closure."

Cold case investigators should cautiously seek guidance and assistance as they re-investigate their cases. Over the past several years, a plethora of nonprofit cold case groups and individuals have offered suggestions and assistance. Many of these organizations and individuals, some with national media television shows, have limited success with cold cases. Their intentions are good, but the goal is to solve cold cases, not simply work them over and over again. Make sure to research these groups beforehand so they do not impede the investigation with their worthy intentions.

I hope you enjoy reading *Solving Cold Cases*. Please know that not one thought or comment in this book is an original idea. They are tips and techniques I learned from working with some of the best investigators on the planet, several of whom I have mentioned. There are countless other investigators, prosecutors, and criminal justice professionals who have taught me how to investigate. There are no original ideas, and investigators are only as good as the mentoring they received from those investigators who preceded them.

—J.D.K.

1

Evolution and Popularity of Solving Cold Cases

In 1991 and 1992 the creation of two grassroots organizations triggered the trend to solve cold cases. During a lunch meeting three men, William Fleisher, Richard Walter, and Frank Bender, started a three-hour discussion about old cases that had not been solved, cases that congealed like aging butter, that investigators abandoned for lack of time or resources. The conversation led Fleisher to propose the idea of forming a club to rigorously tackle unsolved cases.

Fleisher suggested they name the club the Vidocq Society, after Eugène François Vidocq, a nineteenth-century French detective who helped police by using the psychology of the criminal to solve cold case homicides. Vidocq was a former criminal and used his knowledge of the criminal mind to look at murder from the psychological perspective of the perpetrator. Fleisher also supplied the motto: *Veritas veritatum,* or "truth begets truth."[1]

All three men had impressive law enforcement backgrounds. At the time, Fleisher was a police officer turned FBI special agent turned chief of Customs Service in Philadelphia. Walter was a respected crime scene analyst and forensic psychologist for the Michigan prison system, a position Hollywood now calls a profiler. Bender was a forensic reconstructionist, who specialized in taking the skulls of murder victims and sculpting recognizable three-dimensional models of their faces.

The three men hosted the first Vidocq Society meeting in 1990, in a conference room at the Naval Yard in Philadelphia; 26 people attended. After the conference, they scheduled monthly meetings to listen to local law enforcement officials from around the world who brought in cold cases for review. "Vidocq provides pro bono expert assistance to law enforcement agencies across the United States. It does not conduct independent investigations and only acts as a catalyst to assist law enforcement agencies and only at their invitation."[2]

In 1991 Vidocq tackled their first case, the homicide of Huey Cox. Authorities arrested and convicted Derrick Carlock. Vidocq managed to prove that Carlock did not commit the murder but never solved the homicide. Despite their failure to identify the real killer, this case set the stage for Vidocq to successfully help law enforcement agencies solve subsequent cold cases.[3] I will feature three of Vidocq's solved cases in Chapter 4 and Chapter 9.

In 1996 I presented the Kimberley Shawn Vaught case I mentioned in the Introduction to the Vidocq Society at the Old Custom House in Philadelphia. Vaught was a Navy hull maintenance technician assigned to the USS *Moosbrugger* at the Navy base. He'd spent his New Year's Eve at the Enlisted Club and was last seen after the last call at the bar. Two sailors found his body, with metal wire around his neck, at 12:45 p.m. on New Year's Day at the intersection of Bainbridge Avenue and Holland Street. He was missing his shoes, socks, wallet, military ID, and glasses.

The NCIS cold case team interviewed more than 300 people, including the ship's entire crew. No one came up as a suspect, and we never found a motive for his murder. His case still remains unsolved. If you have any information about Kimberly Shawn Vaught, please contact NCIS through the NCIS Tips mobile app or at *ncis.navy.mil*.[4]

A year later, Peter Neufeld and Barry Scheck founded the Innocence Project at the Cardozo School of Law. They were led to start the Innocence Project after their involvement in a 1983 rape case in which they represented the convicted rapist, Marion Coakley. Coakley was arrested for rape and robbery after the victim and two witnesses identified him out of a lineup. At the time, juries relied heavily on the testimonies of a victim and witnesses to determine a defendant's guilt or innocence. At Coakley's trial, the jury disregarded the alibi evidence submitted by the defense attorney and rendered a verdict of guilty; the court sentenced Coakley to a prison term of 5 to 15 years.[5]

That same year Kary Mullis had developed a process for duplicating and matching DNA, a process called polymerase chain reaction.

Law enforcement began applying Mullis's forensic discovery in criminal investigations in which tiny fragments of genetic material were available for testing to identify a person's DNA at a crime scene. Several years later, Mullis received the 1991 Nobel Prize in Chemistry.[6]

In 1988, the Legal Aid Society, which represented Coakley in his appeal, reached out to Neufeld and Scheck, who had previously worked for the organization, to help prove Coakley's innocence. Neufeld and Scheck's strategy was simple. If deoxyribonucleic acid (DNA) technology could prove a person guilty of a crime, it could also prove that people who had been wrongfully convicted were innocent.

The following cases set precedence for Neufeld and Scheck to question Coakley's conviction based on new DNA evidence.

In 1987 the admissibility of DNA in the courts made its debut and led to the conviction of rapist Tommie Lee Andrews. Forensic scientists matched Andrews's DNA with the blood sample and semen found in the rape victim. The court sentenced Andrews to 22 years, and he became the first American ever convicted in a case that utilized DNA evidence. Andrews finished his sentence in 2012, but under the Jimmy Ryce Act, violent sexual predators can be held beyond their sentences until they can persuade a court to release them. Andrews has made appeal attempts for release.[7] A judge released Andrews in 2021 over the objections of his victims.

In 1989, DNA evidence exonerated Gary Dotson. Dotson was convicted for the rape of Cathleen Crowell in 1977. Twelve years later, new DNA tests proved Dotson was innocent. After the DNA result was announced, Crowell admitted that she had made up the entire scenario and inflicted superficial injuries on herself because she feared that she might have become pregnant through consensual sex with her boyfriend the previous day. Her intent to fake the crime had been to create a plausible explanation to tell her parents in the event she became pregnant, which she did not.[8]

Although the DNA tests in Coakley's case were inconclusive, Neufeld and Scheck were eventually able to prove Coakley's innocence through other investigative means. Nevertheless, Scheck and Neufeld realized the potential of DNA technology to reverse wrongful convictions.

The Innocence Project's mission is to free the staggering number of innocent people who remain incarcerated and to bring reform to the system responsible for their unjust imprisonment.

According to the Innocence Project's estimates in 2014, between 2.3 percent and 5 percent of all U.S. prisoners are innocent. The American prison population numbers about 2.4 million. Using those numbers, as many as 120,000 innocent people could currently be in prison.[9]

The Innocence Project also consults on a number of cases on appeal in which the defendant is represented by primary counsel and provides information and background on DNA testing litigation. To date, 375 people in the United States have been exonerated by DNA testing, including 21 who served time on death row.[10]

In addition to the aforementioned organizations like Vidocq and the Innocence Project, public pressure from victims' families has generated renewed media attention to solve cold cases. People do not follow up with phone calls if their relative was a victim of a burglary, assault, or attempted murder that occurred years ago in the same way they do if their loved one has been murdered. The increasing phone calls from desperate family members, especially parents looking for answers about their children's deaths before they themselves died, convinced politicians to embrace the serious threat of unsolved cold cases. If a murder case is not solved, that means the unknown perpetrator may strike again. The public outcry convinced politicians that it was time to allocate funds for law enforcement agencies to create cold case units that specifically solve cold cases in their respective states and cities.

Applications for grant money are now available to law enforcement agencies through organizations like the U.S. Department of Justice and National Institute of Justice. The funding has also allowed law enforcement agencies, prosecutors' offices, and crime labs across the country to establish innovative programs for cold cases.

Since funding began, many cities have been proactive in opening cold cases to improve their clearance rate. Cities such as Detroit have been digging into their files, looking for older cases that might be solved with new techniques. "Fort Worth police increased their emphasis on cold cases in 2002 after the department received pressure by relatives of murder victims. The department conducted a review of 760 unsolved homicides dating back to 1966, prioritizing cases based on evidence and leads. Since then, the department has solved an estimated 128 cases. That includes cases that led to an arrest or where a now-deceased suspect was identified."[11]

Although I have had success in solving cold cases, I'm not the only detective who has contributed to the success rate. Pat Postiglione is one of many cold case pioneers responsible for the recent success rate.

> A tenacious ex–New Yorker, Postiglione headed up Nashville's formidable "Murder Squad"—a dedicated cold-case unit that solved a high number of notoriously nasty crimes, long before true-crime shows, podcasts and documentaries became the national pastime they are today. With the help of his devoted team of diehard detectives, Postiglione solved a whopping fifty-five unsolved murders between 2005 and his retirement in 2013.[12]

The success rate of detectives like Postiglione justified the need to increase funding to solve other cold cases as well as new organizations like the National Registry of Exonerations.[13] It was founded in 2012 by the Center on Wrongful Convictions at Northwestern University School of Law. It provides detailed information of known exonerations in the United States since 1989. "A study by the National Registry of Exonerations reviewed 2,400 exonerations it has logged between 1989 and 2019, nearly 80 percent of which were for violent felonies. Of the 2,400, 93 innocent defendants were sentenced to death and later cleared before they were executed."[14] The University of California Irvine Newkirk Center for Science and Society, University of Michigan Law School, and Michigan State University College of Law are also involved in this project. Not all exonerations are homicide cases. Other cases include arson, child sex abuse, and shaken baby syndrome.

While many homicide exonerations result in cold cases, detectives have been successful in identifying the real killer in some of them, which has been good news for many victims' families. However, there are exonerations that do not involve a perpetrator because further investigation determined the death occurred as a result of self-defense, suicide, or accidental death.

An important discovery I made during the production of the *Wrong Man* show is that many wrongfully convicted inmates had a previous pending trial or criminal record. Often this information about the defendant in court swayed the jury to a guilty verdict. I believe that just because the defendant has an arrest or criminal record does not justify a guilty verdict. But, more importantly, no person should ever serve time for a crime he or she did not commit.

A wrongful conviction is unfair for victims, their families, and society because the real killer is still free. One great example is Christopher Tapp, who appeared in the first *Wrong Man* show. Details of his case are discussed in Chapter 9. In *Wrong Man 2*, which debuted on February 9, 2020, the producers featured three new cases. They were Kenneth Clair, Vonda Smith, and Patricia Rorrer. I will share information about the Kenneth Clair case in Chapter 7. As of the writing of this book, the *Wrong Man* producers are in search of candidates for their third show.

While projects and programs like the Innocence Project and *Wrong Man* have exonerated many inmates who have been wrongfully convicted, the sad reality is that in many wrongful conviction cases the real killer is still at large. But new DNA technology has recently helped investigators identify the real killer in many wrongful conviction cases. Two separate cases were featured in the first two *Wrong Man* shows— the case of Christopher Tapp in the first and Kenneth Clair in the second. The National Registry of Exonerations features on their website a list of many solved cases that involved wrongful convictions.

Hollywood has contributed to the growing popularity by producing television shows and movies that feature cold cases. It is hard to say when the cold case boom started, but filmmaker Joe Berlinger definitely played a part in jumpstarting the public's craving for cold case shows, documentaries, and movies. Berlinger is an Emmy-winning and Academy Award-nominated filmmaker and producer and a pioneer in the genre of true crime documentaries. He has been on a mission to draw attention to social justice issues in the United States and abroad in his films. It all began with a 1996 documentary titled *Paradise Lost: The Child Murders at Robin Hood Hills*, aired by HBO.

Paradise Lost started as a film to chronicle the convictions of three teenagers in West Memphis, Arkansas, for the brutal 1993 murder and sexual mutilation of three eight-year-old boys as a part of an alleged satanic ritual. However, several months after Berlinger and his staff conducted interviews with the victims' families and the three convicted boys, Damien Echols, Jessie Misskelley, Jr., and Jason Baldwin, they felt that something about this case did not add up. "Berlinger recalls looking at defendant Jason Baldwin's 'skinny little wrists' and thinking he would be incapable of using a hunting knife to mutilate and murder anyone."[15]

Berlinger presented the story objectively, showing the trial and reactions from the victims' family members, allowing viewers to make up their own minds about what happened. The documentary inspired a movement to prove the three teenage boys had been wrongly convicted and to set them free.[16]

Fifteen years later, on August 19, 2011, Misskelley, Baldwin, and Echols entered Alford pleas. An Alford plea is a guilty plea in which a defendant maintains his or her innocence but admits that the prosecution's evidence would likely result in a guilty verdict if brought to trial. Judge David Laser then sentenced them to 18 years and 78 days, the amount of time they had served, and levied a suspended sentence of 10 years. All three were released from prison that same day.[17]

The families of the victims as well as the public have mixed feelings about how this case was handled. Steven Branch, Sr., whose son Steven was one of the slain victims, does not believe that the prosecution should have accepted the defense's proposal to employ the rarely used pleas, nor that the convicts should have been released as a result. He referred to Echols, Baldwin, and Misskelley as "animals" who should have remained behind bars, and, in Echols's case, been executed according to his sentence.

Another parent of one of the victims, John Mark Byers, initially felt that these three men murdered his son Christopher and the other two boys, Steven and Michael. However, 14 years after the murder, he had a change of heart and was convinced that the three boys were innocent. Mr. Byers fought to release them from prison and was glad to see it happen. But he was upset about the method in which Arkansas prosecutor Scott Ellington exonerated the men by way of the Alford plea. Mr. Byers felt that the prosecutor should have expunged the men's criminal record before he released them from prison.

After the men were released, Branch Sr. shared his concerns with reporters about the Alford plea and how it sets a dangerous precedent: "It's just going to give a key to everybody that's on death row right now to open up his or her cells and walk out there with the rest of us," he said. "All the killers, the rapists, the serial murderers."

Branch's ex-wife, Pat Hobbs, however, viewed the outcome differently. She doesn't know whom or what to believe anymore. "It's a terrible nightmare that I have to live with from day to day," she explained. "I want to rest, and I want my son to rest."[18]

Despite the mixed feelings, *Paradise Lost*'s influence and legacy have spanned three decades. It has changed the lives of all involved, including Berlinger and his filmmaking staff, the public, and people in the TV and movie industry.

Five years after the debut of *Paradise Lost*, the A&E Network debuted *Cold Case Files*. The show documents the investigation of many long-unsolved murders through the use of modern forensic science, especially recent advances in DNA techniques and criminal psychology in addition to recent breakthroughs in the cases involving previous silent witnesses. Though *Cold Case Files* ended in 2002, because of public demand it was revived in 2006 and again in 2017.

Collaboration between law enforcement agencies; advocates like John Walsh, who founded *America's Most Wanted*; directors and producers like Joe Berlinger; and television networks like A&E have also contributed to cold case popularity. They have all raised public awareness with television shows and documentaries that give viewers opportunities to assist in the investigation with a tip that may potentially lead to the identity of the killer(s). The lure of a reward in many of these shows has also encouraged witnesses as well as bounty hunters and private investigators to help law enforcement solve cold cases.

In 2004 A&E debuted a true-crime detective series titled *The First 48*. The title stems from what most, if not all, homicide detectives and experts claim: If you can't find a lead within the first 48 hours, the chance of solving the case decreases dramatically. "That's when people's memories are best. That's when you have the opportunity of following the clues from clue to clue. As time goes on, evidence gets spoiled, witnesses disappear, and surveillance video is copied over."[19]

Here is how Alexis Robie, executive producer of *The First 48*, reveals what he has learned over the course of 14 years of making the show, which includes 584 cases and 859 arrests.

> It's good old-fashioned fly-on-the-wall documentary work. It's entirely real and authentic. Following a murder investigation, you have a true hero's journey taking an investigation into the great unknown to try to

find someone who does not want to be found. The tension is there; you don't need to manufacture it. The conflict is there; you don't need to create it. Unlike a lot of reality TV these days, this has actual drama. And I think people yearn for that. At heart, we're talking about the real drama about one of the most taboo subjects—taking another person's life—and the people who are sacrificing so much to get to the bottom of it. The good that comes out of showcasing very positive investigative work has had a good residual effect on the communities and police relations. That, for me, is invaluable.[20]

While *The First 48* and other shows like it do well to announce an arrest of the suspect(s) within the first 48 hours, there are also murder cases that remain unsolved for days, weeks, months, or years. It was these unsolved murder cases that influenced Hollywood to produce a show that solely focused on cold cases.

In 2013, TNT debuted *Cold Justice*, an unscripted true-crime series produced by Dick Wolf, the American television producer best known as the creator and executive producer of *Law and Order*. *Cold Justice* follows former prosecutor Kelly Siegler and a team of investigators as they re-open unsolved murder cases with the consent and assistance of local law enforcement. It includes crime scene investigator Yolanda McClary, a veteran of Las Vegas Metro police. This is one of many examples of how real cold cases have influenced the production of fictional TV shows like *CSI* and *NCIS*. As of the writing of this book, the team has helped to generate 49 arrests and 21 convictions, in addition to four confessions, three guilty pleas, and three murder convictions.

In February 2017, *Cold Justice* was acquired by Oxygen and began the fourth season on July 22, 2017. On April 23, 2018, Oxygen announced that the series had been renewed for a fifth season, which aired from August 4 to October 6, 2018. As of the publication of this book, the show was in its seventh season and still aired on the Oxygen network.[21]

The wave of cold cases also inspired Hollywood to produce a movie about a cold case that still has not been officially solved. *Three Billboards Outside of Ebbing, Missouri* debuted in 2017 and received an Academy Award nomination for Best Picture of the Year.

After the 1991 murder case of Kathy Page went cold, her dad, James Fulton, rented billboards to express his frustration with the police and their inability to solve the case and identify his daughter's killer. The billboards still appear today on a road outside the family's hometown of Vidor, Texas. Fulton says he has spent more than $200,000 in the last 25 years on billboards and other expenses. The movie racked up a total of six other Oscar nominations.[22]

Even *People* magazine, one of the top 10 major magazines by circulation, has also jumped on the cold case bandwagon. In 2007 the magazine debuted a list of unsolved mysteries about famous people whose murder cases were unsolved at the time of the *People* articles. It included the following celebrities:

- Jacqueline Levitz, wife of Ralph Levitz, founder of the Levitz furniture chain, who was found dead on her bloodstained king-size bed in 1995[23]
- Tupac Shakur, the American rapper and actor, who in 1996 was shot four times by an unknown drive-by shooter in Las Vegas and died six days later[24]
- Bob Stevens, a photo editor at the tabloid *Sun*, who in 2001 received a letter containing a white powder at his office in Boca Raton, Florida, and died in the hospital of anthrax poisoning[25]
- Chandra Levy, an intern who had an affair with California Representative Gary Condit and disappeared in 2001[26]
- Jason Allen and Lindsay Cutchall, Christian missionaries, who were found shot in the head on a remote, fog-shrouded beach near the tiny town of Jenner in 2004[27]
- JonBenét Ramsey, child beauty queen, who was found murdered in her parents' house in 1996.[28]

Another cold case on the list has special significance because it is another example of the great lengths people, even childhood friends, will go to solve a cold case. Twenty-two years after her childhood friend Andy Puglisi disappeared, filmmaker Melanie Perkins produced the documentary *Have You Seen Andy?* It aired on Cinemax in 2008 and follows Perkins's search for answers to solve the case and find Andy's body. The documentary received the 2008 Emmy Award for Best Investigative Journalism.[29]

People magazine publishes a cold case page on their website that features 28 cold cases, including Kathy Pages's unsolved murder.

People also expanded its true-crime storytelling with the 2016 debut of *People Magazine Investigates*. This TV series on Investigation

1. Evolution and Popularity of Solving Cold Cases   49

Discovery reveals fresh developments in some of the most interesting and mysterious cases in American history. The show "uncovers the heart-wrenching stories behind crimes that transcended headlines and became part of popular culture. Exclusive firsthand interviews reveal shocking twists, new evidence, and unexpected resolutions."

"*People* tells captivating crime stories every day across all our platforms, paying tribute to the victims and investigating the real story behind the crimes that shock America," said Jess Cagle, editorial director of Time Inc.'s Style and Entertainment Group.[30]

Another fascinating aspect of the cold case craze is how wrongful convictions have contributed to it, which was well documented in *Wrong Man*. *Wrong Man* is a groundbreaking, six-episode documentary series produced and directed by Joe Berlinger. The show examines cases of inmates who claim to be innocent.

I'm part of a team that includes renowned civil rights attorney Ronald Ruby, former prosecutor Sue-Ann Robinson, and Ira Todd, a member of Detroit's elite Homicide Task Force. We re-investigated the cases of three inmates. The first is Evaristo Salas. In 1996, at age 16, he was arrested and sentenced as an adult to 33 years in a Washington state prison for the murder of Jose Arreola. His murder conviction was based on two witnesses, including a confidential police informant.

The second is Curtis Flowers, who is on Mississippi's death row list. Flowers was convicted of a quadruple murder. I will feature his and Salas's cases in Chapter 8.

The third is Christopher Tapp. He was convicted of the rape and murder of 18-year-old Angie Dodge. Although he confessed, Tapp claimed that detectives, after multiple and lengthy taped police interrogations, coerced his confession. Dodge's mother, Carol Dodge, also believed detectives coerced his confession and that the wrong man was in prison for the murder of her daughter. Twenty years later, the *Wrong Man* show proved Tapp's innocence. On March 22, 2018, a judge released Tapp from prison. I will feature Tapp's case in Chapter 9. It will include the riveting story of Carol's quest for justice and the part she played in exonerating and freeing Tapp from prison.[31]

Thanks to *Wrong Man*, Christopher Tapp was released from prison in March of 2018. In 2019, the U.S. Supreme Court reversed Curtis Flowers's conviction. Salas continues to petition for his innocence and hopes he'll find legal grounds to challenge his conviction and potentially seek a retrial.[32]

STARZ debuted the first *Wrong Man* show on November 3, 2019, and a second one debuted on February 3, 2020, which featured three incarcerated people, Vonda Smith, Patricia Rorrer, and Kenneth Clair. Information regarding these cases will be shared in other chapters.[33]

Lastly, the detective's obsession to solve the case that I mentioned earlier in the chapter bears repeating. *A detective's obsession with solving a murder case isn't a hazard of the job. It's a core part of doing it well.* The hunger to solve a cold case becomes even stronger when I'm asked to solve a case other detectives were not able to solve. But the real driving force to identify killers and solve cases is the empathy I've acquired for the victims and their families. François-Marie Arouet, known by his nom de plume Voltaire, said it best: "To the living we owe respect, but to the dead, we owe only the truth." Voltaire was a French Enlightenment writer, historian, and philosopher famous for his wit, his criticism of Christianity (especially the Roman Catholic Church), and his advocacy of freedom of religion, freedom of speech, and separation of church and state.[34]

In the next chapter, I will address the emotional toll a cold case can have on the family of the victim as well as the investigators working the cases and reveal why families of murdered victims never really achieve closure, even if the offender is convicted and sentenced. I will also share how our culture needs to practice more empathy for victims and their families.

Throughout this book, I will include stories of the cold cases I have solved or helped solve as well as a few unsolved cases. The first case you read in this chapter is **not** a cold case. It was a fresh homicide case assigned to me that I, along with a team of stellar investigators on my staff, solved in three days. My performance as the lead investigator and success in solving this case is what set the stage for the opportunity to solve my first cold case in 1995.

Fresh Homicide Case: Government of South Carolina v. Gardner—Victim Melissa McLauchlin

My team and I worked this case for 72 hours straight, during which our hard gumshoe detective work paid off quickly. As you read the description of how we solved this case, please keep in mind that much of the work we conducted occurred simultaneously and our success was the result of great teamwork.

Summary

On December 30, 1992, Melissa McLauchlin had an argument with her fiancé at a nightclub, stormed out, and began to walk home. Police gave her a ride home. When she arrived at the front door, her boyfriend's mom was upset that she had been drinking and refused to let her into the house. So Melissa left and started walking down the street.

Later that evening McLauchlin's body was discovered on the side of the road. She had been raped, tortured, shot five times in the face, and left to die.

When my team of investigators and I arrived to help investigate, we determined the time of death had occurred three to four hours earlier, and the manner in which her body was dumped revealed that she likely did not have a personal relationship with the killer(s). If she had been covered up with leaves, branches, or other debris or buried, it would have revealed that there was likely a close, personal relationship between the victim and the killer. If the body had been displayed in some fashion, it would have indicated that the killer did so in order to shock or cause a reaction in the person who found the body, or that the killer had a desire for the body to be found.

After concluding that the killer(s) and victim possibly did not know each other, we immediately set up roadblocks at all the motorways that led away from the location of the victim's body for the purpose of questioning any person driving on these roads who may have seen or witnessed the dumping of the body.

Several hours into the investigation one of the officers reported a person who witnessed a group of men who appeared to be dumping something out of their car on the side of the road. She provided the officer with a partial license plate number and a vague description of the vehicle.

When I returned to the office, I cross-referenced the partial license plate number with the DMV database. As I reviewed the list of cars, I decided to focus on the cars registered to Navy personnel. It seemed like the logical place to start because of the Navy base's proximity to the local community.

My team and I met with Navy officials who provided us with the name of the registered owner of the vehicle in question, Joseph Martin Luther Gardner. Further investigation revealed that Gardner and two other Navy men, Matthew Mack and Matthew Williams, had recently gone AWOL. Therefore, suspicion grew about their involvement in the crime. I immediately requested the home base addresses of all three men because criminals typically flee back to their old neighborhoods to seek help from relatives and friends to cover their tracks and find a safe haven.

Because NCIS has worldwide jurisdiction, I was able to collaborate with NCIS offices in other cities. I coordinated surveillance efforts in the home cities of Gardner, Mack, and Williams. We were able to apprehend Mack in Georgia and Williams in Pennsylvania, along with his girlfriend, Indira Simmons. Unfortunately, during surveillance of Gardner's home in Detroit, Michigan, Gardner managed to escape.

As our focus turned to the three suspects we arrested, I acted as an "air traffic controller" and managed the coordination of all three interrogations. Mack and Williams confessed to the rape of McLauchlin and fingered Gardner as the triggerman who shot and killed her; they also identified two other males, Danny DeWayne McCall and Roger Williams, and a female, Edna Lee Jenkins, who were at the scene of the crime. Simmons confessed to being at the crime scene.

While Gardner was on the lam, he was featured on *America's Most Wanted* and the FBI fugitive list. Because of the publicity, a tip came in from Philadelphia, and police captured and arrested Gardner on October 20, 1994, 22 months after he raped and murdered McLauchlin.

Details of the Homicide

On the tragic night of Melissa's murder, Joseph Gardner and two friends decided to rape and kill a white woman in retaliation for the oppression Black people had suffered over a 400-year span.

After Mack, Williams, and Gardner started a conversation with Melissa, they forced her into their vehicle, drove her to a trailer, and raped her. The men brutally scrubbed her with a nylon brush soaked with bleach and hydrogen peroxide and also forced her to scrub her vagina.

After the rape, the men handcuffed Melissa, blindfolded her, put a heavy coat over her head, carried her to a car, and laid her down on the floor of the backseat. As Melissa managed to free her hands and struggled to get up, Gardner reached over the front seat and fired two shots into her face. Several miles later the men dumped her on the shoulder of the road and Gardner fired three more shots into her body.

Sentence

All eight suspects were convicted and sentenced in 1995. Joseph Martin Luther Gardner was convicted for the murder of 25-year-old McLauchlin, received the death penalty, and was executed on December 5, 2008, by lethal injection. Matthew Carl Mack and Matthew Paul Williams received life sentences. Danny DeWayne McCall served six years; Roger Williams five years; Edna Lee Jenkins seven years and suspended for time served; and Indira Simmons seven years, also suspended for time served.[35]

Cold Case #1: Government of Virgin Islands v. Petersen—Victim Dana Bartlett

As I noted in the introduction, the first cold case I solved was the 1995 homicide of Dana Bartlett, a U.S. Navy Lieutenant. Lieutenant Bartlett was brutally murdered during a robbery by three individuals in St. Thomas, U.S. Virgin Islands, in June of 1993. His case remained unsolved for 18 months and took 33 days for me and my team to solve once we began working on it.

In 1994, I was promoted and transferred from the South Carolina office to NCIS headquarters in Washington, D.C. After several months of working undercover drug and murder cases, NCIS Deputy Assistant Director Jerry Nance convinced NCIS Director Roy Nedrow to assign me to reopen a 1993 murder case in the Virgin Islands. Nance told Nedrow that I was the guy who could solve this case. I really appreciated Nance's confidence in me.

Summary

When I arrived in the Virgin Islands, I collaborated with local law enforcement to build an effective investigation team that consisted of native people whom I could trust without bringing any attention to our undercover work on this case.

I reviewed the 18-month-old case file in great detail to look for any inconsistencies in statements, mistakes that may have been made, and other signs that would point to the people who murdered Lieutenant Bartlett.

One of the strategies I utilize during an investigation is to consider who was in the area when the crime was committed and then determine which of these people did not belong there. Most people are creatures of habit. For example, my sister-in-law visits our house regularly on Monday and Thursday. If someone sees a woman who appears to be my sister-in-law at or near our house on Friday, she doesn't belong there. It is a strategy that requires a process of elimination and a substantial amount of manpower and time.

In my opinion, all crimes are geographic. I look for ways to connect the victim with the potential suspect(s) in the case file and the location of the crime. I draw a triangle for each of them. At the top of each triangle, I write "work." At the base to the left I write "live," to the right "recreation." These three places are the most common locations where a criminal commits a murder or crime. The main reason is that human behavior is such that criminals commit crimes in areas where they feel comfortable and familiar. Somewhere in these three locations the victim and killer(s) cross paths. After I collect information using this triangle about the suspect and victim, I look for a connection between the two in one of these three places. Once I find a connection, I then determine why the victim died there and the motive for the murder.

Resolution

What stood out to me were the interviews with three groups of people conducted by the local police. After reading about the suspects in each group and their statements, I determined that further investigation of one group of people looked more promising than the other two in the possibility of finding a lead and the killer.

The next step was to overlay the triangle for the victim with each person in the group I chose to investigate. This process led me to a possible connection between one of the persons in the group and the victim. One particular person stood out, Nefta Petersen. We discovered that he worked the dayshift for a company located near the crime scene.

I began surveillance on Petersen and created a list of his relatives, friends, co-workers and other people in his social network. I also employed informants I could trust to gather intelligence that might be pertinent to solving the murder.

After several weeks, we caught a break. One of the informants told us that Nefta Petersen was having nightmares. He immediately became a person of interest. During our surveillance of Petersen, we recognized a vehicle he was driving as the one described in the case file that was near the scene of the murder. It was one of many dots that connected the victim to the possible murderer.

Next, my team of detectives performed a key strategic move. We simultaneously brought Petersen, his friends, and anyone else who had knowledge of the murder in for questioning and placed them in separate interview rooms. This strategy is used to prevent the suspects from speaking with one another before the interviews. The person guilty of the murder may collaborate with others involved, relatives, or friends to create an alibi. Another reason is to prevent the suspect from posing a threat to other witnesses who may incriminate him.

While we conducted the surveillances, we orchestrated a trash pull on all the people we suspected were involved in or had knowledge of the murder. The purpose was to learn likes, dislikes, and habits of these people and other intelligence about them. We use the intelligence collected to build rapport with the suspects, which gives a psychological advantage during the interview. (I'll explain in detail the value of the aforementioned strategies and benefits of a trash pull in Chapter 9.)

What we learned from the interviews was that three of the people in this group were identified as the perpetrators of several unsolved robberies on other Navy personnel in which the victims suffered serious injuries. It became clear that these three people planned these robberies that had been going on for some time and that the murder of Lieutenant Bartlett occurred during a robbery.

During the interview with Petersen, he confessed to the robbery and the murder and implicated Ansel Eli Cielto and a minor. The minor was interviewed with his mother present. We convinced the mother that the best thing for her son to do was to tell the truth. He did and confessed to participating in the robbery.

Sentence

The court convicted and sentenced Petersen to 25 years on three federal counts and 25 years on two territorial counts, the 25-year Virgin Islands sentence to be served consecutively with the 25-year federal sentence.

After the resolution of this cold case, NCIS Director Nedrow assigned me to head NCIS's first cold case unit. The following murder case occurred in 1968 and was one of the first unsolved cases the NCIS Cold Case Unit reactivated in 1995.[36]

Unsolved Cold Case: Government of North Carolina v. Pope—Victim Nancy Pope

I've included an unsolved case to demonstrate how difficult it is to obtain an arrest and conviction even when a detective does everything correctly and even when your gut and the evidence, though circumstantial, tell you the person you identified as the primary suspect is guilty. Despite the failure to obtain a conviction in this case, there are lessons I learned from it that eventually helped me solve other cold cases. I will share more unsolved cold cases in Chapter 11. Maybe someone who reads this book has information to share that will help detectives solve a cold case.

Summary

William Pope arrived home from work and discovered his wife's body in the bedroom of their house on a Marine Corps base in North

1. Evolution and Popularity of Solving Cold Cases

Carolina. He and Nancy Pope had an eight-month-old son. Nancy had been stabbed six times with a screwdriver. The murder turned into a cold case because there was no physical evidence to connect the killer to the victim, and all the evidence was circumstantial. Forensic evidence was not as reliable or available as it is today, which made it difficult to collect evidence like DNA or establish a specific and conclusive time of death.

According to William Pope's testimony, he arrived home from work around 11:30 a.m. After he discovered his wife's body in the corner of the bedroom next to the dresser, he said he ran to his neighbor's house to seek help and call 911.

The neighbor testified that when he arrived at the Popes' house, the Popes' eight-month-old baby was still in the baby stroller. Shortly thereafter, the neighbor noted that William punched out the living room window.

After we reviewed the photos in the file we came to these conclusions: Judging by the location of stab wounds in Nancy's body, the killer was right-handed. The killer knew Nancy and likely had an intimate relationship with her because she was partially naked and there was an attempt to cover her face. The scratch marks on the dresser and six stab wounds revealed that the murder was an act of rage and also showed signs of domestic homicide. Therefore, in our eyes, William, who is right-handed, became the prime suspect. We also concluded that William purposely punched the window to manipulate his neighbor into becoming a potential witness to establish an alibi. We also questioned why William didn't call 911 from his house and why he would leave his eight-month-old son at the crime scene while he ran to the neighbor's house.

Because most of the evidence was lost or destroyed, we decided to contact the detective who investigated the case to see if he could provide us with more information that was not in the file. We found the detective living in Henderson, Nevada, and paid him a visit. When we asked him about the case he said, "I know Nancy's husband killed her. I just couldn't prove it."

He told us he saved the file and that it was in his garage. Detectives will often keep a copy of a cold case they were unable to solve, hoping that someday they'll catch a break and find the killer. After cross-referencing his file with our file, we decided to track down Nancy's sister and interview her to possibly obtain more information about the day of the murder.

The sister told us she spoke on the telephone with Nancy the evening before her murder. During the conversation, Nancy told her sister she was baking brownies and installing drapes. In the background, the sister heard a voice say something about a screwdriver. The inference was that William was installing the drapes and had access to a screwdriver.

The sister's comment about Nancy making brownies led us to discover a photo that showed that the brownie mix box sitting on the kitchen table had not been opened. This was a crucial piece of evidence because it established that the murder occurred sometime during the night. It was not possible for Nancy's murder to have happened between the time William left home in the morning for work and 11:30 a.m. when he said he discovered the body. We determined that William's story was as shallow as a kiddie pool and that this cold case had a pulse. We believed William killed Nancy. Now, we had to prove it.

During our interview, Nancy's sister mentioned that custody of the Popes' son was awarded to Nancy's parents. We discovered that the son was serving time in a Maine federal correctional facility for a drug trafficking felony conviction. We contacted him and asked if he would meet with us. He agreed.

At the correctional facility, we asked him what his grandparents told him about his mom. He said they told him they thought she was murdered and that his father had killed her. We also asked him if he had ever met with or talked to his dad since the murder. He said they talked a few times on the phone and met once but only for a short time because neither one felt a deep connection to rebuild their father-son relationship. Then they parted ways.

We asked him if he'd like to help us find the truth about his mom's murder and explained how he'd work as an undercover operative for the government and hopefully help us garner a confession from his dad. He agreed to all the conditions and terms. With cooperation from the federal government, he was released into our custody for a short period of time. Then we transported him to North Carolina.

After arriving in North Carolina, we explained the details of our operational plan to schedule a covert chance meeting with his dad. The plan was for him to call his dad and schedule another reunion and at some time during their conversation persuade his dad to talk about his mom's murder. To prepare him for the covert meeting we rehearsed the script and role-played to increase the chances of a successful operation and avoid any suspicion by William about his son's role as an informant.

Because William was a truck driver, we arranged the scheduled reunion at a truck stop. We asked him to tell his dad he'd reserve a hotel room so they could make the most of the time together. We wired the room with microphones and video cameras.

During the visit to the hotel room, the son asked his dad about his mom's murder. William replied, "That's between God and me."

It wasn't a full confession, but it was enough for us to continue with the investigation.

After William left the hotel room, we made the decision to question William. We told him we reactivated his wife's murder case, had him under surveillance, and wanted to ask him some questions. We questioned him for a while, hoping the reunion with his son might trigger a confession. It didn't. Nevertheless, we submitted our review of the cold case to the United States Attorney's Office, and they felt there was enough circumstantial evidence to arrest William.

We arrested William and were cautiously optimistic because there was no smoking gun or DNA evidence to connect him to his wife's murder. We interrogated William for several hours, but again no confession. Without a confession, the United States Attorney's Office decided not to prosecute. The case was closed again for the same reason it was closed the first time—not enough physical evidence. NCIS agents Sam Worth and Wayne Brown did an excellent job on this case, but there was just not enough evidence to convict Pope.[37]

Lesson Learned

Despite the failure to solve this case, I did learn a valuable lesson. Although the son did a great job and the covert meeting went as planned, we overlooked one important factor that prevented us from obtaining the result I hoped to acquire. I expected that the emotional reunion might play with William's conscience and initiate a confession. But the plan failed because sadly there was no bond or intimate relationship between William and his son. This father-son disconnection lets William get away with murder. And that is still a hard pill to swallow.

2

Empathy for the Victims, Their Families, and Detectives

When a murder case arrives at my desk, I am able to convey sympathy to the victim's family. But when it comes to empathy, I have discovered that it is not as easy to practice, especially when a person needs it the most.

Why is empathy so difficult for people to practice? It requires a lengthy explanation, which is why I devoted an entire chapter to empathy. My hope is that you will carry what I share about empathy for the families of the murder victims throughout the rest of this book.

For the purpose of this book, I will share some of the factors I believe contribute to empathy not being more widely practiced in the law enforcement sphere. These include:

1. misinterpretation of the meaning of empathy,
2. the belief that talking or opening up about one's feelings should come naturally,
3. the viewpoint that temporarily setting bias aside to accept another point of view is a sign of weakness,
4. unwillingness to embrace the learning process it takes to practice empathy, and
5. difficulty in slowing one's life down enough to practice empathy.

I believe most people struggle to define empathy, which is an awareness of the feelings and emotions of other people. It is a key element of emotional intelligence, the link between self and others, and it is how we as individuals understand what others are experiencing.

However, even if you truly understand empathy, it is difficult to practice. It is easy to misinterpret empathy and confuse it with sympathy.[1]

I believe most people do not understand the importance of empathy, why it is a needed practice, and how we all benefit from empathy. It gives the ability to see things from another person's perspective and to connect with their feelings, and it plays an important role in our social lives. Research shows that greater empathy leads to more helping behaviors.

Practicing empathy feels good. When a person is empathetic the pleasure centers of the brain light up, which reduces stress and fosters resilience, trust, healing, personal growth, creativity, learning, and a nourishing connection with other people.[2]

In my role as a detective, it is often a difficult balance because as much as I would like to empathize with the victim and family, there are times I need to refrain for several reasons. First is my sanity. Next is for the protection of my family and the victim's family. I compartmentalize so my emotions do not get the best of me and hamper my ability to solve the case and find the killer. I do not share what I experience as a detective with my family. When I am home, I do not want the tragedies I see daily to affect my personal life in order to make sure I am emotionally present for my family.

Empathy compels me to protect the victim's family. There are details about the crime that I cannot divulge to them or the public because it is information that only the killer knows. If I share this information it can jeopardize my chances of finding the killer.

I do my best to shield family members from the crime scene, details on the brutality of the murder, and gruesome photographs of their loved ones. Nevertheless, most family members request access to the crime scene and information. They want to confront the reality of the murder. When a detective denies family members access to the facts, they are frequently tormented by their imaginations.[3]

As a detective, I immediately focus my attention on finding the killer. Time is of the essence, and it is urgent for me to do my job to get the killer off the streets for the safety of the community. Despite my personal and work-related concerns, I do my best to practice empathy. Instead of the family burying their loved one in a casket, he or she is buried in a file cabinet or database as another cold case statistic. Therefore, I work hard to help bring resolution for the family.

I understand that it is impossible for someone who has never experienced the murder of a loved one to understand or relate to the family's pain and grief. I cannot imagine the enormity of the pain a victim's family feels and how difficult it is to articulate the grief. Mourning of a loved one who has been murdered is dramatically different from grieving a death resulting from an accident, illness, or natural causes. Death, unlike murder, is inevitable and, at some point, everyone will experience a death in the family. No one imagines a murder will happen in his or her family. No one is prepared to deal with the tragic news that a loved one, especially a child, has been murdered.

> In 2020, murders in the United States spiked more than 27 percent—the largest percentage increase in at least six decades. Last year, murders went up again. Those murders resulted in the deaths of thousands more Americans and returned the U.S. to homicide rates not seen since the mid-1990s. While murders and violent crime overall are up, other crimes are down.[4]

However, when you add the effect the murder has on relatives, friends, neighbors, co-workers, and law enforcement staff, the number of those impacted increases dramatically. In 2009 the National Center for Biotechnology Information published an article on a study of a homicide's effect on surviving family members. One of the authors, Dean G. Kilpatrick, director of the National Crime Victims Research and Treatment Center at the Medical University of South Carolina, estimates that about 10 million Americans have endured the murder of a family member or close friend.[5]

One might expect that communities would shower the families of murder victims with empathy. Unfortunately, that is not what happens. While some people do practice empathy to some degree, it quickly fades away. Within a few hours after the murder, all the attention is directed to the killer. Pick up a copy of a newspaper or turn on the television to see the media frenzy that follows every homicide case. Numerous articles appear in the newspaper about the killer's background. The articles attempt to provide an in-depth analysis of the murderer's mental state and what may have happened in his childhood years to trigger the murder; share information about where the murderer works and lives;

and recount interviews with the killer's family, friends, neighbors, and co-workers.

In November of 2018, within a five-day period, the media aired and published coverage of two mass shootings. Both shootings received front-page coverage. One occurred at a Florida yoga studio and the other in a California bar. I realize that there are many murder victims in these shootings, but the press behaves toward a mass shooting much as it does toward a murder case with only one victim.

For two days after the shooting at the yoga studio on November 2, 2018, newspapers across the country featured these headlines: "Florida Yoga Studio Shooter Had History of Allegedly Harassing Women, Authorities Say" (*Wall Street Journal*),[6] "Gunman in Yoga Studio Shooting Recorded Misogynistic Videos and Faced Battery Charges" (*New York Times*),[7] "Yoga Shooter Appeared to Have Made Misogynistic Videos" (*AP News*),[8] and "Gunman at Florida Yoga Studio Had Been Accused of Harassment" (*Reuters*).[9]

Five days later another mass shooting occurred at a nightclub in Thousand Oaks, California. Two days after the shooting at the bar on November 9, 2018, this headline appeared in the *Los Angeles Times*: "'I hope people call me insane': Social Media Posts, Former Teachers Reveal Alarming Mind-set of Thousand Oaks Gunman." The article features a former high school teacher and coach playing Monday morning quarterback about the murderer.[10]

Even more difficult to understand is that the television stations aired a live-stream video of the shooting incident inside the bar. How did this video make it into the hands of the media? Why did the media air the video? Where is the social responsibility?

There was television coverage of interviews with patrons of the bar and witnesses. Several mini docuseries about the shooting aired on television and social media. One included an interview with a person outside the bar giving a play-by-play account of the shooting with the sound of gunfire in the background. The media also aired videos of the murderers' houses.

The following year, after two more mass shootings, *Time* magazine published an article about the recent mass shootings titled "69 People Have Been Killed in Mass Shootings in 2019 Alone." This amount of publicity, which the killers seek, is unnecessary and only encourages other unstable people to consider planning a future mass shooting.[11]

An example of the lack of empathy for families of victims is the number of books, documentaries, and movies that have been produced about murderers that depict their struggles in life and what led them to murder another human being. Even after three decades, Hollywood and the public are still fascinated with the life of serial killer Ted Bundy. Two films debuted about him in January of 2019.

A study of murder in romantic literature may explain it:

> The murderer is a powerful figure who violates one of the tenets of our society without any conscience—*Thou shalt not kill*. What seems to compel most killers to break this commandment is craving for power. When the murderer is the protagonist of a story, a reader can vicariously experience that power. The victim on the other hand is viewed as a defeated soul, a loser in this contest of strength. Subconsciously, perhaps it is easier to identify with the murderer.[12]

Another population affected by a murder that is often overlooked is the family of the murderer. These people are not prepared to deal with the news that their loved one is a murderer and also suffer a great deal of pain. It must feel horrible to hear and accept that your parent, spouse, sibling, or child is a murderer. You do not hear or read how much it affects these family members. Where is the empathy and support for them? I'll feature a case, Government of Iowa v. Carter, at the end of this chapter to shed more light on this overlooked perspective.

In life murder is real. It is not fiction. People really die. Murder is unpredictable and so is the grief caused by murder. It does not unfold in stages. When a family member dies as a result of an accident, illness, or natural causes, there is at least occasionally time to prepare emotionally and feel the anticipatory grief. But when a family member is murdered, it comes without warning.

In the days and weeks right after a murder, the victim's family is often in a state of shock. During the investigation, the survivors may need to go over the details of the crime and relive the murder over and over again. The murder also raises a long list of "why" questions. Why my family? Why did this happen to our loved one? Why did it take place? Why and how did my loved one suffer? Why did the murderer pick my loved one?

And when a case turns cold the list continues to grow. Why can't the police find my loved one's killer? Why don't people who know the killer or about the murder come forward and testify? Why won't the witnesses cooperate with the police?

As the family continues to mourn, friends, neighbors, and co-workers suppress empathy as a matter of self-protection. To avoid the constant grief that surrounds a murder, people tend to turn away and pay less attention to the tragedies around them. Even the most caring people will find ways to distance themselves from the tragedy of a relative or friend's murder because the magnitude of the loss and pain is not easy for them to accept. This leads to the victim's family feeling isolated and ignored.

Even if the murderer is apprehended, the victim's family may face years of legal proceedings before the jury renders a decision. And sometimes, insufficient evidence leaves the prosecution with no choice but to negotiate a plea deal and reduce the sentence of the killer(s) or co-defendants. Each new hearing may also stir up feelings that were seemingly laid to rest. One victim's relative explained: "You never bury a loved one who's been murdered because the justice system keeps digging them up."[13]

Then there are the cases in which the prosecutor drops a murder charge because of insufficient evidence and/or misconduct by the prosecutor and his staff.

How the judicial process operates reinforces the sense of powerlessness that a murderer causes to a victim's family. There are times when the victim's family is barred from the courtroom during a trial, yet the murderer's family is allowed to attend. Even when a trial ends in a verdict of guilty, the family of a murder victim may still be left with a hollow feeling. There are times when family members feel the judge's sentence of the killer is not a harsh enough punishment. These lower sentences are often triggered by plea bargains in which the prosecutor reduces the charge of the killer and, in return, the killer agrees to plead guilty. This is why families of victims often feel betrayed by the criminal justice system as well as by law enforcement.[14]

Even the religious sector struggles to practice empathy. Ministers and priests may alienate the families of murder victims with comments like "the Lord knows best," "everything happens for a reason," and "it is all part of God's plan." While those making these comments mean well, they are not helpful. Murder is difficult to reconcile. Even with faith in God, the pain of losing a loved one to murder is very difficult. Forgiveness, like empathy, is also a hard skill to practice.[15]

We also need to consider the traumatic effect unsolved cold cases and the lack of empathy has on children. This is reflected in the cold case story I shared at the end of Chapter 1 about the murder of Nancy Pope. Her son, at age 30, eventually ended up in a correctional facility. How much was his life affected by his mom's murder remaining unsolved or the possibility that his dad was the killer?

After the killer is convicted or an unsolved case goes cold, everyone returns to the business as usual of ordinary life. Then, when another new murder case appears in the newspaper, the public's fascination with the new murder and killer—stoked by the media frenzy—builds again.

Here is how Lucy N. Friedman, director of the Victim Services Agency in New York City, explains how harmful it is to not practice empathy for the victim's family:

> The survivors of murder victims are often treated like pariahs, avoided like a source of bad luck. They feel cursed. Even the counselors who work with survivors come to feel stigmatized by their jobs. What they have learned contradicts the way the rest of us would like to view the world. We want to maintain an illusion of safety. We want to believe that the children of good parents will never be harmed. Our refusal to acknowledge the plight of murder victims and their survivors is a dangerous form of denial—a flight from reality that allows lethal violence to flourish.[16]

I often hear relatives of the victims share their frustrations and exclaim that the police aren't doing enough when, in reality, the police are working hard every day to collect evidence that will help find the killer within the letter of the law. There are times when I know beyond a reasonable doubt that I have found the killer. However, I need to legally gather the evidence to ensure a conviction by the court. The more evidence a detective collects to tie the suspect to the homicide, the stronger the chance the case will result in a conviction. In order for a detective to succeed in this, he or she must rely on the cooperation of all the people involved in the investigation. That requires people to empathize with the detective.

With a homicide case, the lack of empathy for police officers is exacerbated. Detectives receive very little cooperation from the public and potential witnesses. Yet, a detective marches on because of his commitment to solve the case and find the murderer. Police officers are required to risk their own safety in order to protect and save lives, quiet fears, and preserve peace. They are often the "first responders" to crime scenes, accidents, and medical emergencies. They arrest criminals, quickly comfort victims, administer first aid, preserve evidence, identify witnesses, and stabilize highly emotional moments—often at the same time.

They are also human. They must make split-second decisions in the best interests of citizens and their own lives. Sometimes, as all humans do, they make mistakes and don't make the correct decision. Act too slow or too fast and it could cost an innocent person's life or hamper the efforts to find and apprehend the criminal.

There are people who would say that police officers do not practice empathy, but by the very nature of their job and quest for justice, they do. "You want to bring closure to the family and see justice done," says Jim Parks, a retired Norman, Oklahoma, detective sergeant who recently returned part-time to operate the police department's first cold case unit. "You don't want violent people out roaming the streets, [and] someone needs to be held responsible."[17]

The lack of empathy for police officers and their families exists because of the unfair perception that police officers should not be trusted and should not be viewed as allies. Much of this is caused by the unethical actions of a few officers. When one police officer makes a mistake, the public scrutinizes the entire police agency, rushes to judgment, and then demonizes the whole police community. Whom do the good people turn to for protection from the bad people? The police. Yet, the police don't receive the respect and trust they deserve. Without respect and trust, it is impossible for a person to practice empathy.

Bad people also murder police officers: "In 2020, 295 federal, state, local and tribal officers died in the line of duty. The closest number to 2021's was recorded was in 1930, when there were 312 law enforcement deaths. Officers like Lubbock County, Texas, Sheriff's Office Sergeant Joshua Bartlett was among the 62 officers killed by guns in 2021."[18]

How stressful is a police officer's job and what impact has it had on the law enforcement community? Here is an overview from the Officer Down Memorial Page: As of the end of November, 206 law enforcement officers had been lost in the line of duty in 2022, 58 of which were killed by gunfire. There were 652 line of duty deaths in 2021 and 1,820 in the last five years.

In a 2016 report by The Badge of Life, a police suicide prevention program, 108 law enforcement officers took their own lives. And for every one police suicide, almost one thousand officers continue to work while suffering the painful symptoms of PTSD.[19]

What complicates matters is that there has been very little research on the effect cold cases have on families of homicide victims. In 2008, Ashley Wellman started working as a research consultant in the Cold Case Unit of the Alachua County, Florida, sheriff's department. After listening to a mother whose daughter was the victim of an unsolved murder, Wellman realized that she just needed a receptive ear. One of her most important findings is the acute importance of the relationship between victims' family members and police. As detectives work cases, they often find themselves becoming a source of emotional support for the families of cold case victims. They aren't, however, trained to handle this kind of overwhelming grief and frustration. Even if they do receive training, it is a tough balancing act for the detectives as well as the families.[20]

I believe if families need to direct their anger at anyone, it is the witness or witnesses who withhold information or who are uncooperative. There are several reasons why a witness remains silent. Some are obvious, but others are overlooked. One such reason is that most witnesses would like to avoid revealing a secret that might ruin their reputation and/or profession. A quote on breaking silence and truth-telling explains it best: "For all are silent, before the truth." I'll share an example later in this chapter from the Kathy Page homicide case, which is still unsolved.

With respect to the jury, there are cases in which detectives provide plenty of physical evidence and motive behind the murder. Nevertheless, the jury returns a verdict of not guilty. There are trials in which the defense attorney either finds a loophole in the law or creates theatrics in the courtroom that influence the jury to find reasonable doubt of the suspect's guilt, resulting in a not guilty verdict. Two cases that demonstrate the aforementioned scenarios are Government of California v. Simpson (1994)[21] and Government of Pennsylvania v. Weigel (2007).[22] In these cases, the person the detectives identified as the killer was found not guilty. At the end of this chapter, I will share details of the Weigel case.

Families of victims tend to forget that the final decision for conviction is in the hands of the 12 jurors, not the detective, prosecutor, or judge. Yet, the anger for an unfair sentence or not guilty verdict is directed at the police, prosecutor, and judge.

If you are a bystander or witness to a crime, be respectful, trusting, forthright, and honest with police officers. Imagine one of your loved ones is murdered. Would you want the bystander and/or witness to tell the truth and share everything he or she knew about the murder?

Unfortunately, this rarely happens. Again it's for a selfish reason. In the last 20 years, bystander and witness cooperation has been at its lowest during the course of murder investigations. People fear retaliation by the suspect and fear for their own lives. How does not showing empathy and remaining silent keep a bystander or witness and his or her neighborhood safe? It doesn't. This selfish reason is a double-edged sword because the murderer is still free, which means everyone, including the bystander or witness, becomes a potential victim.

Let's imagine for a moment, in an ideal world, that bystanders and witnesses began cooperating with police in their fresh homicide cases. It would expedite the investigation of murders and the identity of the killer and, more importantly, decrease the number of cold cases dramatically.

If you are a witness, share whatever information you know about the murder or potential suspect. Imagine it is your family member or friend who is murdered. Would you like a witness to come forward to help identify the killer? I understand there are homicide cases in which a witness fears for his or her life, but there are many cases when the reason to not cooperate is a selfish one. The Kathy Page cold case is a good example. After the debut of the movie *Three Billboards Outside Ebbing, Missouri*, Kelly Siegler, *Cold Justice* host, featured Page's case again. During the investigation, she interviewed a witness who stated that he saw the primary suspect near the crime scene on the night of the murder. Detectives asked if he was with another person at the time. He said, "Yes." One of the detectives asked, "Could you give us the name of the person?" "No," replied the witness. "I was having an affair with the person I was with at the time, and I don't want to ruin her or my reputation."[23]

If you are a police officer, one way to practice empathy is to offer families of cold case victims resources available to help them cope with the tragedy. For example, provide the relative with a list of local or national support groups. I have listed some of them at the end of this book. Nancy Kreiner, founder of the William Burnham Jr. Death Scene Awareness Project, will debut in what I believe is the first Conference/Symposium for Families of Cold Case Victims in Pennsylvania.

I have worked with Nancy Kreiner and presented at her symposiums as well as met with many families of victims. An important lesson I learned from them is that the families of homicide victims never receive closure. Therefore, I strongly believe that acknowledgment of the killer's identity and conviction only provides resolution for the family members of homicide victims.

In the next chapter I will share how I read, study, and analyze a cold case as if it were a fresh homicide case; apply the four phases of investigative theory and procedures—analysis, programming, fact-finding, and verification and evaluation; and introduce you to an investigation method I designed called documentation dissection.

Cold Case #2: Government of South Carolina v. Paalan—Victim Annie Tahan

The dynamics of this case are filled with gripping and inconceivable details as well as a valuable lesson in practicing empathy.

Summary

Annie Tahan met Michael Paalan in 1987 when his ship, the USS *Brumby*, from Charleston, South Carolina, was docked in Portland, Maine. At the time that Annie met Michael, she was a single mom with three kids.

One evening Annie left the house and Michael stayed to take care of the three kids—Annie's two sons, Jamie and Sean, and her daughter, Cheyenne. While she was gone the house caught fire. Everyone escaped but Cheyenne, who perished in the fire. Michael claimed that one of the boys started the fire. Investigators thought the fire looked suspicious but had no concrete evidence to figure out exactly what happened. Annie, along with her two sons, moved in with her mom in Portland, Maine, and Michael returned to live in the barracks.

A few months later Annie's mother's house caught fire. The source of that fire was a little bit more suspicious. Investigators found a lighter in the rubble with an engraving that read USS *Brumby*, which was the ship that Michael was stationed on. But again, there was not enough evidence to prove who started the fire.

Because of the suspicious nature of this fire and the first one at Annie's former house, the state of Maine decided that they needed to place Annie's children in protective services with the Department of Social Services and Foster Care. Annie desperately tried to regain custody but to no avail.

Michael moved back to South Carolina and, shortly thereafter, Annie moved down to live with him; there she discovered that Michael had been living a double life. Michael admitted that he had been married to Dawn Breeze, who lived with their three children at his mother's house in Savannah, Georgia, and assured Annie that they were separated and no longer in love with each other.

According to Annie's friend Kathi French, the tension between the two grew and domestic abuse soon followed. Annie considered leaving but decided to stay because she was pregnant with Michael's baby. Several months later Annie gave birth to a baby daughter, Jade.

A month after Jade was born, Annie called Kathi. During their conversation, they talked about domestic abuse. Kathi offered to help her leave Michael and wire money for a bus to return to Maine. Annie said she couldn't leave because Michael threatened to take Jade from her. This was the last time Kathi spoke with Annie.

Around Thanksgiving, Kathi hadn't heard from Annie. She didn't try to call Michael because she was afraid of him. Instead, she called people in Annie's social circle, but nobody knew where she was. Kathi didn't pursue looking for Annie because her life was also in disarray. Annie and her family were not on good terms, so none of her relatives

2. Empathy for the Victims, Their Families, and Detectives

followed up to find out what happened to her. It wasn't until three and a half years later that Kathi decided to look for Annie.

Kathi made numerous phone calls and hired a detective to locate Annie. After several months of no progress, she decided to travel to Charleston, South Carolina, and personally talk to the local law enforcement. She expressed her concerns about Annie to the Berkley County Sheriff's Office and told them about Michael's tumultuous and abusive relationship with Annie. She explained how Annie left Maine and followed Michael to South Carolina and her fears about him. With little to go on, the Berkley County Sheriff's Office asked the NCIS Cold Case Unit for help.

Two of the NCIS agents in our cold case unit, Jim Grebas and Pete Hughes, read the file and concluded that it was worth reactivating the case and speaking with Michael. They found Michael stationed in the Pearl Harbor Naval Station in Hawaii, where he transferred soon after Annie's disappearance. During the interview, Michael claimed that Annie visited him but then left and that he hadn't heard from her since. With no sound evidence, the agents decided to close the case.

Kathi, however, remained diligent and continued to try to convince the agents to pursue their search for Annie. Her role and actions during the investigation are great examples of how to practice empathy. She spent about $16,000 and invested a lot of time to find her friend's killer and bring justice and resolution for Annie's family.

Agent Grebas realized he hadn't searched the missing person files, so he contacted the South Carolina state law enforcement missing person department. He asked a lieutenant in charge if a report of a Jane Doe who had delivered a baby after Annie went missing existed. There was and that Jane Doe turned out to be Annie Tahan.

Annie's burnt dead body had been found on November 7, 1989, along the side of a highway in Jasper County, South Carolina, within about 100 miles of the apartment that Annie shared with Michael in Goose Creek, South Carolina. It was the day after Kathi had her last conversation with Annie on the telephone.

At the time the Charleston police discovered Annie's charred body there was not sufficient reason to continue the investigation because they couldn't identify the body. Without a name, there was no way to connect her to anyone in the area and find the killer. That is why she remained a Jane Doe for three and a half years.

It was a brutal murder. The body was burned beyond recognition and Annie's skull was broken into 124 pieces. It took more than 500 hours to reassemble.

Resolution

The agents subpoenaed Michael's bank records, which revealed a suspicious purchase made on his credit card on the date that Annie disappeared. It had been used to purchase gasoline at the Amoco gas station about 25 miles south of where her burnt body had been found.

The agents also checked Michael's phone records and discovered two early morning calls to his mother's house in Savannah, Georgia, the day before Annie's body was discovered. At the time, Dawn was living with his mother. The detectives discovered that he called Dawn early in the morning, one time at 4:35 a.m. and the second time at 5:17 a.m. They surmised that there must have been some type of problem that needed her help. It's the same day that Michael claimed Annie left the apartment without their child. It was time to find Dawn.

Dawn wasn't easy to track down. She had been living a nomadic life, crisscrossing all over the United States, so it was hard to nail down a final forwarding address. It was as if she was running away from something, and we wondered what. Our gut feeling was that it had to do something with Annie's disappearance and murder.

The agents finally located Dawn in Miami, Florida, and paid her an unannounced visit. During a lengthy interrogation Dawn finally broke down and admitted she had carried the secret of Annie's murder for six years and decided it was time to tell the truth about what really happened to her.

Dawn revealed how Michael brutally bludgeoned Annie in the head with a hammer and tire iron while she was asleep on the floor. The baby, Jade, was asleep next to Annie during the murder. Several hours later in the early morning, as the phone records showed, Michael called Dawn and asked her to stop by the apartment and help him with the baby. Dawn drove back to Michael's apartment to find Annie's dead body still lying on the floor. Michael told Dawn, "I'm sorry for having

2. Empathy for the Victims, Their Families, and Detectives 75

an affair, but that's my child. And that child needs to be with us, and you need to help me raise that child as our own."[24]

Dawn agreed to help Michael dispose of Annie's body and raise Jade. Later that evening Michael and Dawn placed Annie's body in a duffle bag and then in the trunk of the car. After they placed Jade inside the car, they drove to find a place to dump the body. Along the way, Michael stopped to buy gasoline at the Amoco station and used his credit card to purchase it.

After driving 70 miles, Michael found a spot that seemed to suit him and pulled over. Dawn helped him remove the body from the trunk of the car and dumped it on the side of the road. Michael poured gasoline on Annie's body and then set her on fire.

The agents were skeptical about Dawn's testimony because it appeared she had a potential axe to grind with Michael. They needed more evidence to corroborate her story as well as physical evidence and/or a confession from Michael. They invited Dawn to participate in a ruse to help draw out an admission of guilt from Michael for Annie's murder. She agreed.

Dawn did a great job talking to Michael about the murder. It revealed Dawn was being truthful about her role in the homicide. While Michael's comments gave the agents probable cause to suspect him as the murderer, it wasn't a confession. The agents decided to return to the apartment to see if they could gather physical evidence that tied Michael to Annie's murder. It was a long shot because almost four years had passed and several tenants had probably rented the apartment in the interim. Nonetheless, it was worth a try.

The agents dressed Dawn in an NCIS jacket and hat for her safety. They didn't want anyone to recognize her and then warn Michael that she was working with them on the case.

Dawn's description of the crime scene was very concise, detailed, and very specific about the location of Annie's body. The forensic team sprayed the apartment with luminol for evidence of blood. The apartment lit up like a Christmas tree. Although the stained blood proved a murder might have occurred in the apartment, they still needed physical evidence.

The agents recalled that Dawn had told them about a television in the apartment. She remembered Michael had told her, "There's a lot of blood on that TV. You need to make sure you wipe that blood down good."[25] Dawn told the agents that Michael was very cheap and would have never thrown the television in the trash. He would have sold it prior to his move to Hawaii.

The agents thought, if they could find that television and find blood on it they could show that the murder took place in his apartment and create a timeline for the murder. Locating the television and blood on it was going to be like finding a needle in a haystack, and they were running out of time. The agents learned Michael had discovered that we had him under surveillance because Dawn had told him that NCIS had made him a prime suspect. The concern was that Michael might flee.

After Michael had been transferred from Hawaii to Long Beach Naval Station in California, he decided to make a run for it. The agents pursued and arrested him on October 11, 1995, and then transferred him to Naval Station Mayport in Florida to face court-martial charges.

While Michael was being held in the military jail, the agents interviewed everyone they could find who lived in the apartment complex at the time of and after the murder. Three months later, the agents hit pay dirt. One of the people they interviewed said he bought a television from Michael, and he still had it!

The television, which still had Annie's blood on it, was the nail in the coffin that confirmed Michael murdered Annie.

Sentence

In 1996 Michael Paalan was sentenced to 30 years to life in prison at the Fort Leavenworth U.S. Disciplinary Barracks in Kansas. Despite her role in the cover-up, Dawn Breeze was granted immunity for helping NCIS and received no jail time.[26]

During his incarceration, Michael submitted several appeals for early release. Because of good behavior, his request was approved. On August 14, 2013, Paalan was transferred to a halfway house in Savannah and then released on February 4, 2013. Paalan only served 16 years and four months of his 30-years-to-life prison sentence. He didn't even serve the minimum of his initial sentence. His whereabouts are unknown.

After Annie's family heard about Michael's release they expressed their frustration and anger with the court's decision. After Jody Weston, Annie's sister, heard about Paalan's scheduled early release, she watched one of the crime shows that highlighted Annie's murder 10 times. "After watching that show, I just can't understand how they are letting him out," Weston said. "I keep asking myself, 'What planet am I on? Is this a dream, is this real?' I need to wake up."[27]

Weston's attempts to find any possible legal way to keep Paalan in jail failed. Nevertheless, she continues to advocate for justice for Annie and also helps other families who have suffered the same fate as hers.

After the sentence, it appeared Annie's family finally received a resolution for her murder, but because of the judicial system's appeal process, Paalan's incarceration only provided temporary relief. Yes, there was some resolution, but was justice and empathy for Annie and her family properly served?

Annie Tahan is survived by three of her children—Jamie, Sean, and Jade.

Cold Case #3: Government of North Carolina v. Smith—Victim Alanda Jean Yusko

Summary

In April of 1982 18-year-old Alanda Jean Yusko left Slatington, Pennsylvania, and traveled to New Bern, North Carolina, to live with her brother, a marine; his wife, Virginia Constantino; and her father, Warren. She looked forward to leaving behind a troubled past and building a brighter future in New Bern.

Yusko worked as an assistant manager at the Scotchman convenience store in River Bend, a city eight miles from her home. She seemed genuinely happy for the first time in years and was engaged to a marine.

On September 26, 1982, while at work, Yusko had a phone conversation with Constantino. When Yusko didn't return home after the 11 p.m. closing time, Constantino drove to the store to check in on her. After Constantino arrived at the store she noticed the gas pumps had not been shut down and lights were left on in the store.

At 7:30 a.m. the next morning, River Bend police discovered Yusko's Dodge Duster submerged in a nearby pond. After the investigators discovered blood on the back seat, they opened the trunk and found Yusko's bloodied dead body with more than 30 bumps on her head. The coroner's report showed that Yusko died by suffocation and drowned from her vomit while being choked.

River Bend police also discovered that Yusko had engaged in sex with a man but did not tie him to the murder.

Controversy also surrounded the case with the questioning of Constantino, as well as the way River Bend Police Chief David Ellis handled the investigation. Constantino became a suspect after the River Bend police discovered she had left an ominous note at the store on the night Yusko disappeared. She agreed to take a polygraph and passed the test. She also submitted to hypnosis and was ruled out as a suspect.

In March 1983, River Bend Police Chief David Ellis resigned after residents circulated a petition complaining about the unsolved killing. Yusko's case took a backseat after this and turned cold for the next 17 years.[28]

Resolution

In 2000, River Bend Police Chief Duke Pratt made it a priority to investigate Yusko's murder because it had been the only unsolved killing on the department's books. Pratt assigned detectives to reexamine the original evidence with modern technological procedures, such as DNA testing. The detectives discovered physical evidence to connect and identify Carlton Tyrone Smith as the person who murdered Yusko. With this evidence, detectives put an undercover operational plan into action and used a cooperative witness to obtain a videotaped confession from Smith.

When detectives presented Smith with the evidence, he confessed to Yusko's murder. He admitted that he picked up Yusko after work. An argument ensued, and he killed her with a nunchaku—a martial arts weapon consisting of two sticks connected at one end by a short chain or rope. He then stuffed her in the trunk and drove her car into the River Bend pond.

Sentence

In March of 2003, Smith pleaded guilty to second-degree murder and received life in prison without parole.[29]

Cold Case #4: Government of Florida v. Johnstone— Victim Anita Mae Carter Lukander

Summary

Anita Mae Carter Lukander was a Navy administrative clerk. Her husband, Bill Lukander, also worked for the Navy. Anita was assigned to shore duty as an administrative clerk in maintenance control, while Bill worked as an electronics technician and was often at sea.

On March 18, 1988, when Anita did not report to work, authorities were sent to her home. When they arrived at her house, the door was found unlocked and the lights were left on. The officers filed a missing persons report and began their search for her.

At the time Anita disappeared, Bill was in Cuba. After Bill received news of her disappearance, he returned home to help the police search for Anita.

Nine days after Anita's disappearance officers found her truck, with the keys still in the ignition, in the parking lot of a local bar; they then found her mutilated and decomposed body on the shores of the Intracoastal Waterway. The medical examiner said her body had been in the water for about eight or nine days.

The Lukanders' friend Peter Johnstone, who was assigned to the same helicopter antisubmarine squadron at Mayport, became the prime suspect, but there was no physical evidence to implicate him. With no other leads, the local authorities decided to close Lukander's case.

In 1995 NCIS was assigned to reactivate Lukander's case. After further review of Johnstone's statements in the report, the investigators viewed him as a prime suspect again and brought him in for questioning. During the interrogation, Johnstone confessed to Lukander's murder. Based on his confession, the jury found Johnstone guilty and sentenced him to life in prison. The story doesn't end here, however.

Another Trial

Despite the guilty verdict, Johnstone continued to assert his innocence. He claimed that the investigators insisted he committed the murder and that he felt pressured to confess. He said the way he answered the questions—using the pronoun "I"—made it seem as if he murdered Lukander.

Johnstone's persistent demand for a new trial paid off when the public defender felt he might be innocent. The public defender made a desperate decision and hired a psychic counselor, Sharon Johns, in November of 1996. Johns provided the public defender with some new leads to prove Johnstone's innocence who then hired two different private detectives to follow up.

In 2005 the court granted Johnstone another trial, which lasted two weeks. Although the evidence presented by the public defender to the jury didn't lead to another suspect, it did raise enough reasonable doubt that the jury unanimously delivered a verdict of not guilty. Peter Johnstone walked out of jail a free man, and Lukander's case turned cold again.

While reasonable doubt, the bedrock of the judicial system, convicted and sentenced Johnstone to life in prison, it also exonerated him and initiated his release from prison.

The Lukander case is another example, like the Pope case in Chapter 1, of how a detective's best efforts don't always result in resolution and empathy for the family.[30]

3

The Biology and Physics of Cold Case Investigation

When I read a cold case file, I feel it speaks to me just as a psychic claims the dead speak to him or her. I am not a believer in psychic powers, but I believe in the sciences of biology and physics, and I apply them to the way I investigate cold cases.

While biologists study life and living organisms, I study the life of a cold case. I dissect evidence in the file like a biologist dissects a frog. Just as a biologist can't bring the frog back to life, I cannot resurrect a person's life after he or she has been murdered. What I can do is bring the cold case file that has been sitting in storage for years back to life.

I analyze text in the same way a physicist studies the behavior and properties of light, including its interactions with matter and the construction of instruments that use or detect it. I study the behavior of people and their interactions with one another and the use of technology to gather evidence and identify the murderer.

Through my knowledge of biology and physics, I developed a method to dissect the cold case file so that each piece of evidence speaks to me. This methodology helps me assess how and why the victim was murdered; what happened at the crime scene; and ultimately who is responsible for killing the victim. It also ensures that I conduct a thorough investigation of a cold case. I call it documentation dissection, and an example of how it works is included at the end of this chapter.

Documentation dissection is designed to identify investigative leads from written or recorded documents. The best way to describe it is like examining a frog after it has been dissected. Each individual part of the frog is studied to understand the importance of how each body part is connected to the others and why they are important to one another in breathing life into the frog. With a cold case file, which can consist of hundreds or thousands of pages, I examine the contents thoroughly to relive what occurred before, during, and after the crime.

I apply the physics of optics, which is the study of the fundamental properties of light and its interaction with matter, making attention to detail a necessary habit. This perspective helps me shed light on crucial evidence that may have been overlooked or information that may lead me to evidence that is not in the file. The order in which I gather the evidence also plays an important role in making good use of my time to identify the killer. For example, one piece of evidence may lead me to a wild goose chase that leads to lost time in solving the case. That is time lost that could be better spent on more convincing evidence that will lead me directly to the killer. The investigation takes an enormous amount of manpower and hours. Therefore, the sooner I solve the case, the better for the victim's family and community.

Although I designed documentation dissection specifically for cold cases, a detective could apply it to a fresh homicide case, which in turn could decrease the number of cold cases.

Arriving at a fresh homicide scene is quite different from reading secondhand news in a cold case file. Therefore, to gain a better perspective on how documentation dissection works, I'd like to describe how I operate when I arrive at a fresh homicide scene.

I have been told I have a nose for solving cold cases. But I do not just use my nose. I also use sight, hearing, and touch. Of these four senses, sight is the easiest to apply because humans rely on it more than the other senses. If I need verification of what I saw, it is easy for me to refer to the hundreds of photographs taken at every crime scene. My sight, however, kicks in way before I arrive at the crime scene. I'm already looking for clues while I'm en route. I pay attention to what the landscape looks like because it will provide information that will benefit me during the investigation. Details such as the landscape, dynamics of the neighborhood, demographics of the people who live there, what route the killer took to arrive at the crime scene, and his possible escape route are all considered.

When I conduct interviews with people in and around the crime scene, I pay attention to their body language to assess whether they are telling the truth or not. Some examples include nervous twitches, a lack of eye contact, movement of the head, tone of voice, and posture, as well as signs of lack of remorse, narcissistic behavior, or another lie, like in poker, that might indicate the witness is bluffing, lying, or hiding information.

Unlike sight, I need a more acute awareness in using my ears to record noises I hear and my nose to detect odors. Some examples include the sound of the wheels turning on a train track or a factory whistle or the odor of a cooked meal, perfume, cologne, marijuana, or fumes from a cleaning product. Anything I smell may trigger a clue or lead me in a direction towards solving the case.

After all the required photos are taken and the body has been removed, I can utilize my sense of touch by manipulating the crime scene. Sometimes I need to move an item, furniture, and even the body or search areas like drawers or closets that may conceal evidence. For example, I may need to move a bed, table, pillow, or blanket to find the murder weapon or shell casings from the gun. There may also be other evidence like jewelry the killer may have been wearing during the murder or an item that may have the killer's fingerprints on it, like an empty bottle of beer or soda that rolled underneath the couch.

Even moving the body is an important maneuver that may solve the case. One time I arrived to find a woman's dead body. After the photos were taken, I moved the body and discovered that she had died of natural causes. My conclusion of natural death at the scene saved me from spending a lot of unnecessary time trying to identify a killer that didn't exist. Moving the body may also reveal that the person committed suicide.

In another homicide case, the detectives arrived to find two victims in a bedroom. A woman's body was on the floor next to the bed. She was shot and died on the scene. A man lying on the bed had a gunshot wound in his head and was still alive but unconscious. As the detectives continued the investigation, they couldn't find the gun, assumed the killer ran off with it, and treated the investigation as a homicide. One of the officers called the paramedics to transport the male victim to the hospital.

Detectives could not interview the man in the hospital because he was unconscious, so they began interviewing people in the neighborhood and relatives of both victims. A few days later at the morgue, the coroner removed the comforter that was wrapped around the dead woman's body and discovered a gun. Shortly thereafter, the man at the hospital regained consciousness. When detectives questioned him, he was not cooperative. After the detectives reviewed the evidence and testimonies from relatives and friends, they concluded that this case was a homicide and suicide gone wrong and that the murderer was the man in the hospital.

Because the couple had a history of domestic abuse, the detectives concluded that when the girlfriend arrived home from a night out with her girlfriends, an argument ensued, and the jealous boyfriend shot and killed her. He then attempted to commit suicide, but when he shot himself the recoiling action of the gun redirected the bullet's angle into his head and only rendered him unconscious. After the bullet discharged from the gun, he fell on the bed and the gun fell underneath the comforter in a way that it was hidden from view at the crime scene.

If the detectives had conducted a more diligent search and discovered the gun while at the crime scene, they could have saved themselves a lot of time and solved the case a lot more quickly.

In a cold case file, I don't have the luxury of the firsthand accounts that I've described. I must rely on another detective's notes and written report, which presents another list of challenges. The detective who wrote the report might not conduct the investigation the same way as I explained and miss crucial evidence that I may have found. Second, detectives are required to transcribe their notes into an official report, which presents a language change issue.

Different law enforcement agencies have different requirements in the way they write a report, so information about the cold case can get lost in translation. A storytelling game called "Telephone" illustrates how easy it is to lose parts of or fail to grasp the full meaning or significance of translated language.

In this internationally popular children's game, players form a line and the first player comes up with a message and whispers it into the ear of the second person in the line. The second player repeats the message to the third player, and so on. The last player announces the message he or she heard to the entire group. The end result is usually that the last player's message differs significantly from that of the first player. Reasons for changes include anxiousness or impatience, erroneous corrections, the difficulty of understanding whispers, and deliberate alteration of what is being said.

Another obstacle with a cold case file is a change in leadership. The new sheriff or high-ranking police officer will often request that copies of their cold case files be stored elsewhere. The cold case file might also be lost due to a move to another location or destroyed by fire or water damage.

Documentation dissection translates for me the secondhand information into meaningful intelligence that will help solve the case. It's a process that incorporates many fundamental practices I've learned during the course of my work as an investigator. Before I share more details of how I apply documentation dissection in reviewing a cold case, the following is the story of another solved cold case.

Cold Case #5: Government of Virginia v. Whittle— Victim Pamela Ann Kimbrue

Summary

Pamela Ann Kimbrue was a Navy message courier at the Norfolk Naval Air Station in Norfolk, Virginia. Kimbrue had been in the Navy for about two years. She was reported missing on March 25, 1982.

The following day, intensive searches were conducted at the Naval Air Station and in the Norfolk area. Navy divers found Kimbrue's car in Willoughby Bay about 150 feet from the Navy Communications Center. Kimbrue's dead body was in the back seat. She had suffered blunt force injuries and trauma to the head and face. Her wrists were bound with rope, a seat belt had been placed around her neck, and she had been sexually assaulted. The cause of death was drowning following mechanical strangulation. Also found in the car was a green ski mask, two makeshift mittens described as T-shirts stapled together, glass fragments from a broken soft drink bottle, hairs, and latent fingerprint impressions.

Richard H. Whittle was questioned about the murder in April and July 1982. He denied knowing Kimbrue. Investigators did not pursue him as a suspect because they had no evidence to tie him to Kimbrue's death. They did follow a variety of other leads for 12 years but eventually reached a dead end.

Resolution

In April of 1995, the NCIS Cold Case Squad was assigned to reactivate and investigate the Kimbrue case. After a review of the case, Richard H. Whittle became the primary suspect after the NCIS investigative team obtained statements from Whittle's acquaintances incriminating him. Several witnesses told investigators that Whittle lied when he denied he knew the victim. Whittle told at least one former colleague that he was the "last person to see her alive." This was an item to be placed on our list of inconsistencies.

Investigators discovered that Whittle allegedly told various acquaintances, roommates, and others that he knew Kimbrue from work and that he had been in a building she had been in just before and after her death. Whittle allegedly told several people that he owned or had access to a ski mask similar to the one found in the victim's car.

The investigators felt that they needed more conclusive evidence than witness testimony to convict Whittle. With the recent admissibility of DNA in court and advances in technology, the investigators orchestrated an operational plan called a ruse to collect a DNA sample from Whittle without his knowledge.

The investigators assigned a female agent to pose as a door-to-door canvasser. When she arrived at Whittle's house, she asked if he would participate in a shopping preference survey. He agreed. After he answered the questions, the agent placed his answers in an envelope and asked Whittle to seal them to ensure the integrity of the survey. Whittle licked the envelope and returned it to the agent.

Whittle's DNA from the envelope was a match, meaning he couldn't be eliminated as a possible source of the semen. Investigators also discovered that head and pubic hairs recovered from the ski mask were microscopically similar to Whittle's hair.

Recent advances in forensic examinations provided investigators with the ability to compare latent fingerprint impressions recovered from Kimbrue's car in 1982. One of the fingerprints matched Whittle's left middle finger.

After the investigators presented all the evidence to Whittle, he confessed to killing Kimbrue.

Sentence

On January 28, 1997, the court convicted and sentenced Richard H. Whittle to serve one life sentence for murder and a separate life sentence for rape.[1]

When I review a cold case for the first time, I try to imagine I am at the fresh crime scene when the detective first arrived and then picture how four of my five senses would have responded had I been present at the crime scene.

To gain a visual recollection of the murder I take my time when I view the photos of the crime scene in the cold case file. Every photo helps me build a story about the homicide, even those of the victim's lifeless body. The position of the victim's body and the evidence around him or her help me reconstruct the murder. While most detectives look at a photo from a crime scene from the center and outward, I use a magnifying glass and start from the corners of the photo and work inward. I have discovered that this provides me with a different visual perspective that allows me to find clues that were overlooked. It is important to view the photos from every angle and in great detail. This strategy is similar to how people piece a jigsaw puzzle together. The best and most efficient method to finish a jigsaw puzzle is to start with the border pieces and then connect the inside pieces as you move towards the middle. The same holds true with video recordings when they are reviewed for overlooked clues.

In one crime scene photograph, I noticed a cigarette butt that I thought the killer might have dropped. At first glance, it looked like a regular cigarette butt. However, a closer examination with the magnifying glass revealed an unusual twist on the cigarette butt. The investigative file had a list of three suspects who smoked cigarettes. Further investigation disclosed that one of them had a habit of twisting his cigarettes in the same manner as the one found at the crime scene. He was immediately targeted as the primary suspect based on the manner in which he twisted his cigarettes.

When reviewing a crime scene photo, compare it with the original detective's report to confirm the manner in which the murder happened. This is especially true when blood is found at the crime scene. Passive blood flow or droppings will help determine if a body was moved at the scene while vertical blood droplets help determine the path the victim and/or suspect took after the murder.

When reviewing blood evidence, concentrate on the voids. Where is blood evidence not found that it should be and why is it not there? Was the perpetrator standing in a particular position while he or she bled?

Here is a list of other questions to ask while reviewing the crime scene photos. Was there forced entry? Are there signs of a physical struggle? Was the crime organized or disorganized? Why is the body here? What is wrong with the scene? Why did this person die? What is the evidence of planning and premeditation? What are the efforts to avoid detection, identification, and apprehension? Who wants this person dead?

The reconstruction of the crime scene photos will help verify statements of witnesses and suspects and hopefully direct you to the killer.

A valuable skill I utilize is the writing skill used by authors, screenplay writers, and film writers: character development. Every crime scene tells a story and includes characters, a plot, and a beginning, middle, and end. However, in contrast to authors who lead readers to a predetermined ending, the resolution of a cold case depends on how a detective investigates the case.

Developing characters is central to successful fiction writing, screenwriting, and filmmaking—and to writing in general. It plays a large role in determining the success of a writer's storyline. This is also true when investigating a cold case. The more intelligence and personality traits I gather about the witnesses and bystanders at or near the murder scene, the more I will be able to relate to them. Character development helps me create a psychological analysis of each person so I can determine to some degree if the witness is telling the truth or if there are any inconsistencies in the testimony that might lead me to more evidence or to the identity of the killer.[2]

How I read a cold case file is also crucial in documentation dissection. As I noted earlier, there are hundreds and sometimes thousands of pages. Reading them can be very tiresome, but even when a detective is not tired he is prone to human error. This reading exercise explains how important it is to pay attention to every letter and word.

Count the number of times the letter "f" appears in the following sentence: *Finished files are the result of years of scientific study combined with the experience of many years.*

Most people see the "f" appear only three or four times, when it actually appears six times because the brain is trained to overlook the word "of," so most people only see three or four at first glance. If you counted six the first time, you are considered a genius.[3]

Some people feel I have a sixth sense for solving cold cases. I appreciate the compliment, but I feel that I just place more value in the cold case file than most detectives. Like Sherlock Holmes and Columbo, I take great pains to pay attention to detail and focus on what was done and overlooked in an original file as well as what still needs to be done.

How important are details? It is best explained in a *Columbo* episode titled "An Exercise in Fatality."[4] Columbo demonstrates how a simple everyday task everyone participates in solved the case.

The killer is Milo Janus, who has franchised a chain of health spas bearing his name. The spa contracts include requirements to purchase products and services from his other companies at inflated prices. This catches the attention of Gene Stafford, who threatens to bring Janus's little empire crashing down around his ears, with predictable consequences. This is what motivates Janus to kill Stafford and also attempt to establish the perfect alibi.

Stafford is found dead in the health spa's weight room. After he views the crime scene, Columbo wonders why Stafford exercised in the gym after eating a large meal of Chinese food, and something about Stafford's tennis gym shoes grabs his attention.

Columbo explains how someone else had dressed Stafford, based on how Stafford's shoelaces on his gym shoes were tied. He demonstrates how, when right-handed people tie their shoes, the big loop of the lace ends up over the same toe every time. Columbo discovers that Stafford's gym shoelaces show the big loop over the opposite toe, which conflicts with the way his work shoes are tied. This proved to him that after Janus killed Stafford, he dressed him in his gym clothes and tied the gym shoes in the opposite direction. Then he made it look like Stafford had accidentally dropped the weight bench bar on his neck.

By Janus's own admission he was the last person to see Stafford. Witnesses last saw Stafford alive wearing work clothes. Janus testified that nine hours before Stafford's body was found, he had knowledge that Stafford had been dressed in his gym clothes. Columbo concluded that Janus's testimony confirmed he was the killer because only the killer would have known Stafford had his gym clothes on because the killer dressed him.

"You and you alone knew that he was in his gym clothes. You said so. You swore to it in front of five witnesses. How did you know he was in his gym clothes if you didn't change the clothes? You tried to contrive the perfect alibi, sir. And it's your perfect alibi that's gonna hang you," explains Columbo.[5]

In short, with documentation dissection, each investigative document is evaluated thoroughly. You simply read each and every sentence to identify investigative leads that were overlooked or not completed. Inconsistencies are also noted at this time. Documentation dissection ensures that the four critical phases of an investigation are completed. The ultimate goal is a more thorough investigation. This will help focus the investigation on the correct suspect(s) and identify outstanding investigative steps that need to be completed.

Another important technique that I apply is keeping an A-to-Z list of inconsistencies. I have a good memory, but I'm human and thus prone to making mistakes. I'm also forced to digest an inordinate amount of information during an investigation. There is no way to recall all the little ins and outs of a case. The list of inconsistencies helps me see on paper what is not making sense in my head. It helps show that something could not have happened the way it was reported to have happened. The list of inconsistencies may draw on every aspect of information about the crime like the photos; testimony of witnesses, relatives, friends, and bystanders; errors in the detective's report; and case facts or evidence that are inconsistent with what actually could have happened. The list helps me see all the things about the case that simply do not make sense or contradict the established facts in the case. I continuously update it throughout the course of an investigation so that I only utilize the most accurate information that will help solve the cold case.

Inconsistency in an investigation is not a coincidence. There is no such thing as a coincidence in a murder case. There is no set rule in locating inconsistency in a cold case file. It varies from case to case. Once you recognize one, however, it sticks out like a sore thumb. The following examples of inconsistency will help you recognize what to look for in the investigation.

During interrogation, a suspect stated, "I don't know the victim." Later in the investigation, one of the suspect's friends shared a conversation he had with the suspect, in which the suspect said, "The detectives see me as a suspect because I'm the one who saw her alive last." This is what actually happened with the Whittle case I shared before.

The inconsistency here is that the suspect denied he knew the victim to the police and then implied to his friend that he did know the victim. This is an example of a tacit admission. The legal definition is an admission that can be reasonably inferred from the act or statement of a party, or from a party's failure to perform an act or make a statement.

In another cold case murder, one key witness recalled seeing the suspect leave the murder scene at 9:05 a.m., yet another key witness stated a time of 9:40 a.m. The conflict in times indicates that one of the witnesses may be unreliable or is not telling the truth. This inconsistency told me that I needed to question the integrity or the credibility of these two witnesses so I could pinpoint the correct time of the murder.

There is a scene in the movie *My Cousin Vinny* that demonstrates how a person can lose track of time. The attorney in the movie is Vinny Gambini (Joe Pesci) and the witness is Mr. Tipton (Maury Chaykin). Mr. Tipton testified that only five minutes passed between the suspects entering and exiting the store. Gambini asked Tipton if he looked at his watch to determine how much time had passed. He replied, "No." Gambini then asked what he was doing from the time the suspects entered the store to the time they left. Mr. Tipton stated that he had been preparing breakfast, which included cooking grits. Gambini informed the court that it takes 20 minutes to cook grits. Mr. Tipton finally admitted he might have been mistaken about the amount of time.[6]

People are creatures of habit, and another cold case demonstrates how a person's habits can reveal inconsistency. Timothy Crumitie's wife and a man, James Blanks, are found dead in Crumitie's garage.

Crumitie claimed he caught Blanks robbing their house and shot him in self-defense.

When I read the report a comment repeated by several neighbors caught my attention. They pointed out that the suspect always parked his car on the right side of the garage. On the day of the murder, they said he had parked the car on the left side. It raised an important question that needed an answer: "Why did Crumitie park his car on the left side?"

The answer is that he had to park the car there because the murder occurred on the side where he usually parked his car. Answering this question led us to believe that the husband premeditated the murder of his wife and Blanks. After further questioning, we discovered these details about the murders. The husband bought chicken meals at a fast-food restaurant. He then convinced Blanks, a homeless man, to join him for a meal at his house. After Blanks and his wife entered the garage, he shot and killed both of them. I will share more details about this cold case in Chapter 4.[7]

Statement analysis is a critical component for identifying inconsistencies. It will disclose clues to identify the killer and sort out which case facts are correct or false. Look for missing facts and blocks of time that do not provide an alibi for any of the people interviewed during the investigative process and neighborhood canvass.

Another important step to identify an inconsistency is to review the neighborhood canvass reports recorded by the original investigators. This will determine if all of the occupants of a particular location were identified and interviewed. Look closely at individuals who had been interviewed more than once in the original investigation. Look for names recorded in the original neighborhood canvasses for which there is no documentation in the investigative file of an interview. Also, determine who did not belong at the scene of the crime. Before interviewing individuals identified in the original neighborhood canvass or as part of the initial investigation, complete a background check on these individuals.

Essentially the A-to-Z list forces me to keep a record of every step I make in analyzing the cold case file. It increases the chances that I will not miss any critical information that might help solve the case.

Documentation dissection includes three important and necessary

3. The Biology and Physics of Cold Case Investigation

elements I developed from the first few cold cases I solved with NCIS. They are time, technology, and tenacity. I call them the "three pillars of cold case work" because they are the building blocks of solving a cold case. Each pillar makes an important contribution, and I strongly believe the proper application of these three components is essential for the successful resolution of a cold case.

As I noted in Chapter 1, the first 48 hours of a fresh homicide case are crucial because *if you can't find a lead within the first 48 hours, the chances of solving the case decrease dramatically*.[8] With a cold case, however, time becomes an ally because relationships between people change and deteriorate.

A witness may no longer harbor the same fear of or allegiance to the suspect. Time may have made the suspect weaker and less of a threat to the witness. A spouse or friend of the suspect may no longer be on friendly terms with the suspect or may even have turned into an adversary. An example of this is the Paalan cold case story at the end of Chapter 2, in which the suspect's ex-wife assisted the NCIS detectives in the investigation. This change of heart by a witness becomes a valuable commodity and should be used as an investigative advantage.

A witness may have committed or been convicted of a crime. This provides me with leverage to negotiate a deal with the witness to share the truth about the crime. However, I must tread cautiously to ensure that the witness is not lying to save his own skin—to avoid a conviction or make a deal for an early release from jail—none of which is an option I can offer or guarantee.

A witness may have experienced an epiphany that causes them to want to clear their conscience. It could be the result of an event like a near-death experience, a marriage, becoming a parent, or renewed faith in God. Even a heartbreaking event like divorce or separation from a spouse may trigger a change of heart.

A witness may have a change of heart because the trauma of the murder has worn off, making them feel more comfortable about sharing information they withheld at the time of the initial interview with the detective. There may have been a change in the relationship that led to animosity between the suspect and witness(es).

Witnessing (or receiving news of) a murder is a traumatic event. Most people would like to tell the truth or what they know, but the shock and trauma that follows keep them from doing so. An example is a response I often hear from a witness or bystander: "Wow, I can't believe he/she is a killer. He/she seemed like such a nice person." The person's subconscious can't believe the person is guilty, so the witness doesn't voluntarily offer information that might convict the suspect. This is especially true when the witness is a relative. Sometimes, a witness may not have been asked the right questions when interviewed by the original investigators, or there may have been a personality conflict between the witness and the detective.

A witness may become a person the murderer confides in enough to share details about the murder or even a confession. Sometimes a killer's ego will get the best of him or her. Either he or she will brag about the murder, or let down his or her guard and reveal otherwise unknown details about the murder. It is possible that the trauma of the murder, as it is with witnesses, has worn off. The victim's relative may be able to think more clearly about the case as well as provide information about unusual behaviors of potential suspects listed in the file. They may lead me to a person who is not identified in the file or may accumulate additional information over time.

The passage of time has provided detectives with access to the rapidly growing advances of modern technology in forensic science. The most noteworthy is DNA analysis. Scientists originally developed DNA analysis as a method of determining paternity, in which samples taken under clinical conditions were examined for genetic evidence that could link parent to child. In 1986, DNA evidence made its way into the court system, when police in England asked molecular biologist Alec Jeffreys, who had begun investigating the use of DNA for forensics, to use DNA to verify whether a 17-year-old boy was the perpetrator of two rape/murders in the English Midlands. The tests proved that the teenager was not the perpetrator. Police eventually found a match and identified the perpetrator.

Another area of forensic science that has improved immensely because of technology is biometrics. Today, the term "biometrics" is not limited to fingerprints. It also includes palm prints, iris scans and facial recognition. The FBI recently developed the Next Generation Identification (NGI) biometric database, the world's largest and most efficient database of criminal history and biometric information that continues to evolve as user requirements change and new technologies emerge. It is also designed to integrate with other surveillance technology, such as Trapwire.

The NGI system should be used by all cold case investigators, especially when analyzing and comparing fingerprints previously found at crime scenes. The NGI system is superior to the Automated Fingerprint Identification System (AFIS) that has been used since the mid-1990s. NGI is a better system for identifying and linking partial or smudged fingerprints and/or palm prints to a particular individual. Please visit https://le.fbi.gov/science-and-lab-resources/biometrics-and-fingerprints/biometrics/next-generation-identification-ngi for additional information regarding NGI and the advantages it provides investigators when compared to AFIS.

Huge improvements have also been made in ballistics with the introduction of the Drugfire system. Drugfire is a multimedia database imaging system that automates the comparison of images of bullet cartridge cases, shell casings, and bullets. The system allows firearm examiners to quickly retrieve images from unsolved firearm ammunition case files and makes matches in minutes.[9]

The Bureau of Alcohol, Tobacco, and Firearms and Explosives, in conjunction with Forensic Technology Incorporated of Montréal, Canada, developed the Integrated Ballistics Identification System (IBIS), also known as "Bulletproof and Brass Catcher." Old-timers like me refer to it as IBIS, but today's detectives refer to it as NIBIN. Like the Drugfire system, IBIS/NIBIN identifies and creates an image of the marks made by an empty casing or expended bullet. It then attempts to match it to a similar casing or bullet that may have been used in another crime.[10]

The National Institute of Law Enforcement Standards and Technology is currently in the process of making the IBIS and Drugfire systems compatible. Both Drugfire and IBIS can be accessed and utilized at various local, state, and federal forensic laboratories.

Although technology has increased a detective's ability to conduct an effective and productive investigation, the last of the three pillars, tenacity, is the most crucial in solving a cold case. It's the day-to-day grind of repeatedly searching for clues, interviewing witnesses, determining whether a witness is telling the truth or lying, and following one lead to another, which frequently leads to dead ends.

Arthur Conan Doyle describes detective work in his Sherlock Holmes series of books:

> Detectives have to be able to pick themselves up from dead-end clues. Detectives can't be easily discouraged. Holmes went on to say, "A genius is one who has the infinite capacity for taking pains. It's a very bad definition, but it does apply to detective work." In other words, a detective has to be tenacious and accept the fact that not every clue will lead to a pot of gold.[11]

A homicide investigation is hard work. It involves long hours, many disappointments and frustrations, and sleepless nights. A good detective finds a way to make it through the tough times and maintain the motivation and persistence to never give up. "This requires a certain level of tenacity and commitment that is beyond a 9-to-5 mentality" and requires patience as well as being a self-starter.[12]

I feel there is no substitute in police work, especially in cold case investigations, for good old, relentless gumshoe detective work. Author Louis N. Eliopoulos describes the tenacity a detective needs in his *Death Investigator's Handbook*: "The ideal investigator is that individual who knocks on one more door; who misses one more hot meal; who looks at the scene photographs one more time; who makes one more phone call; who makes one last try; who solves one more case."[13]

Why is tenacity so important? One reason is that it provides a perspective to place short-term difficulties in the context of a higher goal. Tenacity is about a commitment to a cause or goal that helps a person look beyond an obstacle and treat it as an opportunity to improve and ultimately achieve success. Tenacity gives a person the confidence and determination to resolve an issue, even if he or she doesn't initially have the know-how. A tenacious person believes that if there is a will, there is a way.

As you will read in the next chapter, tenacity serves as a valuable asset in the psychological chess game that develops between a detective and the prime suspect.

Cold Case #6: Government of Virginia v. Deshazo— Victim Allen McClendon

Summary

In 1992, Jerry Allen McClendon lived near the Little Creek Naval Base in Virginia Beach, and he allowed his Navy buddy, David Allen

Deshazo, to move into his home on Solar Lane, along with his girlfriend, Roxanna Latham. McClendon and Deshazo had recently returned from an overseas deployment, and Latham was preparing to leave the Navy.

On October 2, 1992, hunters discovered McClendon's badly decomposed body in a furniture dump, underneath a couch and wrapped in a bed sheet. A skin sample from the corpse's hand was taken to the laboratory to fingerprint. Police used sophisticated forensics technology to identify the body and determine how long it had been in the trash heap. Evidence indicated that McClendon died a month earlier of asphyxiation. There were high levels of a tranquilizer in the victim's body, which indicated he'd been drugged before being suffocated.

Detectives arrived at McClendon's house and discovered clues that indicated he had fought his attacker. They found a pillowcase of the same material as the bedsheet stained with bodily fluids.

A search through McClendon's financial accounts revealed that there had been withdrawals from it at a cash machine well after he had died. Detectives followed up by reviewing security cameras, which showed a man and woman withdrawing money. The pair were identified as McClendon's former roommates, Deshazo and Latham, who were living two miles from where McClendon's dead body was found. Detectives interviewed Deshazo and Latham as possible suspects, but were unable to collect evidence to make an arrest.

Resolution

It took a few years for detectives to collect enough evidence to issue warrants for Deshazo and Latham and track them down. In 1998, they first arrested Deshazo and then Latham. By this time Latham had ended her relationship with Deshazo and decided to confess to her involvement in the murder, which helped strengthen the court's case against Deshazo.

Latham confessed that, on September 21, 1992, she and Deshazo turned against the man who was providing them shelter. They used Latham's anti-anxiety medication, the prescription drug Xanax, to spike a plate of pasta that they served to McClendon. According to Dr.

Arthur McBay, the drug dose that McClendon ingested was more than enough to kill a person.

After McClendon lapsed into a drug-induced coma the next day, the couple made sure he would not survive by suffocating him with a pillow. They rented a U-Haul truck, packed up McClendon's furnishings, placed his body in the truck, emptied his bank account, and drove two hundred miles to Henry County, Virginia, where they dumped McClendon's body on a trash heap near their new apartment.

Sentence

Deshazo was convicted of first-degree murder and sentenced to life in prison; Latham was convicted of second-degree murder and sentenced to 15 years in prison.[14]

Cold Case #7: Government of Florida v. Hinton— Victim Shannon Melendi

Summary

On Saturday afternoon, March 26, 1994, Shannon Melendi, a 19-year-old Emory University student from Miami, had been keeping score at a softball game for the Softball Country Club in Atlanta, Georgia. At about 1 p.m. Melendi took a 15-minute break before the next scheduled game but never returned.

The next day police found her black Nissan 240, unlocked and with the keys still in the ignition, in the parking lot of a Citgo station and convenience store about a quarter mile away. Detectives did not find any signs of a struggle in her car. Despite an organized search with a tracking dog and a helicopter, detectives were unable to locate her.

After interviewing the softball players and spectators, detectives took a special interest in the comments shared by some of the players. They said that the umpire, Butch Hinton, neglected his duties during their game to look at and talk with Melendi.

When questioned, Hinton admitted that he spoke with Melendi but denied any part in her disappearance. Hinton provided an alibi of his whereabouts after the game and claimed that he had made several telephone calls that afternoon from his home. Phone records showed Hinton's first call was less than 40 minutes after his departure from the softball field, a 25-minute drive from his home.

Witnesses said Hinton reappeared at the softball field between 2:30 p.m. and 3:00 p.m. that afternoon and was seen around that time at the gas station where Melendi's car was found. Another witness saw Hinton around 5:00 p.m. and remarked that he thought Hinton had left, to which Hinton replied he had forgotten to turn in a pay slip and had returned to do so. Another witness said she saw Hinton tending a bonfire in his yard around 3:00 a.m. the morning after Melendi's disappearance.

Hinton became the primary suspect, and detectives searched his home. They discovered three pits in his back yard that contained clothing, wire ties, and a black bag like the one Hinton was seen carrying on the day Melendi disappeared. Hinton claimed he knew nothing about the items buried in his yard and that the previous owner(s) may have buried them. After forensic scientists examined the items, they had no evidence to prove Hinton buried these items.

The following week, the DeKalb Police Department received an anonymous phone call. The person said Melendi was alive and he'd call later with his demands for a ransom. The caller ID led detectives to a payphone where they found a ring that belonged to Melendi in a small cloth bag wrapped in masking tape. Detectives never heard from the caller again and determined it was the killer's attempt to sidetrack the detectives. Although much of the circumstantial evidence pointed to Hinton, without a body or solid physical evidence, detectives couldn't connect Hinton to Melendi's disappearance.

Unfortunately Melendi's case hit a roadblock after police arrested Hinton in 1995 for arson and mail fraud. Hinton set his home on fire to try and collect $185,000 from his home insurance policy. The jury found Hinton guilty and sentenced him to 10 years in prison. With Hinton in prison, prosecutors halted further investigation of his possible role in Melendi's disappearance.

Resolution

Ten years after Melendi's disappearance, prosecutors John Petry and Mike McDaniel reopened her case because they were convinced

Butch Hinton was somehow involved. Petry and McDaniel requested that forensic scientist Mary Miller compare one of the small bags from Butch Hinton's desk to the small bag found with Shannon's ring. Miller determined that the bags were consistent in construction, size, and weave pattern. Both drawstrings were also made of the same cotton polyester microfiber.

Forensic scientists also analyzed the masking tape that had been wrapped around Shannon's ring and compared it to the rolls of tape confiscated from Butch Hinton's garage years earlier. Their findings showed that they were consistent with respect to the width of the tape, the adhesive that was used on the tape, and the coating surface of the tape. They discovered an alloy, clearly visible with an infrared spectrometer, that had been overlooked in the initial investigation. It was an alloy only used in the aerospace industry. Delta Airlines used this alloy to coat jet engine parts. Detectives traced the bag and masking tape to the manufacturer whose only customer was Delta Airlines, where Hinton worked as a mechanic at the time of Melendi's disappearance. Forensic scientists found the same metal alloy particles on the rolls of masking tape confiscated from Hinton's garage, his car, and the tape from the telephone booth.

Petry and McDaniel also discovered shocking information about Hinton from the FBI. Before Hinton moved to Atlanta, he had three prior convictions in Illinois for sexual assault and kidnapping. In one of those cases, his first wife walked in on him while he was assaulting a 14-year-old girl. The court convicted Hinton and sentenced him to four years, but he only served two.

Sentence

With new, solid forensic evidence, detectives arrested Hinton. Although Hinton claimed his innocence, the jury found him guilty of the murder of Shannon Melendi and sentenced him to life in prison.

Years later during a prison interview, Hinton confessed to killing Melendi. Hinton said that during the break between softball games he invited Melendi to lunch at Burger King. After lunch, he faked a leg cramp, asked her to drive his car, held Melendi at knifepoint, and forced her to drive to his home, where he raped her and then strangled her with a necktie. He then burned her body with gasoline on the property, placed her ashes in a bag, and dumped her ashes elsewhere.[15]

4

The Difference Between a Cold and Fresh Homicide Case

Investigating and solving a fresh homicide is a daunting task. Each murder is distinctly different, complex, and complicated. It requires tremendous amounts of patience and expertise developed through years of responding to death scenes. The smallest miscalculation of facts will sidetrack an investigator, which might derail the investigation or result in the case going cold. Some of the reasons a case turns cold are because clues were ignored, misinterpreted, overlooked, and/or contained uncompleted investigative leads.

There are several ways law enforcement defines a cold case. Here is a shortlist of what might count as a cold case:

1. A major violent crime in which all leads have been exhausted
2. Any major case that has not generated a lead within six months
3. Any unsolved major felony that has been stagnant for one year
4. Any case that involves a suspicious death, unidentified remains, or missing person
5. A homicide that has been unsolved for more than three years
6. A death the cause if which is undetermined or that has been ruled a homicide, for which all leads have been exhausted without resolution[1]

One of the biggest differences between a fresh homicide case and a cold case is that instead of (or in addition to) the family burying their loved one's body in a casket or urn, he or she is buried in a file cabinet or database as another cold case statistic. The best way to describe the difference in working a fresh homicide versus a cold case is to compare it to the difference between chess and checkers. While the games of chess and checkers are both played on a game board with 64 squares arranged in an eight-by-eight grid, the similarities stop there.

Checkers is an easy game to explain, teach, and play. It is a simple game with pieces that can only move diagonally and one space at a time. In checkers, a player captures an opponent's piece by jumping over it.

Chess is a more complex game to explain, teach, and play. It is a sophisticated game with six diverse pieces, each of which moves in a unique and different direction. In chess, a player may take an opponent's piece by moving one of his or her own pieces to the square that contains an opponent's piece. The opponent's piece is removed from the board and is out of play for the rest of the game.

No disrespect to checkers players or detectives who work fresh homicide cases, but chess—like a cold case—requires greater use of brainpower to master and is intellectually more demanding. Chess is said to be "the touchstone of the human intellect."[2] Numerous studies have concluded that chess develops mental abilities such as concentration, critical thinking, abstract reasoning, composure, patience, creative thinking, pattern recognition, and strategic thinking.

Chess has some fascinating dynamics that are similar to solving a cold case. Chess is the ultimate game of strategy and is made up of three stages—the opening, middle, and end game. In chess, it is important to understand the terrain and adapt to both gradual and abrupt changes. To play chess effectively and win requires a well thought out and precisely executed plan to attack and defend.

A player who wants to win in chess has to first learn how each piece moves—from the pawn to the bishop, to the rook, to the knight, to the queen and king. A player must learn the unique role and function each piece performs during a chess match.

Bobby Fischer, the American chess grandmaster whom many consider to be the greatest chess player of all time, once said: "Winning in this game is all a matter of understanding how to capitalize on the strengths of each piece and timing their moves just right."[3]

The following tactics of chess can be incorporated into solving cold case homicides. Chess is a psychological battle between two people and personalities. To win the match a player must find and exploit his or her opponent's weakness. It's a win-at-all-cost mentality in which a player will do whatever it takes to win within the rules of the game, even if it means sacrificing one of the pieces, except the king.

To fully harness the power of chess psychology it is important to know your own game. Before you can expect to be able to identify the key strengths and weaknesses in your opponent's game, you will need to assess your weaknesses and strengths. Before you can know your enemy, you must know yourself.

Analyzing your own game with the critical eye you give to someone else's game helps you understand why you do the things that you do and how well it serves you. Maybe there's a move that you consider your "signature" that you like to do in each game, but, upon further reflection, you decide that it really does more harm than good in the long run. Maybe there's a move you never make that would be perfectly appropriate in certain circumstances.[4]

The William Pope cold case in Chapter 1 is an example of a move I made that did not provide me with the desired result. I had expected the biological bond between father and son to initiate a confession. But the plan failed because there was no intimate relationship between William and his son. Nevertheless, given an appropriate circumstance in a future cold case, I would attempt this move again.

Once you have identified your own strengths, weaknesses, and patterns, then look for weaknesses in each suspect's file and look over his or her past with a studious eye. Analyze his or her past with the same laser-like focus you'd apply to a fresh homicide case. If you don't happen to have a suspect, you'll need to rely a bit on your intuition and your own ability to read people. If you don't know anything specific about your suspect(s), you can always fall back on exploiting weaknesses common among murderers.

In the Nefta Petersen cold case from Chapter 1, I exploited a weakness about Petersen that an informant shared with us—that he was having nightmares. I conducted a trash pull to analyze his behaviors, likes, and dislikes. All the information I collected helped to discover

4. The Difference Between a Cold and Fresh Homicide Case

weaknesses about Petersen, which I used during our interrogation of him with great success.

The element of surprise is a way to confuse and intimidate a suspect. This tactic may lead a suspect to make mistakes, which a detective can exploit to his advantage. Once a detective identifies the suspect's mistakes(s), then it's time to plan and conduct an aggressive tactic that will involve a constant assessment of resources, timing, and planning.

The Michael Paalan cold case in Chapter 2 demonstrates how the element of surprise worked with an unannounced visit to the witness and possible suspect, Dawn Breeze. The surprise visit to Dawn caught her off guard, and the relentless interrogation also pressured her to reveal the truth about Annie Tahan's murder. Because she cooperated with the police and identified Paalan as the killer, the court granted her immunity. Although Dawn should have received a sentence for covering up the murder, this is an example of how a person's involvement in the crime was sacrificed in order to guarantee a conviction of the killer.

Another tactic is to draw out the suspect by asking meaningless questions or providing him with senseless information. This may give the suspect a false sense of security and make the suspect feel like he has outsmarted you. It may also lead him to make a mistake or share information the suspect might not normally provide a detective. The suspect may be confused because there seems to be no rhyme or reason to the detective's approach. Do this enough, and the suspect may become less and less cautious of you, thinking that you pose no threat. Then, once you collect enough evidence, it will be too late for the suspect to realize you're ready to arrest him or her.

Bluffing or setting a trap for a suspect is a more subtle tactic but much more difficult to execute. An example of this tactic is an undercover operation, also known as a ruse. I'll elaborate on how to use a ruse in Chapter 7 and provide examples in some of the cases in subsequent chapters. The Whittle cold case at end of Chapter 3 is an example of how I used the draw-out and bluffing tactics.

Regardless of which tactic you use, hopefully the pressure you place on the suspect will wear him or her down enough to make a mistake that will lead to an arrest and conviction.

Another difference between a cold case and fresh homicide is that one must conduct cold cases in a proactive fashion rather than in a reactive fashion. A reactive investigation is used when investigators wait to receive information, which makes it a weaker approach to use than a proactive investigation for these reasons. First, the victims may initially provide information but later refuse to cooperate. Second, informants may provide information that requires an immediate response, enabling those at higher levels of the criminal organization to evade arrest or capture. Third, reactive measures may mean that evidence is lacking or not ready for collection. And lastly, a reactive investigation relies heavily on the response and actions of the suspect. This will cause delays and make it more difficult to arrest and convict the suspect.

The proactive approach is a more efficient way to conduct a cold case investigation for the following reasons. First, the actions taken by an investigator will obtain quicker results from lab reports, intelligence gathering reports from witnesses, and even information from the suspect that will lead to his arrest and conviction. In a proactive investigation, there is also no imminent threat to witnesses. In addition, detectives can remain in control of the investigation.[5]

Cold Case #8: Government of North Carolina v. Crumitie—Victims Michael Gretsinger, Sharon Cook Crumitie, and James Luther Blanks

Summary

The following murder case is an example of how difficult it is for detectives to establish probable cause to arrest a person for murder, even when some of the evidence and instinct tell them the person is guilty. It is an example of poor judgment by people in the judicial system. I say this because I believe the judicial system in this country is a good one and that what impedes true justice for victims and their families is the poor and wrong decisions people in the judicial system make during and after the trial.

Timothy Lavaun Crumitie had a long history of criminal encounters with the law, beginning in 1990 when he was convicted of armed robbery. He served eight years in prison.

In 2005, Crumitie, who had been pastor of a Kannapolis church

4. The Difference Between a Cold and Fresh Homicide Case

for six years, was charged with the murder of Danny Kaye Johnson. Johnson was the owner of Danny Johnson Flooring, where Crumitie worked. It was located beside Crumitie's church. Investigators said at the time that Crumitie borrowed $5,000 from Johnson to repay a church debt and was supposed to meet him at a Charlotte bank. The money was not found, and Johnson never returned home.

Pastor Crumitie was seen with him on bank surveillance camera footage the day Johnson was gunned down on a public boardwalk near Mallard Creek Road. Authorities arrested Pastor Crumitie and held him in jail without bail for five years. Eventually, the prosecutor dismissed the murder charge because of insufficient evidence to take the case to trial.

In 2013 Crumitie was the sole survivor of a shooting that took the lives of his wife, Sharon Cook Crumitie, and James Luther Blanks. Crumitie told police that Blanks had broken into his garage and killed his wife and that he killed Blanks in self-defense. Pastor Crumitie described what happened on the day of the shooting. Authorities did not have any solid evidence to arrest him. The case eventually turned cold.

Resolution

In June of 2015, Anastasia Meaders was reported to police as a missing person. Meaders's car was discovered abandoned at a Mooresville town park approximately 20 miles from Kannapolis. Although Anastasia's sister testified that she observed Meaders and Pastor Crumitie together at a hair salon, police found no evidence in the car to connect Pastor Crumitie to the murder. This case also turned cold.

Around this time Crumitie had a periodic relationship with a woman, Kimberly Cherry. But Cherry fell in love with Michael Gretsinger, a former member of the U.S. Army.

On the night of August 5, 2016, Cherry and Michael Gretsinger were returning to Cherry's apartment in University City to retrieve her phone when Crumitie, holding a handgun, stepped out from behind the front door.

With Gretsinger on his knees, Crumitie shot him in the head. Crumitie then tied up Cherry, placed her in her car, and drove to his Rowan

County home where he kept her for several hours. Then he placed Cherry back in the car, drove back to a construction site near Cherry's apartment, removed her from the car, and shot Cherry twice in the back of the head. Crumitie then placed Cherry in the trunk of the car and drove to the parking lot outside her apartment. Miraculously, Cherry was still alive. After he left the car, Cherry regained conciseness, popped the trunk open, and escaped to a neighbor's home. Nine days later Gretsinger died from his gunshot wound.

Sentence

In 2018 a jury found Timothy Lavaun Crumitie guilty of first-degree murder, assault on a female, first-degree kidnapping, and possession of a firearm by a felon. The judge sentenced Crumitie to life in prison without parole.[6]

Witness Fear

Many witnesses are afraid to testify because of possible retaliation or death threats from the perpetrator. This reluctance of a potential witness makes it difficult to identify suspects and solve a case and makes it difficult for prosecutors to obtain a conviction.

Some witnesses, after being intimidated, simply stop showing up or cooperating in any way. Then there are the witnesses who do show up and change their story. Witnesses who were present during or participated in the murder and are also on trial are reluctant to testify for fear of being housed in the same correctional facility as the killer, who may at some point retaliate.

Although the U.S Marshall Service has been successful since its inception in 1970 in protecting more than 7,500 witnesses and more than 9,500 family members of witnesses, witness intimidation is a huge problem and the courts struggle to find a solution. The problem runs deeper than just the intimidators. Limited funding restricts the use of this service. And when funding for protection is available, many witnesses do not want to leave behind their families, jobs, and lifestyle.[7]

Unreliable Testimony

Even if a witness does cooperate, his or her testimony is not always completely reliable. There are times when a detective follows a lead from a witness that results in exonerating the suspect in question. There are also times when information from a witness leads a detective on a wild goose chase and back to the witness, who sometimes turns out to be the killer. Sometimes a person fabricates a story for a bizarre or an irrational reason. The following is an example from a 2005 murder case that had gone cold for three years.

Early in the investigation, a person contacted police to share information about an unsolved homicide case. He told the detective that he had seen a small, white pickup truck with a horizontal stripe on the side of it and a loud muffler race out of the parking lot before the police arrived at the murder scene. With a detailed description, police felt confident they'd find a suspect. For two days police stopped dozens of trucks fitting this description, checking the interiors for blood and the drivers for any fresh wounds. Then, they received bad news from the witness. He had fabricated his story to impress his girlfriend. That's a week's worth of work down the tubes and valuable time detectives lost in their efforts to find the killer.

Witness Recants Testimony

There are times when a witness will recant his or her testimony. In most criminal cases, a person's recantation will only cast doubt on the credibility of the victim or witness but not on the person detectives believe is the perpetrator. The following is an example that demonstrates how detectives solved a cold case despite the recantation of a witness.

In February and March of 1995 detectives worked two homicide cases believed to have been committed by the same person. Both victims had been bound, gagged, strangled, and stabbed. Items were stolen from their apartments, and the killer set several fires at both apartments. What made the two murders unique was that, of the 6,000 killings committed in Washington and Oregon over the previous two decades, these were the first murders that included rape, theft, and arson.

Seattle struggled for three years to solve these murders. What made them difficult to solve was that after the killer murdered the women, he set fire to their apartments, hoping to destroy any evidence linking him to the murders.

Then in 1998 a woman contacted police and implicated her ex-boyfriend as the killer. The woman said she and her ex-boyfriend had lived near the apartment complex where both murders took place. She provided detailed facts that no one but the investigators, victim, suspect, or someone close to the suspect would know as well as information on how her boyfriend covered up the murders. She said that after both murders he brought items into their home and she still had some of them in her possession. Detectives issued a warrant and found the items stolen from the victims' apartments.

Detectives arrested the ex-boyfriend, who denied that he killed the two women. Although there were no fingerprints, DNA evidence, or eyewitnesses to tie the ex-boyfriend to the murder, the prosecutor filed murder charges based on the girlfriend's testimony. But before the trial began the woman recanted her testimony because she had reconciled her differences with him. She provided a different account of how the personal items from the victims ended up in her apartment, claiming she found them in their neighborhood dumpsters and trashcans.

Detectives and the prosecutor strongly believed they had the killer, but without her testimony, they had little chance of rendering a conviction. Despite the woman's decision not to testify, detectives didn't give up and eventually connected the boyfriend to the murders through good "gumshoe" work. The detectives decided to listen to the recorded tapes they had from their interview with the girlfriend again because they felt it might provide a clue to help find the physical evidence needed to convict the boyfriend. They remembered that the girlfriend had revealed a lot of information about life with her boyfriend, even intimate details about their sex life and his personal hygiene habits. After they had sex, he frequently cleaned up in the bathroom, used a towel to dry himself, and laid the towel on the vanity.

Detectives remembered that they had found two towels on one of the victim's bathroom vanities. Although the towels had been in the fires, detectives wondered if Parker might have used them after he sexually assaulted the victims. Forensic scientists took a closer look at the towels; the towels had been wadded up. When they unfolded the towels, they found four hairs that were visually different from the victims's hair. One hair had the potential to be a goldmine of evidence because it still had the root intact and human tissue. Luck and the killer's personal hygiene habit kept the towels and pubic hair forensic scientists found from burning.

The DNA from the towel matched the boyfriend's DNA profile and placed him at the victim's apartment. The jury found him guilty of two counts of aggravated murder, and the court sentenced him to life without parole.[8]

Forensic Evidence

Collecting DNA and waiting for the results or identifying the victim through dental records or other means requires a lot of time. While the best DNA labs can provide results in one to two days, others can take three to 12 weeks or even longer. If a potential suspect won't cooperate, a detective needs to find other means to collect the DNA. If a detective can't identify the victim through DNA, it makes it harder to find a connection to the killer.[9]

Manpower

A surge of violent crime in a city results in too many cases to investigate and not enough detectives. Some investigators work on as many as five or six homicide cases a week. When a detective has to manage numerous cases, it turns into a juggling act that is often times unmanageable. If there is sufficient evidence to support further investigation of a suspect, he stays on it, but if the evidence trail goes cold, a detective moves on to another case.

Good intentions have even contributed to the reduction in police manpower. While the idea of improving relations between police and communities is an honorable one, it has significantly depleted police manpower. For every police officer involved in a community relations program, it means one fewer police officer able to protect and serve the community or conduct an investigation. While many continue to support this idea, there has been no definitive standard study to prove how well police-community relations programs have substantially reduced crime. Nor has there been any conclusive study to calculate the return on investment of a police-community relations program. Crime rates vary according to such factors as population, demographics, income level, employment availability, level of morality, police and judicial policy, and police-to-population ratio.

Funding

Homicide investigations are inherently expensive. Cities, especially cash-poor cities, don't have enough money in their budget to provide the necessary manpower it takes to police a city. Law enforcement feels the squeeze from budget cuts, especially since the COVID-19 pandemic and national movement to defund the police.

According to the Police Executive Research Forum (PERF), police operations have not confronted such a threat since the financial crisis of 2008, when operations and force numbers were cut dramatically to account for the steep decline in available public funds.

"Unfortunately, the situation this time is only certain to get worse because of the pandemic's resurgence and the convergence of the defund police movement," said Chuck Wexler, executive director of PERF. "It's a combustible mixture for police departments because reform is often achieved by hiring the next generation of officers and acquiring new technology that can assist their work. The unintended consequence of these times is that those reforms will now be held back."[10]

Another financial factor is the huge cost to society. The question is how much, which is difficult to calculate. Researchers at Iowa State University, led by sociologist Matt DeLisi, attempted to estimate the costs in 2010. Just for one murder, they estimated the price tag at a whopping $17.25 million.

In DeLisi's study, he discovered that the bulk of the $17.25 million stems from the public's resulting willingness to pay to prevent future violence. "We aren't shy about punishing people, but we are also very humanistic and want to prevent crime and rehabilitate offenders.

Even if society is very hard on crime, or are crime-control oriented, it seems we'd rather pay money upfront than let it all unfold and pay for it later."[11]

Despite the lack of public funds allocated to law enforcement, there are financial resources available for detectives, like the grant program called the Sexual Assault Kit Initiative (SAKI), launched in 2015 by the Bureau of Justice Assistance. SAKI provides funding through a competitive grant program to support the jurisdictional reform of how to approach sexual assault cases involving DNA from sexual assault kits, or "rape kits," submitted to a crime laboratory. SAKI's mission is to create a coordinated community response that ensures just resolution to sexual assault cases. Because many homicides include sexual assault, SAKI provides another valuable method for detectives to identify a rapist and/or killer.[12]

"Since its launch in 2015, SAKI has been making a difference by improving the response to sexual assault by identifying and apprehending violent offenders and by addressing the problem of unsubmitted sexual assault kits. More than 70 grantees have received SAKI funding over the last six years. From September 2015 to September 2021, more than 146,000 sexual assault kits have been inventoried, over 83,000 kits have been sent for testing, and more than 72,000 kits have been tested to completion."[13]

Cost of New Forensic Technology

While the rapid advances in forensic technologies have played a valuable part in solving homicides and cold cases, the cost is very expensive. It is hard to determine the cost of an average cold case because the cost associated with the investigation, like the forensic methods and amount of manpower to collect evidence, is different in each case.

By far the most expensive portion of obtaining a profile is the lab costs. The cost to extract DNA from the sample and amplify it to determine if there is adequate DNA material costs about $500 per sample. If the forensic scientist proceeds with more testing, the average cost of the full process is about $2,000. Then there is the cost of lab equipment combined with the costs of hiring and training lab staff.[14]

Parabon NanoLabs, a company that offers new technology, has been working with law enforcement since 2015. One service it provides is DNA phenotyping, which predicts physical appearance from DNA and generates leads in cases where there are no suspects or database hits in order to narrow suspect lists and help solve human remains cases.[15] The cost for basic facial phenotyping for hair and eye color along with its genealogy assessment is $1,500. The more advanced package, which includes facial morphology, costs an additional $2,100. An average estimated cost per case is $4,000 to $5,000.[16]

The M-Vac is a sterile wet-vacuum device that collects DNA material from porous areas that are difficult, if not impossible to reach otherwise (like rocks, bricks, ligatures, and clothing items) as well as increases the probability of discovering DNA material randomly located on the surface. The estimated startup cost for the M-Vac ranges from $43,000 to $45,000, while the cost per sample is about $90, compared with less than $15 for the wet swab method.[17]

Political, Media, and Community Pressure

Even "easy" homicide cases are complex, bureaucratic tasks. Yet, politicians, media, and the public expect the police to solve every murder case or at the very least increase the clearance rate. First, it is impossible to solve every murder case, and secondly, murders occur faster than the police can solve them. In Detroit, a city with one of the worst murder rates in the country, investigators admit feeling intimidated by the pressure to keep up. And unfortunately, this pressure, which creates an overzealousness to solve a crime, sometimes leads to wrongful convictions.[18]

Another roadblock is the time and energy directed to the public's demand for police reform. This also creates a tremendous amount of bureaucratic tape that hampers the police's ability to investigate and solve murder cases. Law enforcement spends a large sum of money working with and appeasing police reform advocacy groups. The time and money may be better spent with police officers patrolling the streets and hiring more police officers.

Priority

Sometimes one case takes priority over another case, especially if the victim or victim's relative is a celebrity or high-profile person, thereby leaving other murders in a detective's caseload unattended until the detective is lucky enough to receive another solid lead. When a detective is juggling five or six murder or cold cases and another one arrives at his desk, his time is stretched thin and he or his superiors will determine which cases take priority over the others. This is especially true when a homicide case involves a celebrity, like O. J. Simpson, or a tragic event like the Oklahoma City bombing. Two homicide cases on the *Forensic Files* show illustrate how an ongoing investigation can get sidelined.

As discussed in more detail on Chapter 3, on March 26, 1994, Shannon Melendi, a 19-year-old Miami woman, disappeared after leaving a softball field. Detectives had a prime suspect, Colvin "Butch" Hinton, but no physical evidence or Melendi's body to connect him to her disappearance, and the case went cold. In addition, during the investigation Hinton had been arrested and convicted for insurance fraud and arson. Since he was already in prison, Shannon's case fell by the wayside. Her case was not closed at the time, but there were other priorities.[19]

Unfortunately, at that time much attention was given to high-profile cases like O.J. Simpson and bombings in Oklahoma City and Continental Park. Sadly, as I noted at the end of Chapter 3, 10 years passed before prosecutors reopened and solved Melendi's case.

The second *Forensic Files* show featured the June 1995 murder of Carol Ann Hellar, who lived in Perry, Oklahoma. Doctors who initially examined Hellar believed she died of natural causes due to congestive heart failure. An autopsy was never performed because the medical examiner in Perry was overwhelmed with dead bodies from the Oklahoma City bombing, which happened six weeks earlier on April 19, 1995. In accordance with Hellar's wish, family members cremated her body.

Although Perry police suspected foul play shortly after Carol Hellar's death, it took time for Detectives David Farrow and Russell Busby to get help from doctors and toxicologists and put together a case against Carol's husband, Dennis Hellar. Crucial evidence was collected from Dr. James Cassidy, who ordered a blood test on Carol Hellar a month before she died. Dr. Cassidy did not receive the results of the test—which revealed the presence of ethylene glycol, a major ingredient found in automobile antifreeze—until after Hellar's death and cremation. This new evidence led Detectives Farrow and Busby to believe Dennis Hellar had poisoned Carol, but they needed more evidence.

The detectives questioned the medical examiner again and discovered that although he had not performed an autopsy due to the overwhelming task of identifying the bodies from the Oklahoma City bombing, he had collected tissue samples from Carol's body for analysis. After he tested these, he found calcium oxalate crystals in her brain and kidney samples. Prolonged exposure to ethylene glycol, a raw material in the manufacture of antifreeze formulations, can cause calcium oxalate crystals to form, causing renal failure and death.

After detectives presented this evidence to Dennis Hellar, he confessed to poisoning Carol with antifreeze for a month prior to her death. The case never went to trial. Dennis Hellar agreed to a life prison sentence by pleading guilty to a lesser charge of first-degree manslaughter.[20]

Higher Standards

The public does not realize that clearing murders has become harder in recent decades. Vernon Geberth, a retired, self-described NYPD "murder cop" who wrote the definitive manual on solving homicides, says standards for charging someone are too high. It seems that prosecutors nowadays demand that police deliver "open-and-shut cases" that will either lead to quick plea bargains or a conviction.[21]

Higher standards are the result of the way defense lawyers scrutinize every rule of law; the detective's actions before, during and after the arrest; and written police reports. This places a lot of pressure and stress on detectives to perform an adequate job that will satisfy the court.

Scrutiny of Defense Lawyer

I will openly admit that I dislike the way many defense lawyers practice their profession. But I also understand that a defense attorney's

4. The Difference Between a Cold and Fresh Homicide Case

job is to be an advocate for his or her client and to also protect a client's legal rights. Most defense lawyers are looking for legal loopholes and mistakes made by detectives in order to help their clients avoid conviction and jail time. And I realize that, like law enforcement's thin blue line, there is a fine line a defense attorney treads between seeking the truth and seeking a verdict in his or her client's favor. Nevertheless, I respect and understand the defense lawyer's position, and I work hard to create a friendship with him or her instead of viewing him or her as an adversary.

I have found that my friendly treatment of defense lawyers helps me avoid confrontations with them, which in turn opens an opportunity to create an amicable relationship that helps me become more productive. I embrace their criticism of my investigations. If they point out a legal mistake I made, I don't get upset. Instead, I treat it as a learning experience and look for ways I can improve and strengthen the next case I investigate for the prosecutors. A story of my working partnership with Ron Kuby on the *Wrong Man* documentary series illustrates this concept.

Kuby, well-known civil rights and the criminal defense attorney, is best known for winning cases against Bernhard Goetz and for the Hells Angels and has been a witness for John Gotti's defense. He has helped exonerate many people who have been wrongly convicted and has been a staunch advocate against excessive force by law enforcement.

Kuby and I represent different sides of the judicial system. In many ways we are adversaries. Nevertheless, I approach our working relationship by being open to learning from my friends as well as my adversaries. I likely learn more from adversaries than from "friends" who are going to tell me what I want to hear. I was delighted with the time I spent with Kuby. He is a smart, witty person and one hell of an attorney. The perspective he brings to a case is completely different from my insight on the same case. So, believe it or not, working with Kuby was refreshing to me because he would challenge me and I would challenge him.[22]

When it comes to the nuts and bolts of working a case, I work it from an undercover perspective, which requires a different strategy and a considerable amount of preparation, planning, teamwork, and money. While an undercover operation is not unique to law enforcement, police departments grossly underuse it, mostly because law enforcement limits its undercover operations to narcotics, gang, and organized crime–related investigations.

Human Error

I believe in universal truths. One is that human error is unavoidable in every profession, job, and industry. For example, the analysis of forensic science might be perfect, however, how a person handles, studies, or evaluates it may be imperfect.

Mark Twain said, "There are three types of lies: lies, damned lies, and statistics." Statistics can be manipulated depending on what the analyst is looking for during his or her analysis. Therefore, it is possible for the analyst to provide results that can be misleading even though he or she is mathematically correct.[23]

There are many moving parts to an investigation of a crime, especially in a homicide. There are also many people involved in the handling of evidence and management of the investigation like coroners, medical examiners, forensic scientists, lawyers, prosecutors, and other law enforcement personnel. Therefore, every investigation is prone to human error. It only takes one person's miscalculation or mistake to disrupt the investigation or allow the killer to get away with murder.

Like any other professionals, even good detectives are vulnerable to making mistakes. Many detectives work overtime, so the lack of sleep affects performance. It's possible for a detective to make a typing error in a database search. One wrong letter, number, or entry could be the difference between another wild goose chase and finding the murderer. Tired eyes could also cause a detective to miss crucial evidence during an internet or NCIC off-line search.

Potential witnesses and bystanders are also not immune from human error. In 1971 a man approached two young lovers, Jesse Allen McBane and Patricia Ann Mann, at a lovers' lane near Durham, North Carolina. He held the couple at gunpoint, kidnapped them, then brutally and sadistically murdered them on a secluded rural path just across the Orange-Durham County line. No one was ever charged or tried for the double murder, and the case remained cold for 45 years.

4. The Difference Between a Cold and Fresh Homicide Case   119

In 2016 a new true-crime podcast, *The Long Dance* hosted by Eryk Pruitt, featured the murder case of Mann and McBane. One of the listeners contacted the hosts to share information about the murder. He said that, around the same time, he was also in a similar lovers' lane area with his girlfriend. A man approached his car, knocked on the window, waved a gun, and attempted to kidnap them, but they managed to ward him off and escape. When the couple returned home, they told their parents about the incident. The parents didn't believe their story, so they never brought it to the attention of the police. Investigators are left wondering if this information could possibly have led to the capture of the killer in 1971. Instead, the case continues to remain unsolved.[24]

Although *The Long Dance* podcast did not yet help solve the Mann and McBane murder case, it and other true crime podcasts have captured the public's attention. Podcasts allow listeners to learn more about cold cases, invite listeners to form their own theories, provide opportunities for a potential witness to come forward, and sometimes help investigators solve a cold case. *Jensen & Holes: The Murder Squad, The Gum Shoe Diary, The Vanished, Cold, The Trail Went Cold,* and *Your Own Backyard* are good examples of the best true-crime podcasts.

Forgetting a simple follow-up task led to the following delay in solving a case for over a decade. During the initial investigation of the 1992 kidnapping and murder of Shauna Howe, a 14-year-old girl, detectives considered the O'Brien brothers, Tim and Jim, as suspects. After a policeman reported that the brothers had been arrested days before the girl's disappearance, investigators assumed they were in jail on the night of the girl's abduction and ruled them out as suspects.

Ten years later, however, a detective who had been a patrolman during the investigation reopened the case. As he read the file, he discovered that there had been no documentation to corroborate the brothers being in jail on the night the girl had been abducted. He contacted a trooper he knew and asked him to search for records of the brothers' arrest. The trooper said: "The brothers were arrested but had been bonded out before the girl's abduction." Detectives spent all these years and resources, all the while believing the brothers had been incarcerated.

A search for the brothers led the detective to find both of them in jail. Tim had been arrested for sexually assaulting a girl and Jim for trying to abduct a woman and stuffing her in the trunk of his car. The forensic team collected their DNA. Jim's DNA matched the sample found on the girl. The O'Brien brothers were convicted of kidnapping and murder and sentenced to life in prison without the possibility of parole.[25]

The following is another example of a case that involved human error as well as a witness unintentionally withholding information: On the night of December 10, 1991, Bryan Ruff disappeared during his night shift as a security guard at the Kennecott Mine in Utah. Detectives considered co-worker Dale Bradley as a person of interest in the case because his wife, Kristi, admitted to having an affair with Bryan. When detectives questioned Dale, he insisted he knew nothing about his wife's affair or Bryan's disappearance.

Dale had no criminal history, but the affair gave him a motive to harm Bryan, so detectives issued a search warrant for his red 1974 Camaro. The forensic team checked for blood and gunshot residue but did not find any. Detectives asked Dale to take a polygraph test. He agreed and passed. Without a body or physical evidence, detectives had no probable cause to arrest Dale and dropped his name from the list of suspects. Detectives pursued other potential suspects, but each one had a solid alibi.

A year later hikers discovered Bryan's body, still dressed in his security uniform, in a camping area about 50 miles from the Kennecott Mine. Detectives also found his wallet, five spent shells, and a 22-caliber gun. Evidence at the gravesite showed that the killer shot Bryan five times in the back a few feet from where he had been buried. The next day a dog from the K-9 unit found one of Bryan's work boots.

With no evidence to tie anyone to the crime, Bryan's case remained cold for 14 years until Detective Todd Park received a telephone call from a detective in Carbon County. He told Park that they were investigating Dale Bradley on suspicion of murdering his second wife, Crystal Bradley.

On a hunch, Detective Park contacted Dale's first wife, Kristi, to question her about Bryan's murder. Kristi was surprised, having assumed that Bryan's murder had been solved because Dale told her that detectives had arrested someone. She then told Detective Park

4. The Difference Between a Cold and Fresh Homicide Case 121

something she hadn't mentioned during the original investigation. The day after Bryan's disappearance, Dale cleaned the inside of his red Camaro and trunk. As long as she had known Dale, he had never cleaned his car. (This is an example of a witness withholding information that she didn't feel compelled to share. In this case, it had been because her husband had deceived her.) This is an example of how witnesses provide vital clues years later as relationships change.

Detective Park wondered if Dale might have forced Bryan into the trunk of his red Camaro, so he decided to take another look at Bryan's boot that had been stored in the evidence locker. He discovered a small red scuff mark that looked like paint on the bottom of the boot that didn't catch the attention of the detectives 14 years previously. When he saw that swatch of paint, it flashed back to him that the color looked startlingly similar to the color of Dale's Camaro. He wondered if the red paint smear on the boot might have been caused by Bryan's attempt to kick his way out of the trunk. He discovered that in 1974 Chevrolet painted the inside of Camaro trunks. Detectives began a search for Dale's Camaro to hopefully prove that the color on Bryan's boot matched the paint inside the trunk of the car. They discovered that Dale had sold the Camaro and the new owner had sold it for scrap metal.

Despite the bad news, Detective Park decided to reexamine the other evidence in Bryan's case file and discovered evidence that he had overlooked. During the initial investigation, Detective Jerry Townsend collected paint chips from Dale's Camaro. He took the samples because there hadn't been other evidence to collect. You never know what's going to be important at a crime scene or a suspect's house or in this case in a vehicle, so you collect everything. Sometimes it's the smallest item that you didn't think might identify the perpetrator and solve the case. Regrettably, at that time neither he nor other detectives noticed the red mark on the boot. Therefore, they never considered analyzing the paint on the boot to see if it matched the paint in the trunk of Dale's Camaro.

The paint samples from Dale's Camaro collected by Detective Townsend matched the paint on Bryan's boot. This trace evidence confirmed that Bryan had been in the trunk of Dale's Camaro and clearly linked Dale to Bryan's murder.

Presented with this evidence, Dale Bradley pleaded guilty to second-degree felony counts of manslaughter and kidnapping of Bryan Ruff. Third District Judge Paul Maughan sentenced Bradley to two prison terms of two to 20 years in prison, with the sentences running consecutively for the murders of Bryan Ruff and Crystal Bradley.[26]

Unpredictable Situations

It's rare, but unpredictable situations happen. In this case, the mistaken identity of a vehicle that left a crime scene delayed the arrest of the killer. If it had not been for lady luck, this fresh homicide could have easily turned into a cold case.

During the investigation of a robbery and murder, Miami detectives found a surveillance video that showed a car fleeing the crime scene. The detectives identified the car as a Chevy Impala SS but could not read the license plate number. They felt there was a good chance that finding this car would lead them to the killer because the Impala SS model was much less common than the standard model. DMV records showed that there were only 13 of them registered in Miami-Dade County.

For several weeks detectives methodically tracked down each blue Impala SS, but none of them matched the identifying marks on the car in the video. The detectives also checked other DMV records in the surrounding counties but again didn't find a match.

Several months later the two detectives who worked the case got lucky. On their way to a court hearing for an unrelated case one of them spotted a blue Impala SS parked across the street from the courthouse that exactly matched the car in the video. Both cars had the same rims, tinted windows, spoiler, and door handles.

After the detectives traced the license plate number to a male who had a suspended license, they staked out the car, waited for the owner to show up, took him in for questioning, and impounded his car.

As detectives performed a more thorough examination of the car, they discovered that it was a standard model that the suspect had customized to look like an SS model. The reason detectives couldn't find the car was because it had been registered as a standard model and not an SS model. After a witness identified the suspect, the suspect was prosecuted and convicted of robbery and murder. The lesson learned here is that if a case involves finding the identity of a car, due diligence involves checking DMV registration records for all models of the car brand or even brands with a similar design. Doing so could lead a detective to the killer.

The Jurors

In the end, it is the jury that decides the fate of the accused person, not the prosecutors or detectives, and, like the legal system, the jury system is also an imperfect science. Although a jury provides the best method of judgment for a crime, it is also susceptible to human error, bias, and tampering. Prosecutors and defense attorneys may play to jurors' biases or find ways to distort the facts or sway them to look outside the facts during part of the decision-making process. This is especially true during the jury selection process, where prosecutors and lawyers may stack a jury in their favor so that their desired outcome takes place. It is far easier for a prosecutor to do this than a defendant in most jurisdictions, which means a jury can still convict someone based on their biases instead of the facts involved in the case.

Sometimes a juror from a specific group—a member of a certain race, sex, or income level, or even an alcoholic or drug addict—may be more sympathetic to a defendant who is from the same group. Sometimes a juror may need to rule on a case that is outside of their experience or knowledge. Sometimes corruption breaches the jury when a person motivated by a hidden agenda attempts to influence the outcome of the trial by seating a stealth juror.[27]

One of the most famous murder cases that involved a stealth juror was the Scott Peterson trial in 2004. John Grisham's book *The Runaway Jury* is about a stealth juror in a tobacco-related case. Through a variety of tricks, he manages to get other members of the jury to vote the way he intended. Despite the aforementioned faults, however, the jury system is the best way to render a verdict.

Lastly, an important discovery I made is that most killers in a cold case never murder again because they spend their time hiding from law enforcement to avoid capture. Therefore, it makes finding the killer more difficult.

Regardless of the aforementioned challenges, I march on bound by duty and oath to protect and serve. And just like Bobby Fischer, when I investigate a cold case I'm in it to win it! The next chapter illustrates how much of my success is attributed to good old-fashioned gumshoe work.

Cold Case #9: Government of Virginia v. Coleman—Victim Steven S. November

Summary

Navy Seaman Apprentice Steve S. November (22), Hector Coleman (23), and Carlos Saldana, Jr. (20), all served together onboard the aircraft carrier USS *Theodore Roosevelt*. On April 20, 1998, November received his income tax return check of $2,287 and planned to cash it at the bank. He left the ship with several other sailors but never returned. After two days the Navy questioned other sailors about his whereabouts.

Three days later November's body was found in the grass under a tree in a secluded area next to the parking lot of the Towers Apartment Complex in Newport News, Virginia. The medical examiner testified that November's death resulted from gunshot wounds from a nine-millimeter Ruger pistol. The coroner estimated that November died 24 to 48 hours prior to his body being discovered.

Police questioned Coleman and Saldana about the day November left the ship. Coleman and Saldana denied that they had any contact with November or knowledge of his whereabouts. Further investigation and questioning of witnesses didn't result in any leads, so detectives closed the case.

Resolution

November's cold case was reopened the following year. After the detectives read the report, they conducted an NCIC off-line search about other possible police activity that may have been recorded on the day of November's murder. Detectives discovered that a police officer reported pulling over a vehicle owned by Saldana for speeding and crossing a double yellow line on the day November left the ship. The detective's record of the vehicle stop showed that November and Coleman were passengers in Saldana's car. This contradicted Saldana and Coleman's initial testimony. (During the initial investigation off-line search was available but detectives failed to conduct one.)

Further investigation led them to another witness, Ivan Dockerty, who lived in New York, where Coleman grew up. Dockerty told officers that Coleman sold him a gun during a visit to his old neighborhood. Detectives asked Dockerty if he still had the gun. He said he didn't; he had sold it to another person. Detectives decided to conduct another off-line search to see if the gun had been pawned. It was found at a local pawnshop near Dockerty's neighborhood. The ballistic report confirmed that it was the same gun used to kill November.

Detectives brought Saldana in for questioning and introduced the new evidence. Eventually, Saldana implicated Coleman as the shooter and confessed to participating in the cover-up of November's murder. Saldana said he was driving the car. November was seated in the back seat behind him, and Coleman was in the passenger seat. As they cruised along Interstate 664 in Newport News, Coleman turned around and shot November three times. Then they drove to the woods near the Towers Apartment Complex and dumped November's body. Coleman then shot November again in the back of the head to make sure he was dead.

Detectives concluded that Coleman took the gun on a visit to New York and sold the gun to Dockerty. They also confirmed that the blood samples from the back seat of Saldana's car matched November's DNA.

Sentence

On August 26, 1999, the court convicted Carlos Saldana, Jr., 20, and Hector Coleman, 23, of murder, robbery, and use of a firearm in the commission of a felony. For his part in covering up November's slaying, Saldana, 21, of Winter Park, Florida, was sentenced to eight years in a military jail and given a dishonorable discharge. Coleman was sentenced to life without parole.[28]

Cold Case #10: Government of Texas v. Hamilton and Dunn—Victim Scott Dunn (Vidocq Society: The Texas Bloodbath)

Summary

Scott Dunn settled in Lubbock, Texas, after serving in the military. He worked for MGM Electronics in a job he loved: installing custom sound systems in automobiles. The last time friends saw Dunn was at a party after work.

Dunn had a reputation of being a lady's man and a prankster. It was not unusual for him to date a number of women at the same time. He arrived at a party with a new acquaintance, Shaina, a tall, attractive woman that his friends had not met. Unbeknownst to Dunn's friends, Shaina was a transgender woman. Before the night was over, Scott's friends found out—and were not amused.

Sometime during the party Scott became ill. He was so sick that he was unable to drive home, and friends said he stayed overnight on the sofa. The next day, his live-in girlfriend, Leisha Hamilton, picked him up to take him home. Hamilton said that the next morning Scott felt well enough to return to work. She left for work and never saw Scott again. Two days later Hamilton called Scott's father, James Dunn, who lived in Pennsylvania. She told James that Scott hadn't returned home and asked if he had heard from him. He said he hadn't and filed a missing persons report with the Lubbock Police Department (LPD).

LPD assigned Detective Tal English to investigate Dunn's disappearance. Detective English interviewed Dunn's friends, who said it was out of character for him to not call and contact them. He inquired whether or not any of the friends at the party had been angry enough to harm Scott for the prank he pulled on them. He also discovered that Dunn and Hamilton had a tumultuous relationship. Both had been dating other people. A month before his murder, Hamilton learned that Scott was engaged to another woman. This information revealed that Hamilton might have had a motive to harm Scott or be responsible for his disappearance.

As Detective English searched Dunn's apartment, he discovered some disturbing evidence and history about Hamilton. First, Dunn had left many of his personal belongings. Second, he noticed a patch of carpet whose edges had a red-colored stain that appeared to be blood. This area had been replaced with a piece of carpet from under the sofa. He removed the patch of carpet, which had been held together with duct tape, and discovered what appeared to be a large pool of dried blood. When questioned further about the carpet, Hamilton claimed to have never noticed the red stain.

Forensic scientists sprayed the bedroom with luminol, revealing that someone in Dunn's bedroom had suffered a violent attack. When forensic scientists tested the blood, they concluded that it belonged to Dunn. A background check by LPD revealed that Hamilton had a past arrest in New Mexico for embezzlement. But why did Hamilton bring the patched carpet to the detectives' attention? Hamilton told Scott's father that she thought a man named Tim Smith had something to do with his disappearance. Smith lived near Dunn's apartment, and detectives discovered that Smith had not shown up for work on the day Dunn disappeared.

When detectives visited Smith's apartment, Smith was packing boxes and preparing to move. Detectives asked to search his apartment, and Smith cooperated. During the search they found no evidence to tie Smith to Dunn's disappearance. But as they walked into the living room on their way out, one of the detectives noticed that a roll of tape that had been sitting on the bookshelf had disappeared. They asked Smith what had happened to it. Smith claimed that there was no roll of tape. Nevertheless, detectives searched the bookshelf and found the roll of duct tape hidden behind some books. (This is an example of good detective work. How many times does a detective walk into a suspect's house, see a roll of duct tape, think nothing of it at first, and then on the way out he notices it is gone?)

Detectives sent the duct tape to the forensic lab, where scientists determined that the duct tape used to repair the patch of carpet in Dunn's apartment came from the same roll in Smith's apartment.

Despite the physical and circumstantial evidence, detectives did not arrest Hamilton and Smith because they had no body. Under Texas law at the time, without a body, there was no homicide.

Resolution

A year passed with no progress in the Dunn case, so Scott's father, James, decided to take matters into his own hands. He heard about the Vidocq Society and contacted them. One of the co-founders, Richard Walter, agreed to investigate Scott's disappearance because he was convinced that Hamilton was responsible. It took Walter another five years to collect the physical evidence he needed to find Dunn's killer and solve the case.

Walter sent the crime scene photos to Dr. Richard Shepherd, a forensic pathologist at Scotland Yard in London. Based on the blood splatter patterns, Dr. Shepherd concluded that Scott had suffered blunt trauma injuries in the corner of his bedroom.

Armed with Dr. Shepherd's forensic analysis, Walter pleaded with the Lubbock District Attorney and argued that they had found a part of Dunn's body in his apartment. At the time, under Texas law, without a body, there could not be a case. However, Richard managed to convince authorities that they did have a body part, and that part was blood's connective tissue from the scene at the bedroom.

Walter also discovered evidence that had been previously overlooked: several strands of hair on the duct tape in Scott's bedroom. The FBI lab in Washington, D.C., compared the hair sample to hairs from Hamilton and Smith. No hairs of Scott's were found on the duct tape but hairs of both Hamilton and Smith were. This meant that Hamilton and Smith had been there to line the patch of carpet with the duct tape.

Five and a half years after Scott's disappearance, detectives arrested and charged Hamilton and Smith with murder. The prosecutor believed Hamilton's motive was revenge after she heard Scott was engaged to another woman and that she was the instigator and ringleader who contrived the murder, then attempted to cover it up. The prosecutor determined that Hamilton murdered Scott in the early morning hours of a day in May of 1991. While Dunn was asleep in the bedroom, she struck him four times with a blunt object. She then convinced Smith to help clean up the crime scene, replace the bloodstained carpet, move Scott's body from the apartment, and bury him.

Sentence

In 1997 Hamilton and Smith received separate trials. The court found both guilty of murder and sentenced Hamilton to 20 years in prison. Smith received 10 years probation because the jury felt that he did not participate in Dunn's murder and only helped Hamilton cover it up. Hamilton and Smith never disclosed the location of Dunn's body.

Discovery of Scott Dunn's Body

In May of 2012, Lubbock police found Dunn's body in a shallow grave behind a wooden fence in the Chaparral apartment complex three doors down from his apartment. The reason detectives did not find the body earlier was because of the apartment complex's layout. There were small, fenced areas where law enforcement really did not have the legal authority to search for a body. In addition, detectives didn't believe a murderer would bury a body so close to the crime scene.

Although Dunn's body had been buried for 21 years, it remained in good enough condition to identify him. Ironically, the manner in which Hamilton and Smith wrapped Dunn's body helped to preserve his remains and facilitate his identity. They had wrapped Dunn in blue vinyl material, a bed sheet, and a comforter. This delayed the climate exposure and access for insects to the body, which slowed down the decomposition. The medical examiner said that more than 90 percent of Dunn's remains were successfully collected. This "mummification" of the muscle and skin remaining on the bones made it possible to collect soft tissue samples. Dunn's teeth were also preserved well enough to confirm his identity.[29]

5

Gumshoe Work Precedes DNA Evidence

I'd like to begin this chapter with another sports analogy to help you understand how important it is not to view DNA analysis or genetic genealogy as a miracle science. Unfortunately, DNA testing has garnered so much credibility that it is sometimes given more weight than eyewitness testimony or other physical evidence found at a crime scene. This over-reliance often sidetracks detectives from exercising the same level of due diligence they used prior to waiting for the DNA results and after the arrest.

I have seen many detectives experience an immediate high after they receive news that the DNA sample resulted in a "hit" in the CODIS database, and rightly so. I feel, however, that the other physical evidence that links the killer to the crime scene is just as important and valuable. Granted, the arrest of the suspect(s), preliminary hearing, and trial are huge accomplishments, but, as they say in the sports world, "it's not over until the clock runs out."[1] With a fresh homicide or cold case, "it's not over until the jury convicts."

In the 2017 Super Bowl, the Atlanta Falcons played nearly perfect football for three quarters. The score at the end of the third quarter was Atlanta Falcons 28 and New England Patriots 9. (At one point during the game it was 28 to 3.) At the beginning of the fourth quarter, the Falcons players were all smiles on the sidelines. They assumed that, with only 15 minutes left to play in the game, they had the Super Bowl win wrapped up. Millions of Falcons fans made the same assumption.

As the fourth quarter began, the Falcons coaches' and players' mindsets changed. Instead of sticking to the game plan that led them to a 28–9 score, they got sidetracked, conservative in their play calling, and played to not lose. In the meantime, the New England Patriots didn't give up because there were still 15 minutes of football to play. The Patriots went on to score 25 unanswered points to win the game in overtime. It is the biggest comeback in Super Bowl history.

Solving a fresh homicide or cold case is no different from playing a football game. The ultimate goal is to win. All the physical evidence a detective collects before the DNA result is just as valuable. Collecting evidence does not stop with a "hit" in CODIS. A detective needs to continue to collect more evidence. To prevent being sidetracked and placing too much weight on DNA, I highly recommend a detective make a habit throughout the investigation of asking this question: "If I didn't have the DNA evidence, is the physical evidence I've collected strong enough to render a conviction?"

Since the late 1980s DNA has become the most reliable form of evidence in many criminal cases. What is most impressive about DNA is that it has withstood the test of time. For decades medical examiners properly stored microscopic slides that contained biological evidence found at crime scenes, on victims' bodies during the autopsy, and from the rape kits of victims.

While at the crime scene, the coroner gathers everything on the body as well as within five feet of the body. During the autopsy, the medical examiner collects biological evidence from the victim's clothes and body and other items found near the body. After the coroner completes the autopsy, he stores this evidence in the evidence room.

Evidence has been stored from previous case types including hit-and-run deaths, arson, and serial killings. Freezers are filled to capacity with blood evidence and sexual assault kits and other evidence like shrink-wrapped clothing, bullets, and gunshot residue samples.

The advancement of DNA forensics has created what detectives call a "virtual treasure trove." With this new discovery, law enforcement agencies have worked hard to enter all the old biological evidence into a database. One example is the Los Angeles Police Department (LAPD). Seeing the value of DNA evidence, the LAPD assigned a detective to work at the coroner's evidence facility full-time. "Brown paper bags, manila envelopes, and cardboard boxes are arranged on metal racks to be picked up by police from surrounding cities like Azusa,

Beverly Hills, and La Habra. There are white tennis shoes and a gunshot residue kit from a possible homicide in the LAPD's Rampart Division from 1988, and hair and fingernail kits from a 1980 South Los Angeles hit-and-run. There are 20 years of gunshot residue kits and bullets from 1969 to 1990 in neat cardboard boxes. Sexual assault kits are packed in freezers, and one horizontal freezer is devoted to malodorous material."[2]

For many years most detectives had no idea medical examiners had this inventory of DNA slides. Today, however, microscopic slides serve as valuable reservoirs of key evidence because the new technology also allows forensic scientists to properly examine and test the stored biological evidence with great accuracy even years after the commission of a crime. New computer technology allows crime laboratories to exchange and compare DNA profiles with DNA computerized record systems like CODIS and the FBI's National DNA Index System (NDIS). In the last two decades, detectives have collaborated more often with medical examiners to identify potential suspects and/or the perpetrator of sexual assaults, rapes, and homicides.

While DNA has been the gold standard for identifying murderers and rapists, it is not foolproof or as black and white as it may seem or as people believe. Despite its history of successful convictions, two of my biggest concerns are the judicial system's overreliance on DNA evidence and, more importantly, the lack of reliance on other evidence at the crime scene as well as interviews with bystanders, witnesses, and suspects.

DNA evidence can be clear-cut under ideal conditions, which is when officials have a reasonable quantity of a suspect's well-preserved DNA, it's clear how the DNA arrived at the crime scene, and the labs examining and sequencing the sample do not make any mistakes. There are cases, however, in which one (or more) of these conditions is not met.

The truth is that DNA forensics is not an exact science because it is susceptible to human error. Additionally, the ideal amount of DNA for testing and analysis is not always present on the item of evidence, and sometimes the DNA is degraded or of poor quality, which can impact the ability of the analyst to interpret the sample.

This means that most DNA evidence, oftentimes only a speck of it, presented in courtrooms has some degree of ambiguity to it. This ambiguity of DNA testing methods also means it is hard to know precisely in which cases DNA may have led juries and judges astray. As you will read later in this chapter, just because the person's DNA was at the crime scene doesn't necessarily mean he or she was involved in or committed the crime. As DNA continues to receive credit for solving fresh homicide and cold cases, the public rarely reads about the people who have been wrongly convicted because of mistakes during the testing of DNA.

I believe that most people on a jury—and some judges—would not be able to explain how the process of DNA matching works, but I will attempt to provide a simple explanation. How complex is the analysis of DNA? There is a joke among forensic DNA analysts: If you gave 10 DNA analysts the same DNA profile, you will receive 11 different opinions.

Generally speaking, it takes about half a nanogram, about seven or eight skin cells, of DNA to identify a profile. When you have a DNA profile from one individual, it is very clear-cut. However, when you start talking mixtures, meaning that more than one person's DNA is on a sample, it complicates the analysis of the DNA.[3]

There is always going to be a problem identifying latent DNA on any surface that is tested. For example, if someone entered a house to commit a robbery or murder and touched a doorknob, how do you separate the DNA sample of one person from all the other people who may have touched the doorknob? How much weight can forensic scientists place on the data? How much information can he or she interpret from it? If he or she doesn't correctly assess the data, rock-solid evidence quickly turns into junk science.[4]

Here is an example of how testing a mixture of DNA was explained to me. When a forensic scientist attempts to identify one person's DNA from an item that has a mixture of DNA, it's like trying to name one song while listening to two songs at the same time. Keep in mind that with DNA the mixture isn't always 50-50. One sample may be 70 percent and the other 30 percent of the total DNA. In order to name the two songs, you need to detangle them from each other. Now imagine one song is playing at a higher volume than the other. This will probably make it easier to identify one of the two songs. But the other song becomes more difficult to identify. Now imagine a mixture of three, four, five, or six songs, and they are all playing at different volumes. The same challenge to name the songs exists with a person's DNA.

Another problem arises with DNA when a forensic scientist is asked to examine an amount lower than 25 cells. Let's say 10 cells. The forensic scientist will amplify this small amount of genetic material by artificially generating 15 more cells to properly test the sample. The problem is that each of the cells is not as good as the last. With each copy, quality is lost, and/or there is a chance that a defect may occur. This process does not provide a consistently reliable result.

Just like witness testimony, what is in question is not forensic science overall, but rather the integrity of forensic science. Whether it is a criminal or civil case, two parties and witnesses swear to tell the truth. Each person shares his or her version of the crime and claims he or she is telling the truth. But one or several people are lying or incorrect. Now it's up to a jury or judge to determine who is telling the truth. So, the question is: How do we improve the integrity and reliability of forensic science?

I feel a DNA match should not be viewed as an unambiguous indicator of guilt. While DNA establishes a suspect's presence at the crime scene, it does not establish three other important factors in solving a murderer—motive, opportunity, and means. A criminal investigation is an applied science that involves the study of facts, like DNA, that are then used as "indicators of suspicion." A detective has to establish which individuals had the means, opportunity, and motive to commit the crime and to establish the relationships between the victim and any suspects or known offenders.

Erin E. Murphy, a professor of law at New York University and author of the 2015 book *Inside the Cell: The Dark Side of Forensic DNA*, stated: "People are desperately hoping that DNA will come in to save the day, but it's still fitting into a flawed system. If you don't bring the appropriate amount of skepticism and restraint in using the method, there are going to be miscarriages of justice."[5]

The judicial system's unwillingness to acknowledge some of DNA's scientific shortcomings has compounded the pitfalls and limitations of DNA. Often, when people or organizations invest in a belief, it can be easy to ignore evidence that conflicts or challenges that belief. Admitting that DNA is not as conclusive as it is made out to be is not an easy pill to swallow. That is why the public rarely reads or hears about stories in which DNA evidence wrongly identified an innocent person during a trial. This is different from when DNA exonerates a convicted criminal serving time in prison.

The following 1998 rape case exposed the double-edged sword of forensic science and raised some concerns and questions about its validity in court. A few days after reporting her rape to police, a woman identified two men, Josiah Sutton and Gregory Adams, as the persons who raped her. From the beginning Sutton and Adams denied any involvement. They both had alibis, and neither of them matched the profile from the victim's original testimony. She described her assailants as short and skinny. Adams is 5' 11" and 180 pounds. Sutton is three inches taller and 25 pounds heavier.

Unfortunately for Sutton and Adams, the credibility of DNA testing worked against them. While the report exonerated Adams, it matched Sutton's DNA to the mixture from the vaginal swab. Even more unfortunate was that the forensic lab technician, Christy Kim, used a method that was nearly impossible to differentiate mixtures of DNA. Nevertheless, based on this DNA evidence, a jury found Sutton guilty of aggravated kidnapping and sexual assault, and the judge sentenced him to 25 years in prison.

But fortunately years later, on the evening of November 22, 2002, Carol Batie, Josiah Sutton's mom, was watching a news report about how the Houston Police Department Crime Laboratory had mishandled DNA evidence from at least 500 cases. One of the people the reporter interviewed was William Thompson, an attorney and criminology professor at the University of California at Irvine. While many experts and the public accepted DNA as a silver bullet, Thompson believed that it was not. He stated that Houston police technicians routinely misinterpreted even the most basic samples. Armed with this new information, Batie contacted David Raziq, KHOU's television producer. He, in turn, directed her to contact Thompson.

Thompson graciously took an interest in Batie's son's case and found Kim's conclusion about the crime-scene evidence distressing. After Thompson reviewed the DNA analysis report he concluded that if Kim couldn't consistently identify DNA profiles from a single person, she couldn't be trusted to make sense of a complex mixture of DNA from one saliva and two blood samples. When Thompson examined the test strips, he also concluded that Kim had failed to analyze the other DNA samples found in the back seat. Had she performed this extra test it would have shown that this sample didn't match Sutton's DNA.

In addition to this misstep by Kim, my gumshoe mind questions how the prosecutor and jury did not factor in the fact that there was only one DNA match. If the woman claimed two men raped her, then it is possible to assume that both men ejaculated. If that is the case, there should have been two DNA matches.

Shortly after Batie received Thompson's report about her son's new DNA discovery, Robert Wicoff, the defense attorney, persuaded a Texas judge to have the DNA evidence reprocessed by a private testing facility. The results confirmed that the DNA found at the crime scene didn't match Sutton's DNA profile. But the story about this case doesn't end here.[6]

Three years later, in 2006, the Houston police found the person responsible for the rape after a cold case hit in CODIS led them to a convicted felon, Donnie Lamon Young. When detectives informed Young of the DNA evidence, he confessed and pled guilty to the rape.[7]

DNA has also been regarded as irrefutable proof of direct contact. But a growing number of studies show that DNA does not always stay put and that it is not always possible to tell beyond a reasonable doubt how or when the material got to the discovered location. For example, a person who merely carried a cloth that had been wiped across someone else's neck could then transfer that person's DNA onto an object he or she never touched, according to a 2017 study published in the *International Journal of Legal Medicine*. Another example: if I shake your hand, there is a good chance that I have some of your skin cells on my hand. If I grab a weapon, I transfer your DNA to it.

Cynthia M. Cale, a master's candidate in human biology at the University of Indianapolis, recently reported in the *Journal of Forensic Sciences* that a person who uses a steak knife after shaking hands with another person transfers that person's DNA onto the handle. In fact, in a fifth of the samples she collected, the person identified as the main contributor of DNA never touched the knife.

5. Gumshoe Work Precedes DNA Evidence   137

Jennifer Friedman, a public defender in Los Angeles and DNA specialist, offers these thoughts about DNA: "Although clear cases appear to be quite uncommon, I think it's probably more prevalent than we think. The problem is that what we don't see frequently is the ability to definitely prove that transfer occurred."[8]

At the 2016 American Academy of Forensic Sciences conference, experts spotlighted the case of Lukis Anderson, who was accused of murder after his DNA was found under the fingernail of Silicon Valley millionaire Raveesh Kumra, who suffocated after the perpetrator bound him during a 2012 home-invasion robbery at his gated Monte Sereno estate.

Anderson's public defense attorney, Kelley Kulick, pursued every avenue to prove that Anderson had nothing to do with the crime. He eventually discovered medical records showing that, on the night Kumra died, Anderson was at Santa Clara Valley Medical Center, where he had been taken by ambulance after passing out drunk in downtown San Jose.

Kulick was able to prove that the DNA turned up at the murder scene only because paramedics inadvertently transferred it there from a simple oxygen-monitoring probe they'd clipped onto Anderson's finger first and then onto Kumra's finger, which is the proposed mechanism for transfer. Prosecutors dropped the charges after examining a dossier Kulick put together, interviewing the paramedics and hospital personnel, and reviewing videotape of the crime scene to make sure the paramedics had really treated both men. Anderson walked out of jail five months later.[9]

Scientists and police have long recognized the risks of DNA contamination by lab technicians and of transfers from one object or person to the crime scene. In most uncontrolled, non-experimental samples, experts really don't know for sure how the secondary transfer occurred. *Law Enforcement* magazine warned officers to take great care when collecting evidence if they had a sunburn or dandruff because their DNA could fall into the evidence. In the lab, one experiment showed that it only takes 30 seconds of handling something or someone firmly for skin cells containing DNA to be transferred. Another study demonstrated that semen on one garment could contaminate another if they are washed together in the same machine. Most studies also show that the transfer of DNA is pretty much instantaneous. Additional contact and/or increased pressure and friction can increase the amount of transfer.[10]

While there is no doubt DNA evidence is a valuable asset, it has undermined the value of good old gumshoe investigation methods that have been around longer than DNA forensics. Like any piece of evidence, DNA represents just one part of the investigation process.

Although DNA will confirm the identity of the killer, it won't necessarily find the killer. If DNA is found at the crime scene, a person's DNA must be archived in the CODIS database in order to find a match. Therefore, if CODIS doesn't find a match, the DNA is of no value to the investigation.

DNA can hinder or delay the investigation because a detective must often wait for the results of a DNA test. Turnaround times for various forensic tests vary from state to state. But the average turnaround time estimate for a DNA test result ranges from two weeks to several months depending on the number of cases ahead of your case and the size of the DNA lab.

While a detective waits for the result, there is a chance the suspect may disappear, which results in delays tracking down the suspect or not finding him or her. The police could also discover that the test results do not point to the suspect they originally had in mind. This means the detective has wasted time that could have been spent on other evidence or leads or arrest and conviction.

The following is an example from a 1992 sexual assault case, in which the overreliance on DNA created a bizarre and unfortunate situation for the victim, as well as for detectives and forensic scientists. The results of the DNA test carried more weight than the victim's account of the rape and her identification of the rapist. It led detectives to rule out the person she identified as the rapist and also demonstrated how he duped the detectives and forensic scientists during the DNA test. This case showed how legal procedures hampered the process of properly collecting DNA from the rapist. Detectives did not divulge the victim's real name to protect her identity and referred to her as Candice.

On Halloween night in 1992, after Candice had an argument with her boyfriend, she drove to the hospital to seek comfort and advice from her girlfriend. The girlfriend wasn't working that night, but, because Candice appeared upset, the nurse suggested she see the on-duty doctor.

Dr. John Schneeberger, who was Candice's primary care doctor, was on call that night. Candice said that Dr. Schneeberger recommended a sedative to calm her down. She expected the doctor to give her a couple of pills. Instead, Dr. Schneeberger injected her with a shot. She immediately went numb and passed out.

After she regained consciousness alone in the exam room, she had a strong suspicion that she had been drugged and raped by Dr. Schneeberger. To ensure the possibility of proving the rape occurred, she made a smart move: Before the nurse or doctor returned, she placed her panties in an airtight plastic bag she found in one of the drawers.

After the nurse returned and checked Candice's vital signs, she recommended Candice spend the night in the hospital. Candice did and kept quiet about the alleged rape because she didn't have any real proof.

The next day Candice confronted Dr. Schneeberger and asked what drug he had given her the previous night. "Why, did it give you wild dreams?"[11] Dr. Schneeberger replied.

His mocking reply convinced Candice that Dr. Schneeberger had drugged and raped her and that she needed to establish proof before reporting it to the police. She immediately drove to a rape clinic for testing. The test results showed traces of semen on her panties, jeans, and vagina. A blood test also revealed a drug called Versed in her body. Versed is used as a pre-anesthetic agent to induce anesthesia. It numbs the muscles and eventually puts a person to sleep.

When Candice formally accused Dr. Schneeberger of rape, many citizens in the community did not believe her because he was married with two children and a respected member of the community. They believed Candice, a single mom with only a high school education, was either infatuated with Dr. Schneeberger or that her motive was financial gain.

To end the controversy, Dr. Schneeberger willingly volunteered to give blood for a DNA test. The results showed that his DNA did not match the biological material from Candice's rape test kit. So, the police ruled him out as their primary suspect. Candice, however, insisted that someone had tampered with the DNA test at the hospital and continued to claim that Dr. Schneeberger raped her.

To prove his innocence again, Dr. Schneeberger volunteered to take a second DNA test. This time the police carefully monitored it. Immediately after the nurse collected his blood, the vials were taken directly to the forensic laboratory. Again, the test revealed that Dr. Schneeberger's DNA didn't match the biological material in Candice's DNA rape test kit. With no other evidence to connect Dr. Schneeberger to the rape, the police closed the investigation.

But Candice didn't give up and hired a private investigator. The private investigator broke into Dr. Schneeberger's car in an attempt to collect an item with his biological material on it like hair or saliva. The only viable item he found was a tube of lip balm presumably used by the doctor.

At her own expense, Candice hired a private DNA lab to test the lip balm. The DNA in it matched the DNA in her rape test kit. But there were two problems. The first was that there was no proof that the lip balm belonged to Dr. Schneeberger. Second, the evidence was inadmissible because the investigator broke into the doctor's car without a warrant. Nevertheless, she wondered if the cells on the lip balm belonged to Dr. Schneeberger, why did the DNA from his lips differ from his first two blood samples?

To find the answer Candice filed a civil suit against Dr. Schneeberger and brought charges against him with the local medical society. This prompted the doctor to volunteer for a third DNA test. This time the police videotaped the procedure. When forensic scientists attempted to take blood from Dr. Schneeberger's finger, which is the normal procedure, he politely refused because he claimed he had a disease that causes bruising in his hands. Since this was a voluntary test, the police couldn't force the doctor to do anything against his will.

As the forensic scientist inserted a needle into his left arm she had a difficult time drawing the doctor's blood. Eventually, she did. When she arrived at the lab to examine the blood, she was puzzled because it didn't look fresh. After the examination, she determined that his blood sample was too degraded for DNA testing. Although the police were suspicious about the latest blood test results, they believed so strongly in the science of DNA that they were hesitant to charge him.

Then, five years later, on April 25, 1997, Dr. Schneeberger's stepdaughter accused him of giving her injections for several years and raping her. With the help of Dr. Schneeberger's wife, detectives discovered a box filled with condoms, needles, and drugs, including Versed, in the doctor's home office. This prompted the police to issue a warrant for another DNA test, which gave police the authority to take bodily substances other than blood including hair and saliva. And this time they took the blood from Dr. Schneeberger's finger and not his arm. After the forensic scientist tested the blood, hair, and saliva samples, they all matched the DNA in Candice's rape test kit.

But a big question remained unanswered: How did Dr. Schneeberger dupe the forensic scientists in the three previous DNA blood tests?

During the trial, Dr. Schneeberger admitted he surgically inserted a plastic tube filled with one of his patient's blood under the skin above the inside of his left elbow. This is why he volunteered and insisted the police draw the blood from his left arm. Police looked closely at the videotape of the blood test. They noticed that Dr. Schneeberger had been careful to pull his sleeve only so high, so as to not reveal the incision where he inserted the tube. When the video was slowed for a brief moment the protruding tube is visible on his arm. By the time of the third test, which was five years later, the blood in the tube was old and dark, which explained the forensic scientist's difficulty in drawing the blood and puzzling discovery.

In 1999 the jury found Dr. Schneeberger guilty of drugging and sexually assaulting Candice, obstructing justice, and also sexually assaulting his stepdaughter. The court sentenced him to six years in prison.[12]

The overreliance on DNA analysis exists in other professions and industries. In a case study published in *New Genetics and Society*, Dr. Turney, an expert on the social impacts of forensics, shared her opinion on the forensic testing that took place in the wake of the 2009 Victoria, Australia bushfire disaster.[13]

The official toll of the Victoria bushfire tragedy recorded that 113 of the 173 victims died in their homes, 27 outside their houses defending them, six in their garages, and one in their shed. The people were where they were expected or supposed to be. Yet, authorities first relied on DNA to identify the bodies, which took weeks to complete and made it more frustrating for families to mourn and delayed funeral arrangements. In the end, many victims were identified based on their location and communication with others. Had authorities applied the latter methodology first, they could have expedited the process of identifying the bodies of victims and returned them to their families in a timely manner.[14]

I have discovered that every single scientific discipline has two things that have happened in terms of tremendous progress and the challenges that the discipline faces. This is the nature of a scientific endeavor and what happens when science interacts with the legal system and where there can be some real misunderstandings.

People leave their DNA in the world as they walk through it and leave it behind on every surface they contact. DNA has been given a power that other forensic or scientific evidence has not. The problem with DNA is that if science is misunderstood, science turns into a magic power that people believe works. And that makes the perception of the results and value of DNA as it pertains to each case very dangerous. The underlying challenge with DNA results provided by forensic scientists that is evident with people who testify in a murder trial is that despite the fact that people swear to tell "the whole truth so help them, God," not everyone at the trial is telling the truth. Someone is lying, but who? Then a jury and/or judge must determine the reliability of every person at the trial who swore to tell the truth. Most forensic scientists are truthful and honest in their opinions about their DNA findings. However, I've provided examples of how errors occur during testing and how a forensic scientist's opinion may not be reliable. It now raises this question: How can the integrity and reliability of forensic science be improved?

DNA, however, is not the only investigation method on which there is an overreliance. At one time acquiring telephone landline records through a trash pull was a great way to collect evidence. Changes in technology mean it is rare to find phone bills or any kind of paper trail in the trash, so in today's modern world detectives access a person's cell phone record to determine his or her location at the time of the murder. Despite its use as evidence that has led to many convictions, there has been a huge misunderstanding of how cellular telephone networks operate. Like DNA, pinpointing a suspect's exact location from a cell-tower record is not a perfect science.

According to Michael Cherry, the CEO of Cherry Biometrics, a consulting firm in Falls Church, Virginia, misconceptions about cell phone traceability abound. The false assumption is that when a person uses a cell phone, it automatically connects to the nearest tower, thereby pinpointing exactly where a person used his or her cell phone and proving that he or she was at a particular time and place. That is not how the cell phone system works, however.

When a person hits "send" on his or her cell phone, a complicated sequence takes place during the transmission. A cell phone doesn't send out a radio-frequency signal with pinpoint accuracy. Instead, it sends a signal that covers a radius of up to 20 miles. Because there is usually more than one tower in any one area, this results in the signal being captured by any of the towers in the area, which in turn doesn't provide the exact location of where the phone was at the time of the call. In addition, a tower has a maximum number of signals it can receive at any given time. Therefore, if I used my cell phone and the tower nearest to me is at full capacity, another tower will pick it up. In so doing, it provides false information about the caller's location.

Here is how Aaron Romano, a Connecticut lawyer, explained how imprecise a person's location can be. Cell phone towers' coverage is divided into sectors. If a sector has a radius of 10 miles, that equals an area of about 314 square miles. Most towers have three directional antennae, each of which covers one-third of the circle. Using the 10-mile radius, each sector totals about 104.67 square miles. "That's a huge area," Romano said. "So how can anyone say, with any degree of certainty, that a handset was at the scene of the crime?"[15]

While a cell phone record has helped convict criminals, like DNA it has also proven a suspect's innocence and exonerated convicted criminals.

In 2004 Lisa Marie Roberts, of Portland, Oregon, was convicted of the brutal murder of her lover, Jerri Lee Williams. While there were reasons to suspect her because of her tumultuous, sometimes violent relationship with Williams, the key piece of evidence that convicted her was her cell phone record, which allegedly placed her at the scene.

At the time, Roberts's lawyer, William Brennan, encouraged her to take a plea deal for manslaughter or risk being jailed for life. She accepted the deal. But shortly after her incarceration, Roberts said, she asked Brennan to file for an appeal to overturn her conviction; he repeatedly discouraged her from doing it.

About six years later a fellow inmate urged Roberts to renew the fight. In 2008, her case landed on the desk of a federal public defender named Alison Clark, whose pit bull investigative team worked to dismantle the case over the next six years.

What the new investigation revealed was that Roberts's cell phone record showed that, at 10:27 on the morning of the murder, her phone connected to a tower within 3.4 miles of Kelley Point Park, where Williams's body was found. She made the call, however, while driving a red pickup truck more than eight miles away, a fact confirmed by a witness. The system had routed her call through another tower near the park and she had received another call that came through a different tower. The two towers were 1.3 miles apart. She could not have traveled that distance in the 40 seconds between the calls. Ironically, her cell record helped exonerate her.[16]

There is no dispute that the search of a person's cell phone record is a good investigation method, but judges and jurors must tread cautiously whenever a prosecutor introduces a cell phone record at a trial and avoid an overreliance on it.

While technological advances in forensic science like DNA and cell phones continue to help detectives get closer to reaching the universal truth, the truth is that DNA, cell phone records, or any other technological method is only a supplement to a murder investigation and will never replace good investigative work ethics. Even legal scholars emphasize that additional corroborating facts and evidence should be required to determine guilt or innocence. Nothing replaces asking good questions and interviewing witnesses in search of that missing piece of the puzzle as well as being a good master of detecting deception. However, if you'd like to increase your knowledge of the new DNA technology and/or discover new ways of applying it as evidence, I highly recommend you contact Suzanna Ryan, owner of Ryan Forensic. Ryan appeared with me on *Wrong Man*'s second season during the Kenneth Clair case. I include information about Ryan Forensic and how to contact Ryan in Chapter 12. Detectives should also study and become very familiar with TrueAllele and STRmix. These are computer programs that are used to effectively identify the primary DNA contributor when there are mixtures or mixed stains of DNA from an item at the crime scene or recovered from the victim.

DNA and new scientific technologies will continue to solve lots of cases, but good investigators must rely on a formidable eye for detail, especially when it comes to reading cold case reports. Being persistent, relentless, and finding ways to obtain incriminating statements from suspects are just as necessary for success with cold cases.

Cold Case #11: Government of Philadelphia v. Dickson— Victim Deborah Wilson (Vidocq Society: Foot Fetish Cold Case)

Summary

On November 30, 1984, Philadelphia police found the body of Deborah Wilson, a 21-year-old Drexel University student, lying on her back at the bottom of a stairwell in the campus's Randell Hall. Wilson was fully dressed in jeans and a blouse, with a down-filled overcoat placed carefully over her body. Her face showed the bruises of a severe beating, and the foam-like saliva coming out of her mouth was a sign of strangulation. There was no sign of sexual assault or rape.

Whoever killed Wilson dragged her body from the computer room of the campus building where she worked, carefully placed her in the stairwell, and then did a very curious thing. The killer removed her sneakers and socks and took them from the crime scene. The police never found them.

Philadelphia detectives quickly collected evidence, interviewed friends and relatives, and identified a possible suspect, David Dickson. Dickson was one of two guards on duty at the Drexel University computer lab at the time of Wilson's murder, and he did not have a solid alibi. There was not sufficient evidence to warrant an arrest for Dickson, however. Wilson's case remained cold for eight years.

Resolution

In the spring of 1992, Detective Bob Snyder presented Wilson's cold case to Vidocq. After Snyder described the circumstances surrounding Wilson's homicide, one of Vidocq's members, Richard Walter, offered a short psychological profile of the killer. He described him as the power-assertive type, a macho guy who liked to dominate and control. "This profile fits my guy to a T," Snyder said.[17]

Walter also suggested Snyder focus on the victim's bare feet, and the shoes—or lack of them. Walter described the killer as someone with a foot fetish and advised police to find a man with a history of stealing women's footwear. With Walter's guidance, detectives zeroed in on David Dickson again.[18]

Snyder discovered that Dickson did a stint in prison for robbery and left that important detail out of his university employment application; the university had failed to conduct a background check on Dickson. When detectives dug deeper into Dickson's background, they learned about his military history and that his first active-duty stint ended with a court-martial and discharge from the army in 1979 for burglary. He was accused of breaking into a female soldier's home in Korea and stealing her sneakers and suspected of a string of shoe thefts at the Philadelphia naval base.

Multiple spouses reported that their white sneakers and gym socks had been stolen from their homes, but the military leadership disregarded their accusations because they thought the spouses were "crazy" and "acting up" while their husbands were away. In addition, a local newspaper noted that Dickson was fired from a pharmaceutical company for sending a co-worker a sexually explicit letter and whispering over the phone that he was going to rape her.[19]

It's important to note that Dickson's criminal behavior prompted him to move between the active-duty Army and the Army Reserves. Dickson was able to escape each location without detection, but the behavior followed him from base to base.

Snyder and his team of detectives raided Dickson's apartment and discovered 20 pairs of white women's sneakers wrapped in plastic bags and multiple videotapes containing foot pornography in a storage unit. Detectives theorized that Deborah Wilson stayed late in a computer room in Randell Hall to work on a project that was due the next day. As Wilson exited the room, one of the security guards asked Dickson to escort Wilson to her car. Dickson complied, but on the way out his ego and fetish kicked in and he assaulted Wilson.

Dickson, a fifth-degree karate black belt, struck Wilson on her head and neck area, lunging at her and hitting her on the forehead with a security clock, which explained all the bruises. He then strangled her with a cord, dragged her body to the stairwell, and took her socks and sneakers.

Dickinson remained stubbornly silent after his arrest. His behavior in jail, however, provided more evidence that he killed Wilson. Dickson pasted magazine pictures of sneakers on his cell wall, earning the nicknames "Dr. Scholl" and "Dr. Smell." Fellow prisoners testified that he boasted of killing "the rich bitch" and described how he murdered Wilson.[20]

Sentence

In December of 1995, the jury convicted David Dickson of second-degree murder and the judge sentenced him to life in prison.[21]

Wilson's case is an excellent example of how good old-fashioned "gumshoe" work helped solve a cold case without the assistance of a DNA test and is an argument for the use of the FBI national database to document crime in the U.S. military that can be easily accessed by military law enforcement officials in the world. Since burglary is considered a felony, it would be appropriate to enter the crime into the worldwide system whether or not the perpetrator is known. The FBI national database would help track the clues and solve crimes perpetrated by transient military personnel.

One of the things I love about Columbo is that he popularized the inverted detective story format, which begins by showing the commission of the crime and its perpetrator. Most crime shows and movies, like a fresh homicide, have a "whodunit" element, in which the identity of the murderer is not revealed until the end. But Columbo, like a cold case, has more of a "howcatchem"[22] element in which the plot revolves around how a perpetrator whose identity is already known to the audience will finally be caught and exposed. This format resonates with me because in many of the cold cases I have worked the killer's name was recorded in the first 10 percent of the case file or first 30 days of the investigation report. The number of days is based on how much information the detective who wrote the report collected in the first 30 days after the crime. One report may include fewer than 100 pages while others are hundreds of pages long. Even if I'm able to identify the killer based on what I read in the cold case file, the real challenge is in collecting the evidence to prove he or she committed the murder—which I will discuss in the next chapter.

I love Columbo's interview technique with witnesses and suspects. He is a master at the skill of deploying discrepancies and, like me, conducts interviews without being judgmental. I use the same non-confrontational manner to avoid evoking defensiveness or resistance when investigating the differences between what witnesses and suspects say and their behavior.

There is a purpose to Columbo's seemingly random line of questioning. At the conclusion of every interview, he does something unique. He thanks the suspect profusely, steps toward the door, stops, and then turns back and says, "Oh, just one more thing." Then he asks one last question, a particularly damning question that lets the suspect know that he is onto him or her. Like every form of good communication, sincerity is critical. It cannot be contrived. The goal is to make a strong, memorable point. The process is simple: (1) hold back a critical piece of information and reserve it for the end of the meeting, (2) right before parting company, share the information or ask a question, and (3) enjoy the response you receive.

A 2009 article in the *American Bar Association Journal* reported that the best way to interrogate a suspect is to "Think Columbo."[23] The advice given is to focus on what a suspect says rather than on his or her behavior. After reviewing interrogation tapes, Professor Ray Bull, a British forensic psychologist, told the *Times* newspaper that British police use an investigative interviewing technique that sounds much more like a chat in a bar than an interrogation.[24]

The *American Bar Association Journal* article includes comments from American psychologist Kevin Colwell, who said that suspects who lie in a police interview often prepare a script that does not have a lot of detail. Colwell recommends using interview techniques in which the detective questions the suspect more than once and encourages him or her to retell the event and include details such as sound and smell and to recall the event in reverse. He states:

> Those who tell the truth tend to add 20% to 30% more external detail than do those who are lying. Those who are adept at lying may start to feel more strain if the interviewer introduces evidence throughout the questioning that has been previously uncovered. Detective Columbo, it turns out, was not just made for TV.[25]

Although Columbo is a fictional character, there are many good fresh homicide and cold case detectives who do a stellar job using the same techniques he practices to solve murder cases. Good gumshoe work involves utilizing other investigation methods that require more time and less reliance on technology and the internet. Some examples include an off-line search with the National Crime Information Center (NCIC); trash pulls; mail covers; collecting hard copy documents like a letter, diary, or journal; and cell phone records.

NCIC Off-line Search

While NCIC is technically an online telecommunications system that stores data, it allows investigators to utilize what is called an off-line search. During the course of an investigation, information needs may develop that an online search cannot satisfy. An off-line search is a special technique in which the NCIC system automatically cross-references information that is logged into the database. The NCIC database archives record detailed information for millions of stolen items, wanted persons, missing persons, and unidentified persons records that are instantaneously available to local, state, and federal criminal justice agencies across the United States.

A detective can initiate a search by name, date of birth, license plate, driver's license number, or vehicle identification number, and an item can be searched by its description, serial number, vehicle registration number, or any other numeric identifier. A detective has the ability to request information through a customized word search with a citizen's identification marks such as sex, hair color, height, weight, and age. However, the effectiveness of an off-line search relies heavily on how well a detective submits the information into the NCIC database and his or her level of due diligence.

Unlike CODIS, NCIC archives information about any person who is questioned by the police regardless of whether he or she is issued a ticket or arrested. For example, if a police officer pulls you over in your vehicle because of what he deems to be suspicious activity by you and/or your friends, his first course of action is to enter your names into the NCIC database to see if any of you have a record of previous violations or if there are any outstanding arrest warrants. Regardless of whether the officer issues a citation or not, all the information about you and your friends and your activity during his questioning is recorded into the NCIC database. The information remains on file for at least 10 years.

NCIC created this database for the following reasons:

- To check if any other agency has made an inquiry on an individual or item of property.
- To place an individual at the scene of a crime or miles away from the scene.
- To substantiate or discredit an alibi.
- To track the route of suspects, witnesses, or runaways.[26]

Even in cases in which a vehicle identification or serial number has been obliterated beyond restoration, the off-line search has been of great value. In some cases, the off-line search has provided identifying data on a suspect. The following cases demonstrate just a few of the many insistences in which the off-line search, specifically tailored to the unique needs of the individual case, provided vital information that led to solving the crimes.

Case 1

On April 19, 1995, a bomb exploded at the Alfred P. Murrah Federal Building in Oklahoma City, Oklahoma. Approximately 90 minutes after the bombing, Charlie Hanger, an Oklahoma State Highway Patrol Officer, was driving north on Interstate 35 when he passed a rusted, yellow 1977 Mercury Marquis with no license plate. He stopped the car and found behind the wheel a clean-cut, 26-year-old Timothy McVeigh.

Two days later investigators decided to conduct an off-line inquiry with NCIC to search for a record of police activity in the vicinity of the bombing. In most crimes, the perpetrator is in a hurry to leave. One thought was that maybe the suspect had been pulled over for speeding. The search revealed information about Officer Hanger's arrest of Timothy J. McVeigh.

Authorities contacted Hanger and asked him to describe in detail his reasons to question and arrest McVeigh. Hanger said McVeigh didn't have proof of insurance or a bill of sale for the car. McVeigh told Hanger that he was moving to Arkansas and on his way to get more of his belongings, but Hanger noticed that there was no suitcase in the car or any evidence to corroborate McVeigh's story. And he also noticed that McVeigh was wearing a Glock pistol and six-inch knife under his left arm. At that point, Hanger decided to arrest him.

Investigators speculated that the bombing was an act of terrorism and were looking for men of Middle Eastern descent, but when they discovered McVeigh's arrest through the off-line search, he became a person of interest. While McVeigh was in custody investigators discovered a trail of evidence that connected him to the bombing. The vehicle identification number of the Ryder truck led authorities to the rental agency and then to a motel where McVeigh registered under his real name. Although the detectives may have eventually identified McVeigh as the bomber, the NCIC search expedited his arrest.[27]

Case 2

Police received a call to a private residence where a son found his father's dead body. After the police reviewed the crime scene, they determined that the father was a victim of homicide. The initial investigation produced little evidence that would identify a perpetrator.

After weeks of questioning family and neighbors, detectives began to suspect the stepson who lived several hundred miles away in a different state. During the interview, he claimed that he was not in the area when the homicide occurred. When a neighbor reported seeing a vehicle with an out-of-state license plate near the victim's home about the time of the murder, detectives decided to conduct an NCIC search. Working with the staff at the Department of Motor Vehicles, detectives discovered several vehicles matching the partial license plate number they had been given by the witness. A check of the vehicles revealed that one license plate belonged to the stepson's girlfriend. Detectives contacted the officer who requested the license check. His log indicated that he had stopped the vehicle and questioned several occupants after seeing them drinking. The officer detained them long enough to issue a ticket.

When detectives confronted the girlfriend with the fact that her car may have been used in the commission of a crime, she admitted that the stepson borrowed her car during the month that the killing occurred. When detectives questioned the stepson about the ticket, he confessed to the murder.

Case 3

Detectives reactivated a four-year-old homicide and burglary cold case. One of the items missing from the crime scene was a stereo system. In the initial investigation, detectives failed to trace the serial number to its owner. When they conducted an off-line search to determine if any previous inquiries had been made regarding the stereo system, it revealed one inquiry by another law enforcement agency in the adjacent county two years after the homicide. The log disclosed that an officer had conducted the inquiry for a local pawnshop owner who wanted to confirm the stereo system was not stolen property. Fortunately, the pawnshop owner still had the stereo system in his custody, as well as the identity of the individual who pawned it.

After several months of intense investigation, the individual who originally pawned the stereo system was located and interrogated by detectives. This individual subsequently confessed to stealing the stereo system as well as killing the victim.

The Trash Pull

Another gumshoe tactic that is very effective is the trash pull, also known as "trash cover" or "dumpster diving." A trash pull is simply collecting the trash that has been discarded by a suspect or other individuals identified in an investigation. Most states have existing laws on the books regarding the legality of when the trash is considered abandoned and therefore provide investigators with guidance regarding search and seizure issues. However, in most trash pulls an investigator does not need a search warrant.

A trash pull serves two basic purposes. First, it can be conducted to retrieve physical evidence regarding the homicide. Second, it can be utilized to gather valuable evidence, information, or intelligence about a suspect or key witness.

One of the main benefits of a trash pull is that it reveals a lot about a person's habits, preferences, likes, dislikes, and the events happening in their life. The return addresses on personal envelopes and postcards in the trash also provide contact information of the people they suspect are communicating within his social network or may identify a person unknown to the investigator. This intelligence from a trash pull is strategically used to build rapport with the suspect and discover ways to bond with the suspect in a way that he or she will volunteer information that may be valuable to solving the case during an interview or interrogation. The holiday season is a good time to conduct a trash pull because people receive mail that they do not normally receive at other times of the year.[28]

The following case examples illustrate the benefits of a trash pull.

Case 1

The Central Intelligence Agency (CIA) and Federal Bureau of Investigation have used the trash pull with their foreign counterintelligence investigation and operations. The trash pull played a big part in helping the CIA identify a mole in their agency.

In 1985, the CIA's network of Soviet-bloc agents began disappearing at an alarming rate. The CIA realized something was wrong but was reluctant to consider the possibility of an agency mole. Initial investigations focused on possible breaches caused by Soviet bugs or by a broken code.

Then, in 1986, the CIA assembled a team to investigate the source of the leaks led by Paul Redmond. The team of Jeanne Vertefeuille, Sandra Grimes, Diana Worthen, and Dan Payne examined different possible causes, including the possibilities that the KGB had either bugged the agency, intercepted its communications, or placed a mole. By 1990, the CIA was certain that there was a mole in the agency, but could not find the source. The CIA began conducting trash pulls on people they suspected. It took four more years for the CIA to identify the mole, Aldrich Hazen Ames.

The information gathered from Ames's trash gave investigators valuable information that they were able to use during the interrogation process. They found numerous pieces of correspondence like notes, journals, documents, and receipts that led to Ames's arrest and conviction. Without the trash pulls, federal investigators may never have gathered enough evidence to arrest him for espionage.

On February 21, 1994, agents from the Federal Bureau of Investigation (FBI) arrested Ames outside his Arlington, Virginia, residence on charges of conspiracy to commit espionage on behalf of Russia and the former Soviet Union. Ames is serving a life sentence without the possibility of parole.[29]

Case 2

Four months after reactivating a 10-year-old cold case, investigators identified a viable suspect. From the trash pulls at his residence, the detectives discovered that he liked to drink Pepsi, enjoyed deep-sea fishing trips, and was an avid reader of the local newspaper. The intelligence the detectives collected from the trash pull assisted them in coordinating a script for their interview with the suspect.

When the detectives decided to interview the suspect, they chose the day before his scheduled fishing trip and requested he arrive at the police station early in the morning. The latter request was made to make sure the suspect didn't have time to read the newspaper.

In the interrogation room, the detectives had a local newspaper on the table and offered the suspect a Pepsi, which he accepted. After they gave him the Pepsi, they let him sit alone in the interrogation room by himself for some time before interviewing him. When the detectives returned, they engaged him in a conversation about his upcoming fishing trip before asking questions about the murder case. The strategy was to give the suspect a false sense of security and safety in which he either let his guard down or confessed to the murder. After several hours, the suspect confessed.

The Mail Cover

A similar valuable gumshoe tactic is the mail cover. It is "a process by which a nonconsensual record is made of any data appearing on the outside cover of any sealed or unsealed class of mail, or in which a record is made of the contents of any unsealed class of mail as allowed by law."[30] The process is more than a century old but is still considered a powerful investigation method.[31]

The United States Postal Inspection Service (USPIS) regulates the authority to authorize mail covers. It only issues a mail cover to agencies with the legal authority to conduct a criminal investigation and supervises the mail cover with strict control and regulations. And law enforcement agencies must receive permission to conduct mail covers from the USPIS and treat mail covers as restricted and confidential information.

"The information provided by a mail cover may only be used to protect national security, locate a fugitive, obtain evidence of the commission of a crime, or assist in the identification of the property."[32]

An approved mail cover authorizes the recording of information from the outside of mail pieces, such as the sender's address and name, address of the addressee, and date and place of postmark. The intelligence from a mail cover may reveal information about the suspect that he or she may not voluntarily provide to a detective or information about the suspect that a detective was unable to learn through other investigative steps. Some examples include interaction with people detectives may not know about or evidence that may incriminate the suspect.

"It's a treasure trove of information," said James J. Wedick, a former FBI agent who spent 34 years at the agency and who said he used mail covers in a number of investigations, including one that led to the prosecution of several elected officials in California on corruption charges. "Looking at just the outside of letters and other mail, I can see who you bank with, who you communicate with—all kinds of useful information that gives investigators leads that they can then follow up on with a subpoena."³³

Diaries, Journals, and Letters

Other forms of written material valuable to a cold case investigation are diaries, journals, and letters. It may be hard to believe, but suspects have been known to keep written correspondence about the homicide they committed and share it with other people. Psychologists suggest that this helps a person cope with, or in some cases "relive," the homicide.³⁴

In one murder case, an undercover operative befriended a suspect and was able to view a diary maintained by the suspect. The diary revealed that the suspect was sorry for killing the victim. The undercover operative's testimony was used as probable cause to obtain a search warrant for the suspect's residence. Upon searching the residence, investigators found not only the diary, but also several other documents that implicated the subject in the murder.

Now that you have some insight on what it takes to be a good detective, it's time to introduce you to the 20 investigative steps that are important to investigating a cold case. These steps provide a detective with a clear understanding of how to conduct a thorough review of the cold case file.

Cold Case #12: Government of North Carolina v. Alvarez—Victims Troy and LaDonna French

The following cold case provides an example of the complexities of DNA testing and its credibility to identify a killer. It was one of the first cases in which the court allowed a new forensic DNA test called phenotyping as evidence in a murder trial. This case illustrates the value of good gumshoe work. There is a point near the end of the case in which the detective's deductive reasoning played a crucial role in finding the killer.³⁵

Summary

Troy French and LaDonna Moseley French of Reidsville, North Carolina, lived in an affluent community called Bethany known for its large collection of farms and rural homes with shade trees and ponds dotting the countryside. The Frenches had two children, Whitley (19) and Hunter (12). LaDonna Moseley French's parents and sister also lived in Bethany. Generations of Moseleys have grown up, fallen in love, and raised their families on land given to them by Moseley's parents and grandparents.

The Frenches attended Reidsville Bible Chapel, which is known for being strictly fundamentalist, with a doctrine that women should be submissive to men. So, when Whitley decided to date John Alvarez, a Hispanic boy with a different religious background and view, her parents were not happy.

Whitley told her parents that she wanted to follow Alvarez to Greenville after she completed her senior year. College was always in the Frenches' plans for their daughter, not following a boyfriend three hours across the state. Her mother begged her to reconsider her relationship with Alvarez. They had many arguments, some of them loud and some that spilled over into family events.

Concerns about the relationship of Whitley French and John Alvarez didn't end in the French home. Jose and Elaine Alvarez, John Alvarez's parents, told family members that they, too, objected to the relationship. The Alvarezes owned and operated Alvarez Landscape and Lawn Maintenance in Southern Rockingham County. They had four sons there.

Despite both of their families' disapproval, Whitley and John continued their Romeo and Juliet romance.

In the early hours of February 4, 2012, the Frenches' lives took a tragic turn when an intruder invaded their home and fatally shot Troy and LaDonna French. The murders of Troy and LaDonna French would become one of the most discussed and analyzed murder cases in Rockingham County, North Carolina.

About 1:30 a.m. Whitley French woke up to find an intruder with a hooded sweatshirt lying on top of her. She screamed. The intruder tried to cover Whitley's mouth to silence her, but Troy and LaDonna French heard her scream and ran up the stairs. The intruder heard them coming, climbed off of Whitley, and ran out of her room and toward the staircase, where he ran into Mrs. French and shot her four times. Then the intruder shot Mr. French in the chest. Despite his wound, Mr. French managed to run into the kitchen, where he collapsed. The intruder followed Mr. French into the kitchen and shot him as he lay on the floor. He then escaped through the front door.

After detectives heard about the tension because of Whitley's relationship with John, they considered both of them suspects but eventually ruled them out.

Troy had a gun and rifle collection in his house. A month after the homicides, investigators confirmed that Troy and LaDonna were killed with Troy's missing 9-millimeter handgun.

Eight months after the murder, preliminary tests by the North Carolina State Crime Lab confirmed that the DNA and blood at the crime scene did not belong to Whitley French, her dead parents, or numerous other members of the French family. Detectives learned that a house key was hidden beneath the deck outside the house. They conducted a test on the key, which revealed that the DNA on it came from a male unrelated to the French family. Further identification, however, would need to come from out-of-state labs because the capabilities in North Carolina had been exhausted. Any additional tests would take years.

Investigation of the crime scene and interviews with other people did not lead detectives to a suspect, nor could they find Troy's nine-millimeter handgun. There was not enough evidence to tie any specific person to the murder.

Over the next four years, the case would be handled by two separate district attorneys, investigated by four lead detectives, and analyzed by at least four crime labs.

Resolution

Although the DNA evidence ruled out those initially questioned in the case and quickly excluded others who were not involved, the detectives felt that the DNA they collected would eventually identify the killer. It took advances in technology, as well as deputies and forensic investigators in three states nearly three years to find a DNA match.

In 2014 investigators sent the DNA samples out of state for familial DNA testing because North Carolina's crime lab was not qualified to conduct this kind of test. Familial DNA testing is a type of analysis that allows scientists to match DNA samples to a parent, child, or sibling. Some law enforcement officials expressed ethical concerns and believed familial DNA tests violated privacy laws under the Fourth Amendment.

When a familial DNA test is performed, a scientist takes a DNA sample found at a crime scene and looks for a match to a known criminal in the FBI's database. If there is no match, the unknown DNA profile can be put into another software that looks for profiles that could be related to the suspect sample. That program will then rank the DNA profile to the strongest familial tie.

Scientists then perform a short tandem repeat test on the Y-chromosome, which allows investigators to examine the Y-chromosome—the "male" chromosome—of the DNA. If the DNA sample came from a woman, they would perform a mitochondrial test, which focuses on the portion of the DNA provided by the mother. These tests determine if the two DNA samples are related.

In this case, the sample was compared with John Alvarez's for similarities. Instead of using a database, a scientist closely looked at the two DNA samples to see if there were enough similarities to prove two people were related.

On October 31, 2014, results from DNA tests returned to investigators revealed a partial match to John Alvarez. A partial match shows that there are enough DNA strands to confirm a family relationship. This test confirmed that a parent or child of his most likely left their drops of blood at the scene of the crime. But more analysis was needed.

According to a warrant, one of the labs used by the county recommended a Y-STR test. The best way to tell if the DNA is a brother or father is to run a $40 Y-STR test from him and the sample. The Y-STR results excluded John Alvarez and his parents as sources for the blood drops. The test concluded that the DNA strand likely came from a second-order relative of John Alvarez. Scientists consider parents, children, and siblings first-order relatives. Second-order relatives are grandparents, aunts, uncles, nephews, nieces, and half-siblings.

Detectives obtained another search warrant to perform a new type of test called phenotyping, which breaks down an organism's genetic makeup. The sheriff's office paid $3,500 to Parabon NanoLabs, in Reston, Virginia, for a snapshot analysis, which includes mitochondria DNA tests.

The results of those tests proved two things. The DNA belonged to a Caucasian male who was half–Latino and the DNA came from someone related to Elaine Alvarez, the mother of John Alvarez and his three brothers but not to Jose Alvarez, Sr., their father. DNA experts began searching for a male relative on Elaine Alvarez's side of the family (a half sibling of John Alvarez, an uncle, a grandfather, or a son of a sister).

On May 11, 2015, Rockingham County detectives Marcus Marshall and Ed Smaldone visited the Alvarez house in Stokesdale and obtained DNA samples from Jose Silvano Alvarez, Sr., and Jose Silvano Alvarez, Jr., John Alvarez's father and older brother.

Detectives swabbed inside the cheeks of both men. Their DNA samples, along with samples from John Alvarez and Elaine Alvarez, were sent to the lab at Marshall University for further analysis to support earlier findings. The DNA profile was also sent to the state crime lab for confirmation. That's when investigators found their match.

On June 9, 2015, the tests revealed that Jose Alvarez, Sr., was not the father of their oldest son, Jose Alvarez, Jr. Detectives discovered that Jose Jr. and John Alvarez were born to the same mother, but that they had different fathers, a detail that shocked both families. The DNA identified Jose Alvarez, Jr., as the killer; he was taken into custody on August 25, 2015, and charged with two counts of first-degree murder. Alvarez pleaded guilty to two counts of first-degree murder in the deaths of Troy and LaDonna French.

After detectives interviewed Jose Alvarez, they released details of what occurred before and during the murder.

During a visit to Alvarez's house, Whitley left her driver's license on the counter. After seeing Whitley's address on the driver's license, Jose's curiosity got the best of him and he decided to pay a visit to the Frenches' house. Jose found a spare key beneath the deck outside the house and made a copy of the key. Jose periodically broke into the

Frenches' house for the next six months, sometimes even when the French family was home.

While there was no explanation as to why Jose entered Whitley's bedroom and jumped on top of her, the motive for the murders was to escape from the house. Alvarez told detectives that after the murders he threw the gun and his clothing into a dumpster near his house.

During his sentencing in court Alvarez apologized. "I do regret what happened," he said. "If I could take it back, I would. I am sorry."[36]

Sentence

Judge Ed Wilson sentenced Jose Alvarez, Jr., to two life sentences without parole, which will run consecutively.

6

My Gumshoe Methodology and Cold Case Checklist of Investigative Steps

There are many reasons a person commits murder. Most are fueled by emotions like jealousy, greed, anger, rage, or revenge. Other reasons include intentional illegal acts like robbery, drugs, sexual assault, or rape. It may also be unintentional or mistaken identity and/or a person may happen to be at the wrong place at the wrong time such as in a drive-by shooting.

I believe very few murders are planned crimes; they are often triggered by a victim's hostile or adverse response to the eventual killer. A killer usually spends more time covering up the murder, redirecting the investigation, and/or intimidating witnesses to keep them quiet. Along the way, however, the killer will typically make a mistake or leave a clue that will incriminate him or her.

If a detective is not able to solve a fresh homicide case, it is not always a reflection of ineptness or the inability to solve the case. It just means that the mistake or clue he or she couldn't find still exists somewhere in the cold case file, even years after the murder.

To help cold case detectives identify and avoid the mistakes made in the initial investigation and not repeat them, I created a methodology that includes a detailed list of 20 investigative steps that are instrumental to solving a cold case. There are many layers in a cold case, and a detective needs to be careful how each layer is examined. There are steps a person can take to avoid the pitfalls of the original investigation.

To successfully peel back all the layers in an investigation a detective must execute good deductive reasoning throughout this 20-step

6. Methodology and Checklist of Investigative Steps 163

process. As the saying goes, "if it walks, looks, and sounds like a duck, then it's a duck!" There are some people, like the killer, who will try to persuade you that he or she is not a duck. Like any advice, saying it is a lot easier than practicing it.

Misdirection is a skill that killers use to avoid suspicion and arrest. Therefore, deductive reasoning is a good skill to practice because it proceeds from general premises to a specific conclusion. Deductive reasoning is reasoning where true premises develop a true and valid conclusion. The conclusion must be true if the premises are true. Deductive reasoning will help a detective filter through all the layers of the evidence, witnesses, and suspects to find the specific person who committed the murder.

The following are examples of deductive reasoning as it may relate to investigating a cold case:

- If Dennis misses work, and at work there is a party, then Dennis will miss the party.
- It takes me an hour to get to the mall. If I leave at five o'clock, I will reach the mall by six o'clock.
- That dog is growling, so be careful or you might get bitten. (It is logical if the dog is angry, he might bite.)
- Johnny is a bachelor. All bachelors are single. Hence Johnny is single.

Deductive reasoning may seem simple, but it can go wrong in more than one way. When deductive reasoning leads to a faulty conclusion, the reason is often that the given premise was faulty. Thus, the premises used in deductive reasoning are in many ways the most important part of the process of deductive reasoning, as proven by the help of the aforementioned examples.

Here is an example of faulty reasoning: *All flight attendants know how to swim. Ralph knows how to swim. Hence, Ralph is a flight attendant.* This conclusion is not true because it is not true that only flight attendants know how to swim.

If the premises are faulty, the entire foundation of the line of reasoning is faulty. Therefore, the conclusions derived will be faulty. However, at times, even if the logic is executed properly, the conclusion may be wrong. To minimize the chances of this mistake happening, it is best to not assume anything and to only accept what has been mentioned specifically.

The following progression of steps along with good deductive reasoning will give a detective the upper hand on the killer the second time around. Each step a detective performs in a cold case requires precise and thorough execution. While each step is important, some will require more detailed work than others. Not every step will be applicable. Nevertheless, it is important to consider each one before you move to the next step. Following these steps serves to help a detective avoid or deal with scrutiny from the victim's families, the public, and the media. Before you follow these steps, however, prioritize the cold cases assigned to your department. It's important to apply the solvability factor to determine which cold case takes precedent over another. A copy of the Cold Case Solvability Factors Worksheet is included at the end of this chapter. It's impossible to investigate multiple cold cases because each requires a detective's full attention. This extra work will help relations with the victim's family whose cold cases have been placed on hold.[1]

Step #1: Review the File in a Quiet Place. Studying a cold case is to studying a fresh homicide as chess is to checkers: the former requires much more focus. One good place to undertake this study is the library, which will help avoid any distractions that may cause you to lose concentration and overlook an important piece of evidence that could help you find the killer. Many libraries provide private rooms that will eliminate any distractions.

Make sure you are well rested before reading the file. A tired body and eyes are a bad combination. If you feel yourself getting tired, take a break even if it's only for short time. I suggest at least 20 minutes. Get up and walk around or change your environment. For example, exit the library and walk outside or go for a short drive. This will help clear your mind and give you a fresh start when you return to the library.

As you review the file, confirm that all reports, notes, and related documentation are still available. Find out which people in the file are still alive, where they currently reside, and search for their contact information. Ask for a complete autopsy file and photographs and evidentiary items that are still available that the law enforcement agency can provide. Determine if there is a pulse in the case and what new technological advances you can apply to the investigation. Turn off your cell phone while conducting the initial review. Constantly checking your email and text messages is distracting and will interfere with your ability to "learn" the case and understand what happened during the original investigation. Knowing and understanding the case is critical to successfully solving it.

Step #2: Contact the Evidence Custodian. After you establish that there is a statutory case, confirm the location of the evidence. Then access and personally view the physical evidence to ensure it exists. Make sure you visit the property room or evidence facility and confirm that the evidence exists. Physically view the evidence and compare it to evidence custody documents to determine what evidentiary items still exist and what could be missing.

Step #3: Collaborate with the Prosecutor. Establish a good, friendly relationship with the prosecutor and involve him or her in the investigation as soon as possible. If possible, visit with the prosecutor outside his or her work environment. Get to know each other; the odds are that you'll be working on the cold case for a long period of time. Remember that both of you are trying to accomplish the same objective and be allies for each other. It's a detective's responsibility to sell the case that identifies the killer to the prosecutor who in turn must sell it to the court and jurors for a guilty verdict. Work with the prosecutor to determine if the statute of limitations has expired, the degree of the murder, and if any laws have changed or new ones have emerged since the day of the homicide. Consult the prosecutor about all old and new legal aspects of the case. Procedures that were once lawful may no longer be legal or stand up in court. For example, if during the initial investigation a suspect evoked their right to silence or counsel, do you have to invoke a Miranda warning again before you interview him or her?

Involving a prosecutor as soon as possible is perhaps the most important step for a cold case investigation because things that were not legal issues before may now pose problems. For example, privileged conversations, spousal conversations, and Miranda warnings must be evaluated before approaching the suspect for initial interrogation or re-interrogation. Determine the degree of murder and if there is a statute of limitations and whether the "statute has run."[2]

Step #4: Organize the Cold Case in Three-ring Binders. The binders provide a detective with an excellent, organized reference system. It helps the detective and others on the investigative team stay inherently familiar with all aspects and progress of the cold case. These binders will include contact information and documentation of every law enforcement agency and person who participated in the investigation. Create the binders in these five categories: alphabetical and chronological order, key people, case notes, evidentiary items, and prosecution team. Create timelines and correlation charts, statement time-check charts, comparison graphs and charts, statement and information crosscheck charts, and a list of inconsistencies. Also, consider creating a separate binder for photographs.

Collecting this network of information will provide the element of surprise during the interrogation of potential suspects. Record the information in chronological order and include case notes, timelines, statement crosscheck charts, and link analysis. In order to take full advantage of the element of surprise, it is extremely important for a detective to familiarize him or herself with every detail of the investigation and gain as much knowledge as possible about the suspect's behavior, habits, psyche, and relations with relatives and people in his or her social and working networks.

In the *key people* section record background checks of all the key people in the file. The background checks should include NCIC and social media like Facebook, Instagram, Snapchat, and Twitter to determine whether the people in the file are in contact and still communicating with one another.

In the *case notes* section of the binder file your notes in chronological order by date. Managing all of the data and information is tedious work but it will help minimize or avoid any hindrances during the investigation. Fortunately, today's technology provides software tools to help organize your notes. One called Evernote helps to efficiently capture research, data, and other information and then consolidate, store, and organize it into a single, usable location.

Evernote is an app that works on Android, iOS, and Windows platforms, which means it can be used on computers, tablets, and mobile devices. The app allows a detective to record case notes, research documents, website links, photos, and more. Since the service is cloud-based, investigators can access and enter information into a centralized area when they are in the office or out in the field. This helps eliminate the need to write everything down, then re-enter the information once back at the office. It enables investigators to enter information "at the moment," when the details are fresh in their minds. This helps ensure the recording of more accurate details.

This app will allow other team members of the investigation to interface with it. For example, if two detectives are conducting surveillance on a person from two different locations or angles, they can record case notes simultaneously in the same notebook. This is a huge time-saver and a more efficient way to operate.

Videos, photos, and other visual files are saved safely for anytime access. This eliminates the necessity of a PC or laptop to access files. It can be done on the go via a laptop or mobile device. For example, investigators who are trying to locate a subject can use their mobile device to access the subject's photo and other details of the case using the app.

Another great feature is the offline notebook, which can be used when there is no internet connection. This comes in handy when in a remote area conducting surveillance and there is a need to take notes and update information in case files. Once you can reconnect to the internet, the files can be synced with the cloud.

The Evernote app provides a better overall organization of information and case details. The application helps avoid loss of vital information or case details since everything is stored and backed up on the Evernote account to which it is uploaded.[3]

In the *evidentiary items* section create a complete list of physical items, documentation, and information collected like essays, research papers, assignment evaluations, articles, and recent professional publications.

During this analytical review, background checks will help determine which individuals within the case file are still in contact and communication with each other today.

An important electronic tool to help manage the cold case is CaseMap by LexisNexis. This is an excellent case management software program that is critical to the success of properly managing cold cases.[4]

Step #5: Develop a List of Inconsistencies. Whenever an inconsistency is identified, record it on a list of inconsistencies. This will help visualize all the facts related to why a particular suspect could have or did perpetrate the murder. This list will also help keep track of those small details that are often used to solve a case. The difference between a good detective and a great detective is often in the details, as is in the Virginia v. Peterson case in Chapter 1.

Step #6: Contact the Original Investigator. Contact the original investigator and all participants who worked on the original investigation. If the original investigator is not alive, contact his partner or other detectives who worked with him during his employment. Ask the detective or his partner if a copy of the original file exists. Spend time asking questions about the case. Determine if the original investigators maintain copies of the original case file. This is important, as most investigators keep copies of their old investigative files, especially those unsolved cases that consumed their thoughts.

Many retired homicide detectives keep copies of their old investigation files. Be aware that some detectives can be thin-skinned and sensitive about discussing or sharing information about their old unsolved cases and others can become too involved in a renewed investigation. Therefore, it is important to be careful how you ask for their help. Do not ask them if they *have* copies of the old file. Instead, ask *where* their copies of the old file are located.

Contact all the other people who participated in the investigation like first responders, morgue personnel, policemen, or firemen. They may provide information or different insights on what they witnessed while at the crime scene or working on the case.

Step #7: Reconstruct the Crime Scene. Revisit the initial crime scene during daylight and nighttime hours to conduct a visual re-enactment of the murder and scientific experiments. If applicable, also visit the secondary crime scene, for example where the body was dumped. Determine what the original crime theory was, the updated crime theory, and final crime theory that original investigators pursued. Determine how, why, and when the crime occurred. Analyze all descriptions of the crime scene, photographs, autopsy reports, interviews, interrogations, statements, police reports, case notes, and other related documentation. Interview all of the original first responders, officers, detectives, crime scene technicians, and medical examiners.

6. Methodology and Checklist of Investigative Steps 169

Consult with forensic and psychological experts. Determine if the original investigators followed viable theories and pursued correct suspects.

If there is no access to the original crime scene, visualize in great detail what it looked like based on the photographs and description. Consult with all the detectives in the initial investigation who are still alive as well as other detectives working with you. Their insights will help create the best possible visual description of the crime scene. Refer back to Chapter 3, in which I share information about how I use my senses to help feel what it was like at the fresh homicide scene during the original investigation.

The crime should be reconstructed. Could the crime have happened the way it was reported to have happened? It is important for investigators to get a "feeling" for the case. Determine if the crime scene was altered or staged. A case that involves a staged murder scene may provide a detective with information about the relationship between the victim and the killer.

Since it is impossible to have been at the original scene, avoid the "Why didn't they do this?" syndrome. It will only distract you from determining what the information in the file is telling you about what occurred at the crime scene. Some old files will literally speak in terms of which suspect is likely responsible for the murder while others read like a true whodunit. Separating "white noise" in the file to identify the true suspect(s) can be a challenge.

Step #8: Re-submit Evidence. Make a request for the forensic laboratory to conduct another examination of the evidence. Obtain contemporary evaluations of the original analysis and findings. Use the alternate light source (ALS) as an ally. The use of an ALS could disclose potential evidentiary items (e.g., semen, saliva, etc.) not noted during the original investigation. Remember, many forensic examinations, especially in the DNA arena, that were not available years ago can now be conducted on those evidentiary items originally recovered at the crime scene or from the victim's clothing.

Step #9: Determine the Beneficiary. Make a list of who might have benefited the most financially from the death of the victim. Then contact the National Insurance Crime Bureau at their headquarters in Des Plaines, Illinois, to cross-reference their files to see if any people on this list *did* benefit financially from the murder. This step may lead you to a possible motive or more productive direction.

Step #10: Revisit Background Checks. Update background checks for all the people listed in the file. Look for signs of changing relationships with former spouses, girlfriends, boyfriends, friends, neighbors, co-workers, and other people in the primary suspect's social network. Complete this step before conducting any interviews.

Understanding those "changing relationships" and how to use them to elicit information from witnesses about the crime and suspect is critical to the success of any cold case.

Before I share the last 10 steps, I'd like to share another solved cold case.

Cold Case #13: Government of Florida v. Kuenn— Victim Carol Hutto

Summary

On December 13, 1976, 16-year-old Carol Hutto left her house to shop at a nearby drugstore. Sadly, the Largo High School junior never returned.

The next day Jerry Irwin, Carol's half-brother, found her body weighted with concrete blocks in a pond two blocks from the Hutto family's house. After a search of the crime scene, Largo detectives expanded their search, which led to a nearby house under construction about a block away from the Hutto residence. They found a makeshift bed, Hutto's jeans, a pink blanket, and her watch, stopped at 10:36 p.m.

Initially, detectives suspected Irwin because of his juvenile delinquent record and his lack of an alibi, but detectives did not have enough evidence to connect him to the crime so they ruled him out. After a search of Hutto's bedroom detectives identified another possible suspect. They found Hutto's diary, and in it she had written about a teenage boy named James Brian Kuenn. It appeared Hutto had a crush on him. During the interview, Hutto's parents said their daughter received a phone call from Kuenn before she left the house.

Detectives interviewed Kuenn the day after the homicide. Kuenn told police he had not seen Carol the night before. Although Kuenn had no solid alibi and refused to take a polygraph test, detectives had no solid evidence, so they also ruled him out as a suspect.

An autopsy revealed that Carol had been hit and strangled, lost consciousness, was thrown in the water alive, and that the cause of death was drowning. With no other leads or evidence, detectives closed the investigation on Hutto's case.

Resolution

Two decades later, two Largo detectives reactivated the cold case. When they discovered that Kuenn was an active U.S. Navy Petty Officer and stationed at the U.S. Naval Submarine Base in Groton, Connecticut, they invited the NCIS Cold Case Unit to assist in the investigation.

Detectives traveled to Connecticut and interviewed Kuenn. During the interview, Kuenn contradicted his previous statement about not seeing Hutto on the night of the murder and admitted that he did see her. Detectives had no cause to detain him, so they let him go. Based on Kuenn's answers and behavior, detectives fingered him as a suspect and decided to schedule another interview. Kuenn, however, declined any further interviews and sought legal counsel.

After detectives considered their options, they decided to obtain a search warrant to collect a DNA sample from Kuenn, who, surprisingly, complied with the court order. While detectives waited for the results, they also decided to interrogate Kuenn. They thought the anxiety of waiting for the DNA test result might compel him to confess. He did.

Kuenn described to detectives what happened on the night he killed Hutto. She had agreed to meet him at the house under construction. As the two kissed, Kuenn tried to have intercourse with Hutto. She resisted, screamed, and hit and scratched him. He grabbed her by the throat to get her to stop screaming. When that failed, he found a two-by-four and hit her over the head. Then he undressed her and dumped her into the pond.

Ironically, months later, the test results showed that the hair found on Hutto's jeans did not match Kuenn's hair.

Sentence

On February 9, 2000, the jury found James Brian Kuenn guilty of first-degree murder. The judge sentenced him to life in prison. NCIS Special Agents David Early and Tom Asimos did an excellent job on this investigation.[5]

Step #11: Review the Medical Examiner's File. Confirm that the file is complete. If possible, locate the doctor who performed the original autopsy and establish contact with the family member or person who made the legal original identification of the victim's body. Ask the medical examiner for any retained tissue samples or other specimen slides. Most medical examiners create two specimen slides or smears. This can be especially useful in cases where the victim was sexually assaulted but the original evidence swabs have been used up in earlier serology or DNA testing. The retained slides may contain enough sperm cells to yield a DNA profile. Make sure to read the following article in the *FBI Bulletin* dated November 2000: "The Microscopic Slide: A Potential DNA Reservoir, November 2000." This is the same application that was used to capture the Golden State Killer.[6]

Step #12: Contact the Victim's Family. Contacting the victim's family can be difficult because each family handles the murder of their loved one differently. Be aware that after years of disappointments and frustration, some family members may not want to participate or help with the investigation. Be careful not to falsely raise their hopes in how you approach, deliver, and share information about the reopening of the cold case. If the suspect is a relative of the victim, do not contact any family members.

Step #13: Formulate an Investigation Plan. Collect information about the suspect and key witnesses through any or all of the following resources: social media, trash pull, mail cover, surveillance, subpoenas, credit history, informants, court orders, wiretaps, passive listening posts, ministry and civic outreach organizations, computer databases, public information documents, wills, lawsuits, arrests, booking reports, judgments, cellmates, prison staff, and off-line NCIC checks. Read the article "FBI NCIC—The Off-line Search Revised March 2005" before completing this step.[7]

Step #14: Identify Any Changes in Relationships. Identify the changing relationships and future investigative activities that allow the element of surprise before the interrogation of the suspect.

Before interviewing major witnesses check to see if there have been changes in relationships between the witnesses and the suspects since the murder. Several changes may have occurred. Animosity may have grown between a witness and suspect. Over time a witness's conscience or newfound religion may convince him or her to tell the truth. A witness may be in trouble with the law and willing to agree to a deal, to tell the truth, or become an informant. Collecting this information before interviewing the witness will allow you to maintain the element of surprise before the interrogation of the suspect.

Step #15: Begin Interviews with Peripheral Witnesses. Tread cautiously to not alert the suspect. This is why it is important to follow the instructions in Step #14 first. Demonstrate empathy for the victim and family. Any lack of concern and respect for the victim can make witnesses uncooperative. Do not rush the interviews and be prepared to spend hours, days, and weeks with critical witnesses and potential suspects.

Focus on incriminating statements, alibi information, inconsistent statements, third-party conversations, documents, records, diaries, journals, and digital media. Peripheral witnesses include relatives, friends, employers, co-workers, neighbors, former and present cellmates, members in affiliated clubs and organizations, adversaries, former or present girlfriends or boyfriends, ex-wives or husbands, churches, parole officers, and co-defendants. Interview the witnesses in an order that witnesses will not tip off or alert the suspect about the cold case being conducted by law enforcement. Otherwise, the element of surprise could be lost when interrogating the suspect.

Avoid the "grapevine effect," which is the "informal transmission of information, gossip or rumor from person to person." This manner of communication is informal information that is open to change and interpretation.[8]

Many initial interviews result in false statements and half-truths. Use the half-truths to challenge witnesses so that a more truthful recollection of events is obtained. The second and third interviews of key witnesses and potential suspects will help expose more of the truth. If possible, interview the suspect in a noncustodial environment.

Step #16: Consider Strategic Undercover Operations. Conduct viable proactive law enforcement strategies and undercover evolutions. Incorporate the four phases of investigation: analysis, programming, fact-finding, and evaluation and verification. Schedule a team conference that includes a brainstorming session on how to execute the investigation and undercover operations, and collect evidence. One example is chance meetings. Think outside the box and be creative during covert operations when collecting information and physical evidence.

Think of ways to surreptitiously collect information and/or physical evidence (e.g., DNA, hair, fibers, etc.) from suspects.

Step #17: Interview Witnesses and Suspect. Perform an indirect assessment of the witness or suspect prior to the interview. Develop a theme and rehearse a script and role-play before the interview. Conduct interviews in a strategic and logical fashion. Choose a neutral location like a hotel, library, or park. These kinds of locations provide a non-threatening environment for the suspect and might create a false sense of security. Use props that will remind the suspect of the murder. Acceptable props are photos of the victim before the murder or the location of the murder and maps or newspaper articles. Avoid or use caution when showing photos of the murdered victim, crime scene, or physical evidence from the crime scene because it might jeopardize the investigation, arrest, and conviction of the suspect. However, a replica of an item from the crime scene is an acceptable prop.

The successful utilization of props forces the suspect to relive the crime and creates an emotional advantage to the person conducting the interrogation of the suspect. The proper use of theme development is important for investigators when interrogating suspects. The investigator must rehearse the various themes to utilize during the interrogation.

Also, review the original neighborhood canvassing report. Pay very close attention to individuals who did not belong at the crime scene before or after the murder. There may be a neighbor who always visited the victim at certain times of the day who might provide important information about people or something he saw. It may be fruitful to ask whether everyone present at the crime scene (or in the neighborhood canvass) was expected to be there and, conversely, whether everyone expected was in fact present.

Step #18: Continue Investigation After Arrest. There is a tendency for detectives, as well as prosecutors, to stop further investigation after an arrest. Continue to monitor the suspect's movements and his communication activities through social media, letters, phone calls, email, computers, diaries, and journals. His comments and actions after the arrest may further incriminate him. The more evidence gathered, the more solid the case against the arrested suspect. Thoroughly document all conversations as well as the date and time. After the arrest, most suspects may eventually disclose information or brag about the murder to other people in their social network. It is important to continue collaboration with the prosecutor after the arrest to ensure every piece of evidence that implicates the suspect will stand up in court. Always remember that the suspect is not guilty until the jury officially announces the verdict in court.

Listening to and recording "jail calls" can develop additional incriminating information from the suspect.

Step #19: Re-interview and Re-interrogate. This is another element-of-surprise tactic that will keep the suspect off guard. Interrogate the suspect the next day before he or she has time to consider retaining legal counsel and/or before the suspect's initial appearance or preliminary hearing. The more times you can record the suspect confessing the better.

Step #20: Solicit Public Support and Assistance. It is very important that a detective thoroughly execute all the previous 19 steps before seeking the public's help. Make sure to collaborate with the prosecutor and media and public relations officer in the department. Writing a draft of a press release is also helpful. It will help focus on sharing the information with the public in an amicable way and avoid or minimize scrutiny or criticism about the handling of the cold case from the victim's family, media, and public. One way to gain the public's attention and participation is to advertise a reward for information that will lead to the conviction of the suspect. While people in law enforcement are not in the business of making news or trained in public relations, it is important to create and implement new strategies to improve communications and relations with the families of victims, the media, and the public.

Strongly consider the use of podcasts for your cold cases. Refer to *The Long Dance* podcast and attempt to replicate what was done in that podcast with the cold case you are working. Cold case podcasts are becoming increasingly popular, and many have generated new information and investigative leads for investigators.

Additional tips to support these investigative steps include: In most cold cases, the suspect surfaces early in the police reports, usually within the first 10 to 15 percent of the recorded content in the case file. Over 90 percent of the time the murderer's name is mentioned in the file, and in many cases in the transcripts that document the first 30 days of the investigation. Ghost suspects are normally only exposed through the use of forensic genealogy or a witness coming forward years later with critical information. Pay attention to any person that inserts or interjects him- or herself into the investigation. Original investigators should be interviewed to determine if a particular individual appeared to be overly helpful or showed up unannounced to provide investigators with information about the murder. If a suspect passes a polygraph, do not immediately rule him/her out. Do not ignore other evidence that identifies him/her as the primary suspect. If ruling him/her out, do it through the process of elimination. Do not take the focus off of an individual simply because he or she passed a polygraph during the original investigation.

Pay very close attention to post-offense behavior. Look for major shifts in behavior. Determine which suspect's life has deteriorated or dramatically improved since the murder. Both are potential indicators of guilt. A suspect will often move after committing the murder, either a short distance like two blocks or a long distance, to another state or thousands of miles away across the country. After a murder, a suspect who was normally punctual may suddenly arrive late to scheduled appointments, activities, and interviews; someone who was always tardy may start showing up early. Become familiar with the suspect's normal behaviors and identify any changes in the way he/she interacts with other people. Exercise proper preparation for interviews with solid, reliable witnesses and especially with the suspect, in which the main objective is to obtain a confession.

Every picture tells a story, so pay attention to what the crime scene says and focus on the behavioral clues. Do not try to make your theory fit the crime. Meticulously study crime scene photographs and

6. Methodology and Checklist of Investigative Steps   177

videotapes so as not to overlook clues and evidence the first investigation team missed. When reviewing a photograph, track your eyes from the corners and work inward to the middle of the photograph. This strategy is similar to piecing together a jigsaw puzzle. The best and most efficient method to finish a jigsaw puzzle is to start with the border pieces and then connect the inside pieces moving towards the middle. Every crime scene tells a story if time is taken to properly read what the scene is broadcasting. Use keen observation skills and deductive reasoning when focusing on inconsistencies. Document the inconsistencies and visualize the actions that took place during the crime. Good investigators use keen observation skills to note the clues in the old crime scene photographs.

Prioritize the cold cases assigned to your department. It is important to apply solvability factors to determine which cold case has the best chance of being solved. It is impossible to investigate multiple cold cases; each requires a detective's full attention. The cases with the highest solvability success rate are between eight and 14 years old. Using solvability factors will help relations with the victim's family whose cold cases have been placed on hold. Most family members would like a reasonable explanation as to why their family member's cold case has not been reopened. Be extremely aware of cases that are not solvable solely by evidence. For example, the existence of a video showing that the suspect was near the crime scene close to the time of the murder does not prove he was at the murder scene. This is also true if his/her DNA is found at the crime scene. If solid evidence cannot be found, witnesses cannot be located, and/or suspects refuse to talk, then move on to the next cold case until new evidence appears or a witness or suspect decides to share more information about the case. The older the case, the harder it is to solve. There is a copy of the Cold Case Solvability Factors Worksheet at the end of this chapter.

Search for viable DNA samples from suspects that have been stored in the evidence room and submit them to the forensic laboratory. Be sure to use an alternate light source when reevaluating old evidence. Consult with criminalists at the state or local crime laboratories to help assess which items may contain probative evidence that can be analyzed with current technology. Stay in control of every step by creating a lead tracking sheet the same way as performed in a fresh homicide.

Monitor and evaluate every accomplishment made by the investigative team during the investigation. This leads to building a solid case that identifies the killer. As you collaborate with the investigative team, think outside of the box and find creative ways to increase the chances of solving the cold case. Make the case visual for prosecutors with storyboards, PowerPoints, or other creative methods. Find amicable ways to persuade a prosecutor the cold case is worthy for presentation to a jury at court.

While the 20 investigative steps and related tips are essential in solving a cold case, it's also imperative for a detective to make good use of new valuable resources other people contribute in the law enforcement network like the DNA M-Vac.

In the early 1990s Dr. Bruce Bradley, the owner of a well-known microbiology lab in Idaho, invented the M-Vac. Dr. Bradley's laboratory served the dairy and food industries in that area for over 25 years.

> Since a major part of his business focused on solving an array of microbiological problems in the food industry, it naturally led him to search for better ways to collect surface pathogen samples. Dr. Bradley concluded that surface sample acquisition was the "weak link" in the food safety environment, and the likely cause for undetected microbes in other industries. Since wet-vacuum systems are used to clean a variety of surfaces, Dr. Bradley embarked on a long journey to perfect a hand-held wet-vacuum sampling system that led him to invent the M-Vac.[9]

The M-Vac is a sterile wet-vacuum device that simultaneously sprays a solution onto the surface of an item of evidence and creates a "mini-hurricane" that loosens cellular material and transfers it into a collection bottle, which is then passed through a filter that serves to concentrate and capture the DNA. This new procedure collects DNA material from porous areas that are difficult if not impossible to reach otherwise (like rocks, bricks, ligatures, and clothing items) and also increases the probability of discovering DNA material randomly located on the surface.[10]

At the lab, forensic experts extract the DNA from the filter and test it in the same manner as a cutting or swab. This unique collection method is both more sensitive and scalable so collecting small amounts of DNA is very feasible even when it is spread over a large surface area.

6. Methodology and Checklist of Investigative Steps 179

Another good resource is a perpetual calendar. It will help a detective pinpoint the time of death as accurately as possible. It has 14 one-year calendars, one for each common year that starts on each day of the week, and one for each leap year that starts on each day of the week. A perpetual calendar is a calendar valid for many years, usually designed to look up the day of the week for a given date in the past or future. It is good to use for cold cases so you know the day of the week the murder took place.

There are many more resources available that a detective can access at his or her discretion. One good way to find them is to network with other detectives and law enforcement agencies.

Here is a creative strategy pioneered by Norman Gahn, an assistant district attorney in Wisconsin who has helped detectives keep cases alive that would have otherwise remained closed forever because of the statute of limitations. The main purpose of statute of limitations laws is to make sure that convictions are based on eyewitness or physical evidence that has not deteriorated over time. Statutes of limitations also protect defendants. There are three reasons for their enactment. One is a plaintiff with a valid cause of action should pursue it with reasonable diligence. Second is by the time a stale claim is litigated, a defendant might have lost the evidence necessary to disprove the claim. And third, litigation of a long-dormant claim may result in more cruelty than justice.

For example, in a sexual assault case, a prosecutor has six years to charge a person with the crime. The statute of limitations forbids prosecutors from charging someone for this crime after the six-year period of time has elapsed.

Gahn, who has a master's degree in forensic science from George Washington University, used the advancement in forensic science and a legal maneuver to expurgate the statute of limitations on a sexual assault crime. In the early 1990s, while many prosecutors viewed the statute of limitations as injustice and obstruction of justice, Gahn saw an opportunity to right what he perceived to be wrong. More often than not it is the defense attorney who typically finds a legal loophole to exculpate their clients. This time a district attorney took advantage of a loophole to convict a criminal.

Gahn referenced Rule 4—Arrest Warrant or Summons on a

Complaint—of the Federal Rules of Criminal Procedure, section B1A of which reads: "A warrant must contain the defendant's name or, if it is unknown, a name or description by which the defendant can be identified with reasonable certainty."[11] Gahn felt that since a DNA profile is even more certain than a name, why not create a "John Doe" warrant on an unidentified DNA sample?

Gahn also believed the "John Doe" warrant would allow him to file charges before the statute of limitations expired, thereby, keeping the case open. He also contended that a "John Doe" warrant that cites DNA rather than the usual physical description is more accurate because a criminal can change his or her name and appearance but not change their genetic code. Because CODIS continually updates their DNA database, Gahn felt that there remained potential for a match in the future. He was right!

In 2000 Gahn prevented a 1994 rape case of a 15-year-old girl from exceeding a six-year statute of limitations. He was the first prosecutor to issue a warrant for "John Doe," a suspect known only from DNA taken from the victim of a rape. A year later the "John Doe" #12 was identified as Bobby Dabney. At the time he was serving a prison term for armed robbery. Gahn discovered that Dabney, 38, was required to give the DNA sample in 1996, but it was not until February 2001 that it was matched to evidence in the case. The match of this "John Doe" DNA marked the first time detectives considered Dabney a suspect in the aforementioned unsolved rape case.

The following is a brief summary of the Government of Wisconsin v. Dabney case.

On December 7, 1994, an unknown male accosted 15-year-old Dawana F. at a bus stop in Milwaukee. The man kidnapped and sexually assaulted her. Then he let Dawana out of the car.

Dawana found her mother and called the police. Detectives immediately took her to a sexual assault treatment center where "oral swabs and saliva samples" as well as a "blood standard" were obtained from her. The state crime lab found semen present in the saliva and developed a DNA profile for the unknown male suspect.

On December 4, 2000, the State charged John Doe #12 with kidnapping and four counts of first-degree sexual assault. The DNA profile was included in the caption of the complaint. On that same day, a trial court found probable cause in the complaint and issued an arrest warrant for John Doe #12.

On March 14, 2001, the State filed an amended complaint substituting Dabney's name for "John Doe." The amended complaint stated that the DNA profile had found a match on February 27, 2001. This was reconfirmed on March 7, 2001.

On April 12, 2001, a jury convicted Dabney of kidnapping and sexual assault, and the court sentenced him to 120 years in prison.[12]

Since then the "John Doe" warrant has led to many arrests and convictions. They are important for all cold cases where there are no statutes of limitations. "John Doe" warrants demonstrate how useful thinking outside of the box can be for solving cold cases.

In the next chapter I will share methods of how I collect evidence through undercover work: ruses and strategic interviews with the suspect and peripheral witnesses like relatives, friends, co-workers, employers, adversaries, neighbors, cellmates, clergy, and other people connected to the suspect.

Cold Case #14: Government of Ohio v. Elkins— Victim Judy Johnson

Summary

On the night of June 7, 1998, Judy Johnson was raped and savagely murdered in her own home. Her six-year-old granddaughter was also attacked, raped, knocked unconscious, and left for dead. Fortunately, she survived.

The morning after the attack, the granddaughter regained consciousness and walked to the neighbor's house unclothed with blood streaming from her forehead. She knocked on the door and told the neighbor, Tonia Brasiel, that someone had hurt her and her grandmother. Brasiel told the girl to wait outside and left her sitting alone on the doorstep for 45 minutes before taking her to her mother. (For whatever reason detectives initially neglected to address this neighbor's aberrant behavior. Years later investigation thereof produced crucial information that enabled detectives to solve the case and identify the real killer.)

When detectives interviewed the granddaughter, they discovered she had told Brasiel that the man who attacked her and her grandmother *looked and sounded like* her uncle, Clarence Elkins. Based solely on her testimony, the detectives arrested Clarence.

Clarence claimed he was innocent and his wife, Melinda, believed him. Nevertheless, the district attorney charged him with the rape and murder of Johnson and rape and attempted murder of his niece. Melinda supported her husband's innocence and, in doing so, split the family apart.

One of the challenges Clarence and Melinda faced was that the prosecutor felt he had a strong enough case based on their niece's testimony. In addition, DNA testing was still in its infancy. Therefore, the prosecutor didn't instruct detectives to test the crime scene for DNA samples or search for other suspects to collect their DNA.

At the funeral, Melinda made a promise to her mother to track down the true killer and prove Clarence's innocence. But Melinda didn't know where to start, so she turned to an easy and inexpensive way to learn about the criminal investigation by watching the television show *Forensic Files*. She learned how to create a list of suspects, how to collect and preserve their DNA, and how to perform a ruse. She realized the only way to prove Clarence innocent was to find a DNA sample of another person that matched the DNA at the crime scene.

Through various ruses, she gathered the DNA samples from 12 men she identified as possible suspects. She collected the men's DNA from their discarded beer bottles and cigarette butts, from strands of hair she covertly pulled from their heads. Melinda wasn't sure when or how she was going to raise the money to pay for the tests, or if the results would be admissible in court, so she put the samples in her freezer for safe keeping.

During the trial the granddaughter told the jury *it was* her Uncle Elkins who committed the crime. This situational semantics of her testimony convinced the jury to find Clarence guilty and sentence him to life in prison.

The Appeals

While Clarence's lawyers exhausted their appeals over the next four years, Melinda remained undaunted. She spearheaded rallies, kept her story alive in the media, and organized an internet fundraiser, which raised about $40,000.

Melinda realized she needed more help and contacted the Ohio Innocence Project, led by former prosecutor Mark Godsey. And she also hired a private investigator, Martin Yant, who had worked on cases that led to exonerations of wrongfully convicted defendants.

Godsey realized that, back in 1998, DNA screening had not been sophisticated enough to properly collect DNA evidence from items at the crime scene. Four years later, however, DNA testing had improved immensely. Fortunately, the detectives and forensic team had preserved about 50 items in the evidence locker. They discovered that the male DNA samples forensic scientists found on Johnson's body and her granddaughter's underwear did not match Clarence's DNA.

During this time Yant convinced Melinda to reconnect with her sister. The reunion turned out to be a good move because Melinda's sister revealed that her daughter had admitted that she mistakenly identified her uncle as the killer.

In 2002, armed with this new DNA evidence and the recanted testimony of Melinda's niece, Melinda and Godsey felt confident they could prove Clarence's innocence. But the judge felt that Melinda had polluted her niece and coerced her to change her mind and ruled that prosecutors had convicted Clarence based on compelling eyewitness testimony and that a jury would have reached the same conclusion even if it had known his DNA didn't match the DNA found at the crime scene.

Despite this setback, Melinda did not give up.

Several days later an article in the newspaper caught her attention. It was about Tonia Brasiel and her husband, Earl Gene Mann. Both had been charged with three counts of rape of their three children.

Brasiel was the neighbor Melinda's niece ran to for help. Melinda had always wondered why Brasiel left her niece on her porch for 45 minutes before attending to her. Why didn't she just call 911 right away? When a distraught half-naked child with blood appears on your front doorstep, why wouldn't you invite the child into your home? Why wouldn't you wrap the child up in a blanket? Why wouldn't you call the police when a child has obviously been assaulted? But now she suspected why.

Melinda discovered that Mann, then Brasiel's boyfriend, lived in her house at the time of the murder, had a violent criminal record that included a conviction for rape, and had been released from prison in June of 1998 just before her mother's murder. That is why Tonia told Melinda's niece to wait outside. And when Melinda saw Mann's photo, she saw the resemblance to Clarence.

The Ruse

Melinda needed to find a way to collect Mann's DNA to see if it matched the DNA from the crime scene samples. But how could she collect the DNA from a man in prison? She certainly wasn't going to receive any help from the prosecutor or court. So she devised a ruse. She wrote to Mann pretending to be a pen pal; she hoped to receive a written reply from him, hoped that he would lick the envelope, thereby enabling collection his DNA. Unfortunately, he never replied to the 18 letters she mailed to him. But she did receive a big break and divine intervention by the justice system.

Melinda discovered that the court had transferred Mann to the Mansfield correctional facility where Clarence was serving his sentence. An even bigger stroke of luck was that Mann was assigned to the same cellblock as Clarence.

After Melinda spoke with Godsey, they devised a plan for Clarence to collect Mann's DNA. They asked Clarence if Mann smoked. He said yes.

Melinda taught Clarence how to properly collect and preserve Mann's cigarette butt for testing. It was a risky plan for a couple of reasons. They had no idea if the court would consider the collection of DNA by a civilian admissible evidence. Melinda was fearful of what might happen if Mann, who had a violent past, caught Clarence collecting his cigarette butt. But the risk was worth the chance of acquitting Clarence and getting him released from prison.

Clarence caught Mann putting out his cigarette butt in one of the empty ashtrays. (It was a crucial moment because he had to avoid contamination from other peoples' cigarette butts.) He immediately picked up the butt with a baggie and took it to his cell, where he concealed it in his Bible. The timing was fortunate because prison officials transferred Mann to another prison a few days later.

Two weeks later Clarence managed to smuggle the cigarette butt in a letter to Godsey, who immediately sent it to a DNA lab for testing. The test confirmed that Mann's DNA matched the DNA sample found on the body of Melinda's mother and on her niece's underwear.

The Good Ending

Armed with this new conclusive evidence, Godsey sought help from an unlikely source in order to increase the chances of exonerating Clarence. He contacted Ohio State Attorney General Jim Petro, who was a huge supporter of the new DNA technology and its use to not only convict criminals but also free those wrongfully convicted.

After Petro completed a six-week internal investigation, he publicly pressured the local prosecutor to exonerate Clarence.

In December of 2005, the Summit County Prosecutor's Office dropped the charges against Clarence Elkins and called for his immediate release from prison. Three years later at the trial, Earl Mann pleaded guilty to the murder of Judy Johnson and the rape, assault, and attempted murder of Melinda's niece. The court sentenced Mann to 55 years in prison.

This case demonstrates how an undercover operation can be a viable, efficient, effective, and productive method for solving cold cases as well as fresh homicide cases. However, the best way to expedite the solving of a case and identify the killer is during the interview with a suspect. The next chapter will detail how to prepare for interviews with a suspect, explain the concept of suspect interrogation assessment, and outline strategies for obtaining incriminating statements and/or a confession from the suspect.[13]

Cold Case #15: Government of New Jersey v. List— Victims Helen List, Alma List, Patricia List, John List, Jr., and Frederick List

Summary

In November of 1971 concerned neighbors in Westfield, New Jersey, noticed that the lights at Helen List's mansion remained on for several days and had begun to burn out one at a time. Teachers grew suspicious of the prolonged absence of Helen List's children. After several weeks, the police decided to check on the List family.

When the police entered the house on December 7, 1971, they heard organ music piped through the intercom system. They found a gruesome homicide scene. The dead bodies of Helen List and three children lay on the floor of the grand ballroom, their heads covered with towels and bodies cushioned on boy scout sleeping bags. The three children included Patricia, 16, John Jr., 15, and Frederick, 13. Detectives also found the dead body of Helen's 84-year-old mother-in-law, Alma, in a bedroom on the third floor of the Lists' mansion.

Detectives discovered that the thermostat had been lowered, which explained the lack of decomposition in the bodies and absence of the foul odor that normally follows death. The scene led detectives to believe that it was a premeditated homicide and the killer had methodically shot all of the victims.

As detectives continued their search for evidence in the Lists' house, they found a five-page note from John List, Sr., explaining that the bloodied bodies on the ballroom floor were his family members, whom he killed out of mercy and to save their souls. John's confession confirmed that he was the killer.

After detectives found John's car parked at Kennedy International Airport in New York City, it became evident that John was on the run. Detectives launched a nationwide manhunt. The search was unsuccessful, and it would take another 18 years for detectives to find John.

What Detectives Discovered About John List

John List appeared to be the perfect father, husband and son and he worked hard as an accountant at a local bank. The 19-room mansion where he lived with his mother, wife, and three children was impressive and included a ballroom, marble fireplaces, and a Tiffany skylight. List and his family were the picture of the American dream in 1965. They attended church every Sunday as devout Lutherans; List taught Sunday school. Everything looked perfect on the surface. But his mysterious disappearance led detectives to learn more about John's life and revealed his dark side.

Several months before the day of the murders, John List lost his job as an executive at the bank. Although he attempted to work other jobs, they never panned out or earned enough to provide for his family. He refused to go on welfare to avoid embarrassment in the community and so as not to violate the principles of self-sufficiency he learned from his father. He couldn't bear to tell his family about the loss of his job and income, so he spent his days at the train station reading the newspaper, meanwhile secretly skimming money from his mother's bank accounts to pay the mortgage on their mansion. The money ran out, and the bank started the foreclosure process. To avoid looking like a failure John committed an implausible murderous act.[14]

Description of the Murders

On a November day in 1971, John List methodically shot his wife, Helen; mother, Alma; and three children, Patricia, John, and Frederick. That morning John drove the children to school. When he returned home, he shot Helen in the kitchen. Then, he walked up the stairs to the third floor and shot his mother in her bed. That afternoon John shot Patricia and Frederick after they returned home from school.

John left the house and closed out his bank accounts. Then he attended John Jr.'s high school soccer game. After they returned to the house, John shot John Jr. in the chest.

John lay the bodies of his family members on top of sleeping bags in the ballroom and then wrote the confession note. His rationale was that he feared his family, confronted with a world full of evil and poverty, would turn from God. He felt this was the only way to ensure their safe arrival in heaven. He was not, however, willing to suffer the earthly consequences of his actions.

In an effort to baffle the police, John cleaned the crime scenes and used scissors to remove his image from every photo in the mansion so they couldn't print out a wanted poster with his photo. He canceled all deliveries and contacted his children's schools to let their teachers know the family would be on vacation for a few weeks. He turned on the lights and the radio, leaving religious hymns playing in the house's empty rooms, and lowered the temperature on the thermostat. He slept in the mansion that night, then walked out the door the next morning and managed to hide from the police for 18 years.

Resolution

In 1989, New Jersey prosecutors invited Frank Bender, an expert forensic artist, to create a sculpture of List. To help create an image of what John might look like, Bender sought the help of his friend and profiler, Richard Walter. Walter predicted List would wear a suit and be fond of sunglasses, that he would be remarried, involved with the Lutheran Church, and living no farther than 300 miles from where the crime occurred. With this information, Bender created a masterful depiction of John List.

On May 21, 1989, *America's Most Wanted* aired the story of the List murders. It reached an audience of 22 million people. One of the many tips the show received came from a woman in Richmond, Virginia, 325 miles from Westfield, New Jersey, just as Walter had predicted. The woman felt that her nextdoor neighbor, Robert Clark, bore a striking resemblance to the bust. The tipster also said Clark was an accountant and attended church.

Detectives immediately visited Clark's home and spoke with his wife, Delores Miller, whom he met at a church social gathering. Her story put an end to the 18-year-long mystery about John's whereabouts.

After John left New Jersey, he changed his identity to Robert Clark and moved to Denver, Colorado, where he took on a different career and worked as a hotel cook to avoid any connection to his life as an accountant. As he began to feel comfortable about being Robert Clark, John eventually decided to increase his earning potential by returning to a career as an accountant and landed a job with H&R Block. He also joined the Lutheran church, where he met Delores. They married and then moved to Richmond, Virginia.

Police in Virginia arrested John List on June 1, 1989, nine days after the television show aired his case. Before the trial John confessed to the murders.

Sentence

The judge sentenced John List to five life terms in a New Jersey prison. On March 21, 2008, List died of complications from pneumonia at age 82 while in custody at St. Francis Medical Center in Trenton, New Jersey.[15]

Cold Case #16: Government of Pennsylvania v. Rorrer—Victim Joann Katrinak

Case Featured in *Wrong Man* Season 2

On December 15, 1994, Andy Katrinak arranged to meet his wife, Joann Katrinak, and their three-month-old son, Alex, at his mother's house in Lehigh, Pennsylvania. When they didn't show up, he drove home and found their basement door removed from its hinges and the phone line cut.

Four hours later Andy called the police. After the police searched the neighborhood, they found Joann's locked car in the parking lot of a local tavern near her house. Days, weeks, and months passed with no information of Joann and Alex's whereabouts.

Detectives suspected Andy might have something to do with their disappearance and death. They worked hard to build a case against him, but lack of evidence to connect him to their disappearance ruled him out as a suspect. And so did statements from relatives, friends, and neighbors that convinced detectives that Andy and Joann had a rock-solid marriage.

Four months after Joann and Alex disappeared, a farmer found their dead bodies on a rural horse trail. Joann had been beaten and shot in the face, and Alex died from suffocation or exposure.

As detectives pried deeper into Andy's history, they identified another primary suspect, his ex-girlfriend Patricia Rorrer. Andy and Rorrer had lived together for a short time and parted ways in 1989. Rorrer moved back to North Carolina but stayed in touch with Andy through sporadic visits and phone calls. According to a police affidavit, Rorrer called the Katrinak house days before the murders. Joann answered the phone, and she and Rorrer had an angry telephone conversation. Joann insisted that Rorrer stop calling Andy because he was now married to her.

Detectives also discovered that Rorrer lived in Leigh County at one time where she stabled and rode horses in the same area as the crime scene. This meant she was familiar with the area.

The prosecutor and investigators theorized that the telephone conversation angered Patricia into a jealous rage and she abducted and murdered Joann and Alex.

Rorrer denied any involvement in the murders. Nevertheless, the prosecution extradited Rorrer from Linwood, North Carolina, to face trial for the following reasons:

- She had no alibi and had argued with Joann days before she and Alex disappeared.
- Ballistics experts determined that a bullet removed from Joann's body had been fired from a 22-caliber pistol similar to one Rorrer owned.
- Police obtained samples of her blood and hair, and a microscopic examination revealed similarities to the hair found at the crime scene.
- Her DNA matched the DNA hair samples found in Joann's car and at the crime scene.
- Rorrer had a criminal record. She had been charged with breaking and entering, intoxication, cruelty to animals, and larceny in the North Carolina counties of Davidson, Randolph, Gaston, Anson, and Forsyth.

Sentence

On March 6, 1998, a jury convicted Rorrer on two counts of murder and two counts of kidnapping, and the judge sentenced her to two life terms in prison without parole.

Post Conviction Summary

Rorrer filed and lost two appeals. She had lost all hope. But in 2010 crime writer Tammy Malinowski O'Reilly of Union Dale took an interest in Rorrer's case. O'Reilly found details that did not add up, that had never been made public, and that raised serious questions about the case and Patty Rorrer's guilt:

- What about the compromised crime scenes, contaminated and mishandled evidence, suspects who were never cleared, witness statements that were withheld from the defense, and crucial evidence that was simply dismissed and ignored?
- Why did the police focus on a young mother from another state who lived over 500 miles away, had never met either victim, and whose romantic relationship with Andy had ended more than five years prior?
- Why did the police focus all their attention on a hair found 15 miles from the crime scene but ignore physical evidence left directly on the bodies?
- Why did they refuse to test a hair found in the victim's right hand?
- Why did they fail to test a piece of flesh adhering to a torn fingernail fragment recovered from Joann's chest?
- Why did they refuse to conduct DNA testing on a cigarette butt found with the bodies?

Rorrer hopes *Wrong Man* will prove her claim that the DNA evidence used to send her away is "junk science" and also prove her innocence and warrant her release from prison.[16]

Cold Case Solvability Factors Worksheet
© Joe D. Kennedy

Victim Name _____
Rank Order _____ of _____ Date of Review _____
Date of Murder _____
Reviewing Officer _____

Worksheet Legend

Grade/Points
P (Poor) = 0
F (Fair) = 1
G (Good) 2

Factor #	Solvability Factor	Grade	Points
1	Has the death been ruled a homicide?		
2	Has the victim been identified?		
3	Did the murder occur indoors?		
4	Are all reports, case notes, and photographs still available?		
5	Is there physical evidence that can identify a suspect?		
6	Is there physical evidence still preserved and available?		
7	Can any evidence be reprocessed with new technology to yield further clues?		
8	Can forensic genealogy be conducted on any remaining DNA evidence?		
9	Are main characters and witnesses still alive? Can they be located?		
10	Are there named suspects in the case file?		
11	Were any named suspects arrested for DWI, DUI, or open container after the murder?		
12	Did the suspect "insert" him- or herself into the investigative process?		

6. Methodology and Checklist of Investigative Steps

Factor #	Solvability Factor	Grade	Points
13	Did any suspect physically move residences after the murder?		
14	Have any investigative leads been documented in the last six months?		
15	Are there potential informants who can be utilized?		
16	Are there viable nontraditional investigative techniques to pursue?		
17	Does the case have a pulse?		
	Total		

7

Legal and Proper Ways to Collect Evidence and Intelligence

Most law enforcement departments are structured as paramilitary organizations and train detectives to follow standard procedures. Although it is important for law enforcement agencies to establish a disciplined framework to investigate a cold case, it can restrict a detective's ability to explore other avenues that might lead to the killer.

It is essential to think outside of the box while collecting evidence. Often it is conventional thinking that led the initial murder case to become cold. Outside-the-box thinking gives a detective a view of the case and suspect that he or she may not have considered from conventional thinking. It can give a detective a psychological advantage over the murderer because the murderer expects a detective to follow certain procedures and behave a certain way. Conventional thinking might allow the murderer to prepare a countermove to destroy the evidence, impede the investigation, make it difficult for a detective to build a case against him or her, or evade an arrest. But when a murderer doesn't know what to expect it gives the detective a huge advantage and puts him or her in a better position to expedite the collection of evidence needed to arrest the murderer.

I hold myself to a very high standard and follow the letter of the law. If I don't, it will jeopardize the prosecutor's ability to obtain a guilty verdict and waste a lot of time and money. How evidence is collected is vital to building a solid case for the prosecutor. The evidence gathered must confirm the suspect's motive, opportunity, and means for committing the murder. The evidence must be preserved in such a way that it will stand up in court. Make one legal mistake, no matter how small, and a good defense attorney will exploit it and use it to convince a jury of reasonable doubt, which results in either a mistrial or an innocent verdict.

As mentioned in the preface, I investigate a cold case from an undercover perspective. It requires a different strategy and a considerable amount of preparation, planning, teamwork, and resources. While an undercover operation is not unique to law enforcement, police departments grossly underuse it, mostly because law enforcement limits its undercover operations to narcotics, gang, and organized crime-related investigations.

Undercover work has been largely relegated to the domain of the FBI and a few other federal law enforcement agencies to infiltrate spy networks, terrorists, mafia organizations, illegal weapons, human trafficking, and drug activity. But since the September 11, 2001, terrorist attacks on United States soil, there has been a heightened concern about the growing criminal activity in the United States. The U.S. Congress made a big push to expand undercover operations to more traditional crimes like identity theft, insurance fraud, online solicitation, and human trafficking. This has led state, county, township, and city law enforcement agencies to embrace undercover operations as a powerful new investigative tool to gather evidence in ways that standard law enforcement methods do not offer.

For example, the U.S. Department of Education hires undercover agents from the Office of Inspector General to infiltrate federally funded education programs to investigate financial fraud. Medicare investigators sometimes pose as patients to gather evidence against health care providers. Officers at the Small Business Administration, NASA, and the Smithsonian also engage in undercover operations. The use of undercover operations, however, is rarely utilized and undervalued by homicide and cold case investigators.[1]

The value of an undercover operation, also known as a ruse, is that it can be an alternative and efficient way to collect evidence. This is especially true when a detective identifies a primary suspect but cannot obtain a search warrant to collect his or her DNA or other forensic evidence. A ruse gives a detective the ability to covertly collect testimonial evidence from a suspect or witness. There are no restrictions for developing and implementing a ruse as long as the legal boundaries of the law are not crossed.

Executing a ruse involves good management skills, delegation and coordination duties, and a progression of steps that follows the letter of the law. It requires a considerable amount of teamwork and dedication. The instructions of each undercover operation must be clear and specific. And the course of action must blend in with the environment and reliable resources.

Management of a ruse is like writing a script for a movie or television show. The lead detective plays the role of producer/director and screenplay writer, and the undercover person he chooses is the actor. The detective writes a summary of the ruse, in which he identifies the target suspect. He assigns responsibilities and duties; selects the props; briefs everyone on safety, security, surveillance, and emergency procedures; ensures proper use of electronic equipment; and develops an exit plan in case the person needs to abort the undercover assignment for safety reasons.

The objective of each undercover operation or ruse is to collect testimonial evidence from a targeted suspect through one of the following five methods: incriminating statements, inconsistent statements, alibi information, third-party conversations, or a confession. The latter of which will more likely stand up in court.

The next step is to choose from among several types of scenarios and approaches: deep or shallow cover; chance, yesteryear, and role reversal meetings; and counselor, religious, curious, and confrontational approaches.

Deep and shallow covers are similar in nature. Deep cover requires more time and man-hours than a shallow cover, however, and is suited only for a sworn law enforcement officer. A good real-life example of a deep cover operation was depicted in the 1997 crime movie *Donnie Brasco*. The film is loosely based on the true story of Joseph D. Pistone, an FBI undercover agent who infiltrated the Bonanno crime family in New York City during the 1970s under the alias Donnie Brasco, a.k.a. "The Jewel Man." Pistone, who worked undercover for six years, maneuvers his way into the confidence of an aging hitman, Benjamin Ruggiero, who helps him work his way up the ranks and earn the trust of the Bonanno Mafia. As he moved deeper into the Mafia, he had to be careful not to cross the line between federal agent and criminal. The FBI's former director, J. Edgar Hoover, disagreed with the idea of FBI agents working undercover because he feared it would corrupt the agents. Nevertheless, Pistone's work helped convince the FBI that using undercover agents in lieu of relying exclusively on an informant was a crucial tool in law enforcement.[2]

A shallow cover requires less time and gives a detective the option of assigning a person who is not in law enforcement, like a cooperating witness, friend, co-worker, employer, criminal informant, or a person who has never met the suspect. An example of shallow undercover is depicted in the reality television show *Undercover Boss*. Each episode depicts a person who has an upper-management position at a major business deciding to go undercover as an entry-level employee to discover the faults as well as the strengths in the company. The first season consisted of nine episodes produced in 2009 and first aired on February 7, 2010, on CBS. Companies that appear on the series are assured that the show will not damage their corporate brands. This practice is equivalent to how law enforcement agencies expect people they assign to conduct undercover work.[3]

In a chance or yesteryear meeting the undercover person knows or has an indirect relationship with the suspect. In a role reversal meeting, the undercover person has no association with the suspect. The purpose of these meetings is to influence the suspect to subconsciously relive the murder so that he or she voluntarily shares information about details of the crime that will incriminate him or her. During these meetings the undercover person will attempt to perform one or all of the following objectives: (1) obtain testimonial evidence from suspects or key witnesses, (2) elicit confessions from suspects, (3) enhance interrogation objectives, (4) manipulate the suspect's feelings and mental state before the interrogation, and (5) place as much pressure as possible on the suspect just prior to the interrogation.

Once the cold case team establishes the type of meeting they select the appropriate approach that will give them the best chance for a successful ruse. They will choose one of four approaches depending on the dynamics of the case and the suspect's profile: counselor, religious, curious, or confrontational.

The counselor approach typecasts the undercover person in the role of a therapist who is sympathetic with the suspect. In this scenario the strategy is for the operative to degrade and blame the victim for the murder. An undercover person during the course of his meetings with the suspect will ask questions or make comments like "How are you doing since the police discovered [victim's name]?" or "Have the police ruled you out for the murder of [victim's name]?" or "I'm sorry that the police don't believe you didn't murder [victim's name]." or "I'm sorry the police won't rule you out as a suspect for the murder of [victim's name]." These kinds of questions and statements serve as triggers to jog the killer's memory about the murder and set him or her up to divulge information only he or she knows about the murder or even to offer a confession.

The religious approach plays the guilt card with the suspect. Many religious leaders agree that as people age they often become more spiritual and turn to God for peace and comfort. This is also true with a person who commits a murder, especially with a cold case. Over time many murderers become tired of carrying the burden of this sin and eventually feel compelled to confess to someone he or she trusts. Sometimes they even tell strangers. Religion often becomes the only mechanism of escape for the suspect when he/she is trying to cope with having killed someone. It becomes an avenue for seeking forgiveness. The suspect may either verbally express guilt for the murder or have previously written it in a journal or diary.

The curious approach preys on something that is thought of as a common human trait but which is often dangerous, as captured by the expression "curiosity killed the cat." As a person becomes curious, the brain's chemistry changes and helps retain information and increases the desire to learn. Curiosity is like a mental itch, and the only way to scratch it is to seek out new knowledge. Curiosity will often lead a suspect to test the undercover person with comments about the murder to see how much he or she really knows. The suspect may find it rewarding to play this cat-and-mouse game, which is what this approach is counting on.

A role reversal meeting is complex and requires more detailed planning and preparation. The goal is to create a situation in which someone adopts a role the reverse of that which they normally assume in relation to someone else. For example, if the suspect is a frequent customer at a bar, the detective will assign an undercover person, with the permission of the owner, to take on the role of a bartender.

In a confrontational approach the undercover person confronts a suspect on his or her behavior, attitude, and beliefs. The purpose of this technique is to challenge the suspect to take ownership for his or her behavior, and it urges him or her to be honest. This technique works well on people who are habitual liars and perhaps trying to justify their behavior or actions leading up to or during the murder or who need someone to make them personally responsible for their lies, inappropriate behavior, or illegal actions.

Once the cold case team identifies the suspect in question and chooses a cover, meeting, and approach, they choose an undercover person and brief him or her on a strategy that will best suit the dynamics of the murder case and suspect. The cover needs to provide the undercover person with maximum control and freedom of movement during the investigation.

Undercover work carries serious consequences and life-threatening risks. Therefore, the cold case team must take extra precautions when selecting the law enforcement person or civilian. It takes a specific type of person with certain characteristics to be an effective undercover person. While a background in law enforcement is beneficial, it isn't necessary, and sometimes a civilian is required to perform the undercover operation or ruse.

The following are traits of a good undercover person. He or she needs to have confidence, patience, sound judgment, the gift of gab, imagination, good memory, and strong powers of observation. He or she must be a quick thinker who can adapt to different situations and environments. In many ways this person needs to be a good actor. A good candidate should:

- be able to relate to and work with a wide variety of people;
- be comfortable associating with an entire spectrum of personality types;
- be able to talk to people in a way that builds a level of trust and extracts important information;
- be quick on his or her feet, able to make snap decisions, and a proficient storyteller;

- blend in, which means wearing the right attire, having the right dialect, understanding local culture, and fully inhabiting whatever role is necessary for the assignment;
- pay close attention to detail, compile and retain meaningful and relevant information, and translate information accurately;
- have a keen sense of how to collect, evaluate, and disseminate vital information;
- be knowledgeable and up to date on the latest technology devices, especially social media;
- keep his or her composure and be able to work independently; and
- be able to break temporarily from his or her true persona.

A good undercover person must possess the ability to conceal fear, anxiety, and anticipation; he or she must be able to keep adrenaline under control.

There are three types of people from which to choose, and each has pros and cons. The first is a police officer. The benefits are credibility and experience. The disadvantage is that he/she is a cop, and many criminals seem to be able to sniff out a cop. If the team chooses a police officer, he or she must refrain from carrying any police or personal credentials that will reveal his/her true identity. The second is a person who knows the suspect. While this person provides an element of trust that isn't there with a police officer, he or she lacks experience and some credibility. An example of the latter is that he or she may have a criminal record. The third is an informant. While this person also establishes a certain level of trust with the suspect, the downside is a lack of credibility.

Before covering case examples of undercover methods, the following is a solved cold rape case.

Cold Case #17: Government of Florida v. Brown— Victim Identities Not Revealed

Summary

The Jacksonville Police Department had been investigating two unsolved rape cases since July 1, 2011. The first was a woman who had been raped at her home. She said a man wearing a ski mask appeared in her house, demanded money, and threatened to harm her baby if she didn't comply with his demands. The man raped her and used makeshift condoms comprised of medical tape, plastic wrap, and a Ziploc bag. After the rape, he forced her to take a shower to remove any evidence and drive him to an ATM and withdraw $600.

On May 17, 2012, the wife of a Marine reported being raped in her home. It happened while her husband was on deployment in Afghanistan. She said a man broke into her house, used her husband's knife to threaten her, and raped her. After the rape, he forced her to open a storage unit and stole her husband's Airsoft gun. The rapist left very few clues, so detectives had no suspect.

Resolution

Fourteen months after the first rape, two more women reported an attack and rape in the early morning of September 11, 2012. The first woman said a man broke into her house and beat her with an Airsoft gun, but she managed to escape. After the attack, she discovered that her wallet was missing and fraudulent charges had been made with her credit cards. The second woman said a man beat her with an Airsoft gun, tied her up, and raped her.

From the stolen card's records detectives tracked down footage of a person who used the credit card at a local convenience store and identified him as Willie Abner Brown. Detectives arrested Brown on September 14, 2012, and charged him with fraudulent use of one of the victim's credit cards. But they needed more evidence to charge him for the attacks and rapes.

JPD detectives interviewed the victims to learn more about the rapist's modus operandi and discovered similarities, including the Airsoft gun, credit card theft, and ATM withdrawals. When detectives discovered that three of the victims were military spouses, they invited NCIS to collaborate with them. NCIS had a vested interest because of concerns that there might be a serial rapist on the military base.

JPD and NCIS investigators searched both Brown's house and that of his girlfriend and found items that connected Brown to the victims. Some of the items included a weapon; a Marine wife's phone, which had photos of Brown; an Airsoft gun; and clothes that linked him to two of the victims. In addition to these items, DNA evidence connected Brown to some of the victims.

Detectives interviewed one of Brown's ex-girlfriends, who testified that he used her car every now and then. Detectives introduced evidence from a surveillance video of Brown using her car around the time of one alleged attack.

Brown was charged with the following counts: six counts of first-degree rape, three counts of first-degree burglary, one count of first-degree kidnapping, two counts of second-degree kidnapping, four counts of first-degree sexual offense, one count of attempted first-degree rape, five counts of robbery with a dangerous weapon, one count of felony breaking and entering, and one count of assault with a deadly weapon inflicting serious injury.

Sentence

On March 13, 2014, the jury found Willie Abner Brown guilty of multiple felony charges including rape. He was convicted of assaulting one of the victims with a deadly weapon. The judge sentenced Brown to prison for a minimum of 400 years.[4]

Case #1: Deep Cover

The case involved the rape and murder of a young female. The initial investigation produced little evidence and failed to identify a suspect. Several years later, the cold case homicide unit reactivated the case. Three months into the investigation, after interviews with witnesses, the detectives identified a potential suspect whose name was not in the file. A background check revealed that he had previously been arrested for rape and lived near the victim. A witness told the detectives that this new suspect confessed to her that he had killed the victim. Detectives invited her to serve as an undercover operative to record the confession so it would stand up in court, but she rejected the idea out of fear for her safety.

Detectives assigned a police officer from another jurisdiction to serve as an undercover operative. The suspect worked in a manufacturing plant that made hosiery products. Working with the owner of the company, detectives facilitated the hiring of the police officer. The company placed him in the same department where the suspect worked.

The detective carefully established a relationship with the suspect. Eventually, the suspect agreed to eat lunch with him. In the third month, the detective felt comfortable enough to employ a psychological tactic undercover operatives use to encourage a suspect to volunteer information without causing any suspicion. The detective brought up a conversation about a murder case he read in *Time* magazine. The suspect fell for it and commented that he had been suspected of raping and murdering a woman.

Over the next few days the undercover person strategically struck up several conversations again with the suspect about the topic of murder. He casually made comments like, "I don't know if I could plan a murder well enough to get away with it," "I wonder what it might feel like to murder someone," and "If you wanted to murder someone, how would you do it?" In these conversations, the suspect shared details about the rape and murder of the woman that only the killer knew. Detectives brought the suspect in for questioning, and he confessed to the crime.

Case #2: Shallow Cover

A street prostitute was murdered. The woman had been stabbed with a broken beer bottle during an altercation in a local hotel room and died from her wounds. Based on the initial evidence, the detectives concluded that the perpetrator had also been injured because one of the blood samples was inconsistent with the victim's blood that had been discovered at the scene. Efforts to determine to whom the blood belonged were unsuccessful, and the case went cold. It was reopened 10 years after the murder, and six months later investigators received an anonymous telephone call.

The caller claimed that another female was responsible for the murder. She didn't provide a name but told the detectives the woman worked at the R&M car dealership. Investigators were reluctant to locate this anonymous woman and bring her in for questioning because they felt she might not cooperate or be a credible witness. They concluded that a local citizen made the call after information surfaced in the local community that police officials had reopened the case.

The detectives staked out the car dealership and discovered that two women worked there. They conducted background checks and found that one of the women had been a prostitute. She had cleaned up her act and married.

Detectives needed to collect a blood sample from the woman without her knowledge to confirm their suspicions that she was the killer. They invited an employee at the dealership, who was responsible for cleaning the restrooms, to participate as an undercover person. She agreed.

Investigators devised a plan for her to collect the suspect's tampon from the trash during her menstrual cycle. The witness was successful and delivered it to the state police, who forwarded it to the forensic laboratory for comparison with the unknown blood sample that had been found at the crime scene 10 years earlier. It was an exact match.

While investigators had the legal right to ask the suspect for a blood sample, they didn't want to take the risk of her refusal. If she did refuse, it would delay the investigation and, more importantly, eliminate the element of surprise. But even after detectives exhausted all their options, they'd still need to conduct an undercover operation to obtain the blood sample from the suspect.

With the confirmation of the DNA match detectives now had probable cause to arrest and issue a search warrant of the suspect's home. A search of the suspect's residence produced a journal where she recorded several entries about the fact that she needed to clear her conscience about the murder.

Case #3: Counselor Approach

A 45-year-old white female was murdered in her home. The victim had been suffocated and there were strong indications that the victim had known her attacker. Several suspects surfaced during the original investigation, but investigators were unable to make an arrest.

Detectives reactivated the case as a cold case and did a background check on the three original suspects. One of the suspects had severed contact with his family and friends and also struggled to maintain employment after the murder. As noted, changing relationships with relatives, friends, and employers is an indicator that a person may be the killer. Often without their knowledge, the guilt killers carry affects their behavior and the choices they make.

The detective contacted some of the suspect's old friends and conducted interviews with them. One friend who had worked with the suspect during the time of the murder initially did not believe his friend was responsible for the killing. He did admit, however, that over the years he became convinced that he had murdered the victim. He stated that he hadn't seen the suspect in about three years. During the interview, the detective asked if he would agree to work undercover with the police to collect evidence and intelligence that would implicate the suspect. He agreed.

Because the suspect was an avid car mechanic and enthusiast, the detective arranged for the friend to bump into the suspect at a local parts store he frequented on Saturday mornings. After the suspect entered the store, the friend greeted and engaged him in a catching-up conversation. As the two left the store, the friend asked the suspect how he had been doing since the murder and if the police still thought he did it. After the suspect calmly replied that he was doing okay, the cooperating witness, as per instructions from the detective, made several negative comments about the victim and commented that she deserved to die. The friend also commented that he had a nephew who had killed someone and had learned about the emotional trauma he experienced over the years.

Before the two parted ways, the friend convinced the suspect he was concerned about his health and suggested they meet up again some time. Over the next months they met on a regular basis. As per the script, the friend brought up the murder at each meeting. Each time they discussed the murder the suspect gradually expressed his remorse about the murder. The suspect eventually admitted to killing the victim and claimed it was an accident. He also shared information about the murder only the murderer could have known.

The detective and his cold case team secured enough testimonial evidence from the suspect to obtain an arrest warrant and bring him in for questioning. After the suspect heard all the taped conversations, he provided a full confession of the murder. The suspect also shared how the meetings with his friend forced him to relive the murder and that it became a wake-up call for him to finally accept responsibility and consequences for the murder and remove the burden of guilt he had been carrying.

Case #4: Curious Approach

Detectives established a primary suspect for the murder of a young female. The suspect lived next door to the victim, but detectives did not have sufficient evidence to arrest him and had to close the case.

Two years later detectives reactivated the case and discovered that the suspect had enrolled in a college located in a different part of the state. They worked with the university police department and enrolled a young campus police officer in some of the same classes as the suspect.

The undercover person slowly established a friendly relationship with the suspect by initiating conversations with him over the course of several weeks. In the first meeting, he told the suspect that he had an aunt who lived in his hometown. Then, as their relationship grew, he mentioned the murder that occurred in his hometown, asked the suspect if he knew the young female who had been killed, and said his aunt told him the case was still unsolved. The suspect acknowledged that he knew the victim.

In their next meeting, the undercover person expressed his curiosity as to how it might feel to murder someone. He shared how he had a friend who had previously been convicted of a murder and how his friend had nightmares and shared feelings of remorse with him. The suspect expressed remorse and comments about how he might feel if he had killed someone but never implicated himself for the murder of the young female in his hometown. From this information detectives concluded that the suspect was experiencing nightmares about the murder and brought him in for questioning. About an hour into the interview detectives commented that if he had murdered the young female, the only way to clear his conscience was to tell the truth and admit to killing the victim. A few minutes later the suspect confessed to the murder.

Case #5: Religious Approach

Detectives reactivated an unsolved murder of a gas station attendant. A review of the cold case clarified how circumstantial evidence led to identification of a primary suspect; a lack of solid physical evidence prevented an arrest.

The cold case detectives conducted another background check on the primary suspect to see what kind of changes had occurred in his life since the murder. They discovered that he was married, had two boys, and had stopped attending church. This abrupt change in behavior raised a red flag with the detectives because the suspect had grown up with a firm belief in God. They decided to take advantage of the suspect's change of heart and convinced a person from a local church to participate in an undercover operation.

Per instructions from the detectives, the undercover person contrived to bump into the suspect at the local Walmart where he regularly shopped. As they rekindled their relationship, the undercover person initiated a conversation about religion and his concern for the suspect. A few days later the undercover person, who was wired with a microphone, told the suspect that he was concerned about his health and had recently been led by God to pray for him because God had revealed to him that he was responsible for the murder. God had brought them together, the undercover person told the suspect, because he needed prayer and forgiveness for his sin. He added that God had already forgiven him and that it would serve no purpose for the suspect to turn himself in to the authorities.

The suspect began to cry and shared details of what happened on the day of the murder. He and his friend arrived at the gas station to commit a robbery. But when the attendant resisted, his friend shot and killed the attendant. Detectives arrested the suspect, and during the interrogation he confessed to his participation in the robbery but continued to claim that his friend had killed the attendant. But when detectives asked him to identify his friend he declined. After further questioning, he eventually confessed that he made up the story about his friend and that he committed the murder. He showed the detectives where he buried the murder weapon and admitted the meeting with the undercover person swayed him to relive the murder. He thought about it every day and had a "Polaroid picture" of it that he couldn't erase from in his mind. He finally felt that it was time to clear his conscience.

Case #6: Role Reversal Approach

Detectives assigned a police officer to pose as a bartender at a local nightclub where their prime suspect frequently socialized and drank. The nightclub owner agreed.

After the undercover person established a good relationship with the suspect, he started conversations with him about murder cases. One evening the undercover bartender told the suspect that he had a friend who had killed someone, struggled to cope with it, and finally turned himself in to the police. A week later the suspect admitted he knew someone who had committed a murder and struggled to live with the guilt. The undercover agent suggested that the suspect convince his friend to also clear his conscience and confess his crime to the police. After this conversation detectives brought the suspect in for questioning and he confessed to the murder.

Case #7: Confrontational Approach

Detectives reactivated the murder of a female killed in a rural community. It had gone unsolved because detectives did not have enough evidence to arrest the person whom they considered a prime suspect. He had been a volunteer fireman at the time of the murder but resigned a few months later. Detectives invited a volunteer fireman who had not spoken with the suspect for a while and had been friends with the victim to participate as an undercover person.

After brief surveillance of the suspect, detectives set up a chance meeting at a local convenience store. The undercover person greeted the suspect in the parking lot and delicately confronted the suspect about his involvement in the murder. He told the suspect that the police recently questioned him and he was the primary suspect. Then, he asked how he managed to get away with the murder.

At first, the suspect became somewhat agitated and claimed he was not responsible, but eventually he made several inconsistent statements regarding his alibi on the night of the murder. The undercover person pressed the witness for information about questions that the police had asked him. The two ended up talking for over 90 minutes in the parking lot that night.

Before departing the convenience store, they exchanged telephone numbers. The two met a few more times. In each conversation, detectives discovered several inconsistent statements that were different from the information he had provided to detectives. He shared information about the murder only known by detectives and the murderer. Detectives arrested the suspect.

While detectives have made good use of the ruse, civilians have also executed it to help solve homicide cases. As we saw in Cold Case #14, Melinda Elkins used a ruse to exonerate her husband, Clarence Elkins, who had been wrongfully convicted of rape and murder and sentenced to life in prison.

The next chapter will share techniques on how to interview witnesses and interrogate suspects so as to increase your chances of extracting information from them to solve the case. They include how to rewire your brain, overlook the faults in the witness, find common ground, start a conversation based on common ground, and keep your composure.

Cold Case #18: Government of North Carolina v. Lawing—Victim Lacoy McQueen

This cold case is an example of how forensic geology and rock analysis helped solve a cold case. It demonstrates how important it is to collect and store as much physical evidence as possible—regardless of how insignificant it might be at the time—from an unsolved homicide crime scene and how the constant improvements in forensic technology provide detectives with the ability to collect and examine trace evidence that connects their suspect(s) to the crime scene.

Summary

On May 17, 1996, friends of Lacoy McQueen, a 20-year-old student at Shaw University in North Carolina, reported her missing to the campus police. McQueen's roommate, Stephanie Jeffries, said she heard a conversation McQueen had with her boyfriend, Edwin Christopher Lawing, on speakerphone about being pregnant. During the conversation, McQueen and Lawing agreed to meet and continue the conversation at the Bell Tower on the North Carolina State University Campus, about a 15-minute drive from the Shaw University dorm. McQueen left her dorm room at around 4 p.m. That was the last time Jeffries saw McQueen.

Due to the circumstances of McQueen's disappearance, the Shaw campus police handed the missing persons report to the Raleigh Police Department, who assigned it to Detective Norman Grodi. During Grodi's investigation, Jeffries provided him with additional information about Lawing and what occurred the day after McQueen left the dorm.

Jeffries stated that Lawing called her the next morning on May 17 at 11 a.m. and asked to speak with McQueen. Jeffries said McQueen never came home after her scheduled meeting with him. Lawing told Jeffries they never met at the Bell Tower. Later that day, at 7:30 p.m., Lawing called Jeffries again about McQueen's whereabouts and reiterated that he had not met with her the night before.

The next day, on May 18, detectives visited Lawing's dorm and asked him to go to the police station for an interview. Lawing agreed. When questioned about his scheduled meeting with McQueen, Lawing said they never met. But after detectives presented him with Jeffries's testimony, Lawing admitted that he met McQueen at the Bell Tower. After they talked and argued about whether to keep or abort the baby, Lawing said McQueen left with two other black men whom he didn't know. He provided a scant description of the car and men but couldn't determine which direction they came from or traveled. Detectives asked Lawing if McQueen had been in his dorm room and he said no.

The first interview with Lawing occurred about 2:30 a.m. on May 18. North Carolina State University and Shaw University detectives conducted the interview, where Lawing initially lied and then changed his statement. At 7:40 p.m. on May 18, Raleigh Police Department

Detective Howard interviewed Lawing again and he provided the same statement.

Because Lawing acted nervously, paced incessantly, never made eye contact, lied about not meeting with McQueen, and offered a sketchy story about two black men, Grodi executed a search warrant on his dorm room a few days later on May 23.

During the search, detectives collected some of Lawing's clothes and boots. They noticed bloodstains on the inside of the door near the knob, on the carpet, and on his boots.

A few weeks later, on June 18, detectives executed another search warrant to perform luminol testing to locate additional bloodstains not visible to the naked eye. Crime scene agents noted there was evidence of cleaning in the dorm room. Shortly after, forensic scientists from a private company revealed the results of the DNA test. The blood on the door and carpet matched the DNA blood sample detectives collected from McQueen's mother. And the blood on the boots matched Lawing's DNA.

In the meantime, an interview the detectives had with Lawing's roommate, Jason Hillger, raised more suspicion of Lawing. Hillger stated that he arrived home from work on May 16 at about 5:30 p.m. When he entered the dorm room he saw a woman near Lawing. She excused herself and left.

A few days later detectives showed Hillger a photo of McQueen and he confirmed she was the woman in their dorm room.

Despite all the evidence, most of which was circumstantial, the prosecutor felt they didn't have enough evidence to arrest Lawing and receive a conviction from a jury.

About 10 months later, on March 13, 1997, construction workers discovered McQueen's dead body in the neighboring woods of Kittrell, a city about 40 miles from the NC State campus. Her remains had been scattered, and the forensic team only recovered about 60 percent of her skeleton. They also found remnants of clothing and personal items that appeared to be consistent with the description relatives and friends provided about her personal property. Dental records confirmed it was McQueen's body. Unfortunately, due to the decomposition the medical examiner was unable to determine the cause of death.

Now that detectives had a body, they convinced the district

attorney to issue an arrest warrant on March 19. After they arrested Lawing and put him in the interrogation room, he remained silent and invoked his right to have an attorney present. Unfortunately, law enforcement relied too much on circumstantial evidence. Due to lack of physical evidence and to avoid the possibility of double jeopardy, the prosecutor dismissed the charges and released Lawing on May 2, 1997. Detectives stored all the physical evidence they had collected. And McQueen's case remained cold until 2014.

Resolution

Many detectives have one case to which they become personally attached. It is the one case they want to solve. And for Norman Grodi it was the unsolved case of Lacoy McQueen. For the next 17 years, Grodi continued to spend his off-hours revisiting McQueen's case and trying to find new evidence to reopen the case, find the killer, and get a conviction. But he never made any progress.

Then, in 2014, Grodi made one last-ditch effort to convince the Wake County district attorney to prosecute the McQueen cold case. The DA asked Detective Jerry Faulk to review the McQueen cold case. The case intrigued Faulk, so he decided to look into it. Faulk understood how important this case was to Grodi and that it took a lot out of him emotionally. So he met with Grodi and asked if it was okay for him to reopen the McQueen cold case. Grodi graciously welcomed the idea and provided Faulk with all the files he had stored in his office. Faulk took Grodi's gesture as a compliment and developed a passion for and commitment to solving McQueen's case.

Faulk dove right in and began applying some of my cold case investigation methodologies. The four crucial steps he took were to reorganize the entire case, review all the notes, find and collect new evidence, and rewrite the case presentation to meet the current standards established by the prosecutor.

Faulk reorganized McQueen's case in chronological order so that it made sense to him. This step helps a detective personalize the case and provides a viewpoint as if he first entered the crime scene.

He meticulously reviewed all the notes, especially Grodi's handwritten ones. Back then, when detectives filed a report, they had three copies. The original was white, yellow was for records, and pink was the working copy. The pink copy had handwritten notes that the others did not have. Not all the reports had three copies. Some only had one or two, but he made sure he had one copy, whether it was white, yellow, or pink, of every report.

The third step was a little more difficult. In most cold cases detectives rely on old evidence to convict the killer who at the time was a suspect and hadn't been arrested. But Lawing had been arrested based on old evidence. Therefore, Faulk focused on finding and collecting new evidence. The first new piece of evidence was the testimony of a person the initial detectives did not interview. Her name was Alexa Hunt, one of Lawing's ex-girlfriends. Hunt told detectives that Lawing had visited the area where McQueen's body was found several times before her death. This meant Lawing was familiar with this area.

The most incriminating new evidence that broke the case open was Faulk's focus on finding physical evidence that linked Lawing to and placed him at the crime scene. Faulk was aware of the new forensic technology that was available and knew that other killers had been convicted based on dirt and vegetation detectives found at the crime scene. He decided to have McQueen's clothes and Lawing's boots analyzed. He first contacted the North Carolina State University Forensics Department, since they had collaborated on other cases before. One of the professors recommended that he contact Heather Hanna, who worked for the North Carolina Geological Survey.

Hanna recovered small pebbles from Lawing's boots that looked familiar. She called Faulk and told him about the different types of geological zones and how each zone consisted of material unique only to that location. For example, the geological zone of the North Carolina State campus might be different from that of the surrounding area. Hanna suggested they revisit the area where detectives discovered McQueen's body to collect geological material from there and then compare it to the small pebbles from Lawing's boots.

As luck would have it, this area was known as the Rolesville Batholith. It is the largest body of granite in the southern Appalachian region, measuring about 15 by 50 miles, and occupies the eastern third of Wake County, which makes the terrain there very unique and unlike that of the North Carolina State campus and surrounding areas. After Hanna ran the tests, the results confirmed that the small pebbles from Lawing's boots matched the small pebbles at the Rolesville Batholith. This confirmed that Lawing had been at the location where McQueen's corpse had been found.

Based on the results of the new tests and evidence detectives concluded that Lawing killed McQueen in his dorm room and then dumped her dead body.

Armed with this new physical evidence, Faulk was prepared to deliver his cold case presentation to the DA. He decided to talk with the family first and discuss the new evidence with them and get their approval to move forward before he started the proceedings to arrest Lawing for McQueen's murder. Faulk explained that the new scientific findings of a geological material such as small pebbles had never been used as physical evidence to successfully convict the defendant in a murder trial and that he couldn't guarantee a conviction for Lawing. Nevertheless, McQueen's family decided to move forward with Lawing's arrest and the trial.

Sentence

On Monday, February 29, 2016, the jury found Lawing guilty of first-degree murder and the Wake County judge sentenced him to life in prison without the possibility of parole.[5]

Special Addition

Faulk hadn't had any formal cold case training prior to his new assignment but was fortunate enough to have closed a few cold cases including one from 1971. Nevertheless, he attended my Cold Case Seminar at Myrtle Beach, South Carolina, in February of 2015. As he sat through the course and listened to me explain my methodology, he realized, "Hey this stuff falls right in line with what I had done on the cases I closed." He didn't realize it at the time, but he had been following my methodology. Since then Faulk and I have become great friends and colleagues and have worked together on several different projects particularly related to cold cases.

7. Ways to Collect Evidence and Intelligence

I'd like to thank Detective Faulk for his cooperation and providing detailed information about the case for this book.

Cold Case #19: Government of California v. Clair— Victim Linda Faye Rodgers

Summary

This case was featured on the *Wrong Man* season 2 finale.

On November 15, 1984, Margaret and Kai Hendrickson asked their roommate Linda Faye Rodgers, a mother of one daughter, to babysit their four children, ages two to six, in the Santa Ana home they shared together. At 8:45 p.m. the Hendricksons called to check in on Rodgers and their children. Rodgers assured the couple that everything was fine.

When the Hendricksons returned to their home, they found Rodgers's half-naked dead body in the master bedroom. Her body was found supine on the bed with her hands bound behind her back, naked from the waist down, and with her legs open and a vibrator between her thighs. Rodgers had been tortured, raped, stabbed, and bludgeoned to death. The Hendricksons' four children and Rodgers's daughter were in another room during the murder. Fortunately, they had not been harmed.

Investigators described the killing of Rodgers as vicious, sadistic, and brutal. The deputy coroner determined that Rodgers died of asphyxiation due to a "ligature about the neck."

Detectives quickly focused their attention on a suspect named Kenneth Clair, an unemployed cook and painter. Clair squatted at the abandoned house next door to the Hendricksons' house and had been arrested for burglarizing their home a week earlier.

Clair had also been out of prison for a year after serving six years for purse snatching. Two weeks prior to Rodgers's murder he had been arrested on suspicion of assault with a deadly weapon, trespassing, attempted residential burglary, brandishing a weapon, and possession of stolen property.

Despite a lack of physical evidence like fingerprints or murder weapons to link Clair to the crime scene or rape and murder of

Rodgers, the district attorney moved forward with the trial. What the DA presented to the jury was circumstantial evidence and a controversial taped conversation conducted between Clair and his ex-girlfriend Pauline Flores after Rodgers's murder.

Clair's defense attorney questioned the credibility and believability of the testimony of Flores, whose character and statements were easily assailed. He also noted that Clair made no admission, express or implied, during the taped conversation. But the prosecutor argued that Clair's answers came close to a confession.

Testimony from two of the children also created controversy about Clair's arrest. One of the children, five-year-old Jerrod Hessling, said he witnessed the beating, rape, and stabbing death of Rodgers. He described the man, without hesitation, as white. Another child present during the murder said he saw a white man's tattooed arm reach inside the house to open a sliding glass door. Clair is a black man.

Nevertheless, the prosecution chalked up the children's answers to youth and trauma.

On June 22, 1987, the jury returned verdicts of guilty for murder in the first degree and burglary. The court sentenced Clair to death.

Three decades later the Ninth U.S. Circuit Court of Appeals overturned Clair's death sentence and sentenced him to life in prison without parole.

Resolution

Kenneth Clair has continued to fight to prove his innocence but has lost every appeal. In 2008, even after new forensic testing revealed that DNA found on the murder victim and other clothing found at the crime scene did not match Clair's DNA, Clair's attorney still had difficulty convincing the court of his innocence.

Clair's persistence, however, seems to have paid off. In 2017 his case caught the attention of CNN and the *Wrong Man* producers. On Sunday, April 29, 2018, CNN featured Clair's case on their Headline News network in a show called *Death Row Stories*. Then, on February 9, 2020, *Wrong Man* featured Clair's case. The reinvestigation of his case raised two major questions that might lead to exonerating Clair.

One is why detectives didn't work harder to locate the man who had been dating Rodgers prior to her murder. According to Margaret Hendrickson, Rodgers had been dating a man named John, and he left the area immediately after her murder. But detectives never attempted to locate him.

Second, Flores's testimony is questionable because detectives asked her to wear a wire and scripted the conversation they asked her to have with Clair. In addition, Flores had been involved in a bicycle accident and suffered a brain injury. Therefore, her memory is questionable.

Next, why does the court continue to resist conducting DNA tests on the items in the evidence locker? Suzanna Ryan, a DNA expert, disagrees with the district attorney's claim that the DNA testing completed to date on Clair's case is sufficient, arguing that, with today's technology, it is possible to extract DNA samples from the physical evidence collected at the crime scene that is stored in the evidence locker, even after 35 years. If this crime was indeed perpetrated by Clair, then he probably left his DNA somewhere. But none of the DNA at the crime scene matched Clair. So if you're not convinced that this person committed this crime, then certainly you could test any number of items collected from the crime scene for DNA samples. For example, it's possible to test the clothing used to tie around Rodgers's mouth. A good area to test is the knot like the one on the belt. Other items include her underwear, jeans, and even the hammer and screwdriver that didn't belong to anyone in the house. These are all perfect touch DNA samples.

Soon after the taping of Clair's segment, his attorney filed a motion for a new trial and to obtain new DNA testing.

On Friday, March 13, 2020, Orange County Superior Court Judge Sheila Hanson denied both requests. Clair's attorneys then asked that he be re-sentenced to 25-years-to-life, which, due to his time already served behind bars, would make him immediately eligible for parole. But Judge Hanson believed Clair remains a danger to the public, so she also denied this request. As of the writing of this book, Clair is still serving his sentence at the Pelican Bay State Prison in California.[6]

8

Meeting of the Minds with Witnesses and Suspects

There is a game that kids play where people take turns whispering a message into the ear of the next person in line. By the time the last person speaks the message out loud, it has radically changed because it has been altered each time a person retells the message. The same is true when it comes to an interview with a witness in a cold case.

It's difficult for most witnesses to remember the details of a fresh homicide crime but even more difficult in a cold case that has been sitting around for several years or even decades. Each time a person attempts to recall a crime he or she witnessed the brain alters the recall of it. For each time a person retells the story, one or more details about the event have been forgotten.

Dr. Donna Bridge explains the way a person's memory works. Dr. Bridge is a cognitive neuroscientist with over 10 years of experience using complex human behavior and brain data to understand how people think. "A memory is not simply an image produced by time-traveling back to the original event. It can be an image that is somewhat distorted because of the prior times you remembered it. Your memory of an event can grow less precise even to the point of being totally false with each retrieval."[1]

Dr. Bridge's findings have implications for witnesses giving testimony in criminal trials. "Maybe a witness remembers something fairly accurately the first time because his or her memories aren't that distorted," she said. "After that, it keeps going downhill."[2] The reason for the distortion is that human memories are not static and always adapt. If a person remembers something in the context of a new environment

8. Meeting of the Minds with Witnesses and Suspects   219

and time, or if a person is even in a different mood, his or her memories might integrate the new information.

In a cold case, the degree of difficulty in collecting information from a witness is exacerbated due to the length of time that has passed. Add the truth factor and it becomes more difficult to expect a witness to recall what happened. Nevertheless, there are techniques and procedures a detective can learn in order to get the most or as close to the truth as possible out of a witness or suspect during a cold case interview. Before sharing the techniques and procedures that are productive, it is necessary to address an ongoing problem I have observed in the way a detective prepares for the interview with a witness. Many times a detective will carry a pessimistic attitude into the interview room.

Most detectives view the witness in a negative light, especially if he or she has a rap sheet or is associated with a gang; they believe he or she will not cooperate or provide any information to help solve the case. I've heard comments from detectives like "I doubt this witness is going to cooperate" or "I sense that he's not willing to talk to us."

How has this negative strategy been working for you with previous witnesses? What has been your success rate in the cooperation of witnesses? If the answer to both is "not very well," then why do you continue with the same negative attitude and expect a different result?

It is understandably difficult to avoid pessimism. Over the last three decades, the public has been inundated with news that focuses on the negative and sadness in the world. People in law enforcement witness the worst in people every day. The same, however, is true for the witness, who often has a history of bad experiences with the police and a negative attitude and image of the police. Thus tension and hostility already exist before a detective enters the interview room. But this is not the best way to start a relationship with a witness who might prove to be a valuable asset in solving the case and identifying the killer.

Pessimism can take a toll on a person's thoughts, feelings, emotions, and overall health and affect a person's performance at work. Hearing about the constant negative stories creates ongoing panic, worry, skepticism, scrutiny, and division in people's personal lives and at work.

Bringing a positive attitude will improve your health, enhance your relationships, increase your chances of success, and also add years to your life. This might be a hard concept to embrace because people in law enforcement tend to see and experience the worst in people more than any other profession. There is nothing to lose and a lot more to gain not just professionally but also personally. A positive attitude will help a detective become more efficient and productive during an interview with a witness, and also change the public's attitude and image of police for the better.

The first step is to remove any negative thoughts or preconceived notions or judgments about the witness regardless of whether he or she has a history of arrests or rap sheets or convictions. Start with a clean slate. Any assumptions about the witness might cloud a detective's judgment and, in the end, affect a detective's performance. The negative environment is unnecessary and creates more harm than good.

This is not suggesting a detective appease a witness or let down his or her guard or position of authority, just that the detective treat the witness as a human being. Most witnesses will view a detective as an adversary, a person out to get him or her or a relative or friend who is considered a suspect. Treat the witness like a human being and he/she will be more cooperative and respond with the same respectful attitude.

Instead of viewing the witness as an adversary, embrace him or her as an ally. After all, isn't a detective's ultimate goal to search for the truth and justice for the victim? Invite the witness to be an ally. This is not an attempt to change the person to be a better human being but rather to make peace and encourage collaboration during the interview and throughout the rest of the investigation. Lastly, think about how it makes you feel when a citizen has false preconceived notions about you as a police officer or person without taking an opportunity to really get to know you.

The following tips help encourage a witness to be an ally.

Rewire your brain. Be conscious of the fact that you have a negative impression of the witness, and do your best to remove this perception so that you begin with a clean slate. Imagine that you're meeting this person for the first time and that you know nothing about him or her.

Overlook the faults in the witness. He or she may have many faults that are irritating, but negativity creates a barrier between you and the witness. Instead, focus on how to encourage the witness with positive reinforcement that will remove the barrier. A line of conversation will begin that focuses on helping the witness give his or her best recollection of the murder and, more importantly, tell the truth.

Find common ground. Avi Shatzkes, PhD, an executive coach at ADS Talent, has this advice to offer based on his experience: "I often give people an assignment to learn five facts about a colleague they don't like. For example: where did they go to school, what are their hobbies ... things like that. This forces them to spend more time with the person and ask questions. Often, the result is that they start to find areas of common interest or shared values. Then the areas of annoyance become more superficial in light of these new connections."[3]

Start a conversation based on common ground. Spend the first 10 minutes getting to know the witness before asking questions about the murder. This will create a safe and comfortable environment for both of you and, more importantly, time to adjust to the new positive environment.

Keep composed. Quickly squelch any frustrations that might come up with the witness. Don't take what a witness says personally or allow him or her to push your buttons. Make time to assess your own emotional makeup, which will serve as useful insight into what triggers your frustrations and prevent you from losing your composure. Take deep breaths or excuse yourself from the room for a few minutes to decompress and bring that positive attitude back into the interview room.

In his acclaimed book, *Man's Search for Meaning*, psychologist Viktor Frankl describes the power of perspective: "Everything can be taken from a man but one thing: the last of human freedoms—to choose one's attitude in any given set of circumstances, to choose one's own way."[4]

No matter how horrible a witness treats you, you have the power of choice to practice a positive attitude or a negative attitude. Charles Swindoll, a pastor, author, and educator, put it this way: "The longer I live, the more I realize the impact of attitude on life. Attitude, to me, is more important than facts.... The only thing we can do is play on the one string we have, and that is our attitude.... I am convinced that life is 10% what happens to me and 90% how I react to it."[5]

While there are several interviewing techniques available, the cognitive technique is most effective for a witness in a cold case. The premise of the *cognitive technique* is that open-ended questions tend to produce the best result. As opposed to questions like "How tall was the subject?" or "What color was his hair?" or "Did he have any scars?" questions like "What did he look like?" or "Did he look like someone you know?" provide the detective with a structured approach to help the witness retrieve specific details from his or her memory of the murder. The cognitive technique accomplishes memory retrieval by reinstating the context of the event, recalling the event in a different sequence, and looking at the event from different perspectives.

To reinstate the context of the event begin by asking the witness to relive the events that occurred prior, during, and after the murder. For example, "How about telling me how your day started?" or "Tell me what time you got up, the chores you did, the errands you ran, and anything else that happened before the murder."

As the witness recounts his or her activities, ask what route he or she took on the way to the crime scene and where he or she parked the car. Repeat this line of questioning about the time the witness spent at the crime scene and what he or she did after leaving the crime scene. This process enhances a witness's retrieval of stored information and helps him or her describe details of the murder in its proper context and sequence. It also minimizes or eliminates any accusations of coercion by the detective during the interview.

As the interview continues, lead the witness through a second account of the murder in reverse sequence. This way a witness can describe each stage of the event as a separate entity, much like looking at individual frames from a movie. This will help the witness provide what he or she saw in greater detail. It may help the witness reveal important information he or she overlooked or didn't think mattered during the first line of questioning. It may be worthwhile to ask the witness to change his or her perspective and consider the view of the crime from a different angle or from another witness or victim.

To further stimulate witness memory recovery, ask direct

8. Meeting of the Minds with Witnesses and Suspects 223

questions that associate recollection of details like physical appearance, clothing, and sound with something or someone familiar to them. For example, questions like "You say you heard a scary voice. What was it like? Does it remind you of anybody you know, or perhaps a character you've seen in a movie?" Or "The coveralls you saw the person wearing. Have you ever seen that style before? Was it like a farmer's or a plumber's overall?" or "Does this person you saw remind you of anyone you know? If yes, in what way?" This helps the witness remove the urge to create a description and allows him or her to draw on information with which s/he is comfortable.

Exercising patience is important. Help the witness feel confident that there is plenty of time to think, speak, reflect, and speak again and as often as he or she needs. This will alleviate any tension and pressure a witness may feel during the interview, and, more importantly, set the stage to build rapport.

When a detective builds rapport, barriers gradually disappear and create opportunities to enhance communication with the witness. It establishes trust, which will make the witness feel more comfortable in future interviews and encourages him or her to volunteer other information he or she might recall after the first interview. The witness may be a potential candidate as an undercover person. If the witness turns out to be the killer, good rapport will give a detective an edge during the eventual interrogation.

Many experienced detectives build rapport with a witness through a communication model known as neuro-linguistic programming (NLP). John Grinder, an assistant professor at the University of California, Santa Cruz, and Richard Bandler, a student of psychology, discovered this program after they identified patterns used by successful therapists. NLP embraces three simple concepts. The first is that it recognizes the fundamental idea that all human behavior originates from neurological processes, which include seeing, hearing, smelling, tasting, and feeling. This is because a person experiences a life event through their senses. This is how I review a cold case as well as a fresh homicide case. Second, people communicate their experiences and thoughts verbally through language. Third is that a person organizes their ideas and actions to produce results and each person does that in a specific manner.

During the interview, assess and determine the dominant learning style of the witness. A witness will fall into one of three categories. Visual learners comprise 40 percent of the population, auditory 40 percent, and kinesthetic 20 percent. In the interview ask the following questions to identify which learning style fits the witness.

To identify a visual learner, ask questions that stimulate his or her sight: "What did you see?" or "Could you describe what you saw?" For auditory ask questions that stimulate a person's hearing: "What did you hear?" or "What did the noise sound like?" When dealing with a suspected kinesthetic learner, ask questions that tap into a person's emotions: "How did you feel after you heard about the murder?" or "How did you feel when you heard the shots?"

Another way to identify a witness or suspect's dominant learning style is to pay close attention to his or her eye movements. In NLP parlance, eye movements are "eye-accessing cues" and reflect how a person accesses data. The eyes naturally move in specific directions depending on the person's preferred mode of thinking. A person whose eyes move up and down is visual. If a person's eyes move sideways, he or she is auditory. And a person whose eyes move diagonally is kinesthetic.[6]

After establishing the learning style, the next step in building rapport is to begin "matching" the witness's or suspect's volume, tone, and rate of speech. When a detective intentionally applies this mirroring technique, the witness or suspect is more cooperative in providing information because people like people who are similar to them. This creates a natural, free-flowing conversation that results in an exchange of information. However, be aware that there is a difference between matching and mimicking. Be subtle and cautious about how you match the behavior because it might offend the witness or suspect.[7]

The three matching techniques are kinesics, language, and paralanguage. Kinesics is probably the easiest and most obvious technique. It involves matching gestures, posture, and movements of the body, including hands, arms, and feet. This is similar to partners in a dance; the interviewer and interviewee mirror each other's movements with movements of their own and engage in mutual responsive reactions. The setup in the interview room is important. Two chairs without a table is the recommended configuration. The table creates a barrier and prevents the intimate interaction needed to build a trusting and safe environment for the witness.

The following is an example of how to employ the kinesics aspect of NLP. As the detective enters the interview room, he notices that the witness is leaning forward, head down, her right hand on her forehead and left hand on her left knee. The detective introduces himself, pulls his chair closer to the witness. If there were a table in the room, the detective would not be able to execute this maneuver and the following steps. Just like her, he leans forward with his hands in front of him but is careful not to invade her space. As the witness begins to open up and speak, she gradually raises her head, sits back, and makes eye contact with the detective. The detective follows suit by matching her same nonverbal behavior. Through each succeeding change in the witness's body language, the detective matches it.

The same matching technique holds true with matching language. People use language to communicate thoughts. The words they choose reflect the way they think. When relating experiences people tend to use their dominant representational system of communication, which is visual, auditory, or kinesthetic.

If a person is visual, he or she will respond with phrases like "I see what you mean" or "That looks good to me" or "We see eye to eye" or "I get the picture."

If a person is auditory, replies like these will follow: "Something tells me" or "That rings a bell" or "We're on the same wavelength" or "That sounds okay to me."

If a person is kinesthetic, you'll hear these kinds of comments: "I'll get in touch with you" or "How does that grab you?" or "You don't have to get pushy" or "How do you think I feel?"

In matching language the same observations apply, but the focus is on the language of the witness or suspect. For example, here is a conversation with a woman who witnessed a drive-by shooting. She describes her situation with phrases like "I feel like I'm going to pieces" and "I can't come to grips with what is happening." The detective identifies her kinesthetic comments and responds with words to take the pressure off of her like "I'm sorry you feel that you're carrying this big load on your shoulders" or "What can I do to help you feel better?"[8]

When applying the paralanguage the focus is on the person's

speech pattern. This is perhaps the most effective way to establish rapport. Paralanguage involves how a person speaks, the rate, volume, and pitch of speech. People speak in a slow or fast pace or without pause or a soft or loud volume or in a low or high pitch. A detective need not match a person's voice exactly, just close enough for the person to feel understood.

Slowing or accelerating the rate of speech to correspond with the pace of a witness or suspect allows for recall at his or her pace, thereby relieving pressure and stress for him or her and keeping the relationship between a detective and the witness or suspect in sync.[9]

This description of the same interview with the witness of a drive-by shooting uses paralanguage. As the female witness speaks slowly to find the right words, the detective slows his rate of speech. This gives her ample time to get her point across without feeling anxious. As she changes her pace and speeds up her rate of speech, the detective follows suit. In so doing, this technique demonstrates to her that the detective is interested in her as a person and it allows her to communicate what she experienced in a way that is safe and comfortable for her. This lends credence to the belief that the closer the matching of kinesthetic, language, and paralanguage between the detective and witness or suspect, the better the rapport.

Like any new skill, learning and executing the cognitive technique and NLP will take time. One good training exercise that might help expedite mastering them is to watch videos of other interviews and practice assessing the witness.

Eventually, performing these techniques will become second nature in future interviews with a witness.

After the cold case team identifies the killer, the next step is to conduct a subject assessment of the suspect without his or her knowledge. Evaluating the killer's state of mind will give a detective the optimum psychological advantage over him or her during the interrogation. The assessment involves collecting information about the killer's relationship with siblings, reputation with family, mental health history, educational level, work history, hobbies, interests, religion, birth order, and, if applicable, military service history. Most of this information easily obtained, either through a previous interview with the suspect (perhaps s/he was interviewed as a witness) or by questioning other witnesses and friends of the suspect or through an internet search.

Another method of learning more about the killer and his character is through his or her birth order. The following is a preordained list of traits about birth order.[10]

Firstborn is the "hero" child. He or she tends to be a natural leader, ambitious, protective, responsible, controlling, and cautious. A 2007 study in Norway showed that firstborns had two to three more IQ points than the next child and needed structure in their lives. Firstborns are sensitive to guilt and will tell truth out of guilt.

Secondborn is the "scapegoat" child. He or she is a social butterfly, people pleaser, peacekeeper, and good negotiator; tends to advocate for fairness, thrives on friendships; and is more likely to tell the truth.

The third or last child is the "lost child" or "mascot child." He or she is a free spirit, self-centered, a risk-taker and attention seeker, manipulative, competent, outgoing, fun-loving, and charming. The third child tends to not follow rules, is acutely attuned to other people but also easily disconnects with them, is more likely both to use the internet and to commit suicide.

The only child is the "monarch." He or she is a talker, confident, independent, possessive, and organized. A private person, he or she has high self-esteem, tends to be a high achiever, and enjoys to jamming up people by blaming another person for his troubles and/or causing trouble for other people.

With twins, there isn't a preordained list because there isn't a lot of specific research available about them and they only represent three percent of the population. However, many birth order experts agree that twins tend to organize themselves according to their overall place within the family. For example, if twins have one older sibling, they will both exhibit characteristics of a secondborn. If they are the oldest, they will adopt some traits of firstborns. What is different and important to know about twins is that it will be more difficult to obtain information and confessions from them.[11]

Sometimes it requires more than an assessment alone to collect intelligence about a killer. Which means an undercover operation is in order.

Cold Case #20: Government of California v. Laudenberg—Victims Lois Petrie, Catherine Medina, Anna Felch, Irene Hind, Maude Burgess, and Leah Griffin

In 1972 the Los Angles Police Department (LAPD) discovered the body of Lois Petrie in her San Pedro home. She had been raped and strangled. Petrie had last been seen leaving a bar in San Pedro. The LAPD failed to identify a suspect and dubbed him the "Santa Strangler" because Petrie's body had been found the day after Christmas. Other women the police believed fell victim to the "Santa Strangler" in the years that followed included Catherine Medina, Anna Felch, Irene Hind, Maude Burgess, and Leah Griffin.

In 1974 Catherine Medina was last seen alive at a local bar where witnesses spotted her getting into a van. Anna Felch worked at a hot dog stand on Cabrillo Beach in San Pedro. She disappeared after leaving a bar the month after Medina was killed. Irene Hind was killed after she left the bar she owned. Seven months later, Maude Burgess was raped and strangled in her apartment.

Leah Griffin was found bound, raped, and strangled in a residential hotel on San Francisco's Powell Street. Griffin was the sixth woman in less than two and a half years to be killed in the San Francisco or Los Angeles area.

Detectives who worked these cases discovered strong similarities, both in method and in the kind of victims involved. All of the women had similar lifestyles. They all drank and frequented bars and did not have many friends. Some of the women had been in poor health or had a spouse who had died. The women were raped and strangled, and some of them had their faces covered and were bound.

Whoever killed the six women didn't leave many clues. Detectives only found a partial fingerprint in Burgess's apartment. Semen was collected from the victims, but it only confirmed that they had been sexually assaulted. At the time many medical examiners transferred the biological evidence from these cold cases onto microscopic slides and stored them in the evidence room.

In 2002 the Los Angeles Police Department assigned detectives Richard Bengston and Vivian Flores to reactivate and review these cold cases. In one of the files, the detectives identified a possible suspect, Adolph Theodore Laudenberg, and began a search to find him. Their investigation led them to contact Adolph's daughter-in-law, Darlene Laudenberg. She told Los Angeles investigators that her father-in-law had talked about the 1970s killings to her and his stepson's fiancée. Subsequent interviews with Laudenberg's ex-wife and other people in Laudenberg's network increased the detectives' suspicions about him as the primary suspect. Further investigation into Laudenberg's life history showed that he had lived in the area during the time these murders were committed. It showed that he had worked in a series of odd jobs as a security guard and as a cab driver. But Bengston and Flores needed physical evidence to tie Laudenberg to the murders. The detectives headed to the LAPD evidence room to search for records of physical evidence that had been collected from the crime scenes.

After Bengston and Flores arrived at the LAPD evidence room, they discovered with the help of the clerk a dusty, green filing cabinet that had sat untouched for some time. They opened a drawer, revealing hundreds of microscopic slides from sexual assaults in the 1970s that had been forgotten and never logged into the coroner's database. Unfortunately, the only surviving and admissible samples were from Petrie's body.

Since Laudenberg had no criminal record, there was no record of his DNA on file. Bengston and Flores needed to collect a DNA sample from him but didn't want to ask him for fear he would not cooperate and they would lose an opportunity to arrest him. So they set up an undercover operation to collect a sample of his saliva.

They assigned an undercover agent to start a conversation with Laudenberg about his hobby: carving walking canes. During the conversation the undercover agent invited Laudenberg to join him for breakfast. After they left the detectives collected a sample of Laudenberg's saliva from his coffee cup. Laudenberg's DNA sample matched that of the DNA left at the scene of Petrie's murder.

Sentence

On September 5, 2003, police arrested the 77-year-old Laudenberg. In 2007, the court sentenced Laudenberg to life in prison.[12]

Case #1 Undercover Operation Description

Detectives reactivated a rape and murder cold case of a 25-year-old female, and they identified one of the witnesses as the prime suspect. Although they had gathered a lot of intelligence on the suspect through trash pulls, mail covers, and surveillance, investigators felt the need to conduct an undercover operation before scheduling an interrogation and to ensure a conviction. The mission of the operation was to give the suspect a positive image of the police that he had never before witnessed. Detectives noticed that the killer had been driving with an expired license plate. They assigned a local police officer to pull over the suspect and engage in a friendly conversation with him.

After he pulled over the suspect, the police officer pretended to conduct a background check with the dispatcher. When he returned to the suspect's car he asked if he had ever been arrested. "No," he replied.

The officer then asked if the police had ever interviewed him during an investigation of a crime. "Yes, for the death of a girl."

The officer thanked him for being honest and said, "Because of your honesty and past cooperation with the police I'm not going to write you a ticket as long as you promise me you'll contact the DMV and pay the registration fee."

Resolution

The patrol officer noted that the suspect acted friendly and respectful but nervous. He also noticed that the suspect had empty Coke cans in his car.

Two days later the detectives brought the suspect in for questioning and had Coke available for him. After they casually built rapport with some of the cognitive and NLP techniques, they presented the evidence. The suspect confessed to the murder. After the confession, the suspect stated that the good experience he had with the patrol officer who pulled him over persuaded him to cooperate with the detectives on the day he was interviewed.

Case #2 Undercover Operation Description

Detectives discovered the body of a young man at a construction site. He had been beaten with a metal pipe to the head and face. The pipe contained a piece of human skin, which had been ripped from the perpetrator, but there was no DNA match through a CODIS search. Four years later detectives reactivated the case and identified a possible suspect but didn't have his DNA on file. Detectives decided to use the water bottle trick to collect the suspect's DNA.

Resolution

In the initial interview, the suspect denied any involvement in the murder. Detectives kindly invited him for a second interview to discuss further details about the investigation and gave him the impression he'd only be there for a short time. He accepted but was unaware that the detectives considered him as a suspect and they had a plan in place to collect his DNA.

An hour before the scheduled interview detectives turned up the temperature on the central heating system and also placed electric heaters in the interview room to literally turn up the heat on the suspect. Before they escorted the suspect into the room they removed the heaters and also gave him a bottle of water. After a short conversation, detectives excused themselves and left the room. When they returned the suspect had drunk much of the water in the bottle. They thanked him for his time, apologized for the inconvenience, and said they'd throw the water bottle in the trash for him.

After the suspect left, detectives cut a hole in the bottom of the plastic bottle to empty the rest of the water and sent it to the forensic lab for DNA analysis. The results showed it matched the DNA collected from the crime scene. This gave them probable cause to arrest the suspect, who was subsequently convicted of the murder.

Case #3 Undercover Operation Description

A cold case was reactivated to submit DNA into the CODIS database. In the initial investigation detectives only had circumstantial evidence on a man they identified as the likely killer. With the new DNA technology, they collected DNA from the victim's shirt, which had semen stains and had been stored in the evidence room. After a search in the CODIS file did not find a match, detectives submitted a warrant request to collect DNA from the original primary suspect. But the judge denied the warrant because detectives lacked sufficient probable cause.

Resolution

Without a court order, detectives arranged an undercover operation to collect the suspect's DNA. During surveillance of the suspect, detectives discovered that he smoked Salem cigarettes and regularly shopped at a local grocery store.

On a Saturday morning detectives set up a promotional booth for Salem cigarettes in front of the grocery store. The undercover person posed as a Salem cigarettes representative and invited customers to participate in a cigarette tasting survey. He also placed ashtrays on the table for customers to extinguish the cigarettes. If the customer correctly identified which one of the three cigarettes was a Salem, he or she would receive a free pack of Salems.

The undercover person successfully persuaded the suspect to participate in the cigarette survey. After he finished smoking each cigarette, the undercover person handed him an empty ashtray, in which he extinguished all three cigarettes. The undercover person announced he had chosen the Salem cigarette and gave the suspect a free pack. After detectives submitted the suspect's cigarette butts to the forensic lab for analysis, the results showed that the DNA matched the semen on the victim's shirt. When detectives showed the suspect the DNA evidence, he confessed to the murder.

Interview all the people in the file the same. In the initial interview avoid viewing or treating any of the witnesses as the potential killer for the following reasons. In most cold cases the name of the killer is in the file or has already been identified. By drawing suspicion away from him or her, it might possibly cause the killer to let his or her guard down or make a mistake and unknowingly offer valuable information that will

8. Meeting of the Minds with Witnesses and Suspects

implicate him or her and create probable cause later in the investigation to warrant an arrest for the murder. This will give a huge advantage when it is necessary to conduct surveillance and/or an undercover operation on the killer or interrogate the killer.

Never ask a suspect why he or she committed the murder. A husband is caught having an affair. If you ask him why, he is not going to say "I had the affair because my wife would not have sex with me anymore" or "I don't find my wife attractive anymore." Although either one of these reasons might be true, he is most likely not going to admit it. In some cases the suspect does not even know the answer. Obtaining a confession from the killer or collecting evidence that will convict the killer is more important than why the killer did the deed. Most people who commit a crime have no desire to tell you why. It makes them feel uncomfortable, which will likely agitate the suspect and cause him or her to become uncooperative or, in the worst case, shut down. Avoiding the why question is extremely important for murder cases. Of course, after suspects confess to the murder, it is okay to ask them why they did it. If possible, conduct the interviews with witnesses in a way that prevents them from being able to make contact with one another or the person you suspect to be the killer. This may be difficult to do, but the less contact the people in the file have with one another the better.

Another good way to build rapport and determine the value of a witness or suspect is to find out the titles of movies he or she has watched. During the interview or interrogation, subtly mention a movie the witness or suspect has seen. The same works with political views, sports teams, and other hobbies or activities. This is a rapport-building technique and can be quite effective if properly utilized.

Wear clothes similar to the fashion or style of the witness or suspect. This will make the witness or suspect feel more comfortable. If a detective wears contrasting clothes, it will subconsciously encourage the witness to view and treat a detective as an adversary and not an ally.

Avoid distractions or interruptions like extraneous noises or movement or interrupting the witness's concentration by asking too many questions.

Schedule the interview or interrogation based on sleeping habits, work schedule, or family dynamics. If the person is an early riser, then schedule the meeting in the morning. If the person is a late sleeper or works the graveyard shift, then schedule later in the day. If the person is divorced and has visitation on Friday, don't schedule on that day.

Rehearse the interview or interrogation. Select people to role-play as the witness or suspect. It's a good way to practice and improve interview and interrogation skills.

Finally, the most important piece of advice for a successful interview is to listen more. As detectives, we are trained and conditioned to ask questions. Therefore, listening is the least developed skill. It is said that silence is golden, but that's only part of a much older proverb: "Speech is silver and silence is golden." This is especially true when it comes to interviewing or interrogating a man. In my experience, a man needs more time to collect his thoughts and answer a question. I've discovered that once I listen more to a suspect or witness he or she tends to feel more comfortable about sharing information. It encourages a witness or suspect to continue the conversation on his or her own terms. This could result in him or her voluntarily or accidentally offering information he or she might otherwise not share. Listening creates a safe environment and builds trust. This ultimately creates an amicable conversation between two human beings instead of two adversaries—a suspect and a detective.

As you conduct the interview or interrogation it is important to keep your composure and stay in control of every aspect of the interview with the witness as well as the interrogation with the killer. There is a lot at stake for both the suspect as well as a detective. For the killer, his or her life is on the line. And for detectives and families of the cold case victim, it is justice and resolution.

The next chapter will share information about a new resource available to law enforcement that received national attention in April of 2018 when it helped solve a five-decade-old cold case. Then, in 2019, it made headlines again. In June of that year, William Talbott II became the first person convicted of murder after being singled out with the use of this new science. The following month it exonerated a wrongfully convicted man and also identified the real killer. It's called forensic genealogy.

8. Meeting of the Minds with Witnesses and Suspects

Cold Case #21: Government of Florida v. Hartley— Victim Verle Lee Hartley

Summary

In November of 1982, while he was serving onboard the USS *Forrestal* aircraft carrier, Lieutenant Verle Lee Hartley was admitted to the ship's hospital with a mysterious illness that baffled the doctor. Lieutenant Hartley's symptoms included diarrhea, vomiting, and abdominal pain. His condition worsened, and after weeks of constant pain and multiple organ failure, he died on November 18 in a stateside hospital at the age of 37.

A postmortem test of Lieutenant Hartley's hair and blood revealed that he had a lethal level of arsenic in his system believed to have been in his body for at least five months. The victim had spent the last six months at sea, and naval investigators had no idea how Lieutenant Hartley digested the arsenic or why someone would want to kill him. The aircraft carrier employed more than 5,000 sailors, and naval investigators had no leads or suspects.

Naval investigators questioned Lieutenant Hartley's wife, Pamela. She had no idea how her husband digested the arsenic and denied any involvement in his death. Despite the naval investigators' suspicions of Pamela, the Navy issued her $35,000 in insurance money, $10,000 a year in veteran's benefits, and free military medical benefits. While Pamela appeared to have a motive, naval investigators didn't have enough evidence to arrest Pamela and had to close the case.

Resolution

In 1995 NCIS cold case agents from Mayport, Florida, started reworking the unsolved homicide. The NCIS cold case squad had a difficult time locating Pamela Hartley, so they used a database and internet search to locate people who knew Lieutenant Hartley. As NCIS agents proceeded with the case, they interviewed relatives, neighbors, and friends who did not speak up during the initial investigation. They shared information they had not previously revealed. One person said that Pamela had thought about hiring someone to kill her husband.

Some said that Pamela had an unhappy marriage. And many of them thought she murdered her husband.

NCIS agents eventually found an unemployed Pamela in Augusta, Georgia, living with her mother. After detectives questioned Pamela about her husband's death, she confessed. She told detectives that she had a miserable marriage but didn't want to give up being a Navy officer's wife, so she decided to be a Navy officer's widow. Pamela confessed that she had sent her husband care packages that included baked goods laced with rat poison.

Sentence

At her arraignment in the fall of 1996, Pamela pleaded guilty to second-degree murder. The court sentenced her to 40 years. However, Pamela only served 16 years of her sentence and was released from the Bradenton Transition Center on April 2, 2012. Records show that she moved to Martinez, Georgia.[13]

Cold Case #22: Government of Mississippi v. Flowers—Victims Bertha Tardy, Carmen Rigby, Robert Golden, and Derrick "Bobo" Stewart

This case was featured in *Wrong Man*, season 1.

Summary

In Winona, Mississippi, on the morning of July 16, 1996, a retired employee of Tardy Furniture entered the store and found four people who had been shot in the head, execution-style. The four victims were Bertha Tardy, 59, the owner of Tardy Furniture; Carmen Rigby, 45, a full-time employee of over 20 years; Robert Golden, 42, a part-time employee; and Derrick "Bobo" Stewart, 16, a part-time employee and high school student.

Two months after the quadruple murder detectives identified a former Tardy employee, Curtis Giovanni Flowers, as a primary suspect. Detectives learned Tardy had fired Flowers two weeks before the

8. Meeting of the Minds with Witnesses and Suspects 237

murders, and they had eyewitnesses who testified that they saw Flowers near the front of the store on the morning of the shootings. Detectives found Flowers in Texas, brought him back to Mississippi for questioning, and then arrested him based on the following circumstantial evidence.

- Bloody footprints found at the crime scene matched Flowers's shoe size and the FILA brand shoes witnesses said Flowers wore the day of the murders.
- Forensic investigators determined that the shells at the crime scene came from a 380-caliber gun, the same kind of gun Flowers's uncle reported stolen on the morning of the murders. Forensic evidence revealed gunpowder residue on Flowers's thumb.
- Detectives found $255 in cash hidden at Flowers's girlfriend's home and claimed it to be some of the money stolen from Tardy's cash register.
- Two of Flowers's cellmates testified that he had stolen the money and committed the murders.

Flowers, who had no prior criminal record, maintained his innocence. He claimed he stopped going to work and didn't know he had been fired. He also said he wore Nike, not FILA shoes that day; that the clothes he wore did not match the description given by eyewitnesses; that the powder on his hands resulted from fireworks he handled the day before the murders; and that he never admitted any crimes to his cellmates.

Detectives never found any physical evidence like DNA, a gun, or bullets to directly connect Flowers to the crime scene. Nevertheless, the prosecutor charged Flowers with the robbery and murders and portrayed him as a disgruntled employee who sought revenge. One year later the jury convicted Flowers of robbery and quadruple murder and sentenced him to death. After his sentence Flowers continued to maintain his innocence.

Over the next three decades, Flowers filed six appeals to retry his case, which resulted in four convictions and two hung juries.

In June of 2019, the United States Supreme Court reversed Flowers's conviction because of the prosecutor's racial bias during jury selection.

Six months later Flowers received an early Christmas present. On Monday, December 16, 2019, a Mississippi trial judge released Curtis Flowers on $250,000 bail. After an anonymous donor posted Flowers's bond, he officially became a free man and returned home to his family in Winona. Although he is no longer in prison, he must wear an electronic monitor and may only leave his home to attend court or a doctor's appointment. While he is under house arrest, he waits to see if the prosecutor decides whether to try him a seventh time for a quadruple murder he has long maintained he did not commit. Flowers's lawyer has filed two other motions. One is seeking dismissal of the charges against Flowers and the other asks for the removal of District Attorney Doug Evans from the case. Evans's misconduct resulted in the reversal of four of Flowers's convictions and a stern rebuke from the Supreme Court.[14]

Cold Case #23: Government of Washington v. Evaristo Salas—Victim Jose Arreola

This case was featured in *Wrong Man*, season 1.

Summary

On November 15, 1995, Jose Arreola drove into the parking lot of his apartment on Saul Road in Sunnyside, Washington, with his girlfriend, Ofelia, and their infant son. After he parked his Mazda pickup truck, someone walked up and fired two shots into his head through the driver's side window. The next day Arreola died of his wounds at Harborview Medical Center in Seattle.

The investigation of Arreola's murder is filled with conflicting testimony and stories, as well as information that raises questions about Ofelia's behavior after the shooting.

Four days after the shooting Ofelia convinced the towing company to release the truck to her. She had the truck cleaned and replaced the window. This contaminated the crime scene and did not allow detectives to collect and process potential physical evidence that might lead to the killer. Only the lead detective or the prosecutor is authorized to release a vehicle. Information about this misstep was not presented when a suspect was brought to trial.

Initially, police thought the motive for Arreola's death was retribution for a previous gang killing. Six months later, however, police arrested Evaristo Salas because Ofelia and a confidential informant identified him from a photo a detective showed them. How detectives presented the photos to Ofelia and the informant has also been questioned.

The case against Salas was built around conflicting eyewitness accounts of the shooting. Some claimed the shooter had a Chicago Bulls hat, and others said it was White Sox or Braves. Some said the shooter was white, while others claimed he "looked Mexican." Some, like Ofelia, said the killer's age ranged from 15 to 16 years old. Some claimed him to be between 25 and 30 years old. While such details may seem minor, in a criminal trial it can be the difference between innocence and guilt.

Salas denied shooting Arreola and had an alibi from a 7-Eleven clerk, who stated that Salas had been at the store located on the other side of town during the shooting.

Although the prosecutors never established a motive or found the gun or had any physical evidence to connect Salas to the murder, the jury rendered a guilty verdict and sentenced him to 33 years in prison. As of the writing of this book, Salas still awaits an opportunity to appeal his case and secure a retrial.[15]

Cold Case #24: Government of Tennessee v. Smith— Victim Jessie Nicole Morrison

This case was featured in *Wrong Man*, season 2.

This was a complicated case, and it became much more complex after the convicted woman, Vonda Smith, dropped a bombshell during the *Wrong Man*'s taping of her post-conviction interview. She made a claim about her son that he denied, which raised speculation that although she may not have committed the murder, she may have been involved somehow. Smith's case is an example of how, despite good interview and interrogation techniques, witnesses find a way to hide the truth or make it even more confusing for a detective to find the truth.

Summary

Vonda Smith rented a mobile home at Cross Anchor Trailer Park in Greenville, Tennessee, for her daughter-in-law, Jessie Nicole Morrison, so she could be close to her grandson, Channing. Morrison, who was four months pregnant, lived in the trailer with her fiancé, Gary Ealey, two sons, Channing (3) and Kamdyn (1), and Gary's father, J.D. Ealey.

On the afternoon of Friday, August 12, 2016, Smith accompanied Morrison and the two boys to buy groceries. Surveillance videotape from the Snapps Ferry Road City Supermarket shows them leaving the checkout aisle at about 3:30 p.m. and pulling out of the parking lot in Smith's white Pontiac at 3:43 p.m.

According to Smith, they dropped the groceries at Morrison's home and returned to her house. Smith gave her $1,000 to pay her bills, babysat the two boys, and loaned her white Pontiac to Morrison. Morrison left Smith's house between 4:30 p.m. and 4:45 p.m.

Earlier that day Morrison's mother, Tammy Morrison, received a text message from her daughter. They had planned to meet in Greene County that night so she could spend time with her grandson, Kamdyn. But Tammy never heard back from her. She drove to Morrison's home, but there was no sign of her.

Tammy called Smith several times, but she didn't answer the phone or return her calls. So she drove to Smith's house. When Tammy arrived there, she asked Smith if she knew of Morrison's whereabouts. Smith said she hadn't seen Morrison since 4:30 p.m. when she left to run errands in her white Pontiac. Tammy left the Smith house and drove to the Greene County Sheriff's Department, where detectives took a statement from her.

As Morrison's family, friends, and detectives continued their search for her, a man walking his dog along Jud Neal Loop in Afton about 15 miles from Greenville discovered the body of a dead woman around 7:30 p.m. When detectives arrived, they had no clue of her identity but eventually confirmed that it was Morrison.

The autopsy revealed defensive wounds, which meant that

8. Meeting of the Minds with Witnesses and Suspects

Morrison put up a fight against her attacker. She suffered several skull fractures along with cuts, bruises, and other lacerations. It showed that the blunt force trauma to her head was what killed her. The forensic department discovered DNA of three unidentified males underneath her fingernails and DNA of two males in her panties. Despite the male DNA evidence, detectives turned their attention to Smith because she had been the last person to see Morrison alive.

As detectives continued their investigation, they found Smith's white Pontiac near her house with Morrison's blood inside and outside of the car. Based on the testimony of family and friends, they discovered a possible motive for why Smith might have killed Morrison. Smith had been deeply upset when she learned of Morrison's plan to marry Ealey. To Smith, the marriage meant she would see less of her grandson. They believed that, as the days and weeks passed, tension grew between Smith and Morrison, which eventually led to a confrontation and Morrison's death on that Friday night.

Smith denied involvement in Morrison's murder. And two witnesses provided information to support her whereabouts at the time of the murder. One was Smith's husband, Roger, who had been home with Channing. He confirmed that she left the house around 6:15 p.m. to pick up her granddaughter, Emma, at Sharon Burgner's house. The other was Burgner, who said that Smith picked up Emma at her house around 7:00 p.m. This time frame is important because it is about a 40-minute drive from Smith's to Burgner's house.

Morrison's neighbor, Mr. Hutchinson, testified that he had seen her with two white males at her house around 5:30 p.m. and that all three eventually left in a white van but left Smith's car parked near Morrison's house. Despite Hutchinson's testimony, detectives found no connection between the white van and Morrison's murder.

Detectives never recovered the murder weapon, which the coroner believed to be a metallic blunt force object; nor did they discover Smith's DNA at the crime scene. Nevertheless, the prosecutor charged Smith with Morrison's death.

Sentence

On Monday, June 25, 2018, the jury felt there was enough circumstantial evidence to find Smith guilty of one count of first-degree murder for Jessie Morrison's death and one count of second-degree murder for the death of her unborn child. Judge John D. Dugger sentenced Smith to life in prison.

Post-Conviction Summary

Vonda Smith's case raises more questions than it answers. Regardless of what people believe when they watch the show, her case needs to be reopened and reinvestigated because the narrative of this case has too many inconsistencies in it. One is the bombshell Smith dropped during her interview with Detective Ira Todd. Smith told investigators she lent her car to Morrison hours before her body was found and did not see Morrison afterward. Two witnesses at the trial testified about seeing Morrison in a white van leaving the trailer park she lived at with her boyfriend, who was ruled out as a suspect.

Vonda initially claimed that she did not see who returned her car, then said it was Gary Ealey, and finally claimed it was her own son, William.

When Detective Todd interviewed William he denied his mother's claim.

So who is telling the truth?

While lying doesn't make a person a murderer, it also doesn't make him or her trustworthy. Nevertheless, the truth needs to be found.

The person who returned Smith's car did not necessarily kill Jessie, but one thing is certain: one person cannot drive two vehicles at once.

Another question is the blood splatter in the white Pontiac. According to Johnny Lawrence, the blood splatter expert, two things were true of the bloodstains found in Vonda's car. The blood was not planted and the car was used only to transport Jessie. So this created confusion about where Morrison was murdered.

Based on what has been revealed in the *Wrong Man* show, perhaps it may never be known what the absolute truth of this case is or what truly happened to Morrison. An effort should be made to reveal the truth and bring justice for Morrison and her unborn baby. Smith is working on filing an appeal to retry her case.[16]

9

Forensic Genealogy's Role in Law Enforcement

As you read this chapter it is important to understand that forensic genealogy, with its use of DNA evidence collected at the crime scene, is not meant to identify the perpetrator but rather to exclude 90 percent of the population quickly. Detectives must look at so many suspects. Therefore, this is another tool to help them work more efficiently against the list. It is the elimination of people on that list that may lead to a possible match of the suspect. When it does, detectives must rely on traditional investigative work to collect more evidence to prove the new suspect is the perpetrator. Since 2011 forensic genealogy has played a major role in helping law enforcement solve cold cases. The cold case that legitimized forensic genealogy as a viable investigation tool for law enforcement was the Golden State Killer. In April 2018, the Sacramento County District Attorney's Office announced the arrest of 72-year-old Joseph James DeAngelo, whom they believe to be the Golden State Killer. DeAngelo is accused of committing at least 13 murders, more than 50 rapes, and more than 100 burglaries in California from 1974 to 1976.[1]

The break that led to identifying DeAngelo came when Detective Paul Holes received approval from the Contra Costa County Sheriff's Office to upload the DNA profile collected from a rape case to GEDmatch, a genealogy company founded in 2010 by Curtis Rogers, a retired businessman, and John Olson, a transportation engineer. GEDmatch offers a free service to consumers who are trying to find their relatives. Since then interest in using forensic genealogy to solve crimes has exploded. For the next year genealogists helped police identify suspects in more than 40 cases.[2]

In June 2019 William Talbott II became the first person convicted of murder after being singled out with the use of forensic genealogy. Talbott was charged with the 1987 murders of Jay Cook and Tanya Van Cuylenborg. One month later forensic genealogy reached another milestone when it helped exonerate Christopher Tapp, who was featured on the first *Wrong Man* show, for the 1996 murder of Angie Raye Dodge. The process also identified the real killer, Brian Leigh Dripps, who confessed to the murder. Both groundbreaking cold cases are featured later in this chapter.[3]

The success of these cases should have ushered in a triumphant time for forensic genealogy. But instead it sparked controversy about its use in law enforcement. This book will not go into details regarding the public and politicians' trepidation about forensic science because the focus is to help detectives utilize and maximize all the resources and tools possible to solve cold cases.

Since 9/11, law enforcement has had to go through some radical changes. Three factors that have driven this are (1) the threat of terrorism, (2) intelligence-led policing, and (3) DNA analysis.

Change is difficult, especially when a new tool for accelerating the achievement of a strategic initiative—like forensic genealogy— appears in a rapidly changing environment like law enforcement. Not only are changes occurring in the environment that may affect the structure of policing but *police* themselves are in the process of changing the way they work.[4]

I am not an expert in forensic genealogy. Therefore, I will not attempt to explain how it works. Instead, I will defer to two well-known forensic genealogy experts, Dr. Colleen Fitzpatrick and CeCe Moore,[5] both of whom I feature in this chapter along with information on how to contact them. Before sharing information about Dr. Fitzpatrick and Moore here are synopses of the Talbott and Tapp cold cases that I mentioned earlier in this chapter, both of which used forensic genealogy to identify the killer.

Cold Case #25: Government of Washington v. Talbott—Victims Jay Cook and Tanya Van Cuylenborg

Summary

On November 18, 1987, Canadian high school sweethearts Jay Cook (20) and Tanya Van Cuylenborg (17) left Victoria on a trip to Seattle, Washington, in Jay's father's Ford van. Jay's father ran a furnace business and asked him to run an overnight errand to pick up parts at a store in south Seattle. When they didn't return home the next day as expected, their parents began to worry. The following day they filed a missing persons report. At the police station, Tanya's father told the police that it was unlike her to be late and not call him.

Tragically, on Tuesday, November 24, a citizen discovered Tanya's partially clothed dead body bound with plastic wire ties in a ditch by a rural road near Alger, Washington. Police said she had been raped and shot in the head with a 380-caliber gun. The next day police found the Ford van in downtown Bellingham. Inside the van were plastic ties of the same type used to bind Tanya, plastic gloves, and two ferry receipts. They also found Tanya's wallet, keys to the van, a pair of surgical gloves, and a box of 380-caliber ammo under the back porch of a tavern called Essie's.

On November 26 a pheasant hunter's dog found Cook's body by a bridge near the Snoqualmie River southwest of Monroe, 60 miles from where Tanya's body had been found two days earlier. Jay had been wrapped in a blue blanket that didn't belong to the couple. He had been strangled to death with twine. The killer also packed tissue and a pack of Camel cigarettes down his throat.

Detectives interviewed several witnesses who reported seeing Jay and Tanya board the Port Angeles ferry in Hoodsport and then a second car ferry in Bremerton to Seattle. That was the last time anyone saw or heard from Jay and Tanya.

In the months after the murders, both victims' families received a series of greeting cards, in which the author claimed responsibility for killing Jay and Tanya and included graphic descriptions of the murders. A handwriting analysis revealed the same person wrote all of them. The cards bore postmarks from Seattle, Los Angeles, and New York. This trail of evidence, however, did not lead detectives to the killer.

Although detectives collected DNA evidence, they found no match in any of the criminal databases. Nevertheless, over the next three decades as new DNA testing technologies developed, they continued to search for a match in federal databases in the U.S. and Canada with no success.

The Snohomish County Sheriff's Office featured the couple in a deck of playing cards that they handed out to inmates, in hopes of conjuring new tips in 52 cold cases. Jay and Tanya's names were on the king of hearts. But again it did not result in any new clues to the identity of the killer.

In 1990 police located the camera lens that belonged to Tanya's missing camera at a pawnshop in Portland, Oregon. Unfortunately, the owner was unable to determine who originally pawned the lens. Without any more leads, the double homicide remained unsolved for the next three decades.

Resolution

After Jay's father passed away, Tanya's brother, John Van Cuylenborg kept in touch with the sheriff's office in Snohomish County and became the spokesman for the family. John said the family struggled to accept that the police might not solve the case. But the family never gave up hope that someday a break in the case would help detectives find the killer.

Then in 2018 genetic genealogy received a lot of media attention. Using genetic genealogy as a tool in law enforcement, detectives submitted the DNA samples they collected from the bodies and van to Parabon NanoLabs. In addition to testing the DNA, Parabon also provided a service to build a rough digital sketch of a suspect's face from DNA samples. Parabon had recently hired CeCe Moore, an independent genealogist, to head up its new genetic genealogy services division to identify suspects through their family ties.

Parabon uploaded the genetic profile on GEDmatch. The GEDmatch report turned up a pair of second cousins that shared genetic material with whoever had left DNA at the crime scene. Moore spent the course of a weekend sorting through obituaries, census records, newspaper archives, and social media posts to figure out the marriage that connected them. She followed branches of their descendants and traced it to a Mr. and Mrs. Talbott, who lived in the Seattle area during the time of the murders. She also discovered that the Talbotts had two daughters and one son, William Earl Talbott II, now 52 years old.

After Moore submitted Talbott's name to the Snohomish County investigators, they located him in Seattle and placed him under surveillance. A background check revealed that Talbott had lived with his parents in Woodinville, seven miles from where detectives found Jay's body.

Detectives discovered that Talbott, who was 24 years old at the time of the killings, worked as a delivery truck driver in and around Seattle and had been convicted of a misdemeanor assault in 1985, in which the court required him to attend an anger management class.

Undercover officers followed him on his driving routes for days. Then, on May 8, 2018, Talbott threw out a paper cup from his work truck. An officer grabbed the cup and delivered it to the forensic lab for testing. The lab confirmed that his DNA matched the DNA collected from the bodies and items at the crime scene.

On May 18, 2018, detectives arrested Talbott and charged him with two counts of aggravated first-degree murder. After Talbott's arrest, they swabbed his cheek to obtain another DNA sample, which matched.

Detectives asked for anyone who knew Talbott around the time of the murders to come forward. Several of his former friends contacted police. One of them, Michael Seat, Talbott's former roommate, provided some very damning evidence. He told police that he had seen a blue blanket, similar to the one found on Jay's body, in Talbott's home and car and that Talbott had taken photos with him along a riverbank south of Monroe, in the general area where Cook's body was found. He also noted that Talbott had a tumultuous relationship with family members, was involved in drugs, and had personality changes when he drank alcohol. Seat recalled seeing a bronze van outside of Talbott's home on a misty day in the fall of 1987. Other friends said that Talbott had worked as a delivery driver and that the route he took for his deliveries matched that of the couple's travel plans at the time.

Sentence

On Wednesday, July 25, 2019, a jury found William Earl Talbott II guilty on two counts of first-degree aggravated murder. After the Snohomish County judge sentenced him to life in prison without parole he became the first person arrested and convicted through genetic genealogy. The case set precedent for future fresh homicide and cold cases.[6]

Cold Case #26: Government of Idaho v. Tapp and Dripps—Victim Angie Raye Dodge

Summary

In this situation the case went from a wrongful conviction, to a cold case, to a solved case.

Angie Raye Dodge had recently graduated from Idaho Falls High School, had moved from her parents' home to an apartment, and had gotten a job. Three weeks later on June 13, 1996, Dodge did not show up for work.

A co-worker and friend decided to visit her apartment and check on her. When she arrived, the front door was unlocked. She entered the apartment and found Dodge's bloody, half-naked body on the floor. There had been no sign of forced entry, but there were signs of a struggle. Dodge had been stabbed and cut 14 times. There were no signs of rape, but the killer had ejaculated, leaving a good semen sample.

Idaho Falls investigators interviewed dozens of young men in the city, particularly those who hung out at the recreational boat docks on the Snake River, a place frequented by teenagers and young adults. They took DNA blood samples from more than 20 men. None matched the semen collected from Dodge's body. But a few months later investigators identified another suspect, Christopher Conley Tapp, a 20-year-old Idaho Falls High dropout.

Tapp cooperated with police, showing up at the police station for an interview and voluntarily giving his DNA sample, which did not match the DNA found at Dodge's apartment. Nevertheless, police questioned him again. After more than 20 hours of interrogation and multiple polygraph tests over three weeks, Tapp confessed to Dodge's rape and murder. On January 29, 1997, police arrested Tapp on charges of rape and first-degree murder.

During the trial, Tapp's public defender argued that no physical evidence, including his DNA, linked him to the crime scene. Tapp also recanted his confession and claimed detectives pressured and manipulated him to confess to Dodge's rape and murder. Bonneville County prosecutors also withheld exculpatory evidence including videotapes of Tapp's confession.

Unfortunately, at that time there was an inflated value placed on confessions, which caused detectives to be overzealous in trying to obtain them. But today, while a confession is still the best evidence to obtain from a suspect, law enforcement is very careful and judicious in how it obtains a confession from a suspect.

Despite the lack of physical evidence and the DNA at the crime scene not matching Tapp's DNA, the jury found him guilty. The court sentenced him to life with a minimum of 20 years; he would be eligible for parole in 2027.

After the jury read the verdict, Angie's mother, Carol Dodge, felt some resolution. But she expressed anger towards Tapp for killing her daughter. At the same time, she asked the judge that he spare Tapp's life by not sentencing him to death. She left the court angry, crying, and feeling as if justice had not been served for Angie.

Throughout his incarceration, Tapp continued to claim his innocence. He filed five post-conviction relief pleas. By 2012, three had failed, and two were still pending. Also in 2012, two wrongful-conviction advocacy groups continued to work on behalf of Tapp. One was the Idaho Innocence Project. Tapp's case was one of the first taken by the Idaho Innocence Project led by Greg Hampikian, a Boise State biology and criminal justice professor.

The second was Judges for Justice, who identified numerous problems with the police interrogation of Tapp. Judges for Justice claimed that detectives violated every principle and the law regulating interrogations and confessions, used threats of force and promises of leniency, and threatened Tapp with the death penalty. The problem with the confession was that Tapp never provided a single detail of the attack, the crime scene, or any other pertinent part of the case that the investigators had not first introduced to him. A bigger issue was that the killer had ejaculated on Dodge's body, and Tapp was not the donor of that DNA source.

That same year NBC's *Dateline* featured Tapp's case in a two-hour special. The show sparked nationwide interest in Tapp's case and inspired an outcry from advocates calling for Tapp to be released.

While Tapp advocated for his innocence and release from prison, Carol Dodge focused her attention on the DNA evidence. If the DNA from the crime scene didn't match Tapp's DNA, then whose was it?

Although the court only convicted Tapp, detectives believed another person was with him during the murder. While detectives began their search for him, Carol felt compelled to begin her own investigation to search for the person who matched the DNA profile found at the crime scene. She remembered that in Tapp's videotaped confessions he talked about a guy who hung out in a neighborhood where people were cooking meth. She began surveillance on the houses. When the Idaho Falls Police Department (IFPD) found out what she was doing, they placed a tail on her for protection.

For the next three years, she parked her car and videotaped people entering and exiting the houses. Every night she lived on the streets she recorded all her findings from all the drug houses. All this time the police kept telling her they didn't know who killed her daughter. Nevertheless, she stayed vigilant.

When she lived out on the streets, she met the roughest and toughest people. She built friendships with people who would do anything for her with a snap of a finger. One night she received a telephone call from a prison inmate who said, "You'll never believe who arrived here tonight."

It was Christopher Tapp.

"What do you want done with him?"

"I said nothing. I just want the name of the guy who murdered my daughter."

Soon after the phone call, Carol received a letter from Tapp. In it he wrote:

"Dear Mrs. Dodge, I do not know who killed your daughter. Honest to God I don't know."

Carol realized he did not know and began to question the way the police handled the investigation. She decided to watch the interrogation videotapes until she wanted to put her fist through the TV. It confirmed her revelation that the police arrested and charged the wrong man. Now she directed her anger at the IFPD because they had programmed her for 13 years that Tapp played a part in Angie's murder. And that is when she began a campaign to say: *The IFPD wronged Tapp, Vera (Tapp's mother), and me. They arrested the wrong guy. I want him out of prison.*[7]

In 2017 the *Wrong Man* show featured Tapp's case, which also included an interview with Carol. During the filming of *Wrong Man*, the Idaho Innocence Project announced the results from the new M-Vac DNA, which exonerated Tapp as the person who raped and killed Angie Dodge.

In a 2017 plea agreement, the court reduced Tapp's sentence to time served and vacated his rape conviction. The judge ordered Tapp's release from prison 10 years before his eligible parole hearing. The judge also waived the order to serve probation. However, the murder conviction remained on his record.

After Tapp's exoneration and release from prison, as it is with every wrongful conviction, there remains an enduring question. Who killed Angie Dodge?

Resolution

The Bonneville County Prosecutor's Office continued to pursue justice for Angie Dodge. New DNA evidence from the M-Vac and a technique called "snapshot kinship inference" invented by Parabon NanoLabs led detectives to one of the initial suspects in the case.

"Snapshot Kinship Inference provides highly accurate inferences about the familial relationship between two people based on their DNA, even if they are distantly related. Unlike traditional forensic DNA methods... Snapshot can detect relatedness out to ninth-degree relatives (fourth cousins)."[8] These types of results give investigators valuable information about DNA samples from crime scenes that was often previously unobtainable. This information can save time and money as well as lead to more solved murders.

Parabon's lead genealogist, CeCe Moore, drew up three family trees from partial DNA matches at GEDmatch, which converged on a single couple that seemed to be the perpetrator's great-grandparents. This couple's descendants led to a handful of suspects. "We originally had it narrowed down to about six men, but it turned out there was a seventh," Moore said.[9]

Moore discovered that one woman in the family had conceived a son shortly before she divorced. That child was Brian Leigh Dripps, who had taken the last name of the woman's new husband. After a review of Dripps's background, detectives discovered that at the time of Dodge's rape and murder he lived across the street from her apartment.

Detectives tailed Dripps and picked up a cigarette butt thrown from his vehicle. When it was tested for DNA, it matched the DNA and semen from the crime scene.

Fourteen months after Tapp's release from prison, detectives arrested Dripps on May 5, 2019. Dripps initially denied involvement in the Dodge case but eventually confessed to the rape and murder of Angie Dodge. He said that he entered Dodge's apartment, threatened her with a knife, and then raped her, but didn't mean to kill her.

On February 9, 2021, Brian Dripps pleaded guilty to first-degree murder for killing Dodge. Four months later, on June 9, 2021, District Judge Joel Tingey sentenced Dripps to 20 years to life.

Christopher Tapp is the first person in the United States to be exonerated of murder through the use of forensic genealogy.

The Christopher Tapp case is a perfect example of how most people cannot grasp the severe collateral damage that comes with wrongfully convicting a person. Steven Drizin, an attorney and confession expert, said it best: "Police work and the justice system is not about closing cases. It's about getting it right. Because everybody suffers when the wrong person is locked up."[10]

Cold Case #27: Government of California v. Davis and Green—Victim Jane Hylton

The Ricky Davis wrongful conviction case is an example of two of the most dramatic and traumatic extremes a person can experience. On one hand, the criminal justice system worked in the worst possible way, and, on the other hand, in the best possible way. It is a good example of how DNA and forensic genealogy led to freedom for a wrongfully convicted man and also the identity and arrest of the three people who did murder Hylton. DNA and forensic genealogy are resources of the law enforcement trade. Often both are used as resources for conviction. But, in this case, both served as resources for justice.

Ricky Davis is the second person in the United States and the first person in California to be exonerated for murder through the use of forensic genealogy. In 2019 Christopher Tapp was the first person in the United States. What makes Davis's case unique is that the El Dorado County district attorney, Vern Pierson, collaborated with Davis's North California Innocence Project lawyers to free Davis and find the real killers.

Summary

On July 7, 1985, El Dorado County Sheriff's Department discovered the dead body of Jane Hylton, a 54-year-old columnist, in the master bedroom of a friend's El Dorado Hills house. Hylton had been stabbed 29 times. An autopsy report revealed that she had also suffered a bite mark on her left shoulder.

Hylton lived in the house with her teenage daughter, Ricky Davis, and his girlfriend, Connie Dahl. Davis's grandmother owned the house, and she had allowed Hylton and her daughter to move in temporarily because the columnist had been having marital trouble.

Davis and Dahl told detectives that they had gone to a party the night before and returned home at 3:30 a.m. When they arrived at the house, they found Hylton's daughter waiting outside. The teenager explained that she had gone out with a group of boys that night and was afraid her mother would be upset with her for being out too late, so she waited outside until they returned home.

After the three entered the house together, Davis saw blood in the hallway and followed it into the master bedroom, where he found Hylton's bloody body on the bed. Davis and Dahl immediately called 911 to report the crime. All three maintained that they were not involved in the murder and did not know who committed the crime.

Because of her marital problems, detectives questioned Hylton's estranged husband but ruled him out as a suspect. Detectives had no other suspects, so they ended the investigation.

Fourteen years later the El Dorado County Sheriff's Office reopened Hylton's case. Detectives interrogated Dahl four times over the next 18 months. During the last interrogation Dahl implicated Davis as the killer. Dahl also implicated herself in the crime, told detectives that she bit Hylton during the attack, and claimed Hylton's daughter helped the couple move her mother's body.

Based entirely on Dahl's testimony, the jury convicted Davis for second-degree murder in 2005 and sentenced him to 16 years to life in prison. Dahl, meanwhile, received a sentence of a year in county jail for her purported role in the crime.

Resolution

After Ricky Davis contacted the Northern California Innocence Project (NCIP) in 2006 to review his case, his lawyers began a thorough re-investigation. As the lawyers reviewed the transcripts, they discovered that the detectives used an aggressive, confession-driven interrogation to coerce a confession out of Dahl. But they felt this revelation wasn't enough to convince the court to exonerate Davis.

Eight years later the NCIP focused their attention on the physical evidence because the lawyers had heard about a new sophisticated DNA and forensic genealogy testing technique. NCIP hired forensic experts to begin an extremely meticulous process of examining the evidence from the crime scene and found DNA that did not belong to Davis. With the cooperation of the El Dorado County District Attorney's Office, NCIP obtained post-conviction DNA testing on articles of Hylton's clothing and material from under her fingernails.

The DNA test results revealed an unknown male DNA profile on the nightgown, in the area of the bite mark, and under the victim's fingernails. The test results excluded Davis, Dahl, and Hylton's daughter as the sources of the DNA. The unknown male DNA profile found on the nightgown indicated that Dahl did not bite the victim, contrary to her testimony at trial.

In October of 2016 NCIP filed a petition for writ of habeas corpus in the El Dorado County Superior Court on Davis's behalf. Despite the new evidence, Davis had to endure many court delays for the next two years because at that time the California court required that new evidence point unerringly to innocence, which at the time had been the highest hurdle in the country, a nearly unattainable standard. Despite the setback, NCIP took matters into their own hands and co-sponsored Senate Bill 1134 championed by former California State Senator Mark Leno, to put California's standard in line with that of 43 other states. The bill passed in January 2017 and allowed wrongfully convicted inmates like Davis to instead prove that the new evidence would likely have been compelling to a jury. The court immediately issued an order to show cause and an evidentiary hearing was ordered in 2018. Because of unforeseen court delays, Davis had to wait until 2020 for the court to hear his case.

In February of 2020 NCIP successfully convinced the court that, had the original jury heard the DNA results, it would likely have reached a different outcome. Because of the new evidence, District Attorney Vern Pierson filed a motion to dismiss all charges against Davis and asked for a finding of factual innocence. He expressed to the court that the DNA evidence exonerating Davis led his office to go over the murder case again as though it had never been solved instead of trying to prove Davis was the killer. El Dorado County Superior Court Judge Kenneth Melikian granted the request and scheduled a new trial.

Pierson's office teamed up with the Sacramento County Crime Lab to use forensic genealogy to trace the unknown DNA found at the crime scene to potential family members who had submitted their own genetic profiles to one of the public genealogy websites FamilyTreeDNA. It didn't take long to find that the DNA matched 51-year-old Michael Green. Detectives also discovered that Green, age 17 at the time, was one of the three young men who had been with Hylton's teenage daughter at a park on the night of the slaying. After Hylton's daughter confirmed the identity of Green and the other two boys, detectives conducted a ruse to collect Green's DNA. The test confirmed that Green had been at the scene of the crime.

Detectives arrested Green on Tuesday, February 11, 2020, outside his Roseville home and booked him for murder on Friday, February 14, 2020, into the El Dorado County Jail. Although detectives know the identity of the other two suspects, they did not reveal their names. One of the men is cooperating and the other is deceased.

Ricky Davis was released from the El Dorado Jail in Placerville, California, on Thursday, February 13, 2020.[11]

The three aforementioned cold cases are examples of how forensic genealogy has become a useful tool in helping investigators identify the killer. One of the pioneers of this new genetic technology is Dr. Colleen Fitzpatrick.

Dr. Colleen Fitzpatrick's passion for genealogy began at an early age. She was very close with her grandparents and also knew some of their brothers and sisters and aunts and uncles quite well, and her grandparents often spoke about the ones who had already passed. As she got older, she developed a precocious interest in family roots, combined with an inborn knack for scientific inquiry. It led her to Duke University, where she received her PhD in nuclear physics.

In the following years, she developed an interest in high-resolution laser measurement techniques and eventually founded her own high-tech optics company, Rice Systems, in the late 1980s. Rice contracted work with NASA, the U.S. Department of Defense, the National Science Foundation, and other government and civilian organizations. In 2005 Rice Systems was chosen to subcontract with Northrop Grumman on the sensor design for the Jupiter Icy Moons Orbiter (JIMO) project, the next spacecraft to Jupiter.

When Dr. Fitzpatrick was forced to close her company, she published her first book, *Forensic Genealogy*. She wrote the book as a guide to applying the principles of forensic science investigation to genealogical research. It includes insights into how photographic analysis, database mining, and DNA analysis play important roles in solving genealogical puzzles and also provides case studies to illustrate investigative techniques.

Dr. Fitzgerald teaches that genetic genealogy can be regarded as a sub-discipline of forensic genealogy when genetic genealogy is applied to forensic identification. Forensic genealogy is broader and can include heir searching, mineral and land rights, and other areas of legal work. It is useful in a casual sense by genealogists, applied to identifying old family photos, and historical research. As Dr. Fitzpatrick educated people through conferences and media interviews about forensic genealogy, people described it as *CSI* meets *Roots*.

Dr. Fitzpatrick had a great yearning desire for the genealogy

9. Forensic Genealogy's Role in Law Enforcement   257

industry to be more scientific-minded, with higher proof standards, so that it could be used in legal contexts beyond the collection of family history. She was constantly searching to improve and refine her scientific techniques in forensic genealogy. In so doing, she discovered a way to compare the Y-STR profile developed from DNA found at a crime scene to the genetic genealogy Y-STR databases, which were organized around last names, ethnic backgrounds, historical figures, etc. She didn't need a DNA sample to do this since the law genealogy community used the same markers as the law enforcement community, and there are thousands of public Y-DNA databases found online. There were also new SNP tests developed by 23andMe and Ancestry, based on the biomedical industry. These tests tested markers on all the chromosomes, not just the Y chromosome. Both men and women could take the test. Therefore, she could look through the databases for matches.

It was well known in the industry that the genealogy companies would not accept forensic cases and did not have publicly accessible databases. Nevertheless, she found a way to circumvent the need to rely on them to locate and identify missing people, relatives, criminals, or a corpse. This led her to start Identifinders International in 2011.

Identifinders is a forensic genealogy company that primarily works with law enforcement agencies to apply genetic genealogy to cold case homicides and rapes. It works on Child Doe cases that might lead to criminal charges against the child's parents or caretakers.[12]

Identifinders tackled its first forensic case in 2012, attempting to identify the killer of 16-year-old cheerleader Sarah Yarborough, who was strangled near her high school campus in Federal Way, Washington, in 1991. More information about this case is highlighted at the end of this chapter.

In 2014 the Phoenix Police Department hired Identifinders to help them identify a serial killer. Using techniques Identifinders had developed, it linked the Canal Killer to the murders of 22-year-old Angela Brosso in 1992 and 17-year-old Melanie Bernas in 1993. When they sent the Y-STR profile developed from crime-scene DNA to Dr. Fitzpatrick, she was able to narrow down a list of 2,000 suspects to five matches with the name Miller.

One of these was Bryan Patrick Miller, whom detectives had already interviewed. After a DNA sample obtained from Miller was found to match DNA found at the crime scene, detectives arrested Miller and charged him with two counts of first-degree murder. This case is highlighted at the end of this chapter as well.[13]

In 2017 Dr. Fitzpatrick partnered with Dr. Margaret Press and founded the DNA Doe Project (DDP), a nonprofit organization that uses genetic genealogy to identify John and Jane Does and reunite them to their families. DDP has never turned down a case, and does fundraising to help smaller and less-well-funded agencies to cover the fixed costs of DNA testing.

DDP's work is valuable to law enforcement because detectives cannot solve a crime unless they know the name of the victim. Once DDP identifies the victim, law enforcement can begin an investigation to determine if the victim died as a result of murder, suicide, or natural causes. Therefore, it either confirms a murder or rules it out. Even if the identification does not lead to a killer—as in the case of suicide—at least it answers the "why" for the families of the victims. DDP's work has also helped with the misidentification of a corpse. To learn more about Identifinders International and DNA Doe Project's services or to contact Dr. Fitzpatrick visit the websites at *www.identifinders.com* and *www.dnadoeproject.org*.

High profile or not, forensic genealogy is turning into a useful resource for law enforcement. For the sake of all the victims and their families and the safety of all citizens, it is imperative that politicians, law enforcement, and the public quickly develop policies and procedures for the use of forensic genealogy by law enforcement.

While forensic genealogy has proven to be a valuable resource to help law enforcement solve cold cases, it has not legally been deemed reliable. For now, it only serves as a tool to direct a detective to a potential suspect. To date, it has only solved about 700 of the 250,000 cold cases in the past two years.

At the end of the book in the Resources and Support Services section, more information is provided about Identifinders International and the DNA Doe Project and how to contact Dr. Fitzgerald. Here are the cold cases and Jane and John Doe cases Dr. Fitzpatrick helped solve.

Cold Case #28: Government of Arizona v. Miller— Victims Angela Brosso and Melanie Bernas

Summary

On the evening of Sunday, November 8, 1992, Angela Brosso, 22, left the apartment she shared with her boyfriend for an afternoon bicycle ride along a bike path that snakes through Phoenix along the Arizona Canal. When Brosso didn't return home, her boyfriend, Joseph Krakowiecki, phoned the Phoenix Police Department to report her missing.

A few days later the police discovered Brosso's headless body in a field near her apartment. She had been stabbed several times. Police never found her bicycle. One week later a man walking along the canal found Brosso's head floating in a canal grate near Metro Center.

On September 21, 1993, Phoenix PD discovered another female body floating in the Arizona Canal under the Black Canyon Freeway, north of Dunlap Avenue. Her name was Melanie Bernas, a 17-year-old high school student. Like Brosso, she had been stabbed several times, and her bicycle was also missing. Police believed the same person killed both women.

The Phoenix PD placed flyers along the Arizona Canal path where the bodies had been found. They followed hundreds of tips, but all of them led to dead ends. As a result Phoenix PD stopped the investigation.

Phoenix PD reopened the case and enlisted the help of the Vidocq Society in 2013. The Vidocq Society's profiler speculated that the killer was probably still in the Phoenix area, that police had likely previously run into him, that he had probably committed another crime prior to the two murders, and that he might be a serial killer. But the Vidocq Society staff were unable to help Phoenix PD solve these two murder cases. Again both cases remained cold until Phoenix PD received a big break the following year.

Resolution

In 2014 Phoenix PD received a break when they met Dr. Colleen Fitzpatrick at the International Symposium on Human Identification

(ISHI). ISHI is the largest conference on DNA analysis for human identification. After they learned about Dr. Fitzpatrick and her company, Identifinders International, they hired her to analyze the DNA profile they collected from the crime scene.

Dr. Fitzpatrick narrowed down a list of 2,000 suspects to eight matches, all with the same last name, Miller. When detectives checked the cold case file, they discovered that one of the suspects on the list was Bryan Patrick Miller, whom detectives had interviewed after the murders occurred but could not tie to the case for lack of evidence. Before Phoenix PD arrested Miller they conducted a ruse to collect Miller's DNA and test it. When the results confirmed a match, they arrested and charged Miller with two counts of first-degree murder on January 13, 2015.

Miller denied involvement and admitted that he lived near the bike path and frequently traveled there but had no explanation of how his DNA matched the profile found on the victims.

After Miller's arrest, Phoenix PD conducted a background check on Miller and discovered that he had been arrested and charged on May 23, 2002, in the state of Washington for a knife attack on a woman, Melissa Ruiz-Ramirez. But Miller was acquitted because he said the woman tried to rob him. So his DNA had never been entered into CODIS. They also discovered that, in 1990, when he was 16 years old, he had a stabbing incident with a woman at Paradise Valley. This corroborated Vidocq's precursor crime prediction made in 2013. Shortly after the incident, Miller quietly resumed his life in Phoenix.

As the investigation progressed Phoenix police also believed that Miller might be responsible for other murders. The list includes Brandy Myers, 13, who vanished on May 26, 1992; Adrienne Salinas, 19, who disappeared on June 15, 2013 and whose body was discovered in a wash near Apache Junction on August 6, 2013; and Shannon Aumock, 16, vanished when she ran away from a group home not far from Brandy Myers North Phoenix neighborhood. Aumock's body was found on May 27, 1992, in the rural area of Dear Valley Road and 26th Street. She remained unidentified until 2011.

Trial

The court scheduled Miller's trial for April 28, 2016. Unfortunately, due to unforeseen delays, the court had to reschedule his trial. Miller's trial began in Phoenix on October 3, 2022, and is expected to continue into 2023.[14]

Cold Case #29: *Government of Washington v. Nicholas—Victim Sarah Yarborough*

Summary

On the morning of December 14, 1991, two 12-year-old boys saw a man emerge from the bushy hillside near Federal Way High School's tennis courts. After the man walked away, the boys noticed a body dressed in a drill team uniform by the hillside not far from where the man exited the bushes. The boys ran home and told their parents, who called 911.

When King County sheriffs arrived they identified the female body as being that of 16-year-old Sarah Yarborough. She had been raped and strangled to death with her stockings. After a search of the area, police found her car in the school parking lot.

Yarborough was last seen alive on a Saturday morning in December 1991, when she left home to take part in a dance-team competition. About six people came forward and said they saw the suspect. They identified him as a man in his twenties, about six feet tall, with long blond hair, clad in a black trench coat and dark pants. One of the witnesses saw him interacting with Yarborough, and some saw him leaving the brushy area where her body was found. Another witness said he jogged by the area that morning and saw a man kneeling over a girl. He didn't question what was going on because he thought they were a couple so he kept jogging. Another witness helped the police draw a sketch of the man. And another said he saw a man driving away in a tan 1970 Chevy Nova.

The forensic team discovered semen on Yarborough's clothes and collected a DNA profile. Detectives searched regularly in state and national DNA databases, but no match was made for decades. Despite all the tips, detectives never found a suspect and the case went cold.

In 2012 the King County Sheriff's Office (KCSO) sent the DNA evidence to Identifinders International. By comparing the Y-STR profile obtained from crime scene DNA to the Y-STR genetic genealogy databases, Dr. Fitzpatrick was able to provide a possible last name of Fuller for the unknown assailant. Unfortunately, the lead didn't result in any arrest because the KCSO was unable to link the name to any suspects. The case remained cold.

Resolution

In 2018, with new advances in genetic genealogy, Identifinders led the KCSO to a man named Patrick Nicholas. After detectives did a background check on Nicholas, they discovered that he had a prior rape conviction and had served time in prison for a 1983 rape; he was released from prison in 1987. He was also charged in 1994 with first-degree child molestation but later pleaded guilty to fourth-degree assault. The reason detectives didn't get a "hit" on Nicholas was because he was never asked to submit a DNA sample for entry into CODIS.

When detectives located Nicholas, they placed a surveillance team on him. Detectives observed him smoking several cigarettes outside of a Kent business where he worked and they collected the butts and tested his DNA. It matched the DNA found on Yarborough's clothes.

Detectives arrested Nicholas without incident for first-degree murder on October 2, 2019, and booked him into King County Jail. At the preliminary hearing Nicholas pleaded not guilty, and the judge set his bail at $5 million. As of the writing of this book Nicholas's trial date is pending.[15]

Cold Case #30: Government of Iowa v. Burns—Victim Michelle Martinko

Summary

On the evening of December 19, 1979, 18-year-old Michelle Martinko attended a banquet for the Kennedy Concert Choir at the Sheraton Inn in Cedar Rapids, Iowa. After the event, she asked a friend if she'd like to join her on a shopping trip to the Westdale Mall, where she had a part-time job. Her friend declined, so Martinko left without her. Martinko had $180 and intended to purchase a new winter coat. Witnesses said they had seen Martinko shopping and speaking with friends and co-workers up until about 9 p.m. outside of a jewelry store in the mall.

When Martinko didn't return home at a reasonable time her father began to worry and called the police at 2 a.m. Together with the police, he headed to the Westdale Mall to search for her. When the police arrived they found the Martinko family's tan and green 1972 Buick Electra in the northeast corner of the mall parking lot by a JCPenney. Inside the car was Martinko's fully dressed dead body collapsed over the passenger seat. She had been stabbed 21 times in her face, neck, and chest. Based on the defensive wounds on her hands, police determined that she had fought back against her killer; because of the lack of blood outside the car, they surmised that Martinko had been killed while inside the car. The police found no fingerprints, which led them to believe the killer wore gloves.

Because Martinko's purse contained cash police concluded she had not been robbed. The medical examiner determined she had not been sexually assaulted and estimated her time of death between 8 and 10 p.m. the previous evening. But he couldn't determine the type of sharp weapon used to kill her. Based on the location and number of stab wounds, police considered the killing to be personal in nature.

Five months after the murder a woman came forward and said she had driven by the mall parking lot in the early hours of December 20 and had seen a man standing next to the open driver's side door of Martinko's car but couldn't identify him. When detectives asked why she hadn't shared this information earlier in the investigation, she said she told the public safety commissioner. Unfortunately, the commissioner didn't report her eyewitness account of that night, and it didn't provide any substantial lead for the detectives.

On June 19, 1980, police released a composite sketch of a man believed to have killed Martinko. The sketch was drawn from descriptions provided by two witnesses under hypnosis. They described a white man in his late teens or early twenties, around six feet tall and weighing 165 to 175 pounds, with brown eyes and curly brown hair. But no one came forward to identify the man in the sketch. Without any more viable leads, her case languished for 26 years.

As the years passed Martinko's parents struggled to deal with their daughter's death. They went into seclusion and suffered health problems. Sadly, Martinko's parents died not knowing who killed their daughter or why. Her father, Albert, died in 1995 and her mother, Janet, died in 1998.

Then, in 2006, the Cedar Rapids Police Department reopened Martinko's case. Detective Doug Larison received a tip about a suspicious person with a possible connection. The tip didn't produce any solid leads, but it provided Larison another chance to meticulously review Martinko's file and the physical evidence that had been stored in the evidence room. In so doing, Larison found traces of blood he thought might belong to the killer. He also re-examined evidence in Martinko's car because he theorized that the killer might have bled from injuries sustained during the attack. And he also found blood on the gear stick.

Larison sent the blood sample to the crime lab for DNA testing, where forensic scientists were able to build a DNA profile. He entered it into CODIS but did not get a hit. Although the case went cold again, the extra gumshoe work by Larison to collect and create a DNA profile offered a glimmer of hope that Martinko's killer would be found. It paid off 11 years later.

Resolution

In 2017, Cedar Rapids Cold Case Unit hired a company specializing in a new DNA technology called phenotyping. It created additional images of the killer based solely on DNA clues about facial appearance and ancestry. But it did not provide any new leads.

Investigators submitted the unknown DNA profile data into GEDmatch and found one person who shared DNA markers with the suspect in Martinko's murder. This DNA marker was given to a forensic genealogist who created a family tree that led them to four sets of the woman's great, great grandparents and reported that the killer might likely be a descendant from one of those couples.

As detectives contacted the people in the branches of the family tree, it led them to three brothers who had grown up in Manchester, Iowa. The brothers were placed under surveillance, and investigators began to attempt to secretly collect their DNA.

On October 29, 2018, a detective observed one of the brothers, Jerry Lynn Burns (64), drinking multiple sodas using a plastic straw. When Burns disposed of the straw, the investigator collected it and sent it to the crime lab for testing. The results revealed that Burns's DNA profile matched the blood found at the Martinko crime scene.

On December 19, 2018, investigators went to Burns's business in Manchester, Iowa, to interview him. After he refused to voluntarily provide a sample of DNA, detectives issued a search warrant to collect his DNA. When they returned to collect Burns's DNA, he showed almost no emotion. Detectives examined his hands and arms for scars possibly left by a cut he might have sustained during the attack.

When detectives told Burns his DNA test result matched the DNA found at the crime scene, he denied killing Martinko and was unable to give a plausible explanation for why his DNA was found at the crime scene.

On December 19, 2018, 39 years after Martinko's murder, detectives arrested Burns and charged him with first-degree murder. At the preliminary hearing Burns entered a plea of not guilty and the judge set Burns' bail at a cash-only $5-million bond. Fourteen months later, on Monday, February 17, 2020, a jury convicted Burns of first-degree murder. On Friday, August 7, 2020, Burns was sentenced to life in prison.[16]

Cold Case #31: Government of California v. Curry—Victim Mary Edith Salvani

What made this case so compelling is that detectives struggled to identify the Jane Doe body because she was a homeless drifter, estranged from her family, who didn't have a social network or a job. Her killer was also difficult to find due to different challenges the forensic genealogists encountered during his family tree search.

Summary

In the summer of 1982 a group of hikers discovered the body of a female on a trail in a popular meadow called Sheep's Flat along Lake

Tahoe in Washoe County, Nevada. They found her lying face down on the ground with men's underwear concealing two gunshot wounds to the back of her head. She was fully clothed wearing blue jeans, cream-colored tennis shoes with yellow toes, and a blue tank top with a one-piece blue swimsuit beneath. Detectives estimated her age to be between 25 and 35 years old, height at five feet, and weight around 112 pounds. She had hazel eyes and long, medium brown hair.

Police searched her body and the area to look for clues as to her identity but didn't find any identification. However, they found a set of footprints and followed them to a parking spot. A further search of the parking lot led them to tire tracks that led out to the highway and another set of two footprints that led back to the crime scene. Police canvassed the area and interviewed people, but nobody recalled seeing her.

An autopsy revealed evidence of both a sexual assault and a cesarean section.

After fingerprints did not match anyone in the missing people database, detectives named her "Sheep's Flat Jane Doe."[17]

With no identification, clues, or witnesses, her case turned cold. For the next four decades, Sheep's Flat Jane Doe lay unidentified in an unmarked grave at Our Mother of Sorrows Cemetery in Reno.

Resolution

In February 2018, criminalists with the Washoe County Sheriff's Forensic Science Division attended a lecture on forensic genealogy presented by Dr. Colleen Fitzpatrick of Identifinders International and the DNA Doe Project during the annual meeting of the American Academy of Forensic Sciences in Seattle. Detectives and criminalists believed these organizations could help with the Sheep's Flat Jane Doe investigation and the sheriff's office began working with them in April 2018 to try to identify the victim and the suspect.

DDP sent samples from Sheep's Flat Jane Doe to a private DNA lab, uploaded the results into GEDmatch, and found that the DNA belonged to the biological daughter of John and Blanche Silvani of Detroit, Michigan. The Washoe County Sheriff's Office (WCSO) uploaded Sheep's Flat Jane Doe's fingerprints into the Detroit Police Department database, identified her as Mary Edith Silvani, and discovered that she had been arrested for loitering when she was 25 years old. She was born in Pontiac, Michigan, on September 29, 1948.

Detectives chose not to release her identity at that time as the murder investigation was ongoing and the identity of the suspect was still unknown. Police waited until May 7, 2019, to officially announce her name to the public.

Silvani's extended family and friends did not report her missing as they believed she had just moved away of her own accord. She had not had an easy life, and friends said she didn't talk about her family.

Silvani had a homeless father and absent mother, who had been in and out of psychiatric institutions. Her parents died when she was 16, and she was left homeless, along with her two siblings, Charles and Bob. At age 24 she became pregnant and gave the child up for adoption because she felt unfit to keep the child. Silvani relocated to California with her brothers but slowly drifted away and eventually fell out of contact with them. Her whereabouts and what she did between 1974 and 1982 are unknown.

Now that WCSO had the identity of the victim, they had to focus on finding the killer. Detectives entered the DNA evidence from the crime scene into the FBI's criminal DNA database CODIS but didn't get a hit. As with Silvani's DNA, they worked again with the DDP staff. After they received the DNA testing results from a private lab, DDP uploaded them to GEDmatch.

Although they discovered a connection to a family, they spent more than two thousand hours on this case enduring some roadblocks along the way. The genetic profile led them to two sisters in Texas. One of them had a son out of wedlock and raised him under a different family name. But their tenacious work led them to the grandson of a couple who lived in Dallas. The couple had three sons but only one known grandson. The additional investigation cleared that grandson of being the suspect in the Sheep's Flat case and indicated that the suspect was an illegitimate child fathered by one of the sons. Investigators now had a possible suspect, James Richard Curry.

Curry had two children, who voluntarily provided DNA samples to a WCSO detective. The test results from the forensic science division confirmed that Curry's children's DNA matched the DNA at the crime scene.

A background check revealed that Curry was born in Texas in 1946. During his time in Texas, police arrested and convicted him for robbery, and the court sentenced him to prison in Huntsville. After his release from prison in 1977, Curry moved to Waukena, California, where he worked at J & M Locksmith. In 1983 Curry had been arrested as a suspect for a murder in the Bay Area. During the interview Curry confessed to the murder as well as two other murders. Two of them occurred around the time Silvani had been murdered on January 2, 1983, in the San Jose area, and the third occurred in early January of 1982 in Santa Clara. But the FBI did not have his DNA profile in CODIS because he had not yet been convicted.

When Curry worked as a manager of a storage lot in Santa Clara, he said he killed a married couple, Gerald and Sharon Novoselatz, who operated a nearby rival storage facility. While in custody, Curry also confessed to killing Richard Lemmon, Jr., of Bakersfield, California, and led detectives to his body, which he stashed in the Santa Clara storage unit.

Arrest

After police charged and arrested Curry with the murders and placed him in jail, he attempted suicide but failed. In the hospital, Curry succumbed to his injuries and died on January 7, 1983.[18]

DNA Doe Project Alias Case #1, Victim Lyle Stevik

In September of 2001, the Grays Harbor County Sheriff's Office received a call about a dead man at a motel in Amanda Park on the Olympic Peninsula in the state of Washington. When police arrived they found the man dead and hanging in the closet of his room from an apparent suicide. According to the motel registration book, he checked in under the name Lyle Stevik.

Conducting a background check on Stevik, detectives surmised that the name the dead man had given, which had no connection to any names in their missing persons database, was an alias. Detectives concluded that the name appeared to be drawn from "Lyle Stevik," a character in a 1987 Joyce Carol Oates novel, *You Must Remember*. They spent countless hours in search of the man's true identity, but to no avail.

In 2018, the DNA Doe Project took the case at the request of the Grays Harbor County Sheriff. In order to raise the funds required to complete the necessary DNA analysis, the DDP set up its first-ever "Doe Fund Me" campaign on behalf of the victim. The campaign was a quick success, as by this time "Stevik" had gained internet fame among web sleuths. Adequate funds were raised within 24 hours.

By March 22, 2018, DDP had obtained his DNA results and began analyzing them through GEDmatch and related genetic genealogy research. DDP's search led them to the victim's possible grandparents in Rio Arriba, New Mexico, where many of his DNA cousins' families originated. After hundreds of hours of following the branches in the family trees, it led them to a possible candidate, a 25-year-old man from California.

The Grays Harbor County (GHC) detectives contacted the man's family, who then conclusively verified his identity using fingerprint samples taken in his childhood. Per the family's request, GHC has kept his true identity confidential.

DNA Doe Project Alias Case #2, victim confidential

On May 2, 2014, the Kennebec County Sheriff's Office received a call from a landlord about a deceased man at an apartment located in Oakland, Maine. The forensic team determined that the man was between 40 and 46 years old and that he died from natural causes. In his lease application, the victim registered under the name "Alfred Jake Fuller" and provided a birth date of November 8, 1970. The personal items detectives found in his apartment included a prepaid Visa card and a "fugitive recovery agent" document. Detectives were unable to find records to match this information, which led investigators to speculate that he used an alias.

In 2018 the DNA Doe Project took on his case. After DDP uploaded the victim's DNA profile to GEDmatch, it led them to a name. His family confirmed his identity and they also requested that his true identity remain confidential.[19]

DNA Doe Project Alias Case #3, Victim Tracey Coreen Hobson

In August of 1987, a hiker discovered skeletal remains of a female corpse in a grassy area off of Santa Ana Canyon Road near Yorba Linda, California. Anthropological investigators estimated that her body had been there for about two months and that the young woman was in her early twenties. They determined she had been stabbed twice in the ribs and did not find any skeletal remains of her hands. The only items found were a red handkerchief and a cord. With no physical evidence available to identify her, detectives listed her as "Anaheim Jane Doe."

Eighteen years later detectives extracted DNA from the woman's remains and uploaded the results into the missing persons databases but it found no match. An attempt to identify Anaheim Jane Doe through facial reconstruction of a clay model also did not lead to her identity. She remained unidentified until January of 2019.

In November of 2018, the Orange County Sheriff's Department (OCSD) hired the DNA Doe Project to help identify Anaheim Jane Doe. For the next two months, Dr. Fitzpatrick and Dr. Press checked her DNA profile for matches in a genealogy website and narrowed down the possibilities of her identity to one surname. Then they contacted and invited one of the relatives to upload their DNA profile, and it matched. The Orange County Coroner's Office also used forensic dentistry to legally confirm Anaheim Jane Doe's identity as Tracey Coreen Hobson on January 15, 2019.

Hobson was 20 years old at the time she disappeared in the summer of 1987. She graduated from La Mirada High School and lived in Anaheim. It is unclear whether a missing persons report had been filed on her, and the circumstances of her disappearance and death still remain a mystery.

The OCSD has turned its focus to solving Dobson's murder, but the case still remains cold. Anyone with information related to this case is encouraged to contact Orange County Crime Stoppers at 1–855-TIP-OCCS or *crimestoppers.org*.[20]

While Dr. Fitzpatrick contributed her genealogy expertise to law enforcement agencies, another genealogist, CeCe Moore, was collaborating with them. Moore's path to forensic genealogy was quite different from Dr. Fitzpatrick's. Moore was an actress for over two decades. She performed leading roles in professional musical theater such as *West Side Story* and *Phantom*, appearing in numerous television commercials, as well as producing and casting many advertising campaigns for broadcast. Moore worked with many celebrated people in the entertainment industry, like Francis Ford Coppola, Michael Jackson, Jack Black, Dennis Hopper, Dick Van Patten, and Ed McMahon.

Moore's interest in genealogy began around 2000 when she took it up as a casual hobby. In 2003, her interest in genealogy grew when she discovered and read about FamilyTreeDNA, as well as other genealogy companies like Family Finder, 23andMe, Geno 2.0, and AncestryDNA. As she followed these companies' progress for the next few years, she turned genealogy into a full-time career.

In 2013, Moore started her full-time genealogy gig on the PBS television documentary series *Finding Your Roots* with Henry Louis Gates, Jr.

In May of 2018, Moore joined forces with Parabon NanoLabs to create and lead their Genetic Genealogy Services for law enforcement unit, boasting the unparalleled record of more than 100 successful identifications in the first 22 months. Her work has led to the first conviction, the first conviction through jury verdict, and the first exoneration in criminal cases where the suspect was identified through investigative genetic genealogy. Moore is the founder of the DNA Detective, with an online following of more than 130,000 people. She has helped law enforcement agencies in identifying suspects in more than 50 cold cases in one year using DNA and genetic genealogy.

On May 26, 2020, ABC debuted a new show titled *Genetic Detective* that features Moore. *Genetic Detective* follows Moore as she uses her unique genetic research skills to transform the face of crime solving. "By working with police departments and crime scene DNA, Moore is able to trace the path of a violent criminal's family tree to reveal their identity and help bring them to justice."[21] Two of the cold cases featured on Moore's show are in this book—the 1987 murders of Jay Cook and Tanya Van Cuylenborg and the 1996 murder of Angie Dodge. To contact CeCe Moore, visit the DNA Detective website (*www.thednadetectives.com*) or email her at *cece@theDNADetectives.com*.[22]

10

Lessons Learned

I have been blessed with a successful career in law enforcement, but I did not do it alone. I believe the major reason for my success has been the other successful people I worked with who embody the same passion, pride, work ethic, and high standards for their profession as I do. Each person contributed their unique skills that helped me solve cold cases. Along the way, they taught me some valuable lessons that I would like to share with you in this chapter. I hope these lessons along with the information I shared in the previous chapters will serve you well in solving cold cases. These lessons learned are dedicated to the victims and their families as the media rarely publishes detailed information about the victims.

1. It is very difficult to solve a cold case. Only one in five cases will turn up a "conclusively identified" suspect. Only one in 20 cold cases will result in an arrest, and only one in 100 cold cases will result in a conviction. There are more than 250,000 unsolved murders in the United States dating back to the 1950s.

2. Determine if correct investigative assumptions were made during the original investigation. Try and establish if the original investigators were on the right track and pursuing the "true" suspect(s).

3. There are too many suspects for many cold cases. Narrowing the pool of suspects and eliminating "white noise" is critical at the onset of the reactivated investigations. Ask why this person became the victim and what made the victim stand out (e.g., lifestyle, habits, hobbies, etc.). Determine where the victim and suspect intersected in life (e.g., work, residence, recreational activities, etc.).

4. According to the Pew Research Center, as the murder rate rose 30 percent between 2019 and 2020 in the United States, the clearance rate declined from 62 percent in 2019 to 54 percent in 2020.[1]

5. Forensic genealogy is a game-changer for cold cases (circa 2016); however, it will only solve a limited number of cold cases. Investigators must learn as much as possible about the possibilities and limitations of forensic genealogy, including "ghost" suspects and the importance of "common ancestors."

6. Contrary to popular belief, expended shell/cartridge casings recovered at crime scenes can sometimes yield touch DNA if evaluated by the forensic laboratory.

7. All fingerprint evidence should be evaluated with the FBI Next Generation Identification (NGI) system. The use of the NGI system has resulted in positive hits with fingerprints that AFIS/IAFIS did not link to a particular individual.

8. "Smudge prints" should be evaluated to determine if DNA can be extracted. Although these latent fingerprint impressions previously collected at the crime scene were unidentifiable, they still may contain DNA. The FBI and state forensic laboratories maintain photographs of fingerprints previously developed at crime scenes that may be unknown to investigators.

9. Look for pronoun changes in old witness statements. Pay close attention to individuals using past tense statements or "talking in past tense."

10. The majority of murders are not premeditated. Planned murders can be more difficult to solve. Consider this fact when selecting cases for reinvestigation.

11. A case is more likely to be solved if the victim died at a private residence.

12. Consider soil analysis that was potentially overlooked during the original investigation.

13. There are separate and distinctive clues for buried, concealed, dumped, or displayed bodies. These clues are important when evaluating and eliminating potential suspects.

14. Pre-event stressors for the suspect (e.g., lost job, divorce, financial problems, eviction, etc.) can be just as important as post-

offense behavior when evaluating suspects. Remember to focus on the following six groups of individuals: family, friends, co-workers, neighbors, associates, and acquaintances.

15. Look for the absence of the usual and presence of the unusual with the cold case you are working. Ask what is possible versus what is probable. Focus on what probably happened as opposed to what possibly happened.

16. Technology (e.g., pacemakers, fitness trackers, etc.) used by victims/suspects can reveal overlooked clues.

17. Cases are harder to solve if the victim was a drug user.

18. Do not conduct a "million-dollar investigation" and then complete a "10-cent" interview and interrogation of the suspect.

19. Multiple approaches for suspect interviews and interrogations can be fruitful, especially when conducted in nontraditional locations.

20. In most cold case investigations, the suspect surfaces early in the report and investigative files, usually within the first 10 to 15 percent of the recorded content in the original investigative file. Pay close attention to individuals who were identified, recorded, and/or interviewed early in the investigation. The suspect's name is typically recorded somewhere in the investigative file within the first 30 days of the investigation.

21. Be aware of cases that are not solvable solely by evidence. For example, the existence of a video of the suspect showing that he was near the crime scene close to the time of the murder does not prove he was at the murder scene.

22. Exercise proper preparation for interviews and interrogations by knowing the facts and what transpired during the original investigation.

23. Use an investigative tracking lead sheet for cold cases just like they are used for fresh homicide cases.

24. In most homicides, the murderer had some sort of relationship with the victim, whether short- or long-term. A suspect with close ties to the victim or the victim's family can hold the key to solving cold cases in which there is no apparent motive or prevailing theory as to why the victim was murdered. But be careful to not assume there is a close personal relationship between the suspect

and victim based on overkill at the crime scene, such as excessive stab wounds or extensive blunt force trauma.

25. A vehicle is often used by the suspect/victim during a homicide, and stranger-on-stranger murders are relatively rare.

26. As you read the investigative file, look for individuals who appeared to zealously insert or interject themselves into the investigation. If possible, ask the original detective if a particular person appeared to be overly helpful or showed up unannounced to provide additional information or inquire about the progress of the investigation.

27. Human behavior does not change regardless of the activity being performed, including the murder of a human being. Do not focus on looking for monsters, as often the killers are as normal as anyone else.

28. Everyone has a pattern of life. Focus on the person whose pattern of life changed after the murder. Familiarize yourself with the suspect's normal behaviors and identify any changes you see in the way he or she interacts with other people. For example, after a murder, a suspect who was normally punctual suddenly arrives late to scheduled appointments, activities, and interviews. The same is true vice versa.

29. Be aware of post-offense behavior and major shifts in behavior. Determine which suspect's life has deteriorated or dramatically improved since the murder. Both are potential indicators of guilt. A murderer will often move after committing the crime. Some will move a short distance (like two blocks), while others relocate to another state or thousands of miles away across the country. Comments recorded in the field notes or original investigative file that a particular follow-up interview was never completed because the witness had moved across town or to another state or county should be fully evaluated. The killer might move and leave the immediate area days or weeks after the murder to avoid suspicion and further contact with law enforcement. But this does not apply to a person who was scheduled to move before the murder.

30. Learn as much as possible about the victim's relationships with everyone in his or her social network. These include (1) family and friends, (2) neighbors and co-workers, and (3) associates

and acquaintances. The facts of the case and the suspect's prior relationship with these individuals will dictate the order of the interviews. The victim's history and background with these people will help collect information that might assist detectives in determining the motive for the murder.

31. Identifying the small details of witness statements and finding the inconsistencies will help narrow the pool of suspects.

32. Murderers do not tend to break up long-term friendships and associations unless there are underlying suspicions. Try to determine pre-murder and post-murder relationships and behavior changes of the suspects. Find out how the relationship changed after the murder or which friends and family members no longer associate with a particular person or group of individuals. Ask questions like the following: Was the person a high- or low-risk victim? What level of control did the offender use to restrain the victim? What type of relationships did the victim have with the people in her social network? What relationship exists between the location of the crime, victim, and killer?

33. Some cold case suspects may be unable to maintain stable employment and often move from residence to residence. Others may never leave their neighborhood or never change jobs. Some may turn to alcohol and drugs to cope with the murder, so consider suspects with DUI, DWI, or open container citations received after the murder.

34. The so-called "ghost suspect" is the exception and not the rule. A "ghost suspect" is a person not listed or recorded anywhere in the original investigative file as a possible suspect but who turns out to be the killer. Very few solved cold cases involve a "ghost suspect," though occasionally one comes to light via forensic genealogy.

35. Search for viable DNA on artifacts stored in the evidence room and submit it to the forensic laboratory for testing with the latest available technology. Be sure to use an alternative light source when you reevaluate old evidence. Consult with criminalists at your state or local crime lab to help you assess which items may contain probative evidence that can be analyzed with the current technology.

36. Every picture tells a story. The crime scene will tell you

a story if you just read it and focus on the clues. Document the inconsistent behaviors, visualize the actions that took place during the crime, and use your keen observation skills to note the clues in the old crime scene photographs.

37. Recognizing manifestations of behavior patterns in crime-scene photos provides insight into the killer and assists in linking crimes committed by the same person. It is also a means by which investigators can distinguish between different offenders committing the same type of offense. Three manifestations of crime scene behavior are modus operandi, signature, and staging. Become familiar with these concepts and the importance they play in evaluating cold cases.

38. When viewing the photos of a crime scene, allow the evidence to lead you to the correct suspect. For example, if the injuries sustained by the victim were on the right side of the victim's head and body, this could suggest that the killer might be left-handed. While this seems like a no-brainer, this is an example of how a detective whose focus is on a suspect-based investigation is so convinced about another suspect, who is right-handed, that the killer is overlooked for this minor detail.

39. When there is a significant amount of slashing and stabbing to the victim coupled with a sloppy crime scene that consists of blood transfer, signs of a physical struggle, overturned furniture, or misplaced objects, a detective should place suspicion first on a young person during the elimination of suspects process. A murder with ligatures, strangulation, or restraining devices will likely involve a sexual component.

40. Outdoor murders account for about two-thirds of homicide cases, indoor murders the remaining third. If the victim is found in a private residence, the case is more likely to be solved. If the victim found in the private residence is a female, the case is more likely to be solved than if the victim is a male.

41. The criminal history of a person who kills a prostitute is likely to include prior arrests for solicitation or solicitation of a prostitute charges.

42. Success rates for a cold case decrease if it involves illegal drugs, a drug user, a prostitute, or a homosexual.

43. A cold case that involves an unidentified body, skeletal remains, or an old missing person with no DNA or use of forensic genealogy presents the biggest challenge, which makes it a low priority on the reactivation list.

44. Many murders happen during the commission of other crimes. Most are committed by a single perpetrator and involve a single victim. The most common type of murder involves an altercation, involving a firearm or a sharp instrument.

45. Criminals think differently. They commit a crime to fulfill their needs and fantasies. The method and the manner of how the crime is committed directly reflect the criminal's personality. Complex crimes are typically committed by more intelligent killers. The smaller the crime scene, the more likely the murder was planned.

46. While most detectives focus on motive, spend time evaluating the crime scene to determine the real story of what happened.

47. Even if a suspect passes a polygraph test, do not immediately rule him or her out. And do not ignore other evidence that identifies him or her as the primary suspect. If you rule him or her out, do it through the process of elimination.

48. Monitor and evaluate every accomplishment made by you and your investigative team during the investigation that leads to building a solid case that identifies the killer. As you collaborate with your investigative team, think outside of the box and find creative ways to increase your chances of solving the cold case.

49. Make the cold case visual for a prosecutor with storyboards, PowerPoints, or other creative technological methods that will convince him or her that you have identified the killer. Anticipate resistance and rejection from a prosecutor and keep the lines of communication open. Find amicable ways to persuade a prosecutor the cold case is worthy and solid enough to present in court. View and treat the prosecutor as your ally because both of you are working towards the same end result—a conviction.

50. If you cannot find solid evidence or witnesses and/or suspects refuse to talk, then move on to the next cold case until new evidence appears or a witness or suspect contacts you and decides to share more information about the cold case.

51. Most family members would like a reasonable explanation of why their family member's cold case has not been reopened. Be empathetic to the family's interest to solve their loved one's cold case.

52. There is no "perfect investigation." A detective will make mistakes. One of the most common is when a detective's tunnel vision influences him or her to make the suspect fit the narrative of the crime. To avoid mistakes let the narrative direct you to the suspect.

53. The evidence-based investigation is more precise because it relies on evaluating all information and evidence for all the potential suspects to determine who is responsible for the crime. Focusing on a particular suspect or following your theory likely results in frustration, disappointment, and an unsolved case. But following the evidence will minimize mistakes, prevent you from wasting time, lead you to a suspect, and increase chances of solving the case. Do not try to make your theory fit the crime.

54. You must learn the case before you can start investigating it as a cold case. Therefore, review it over and over in a quiet place like the library.

55. Crime scene photographs and video recordings contain clues that were overlooked in the original investigation. When reviewing old photographs, start from the corners and work inward.

56. Identify and list all of the inconsistencies that were identified during the original investigation and during the follow-up investigative leads that have been completed as part of the cold case process. This will help you visualize the case and reveal the strengths and weaknesses.

57. When cold case suspects confess, it is normally a very matter-of-fact confession.

58. Remain in constant contact with the prosecutor who will be responsible for prosecuting the cold case.

59. The most logical explanation for what happened at the crime scene and how the victim was killed is normally the best theory to follow.

60. Never stop investigating and remember that an evidence-based investigation is far superior to a suspect-based investigation.

11

Unsolved Cold Cases

The information in this chapter is being shared about cold cases that remain unsolved as of this book's publication to offer a glimmer of hope for the victims and their families. Perhaps you have information that can help solve a case. Or maybe it will motivate you to visit some of the nonprofit cold case organizations in the Resources and Support Services section at the end of this book.

Unsolved Cold Case #1 Orange Socks— Victim Debra Jackson

On Halloween in 1979 detectives discovered the dead body of a woman in a concrete drainage ditch on the southbound side of Interstate 35 north of Walburg Road in Georgetown, Texas. She was found nude with only a pair of orange socks on her feet. Based on the track marks found in the patch of grass, it appeared that she had been dragged to the culvert and thrown over the guardrail. The autopsy report revealed that she had a large amount of bruising on her neck as well as other bruises caused by her body having been dropped from the overpass. She had been sexually assaulted and strangled to death.

The medical examiner described her as a white female in her late twenties, approximately 5' 4" and 125 pounds, with very long toenails and fingernails, long brown hair with a reddish tint, and hazel eyes.

Despite their best efforts, detectives were unable to identify the woman. Although she was a Jane Doe, she became as known as "Orange Socks."

In 1982, serial killer Henry Lee Lucas confessed to her murder. During the interview, Lucas stated that he thought her name was Joanie or Judy. He picked her up in Oklahoma. They had sex, and then he killed her and dumped her body. After Lucas described how he had dragged her body over the guardrail detectives felt he might indeed be the killer because it was a detail that had not been shared with the public. Detectives discovered, however, that someone had shown him images of the crime scene.

A further investigation ruled him out as the killer because Lucas was working in Florida at the time the woman had been killed. Detectives learned Lucas had a history of dubious confessions, upwards of 3,000. Eventually, Lucas recanted this statement.

In December of 1998, after the *America's Most Wanted* television show featured Orange Socks, an anonymous woman called in to the program and claimed that she had seen the unidentified victim hitchhiking the day of her murder. This tip didn't generate any leads.

In 2001, a missing woman's photograph surfaced that resembled Orange Socks. DNA testing, however, determined that there was no match.

In 2016 the National Center for Missing and Exploited Children entered her information into the database but failed to identify her.

In 2017, Williamson County Precinct 1 Constable Robert Chody ran for Williamson County Sheriff on a campaign to reopen cold cases and won the election later that year. Sheriff Chody immediately created the Williamson County Sheriff's Cold Case Unit in early 2018. It included a paid sergeant and detective and 21-person volunteer contingent that included retired detectives and law enforcement reserves. He appointed Sergeant John Pokorny to lead the unit. Prior to this assignment, Sergeant Pokorny worked cold cases in the homicide unit, then transferred to patrol sergeant and landed the leading detective position in the Williamson County Sheriff's Cold Case Unit.

Although Sergeant Pokorny had experience investigating cold cases, he decided to attend my seminar on how to solve cold cases. Pokorny said the seminar taught him how to approach witnesses and suspects, how to leverage the M-Vac, where and how to take advantage of the advances in DNA technology, how forensic genealogy works, and how to be empathetic and collaborate with the victim's family.

After the seminar, Sergeant Pokorny wrote a cold case policy for the Williamson County Cold Case Unit and prioritized the cold cases they had on file. He established a program to invite families of the victims to attend a presentation at the sheriff's office. Sergeant Pokorny's goals were to create a fresh start with the families of the victims, include them in the investigation process, and build a trusting relationship with them. During the program, he introduced the families to the cold case unit staff, explained their specific duties, how the cold case unit operates and how to contact each of them, and assured the families that their loved ones would not be forgotten by the cold case unit. The program was well received by the families.

One of the first cold cases Sergeant Pokorny decided to reopen was the "Orange Socks" case. He sent the victim's fingernail clippings to Sorenson Forensics, an independent lab in Utah. The test result revealed that there wasn't enough DNA to create a genetic profile. So Sergeant Pokorny sent additional fingernail clippings. Although the test returned with male DNA, he obtained a DNA extract from the University of Texas for additional testing. With assistance from the DNA Doe Project, the DNA was uploaded to GEDmatch to incorporate it into a family history search.

While he waited for the GEDmatch results he assigned forensic artist Natalie Murry to reconstruct an image of Orange Socks's face. He released it to the media in hopes that someone might be able to identify her. Someone did. A woman called the sheriff's station and claimed that Orange Socks was her missing sister, Debra Jackson.

Jackson's sister told the detectives that in 1977 Debra left her home in Abilene, Texas. Days, weeks, months, and years passed with no sign of her whereabouts. Her parents didn't file a missing persons report because Debra had a history of running away from their home.

To verify the sister's claim, detectives collected photos and also compared physical characteristics from Jackson's family. The scars on Orange Socks's lower legs shown in autopsy photos were consistent with scars from impetigo, a bacterial infection the family said Debra had contracted as a child. The Jackson family also recognized her abnormally long toes and uniquely shaped ear lobes.

Detectives collected Jackson's sister's DNA and sent the sample for a mitochondrial DNA test to focus on the maternal link and then sent the results to the DNA Doe Project, for further genealogy research.

Further investigation by detectives, via Jackson's social security number, revealed her employment history in the cities of Amarillo and

Azle, Texas. After her disappearance and before her untimely death, Jackson had been employed at the Ramada Inn and an assisted living facility called BUR-Mont Inc. Her last employment record in 1979 was with R. E. West & C. G. Cole Admiral PTR, Realty Investment LTD. Her social security activity stopped after her death in 1979.

In August of 2019, the DNA Doe Project confirmed the identity of Orange Socks as Debra Jackson.

While the discovery of Debra Jackson's identity was a huge breakthrough, it is only one small step to solving her cold case, finding a DNA match, and identifying her killer. If you have any information about Jackson that may help solve this case, please contact the Williamson County Sheriff's Cold Case Unit in Georgetown, Texas, at (512) 943-5204 or *coldcasetips@wilco.org*.[1]

Unsolved Cold Case #2—Victim Officer Jason Ellis

Officer Jason Ellis was 33 years old and joined the Bardstown Police Department in 2006. In 2008, he partnered up with a German shepherd, Figo, to be a canine officer. Former Bardstown police chief and current Shepherdsville Chief Rick McCubbin described Jason as a chief's cop: "What I mean by that is he loved the profession. He was dedicated. He was as active when it came to proactive policing as he was with reactive policing."[2]

On May 25, 2013, Officer Ellis had just finished his shift at 2 a.m., but Figo was not with him. He was driving a pool car so he did not have a camera mounted on the dash. On his way home at about 2:30 a.m. Officer Ellis left the Bluegrass Parkway on Exit 34, where he found the ramp blocked with tree limbs. He turned on his overhead lights, parked his patrol car to block the ramp, and began clearing the limbs. As he cradled several branches in his arms, shotgun blasts rang out from the embankment nearby. Pellets tore into his arm, side, neck, head, and other areas not protected by his bulletproof vest.

Soon afterward, a passerby pulled over with the intention of helping Officer Ellis. Instead, he saw him on the ground in a pool of blood. The man ran back and asked another motorist who stopped to call for help. The man did what he could to comfort Officer Ellis until help arrived.

After Kentucky state trooper Mike Garyantes arrived he found that Officer Ellis he had been shot multiple times with a 12-gauge shotgun and his service weapon was still in its holster.

The police received many tips that did not result in any good leads or suspects. Investigators also reviewed many of Officer Ellis's past cases and interviewed people he arrested to see if any of them might have committed the murder.

Six months after Ellis's murder, the Kentucky State Police featured a video asking for the public's help in identifying those responsible. At the two-year mark, the department issued a second video, this time featuring a plea directly from Officer Ellis's wife, Amy. But no one answered the call.

Finding a motive has been difficult, but police believe that whoever killed Officer Ellis knew the route he took home and his work schedule. They also knew enough about the area to realize that the highway exit ramp provided good cover, nestled between brush-covered rock walls. Detectives believe the killer planned the ambush and placed the debris on the road. In September of 2018, an anonymous inmate claimed he knew the motive behind Ellis's murder. He explained that Ellis had been shot because he was close to solving a burglary investigation of storage-shed units that contained high-end antiques and drugs. He stated that at least four men had been hired by an unidentified person to carry out Ellis's murder. However, he did not disclose their names or how he knew them. When asked why this information had not come out before, the inmate explained that the men involved were killed to keep the investigation quiet.

The Kentucky State Police invites anyone with information about the shooting of Officer Jason Ellis to please come forward and contact the them at the following email address: *EllisCaseETips@ky.gov*. You can also call the state police post in Elizabethtown at (270) 766–5078, the state police tip line at 1–800–222–5555, or the Louisville office of the FBI at (502) 263–6000 (wait for a pre-recorded message to start, and then press 2). The Kentucky State Police and other agencies have offered a reward of $218,000 to anyone who helps them find and convict the killer.[3]

Unsolved Cold Case #3—Government of Iowa v. Carter—Victim Shirley Carter

In this case as well as the O. J. Simpson case the families of the victims filed a civil suit against the alleged killers. The civil lawsuit trial of Brown and Goldman v. O. J. Simpson occurred after the criminal trial returned a verdict of not guilty, whereas the civil lawsuit trial of Bill Carter v. Jason Carter occurred before the criminal trial. What makes this case so unique is that Bill Carter is the father of Jason Carter, who was accused of killing his mother, Shirley Carter.

Summary

On Friday, June 19, 2015, Shirley Carter, a 68-year-old grandmother, was shot and killed inside her home in rural Lacona, Iowa. Officials said the killer shot Mrs. Carter sometime between 7 a.m. and noon. She suffered two gunshot wounds to her back.

Shirley's husband, Bill Carter, told officials he had dropped off Shirley at the couple's 132 Perry Street home after a morning coffee run before heading out to haul corn with his son, Jason Carter. Bill said Jason was 17 minutes behind him and that while Bill went on to haul another load from elsewhere, Jason went to his parents' house.

On his way home, Bill received a phone call from his daughter, Jana Lain, who said she had just received a phone call from Jason, who had told her he had found their mother dead in the kitchen. When Bill arrived at the house he found his wife's body on the kitchen floor in a pool of blood, her arms folded across her chest.

The county sheriff arrived at the home just moments after Bill and asked him to leave the house; the home ended up sealed for several days. Because he was not allowed to look around, Bill could not see that drawers in the office and bedroom had been pulled out, their contents dumped on the floor. Nothing, however, appeared taken; investigators found Shirley's purse, containing credit cards and $140, undisturbed, as was an envelope on the dresser containing $1,700 in $100-bills. Officers did not allow him to check his safe in the basement to see if the gun he kept there was missing.

As time passed without any progress or suspect, Bill's grief morphed into frustration, despair, and suspicion towards his son, Jason. Bill had provided officers with bullets previously fired from the rifle, which matched those recovered from Shirley's body. He accused officials of bungling the gathering of evidence and not collecting Jason's clothing and boots, which might have shown traces of gunpowder and blood, until 10 days after the crime. He spent $160,000 to hire an attorney and a private investigator. The results of their investigation led Bill to file a wrongful death suit against his son, Jason.

Bill alleged that his son used the rifle from the basement safe, which has never been found, to kill his mother, hid it on the property, and then retrieved it days later before authorities realized it was missing. Bill claimed Jason failed a lie detector test given by the Division of Criminal Investigation and sheriff's office.

The Civil Lawsuit

Given all the evidence Bill collected, he and his other children filed a wrongful death suit against Jason on January 5, 2016, and named him as the killer. Bill based the allegations against his son on a combination of potential motivations and circumstances. Jason was having financial troubles and had family farmland worth $5 million to gain. Bill also said Jason had been having an extramarital affair and that Shirley became aware of it and may have confronted Jason. He had not known about his son's affair until after Shirley's death.

The civil trial produced evidence and testimony from Jason that detectives did not previously possess. Court documents indicated that Jason incriminated himself by giving multiple inconsistent statements. Jason testified that he never touched evidence at the crime scene, but authorities later found his fingerprints on the evidence. He also shared knowledge about details of the murder that no one other than a person present at the time of the crime could have known and withheld information during the initial interviews after his mother's murder.

On Friday, December 15, 2017, a Marion County jury sided with Bill Carter and ordered Jason Carter to pay $10 million to his slain mother's estate.

Criminal Trial

After the civil suit verdict, allegations and accusations grew about Jason's possible involvement in his mother's murder. Although detectives struggled to determine a clear motive, Marion County officials and the Iowa Division of Criminal Investigation arrested Jason for first-degree murder. At the arraignment Jason pleaded not guilty.

The prosecutor claimed that the burglary was staged at Shirley Carter's home during the time of her death. I testified that the way the crime scene looked in Shirley Carter's house left no doubt in my mind that it was staged. The killer did not take any of the items—firearms, credit cards, money, jewelry—that a burglar normally steals. In my expert opinion, the act of burglary was never carried out at that crime scene.

Verdict

The jury decided that the prosecutor failed to prove Jason Carter killed his mother Shirley Carter and returned a verdict of not guilty. The identity of Shirley's killer is still unknown. In May and June of 2020 A&E's *Accused—Guilty or Innocent?* aired two episodes about Shirley Carter's unsolved murder. If you have any information that will help solve this case, please contact the Iowa Division of Criminal Investigation at (515) 725-6010 or the Marion County Sheriff's Office at (641) 828-2220.[4]

Unsolved Cold Case #4—Government of Pennsylvania v. Weigel—Victim William Burnham, Jr.

The following case is an example of how, despite all the evidence, work by detectives and prosecutors, and suspicion that the suspect on trial is the murderer, it is the people on the jury who make the decision of guilty or not guilty.

Summary

On the afternoon of June 25, 2006, police discovered the dead body of William Burnham, Jr., on the living room floor of his condo. The bloodstains on the carpet, window, and moldings revealed that Burnham had been brutally attacked with a blunt instrument. Burnham, 27, was a father of two and had recently started his own construction company.

According to the police report, Diana Weigel had been in Burnham's condo during the time of his murder. Diana, who is married to Dustin Weigel, told detectives that she had been having an affair with Burnham. On the evening before his death, Diana met Burnham at his condo. They had sex and both fell asleep. Later that evening a sound woke Diana up and she saw a man standing over the bed wearing dark clothing and a hooded sweatshirt over his head. It was her husband, Dustin.

Burnham also woke up, and a fight between the two men ensued. Dustin appeared to have some sort of weapon in his hand. During the tussle, Burnham managed to hold Dustin on the ground and said, "Let's talk about this." Burnham then stood up and walked out of the bedroom and into the living room. Diana fled into the bathroom. After she closed and locked the door, she heard noises that sounded like metal hitting an object followed by a gurgling sound from Burnham. Moments later Dustin burst into the bathroom, hit her in the face, and then told her to get out of the house. She left the house—without checking on Burnham—wearing only her underwear and a shirt and drove off in her car.

About 2:45 a.m., she tried calling Burnham from her cell phone to make sure he was okay but got no answer. She then called Dustin to tell him that she had left her pants and purse at Burnham's. He told her to meet him in the parking lot of a church. When Dustin arrived he had her belongings. He told her he had killed Burnham and would kill her, too, if she did not go straight home and not tell anyone what happened.

Police arrested Weigel and charged him with first-, second-, and third-degree murder, voluntary manslaughter, burglary, two counts of simple assault, and terroristic threats. He was remanded without bail.

Trial

The prosecutor, Bill Graff, argued that Dustin killed Burnham in retribution for a two-week affair with his wife, Diana. He built the case on cell phone records indicating that Dustin had been near Burnham's home at the time of his murder, DNA evidence from Weigel's truck that experts testified likely came from Burnham, and a baseball bat that police found after Diana notified them of its location in a nearby creek called Yellow Breeches.

Dustin's attorney did not deny that Dustin was at Burnham's home on Spring Road but argued that his client's DNA was not found in the house and that two spots of blood, one in the kitchen and one on a wall leading to the basement, were never identified as belonging to Dustin.

Verdict

Despite all the physical evidence and Diana's testimony, the six-man, six-woman jury acquitted Weigel. Burnham's murder case still remains unsolved. If you have any information that will help solve this case, please contact the Biglerville Police Department at (717) 677-9101.[5]

Unsolved Cold Case #5—Victim Elizabeth Hills Grant

Summary

Elizabeth Grant, a 55-year-old grandmother and prominent citizen in Winston-Salem, North Carolina, planned to visit her daughter, Alice Grant Chambers, in Connecticut. Instead, her daughter arrived in Winston-Salem for her funeral.

On July 29, 1969, when Grant did not show up for work, her sister went to her house and found her body lying in a pool of blood on her bedroom floor and blood spatter six feet high on the walls.

After police from the Forsyth County Sheriff's Office arrived, they discovered that Grant had been stabbed multiple times. Detectives noticed that her back window had been pried open, leading them to believe that the attacker had been lying in wait. They found four bloody knives, including a 16-inch butcher knife, near Grant's body, Grant's car keys in the car ignition, milk on the counter, and a pair of men's gray boots carefully positioned near her dead body.

Based on the description of the crime scene in the house, detectives surmised that Grant fought her way through the house, leaving a trail of blood before dying on the bedroom floor. Detectives were baffled at how the attacker was able to leave without tracking any blood across the floor. An autopsy report revealed that Grant, a widow who lived alone, had been savagely stabbed 54 times; there were no signs of sexual assault.

The forensic crime scene team recovered 15 sets of fingerprints in the house and strands of hair on Grant's stockings. DNA technology was not available at the time, but extensive tests by the crime lab identified the hair as belonging to an African American man.

Detectives discounted robbery as a motive because Grant had little cash and two valuable diamond rings were still on her fingers when police found her body.

According to people interviewed by Winston-Salem detectives, one neighbor reported that he heard a car door slam and engine noise from a car about 10:30 p.m. but never any screams for help. Another man said he saw an old green Falcon car with the license plate in the rear window instead of on the bumper and that the driver was middle-aged, with long, light-colored hair brushed back on the side.

After two boys turned in Grant's wallet that they found near a barbershop, detectives thought it odd that it had been in a predominantly African American neighborhood. Five months later construction workers found Grant's white handbag in a creek near 10th Street.

Detectives believed Grant knew her killer. A prominent New York psychiatrist, James A. Brussel, who often helped police solve cases by creating psychological profiles, echoed the theory. He described the killer as a mentally unstable white man between the ages of 30 and 50 years old.

Because of the 54 stab wounds to Grant's body, Brussel believed the killer had a deep-seated hatred and long-standing grudge but not necessarily against her. He was not there to kill but rather to plead or argue something because he used the four knives from Grant's kitchen. The attacker knew her habits, like when she would be home. Therefore, he concluded that it had to be someone from Winston-Salem.

Brussel deduced that the killer left the gray boots behind in the bedroom as a sinister and triumphant symbol of "I win." He ascertained that the man who wore the boots weighed between 140 and 165 pounds and was right-handed and flatfooted with a slight limp. Because detectives yielded few clues and were unable to establish a motive or even a concrete suspect, they had to stop the investigation.

Then, 25 years later, detectives received a tip that reopened Grant's case. Detectives recalled a man in his mid-fifties who had been interviewed in 1977. The man, whose name had never been released, lived in Winston-Salem with his wife and had no criminal record at the time. Detectives called him in again for questioning. When they asked him if he remembered anything from 1969, he responded, "That was the year the lady was murdered." His answer made the detectives suspicious, and he fit the profile for a theory brought up during the initial investigation postulating that a man 18 or 19 years old killed Grant after she had him fired and that the murderer's father protected his son by helping him cover his tracks. The man also fit the description given by one of the witnesses, which meant he might have been the father. Alice Chambers said she offered to confront the unidentified man to try to elicit a confession, but detectives didn't allow it.

If you have any information that will help solve this case, please call the Carolinas Cold Case Coalition at (336) 813-3299.[6]

Unsolved Cold Case #6—Victim Officer Kevin Brame

Officer Kevin Brame followed in his father's footsteps and joined the Dayton Police Department in 1993. Prior to that, he had served in the Air Force Reserves.

November 1, 1999, started out as an ordinary day off for Officer Brame. After he left a job-related court appointment, he received a call from his estranged wife, Carla Brame. She told him that his two sons, Antonio, 8, and Dominique, 5, wanted to see him and scheduled a time for him to see the boys that evening. Officer Brame took the boys out for dinner and shopping and then dropped them off at their mother's house around 8:45 p.m.

As Officer Brame left the house to return to his car, Carla and a neighbor heard gunshots and called the police at 8:54 p.m. She hung up the phone and ran outside to find her ex-husband lying down in the front yard.

When the Dayton police officers arrived, they discovered that Officer Brame had died of his gunshot wounds. It appeared that he had been ambushed and shot in the back as he was walking to his vehicle.

During the investigation police received only a vague description, like dark cars and a shadowy figure. Although a few people heard the gunshots, nobody clearly saw a suspect. It was a rainy night, so any evidence had likely been contaminated or washed away. Without witnesses or physical evidence, the detectives had no leads to identify a possible suspect.

Then, in 2003, detectives received a tip from a retired autoworker who said he had worked with Carla Brame at Delphi Corp. He said Carla and another co-worker, C. D. McCoy, had an affair and that he believed McCoy killed Officer Brame for $2,000. This information created a possible motive. Detectives questioned McCoy, who denied the affair and any involvement in Officer Brame's murder. McCoy was never arrested or charged. He died nine years later.

Officer Brame's family created a website called Justice For Kevin Brame in cooperation with the Dayton Police Department to gather facts on the case, news articles, and information about Kevin's life with the hope of justice being served someday.

There is currently a reward of up to $100,000 for information leading to an arrest in Officer Brame's case. If you have any information concerning what happened to Kevin Brame, contact the Dayton Police Department at (937) 333–7109 or email Detective Patricia Tackett at *patricia.tackett@daytonohio.gov*.[7]

12

More Cold Case Success Stories

This chapter includes additional cold case success stories.

Cold Case #32: Government of California v. Lazarus—Victim Sherri Rasmussen

About Sherri Rasmussen

At the time of her death, Sherri Rasmussen was the newlywed wife of John Ruetten, whom she dated in college. The two married in November 1985.

Rasmussen was an athletic, tall Scandinavian beauty, with light-brown hair, a broad face with high cheekbones, and wide-set eyes under dark, arching eyebrows. Her family and friends described her as brilliant, confident, and a goal-oriented person.

Rasmussen's compassion for other people motivated her to attend Loma Linda University School of Nursing at age 16. She began her nursing career at age 20. By age 27 she was named director of critical care nursing at Glendale Adventist Medical Center and served as an instructor and lectured internationally on critical-care nursing.

Rasmussen was a highly respected nurse. She enjoyed taking care of the patients and making sure they received quality care and treatment. One of her goals was to elevate the stature of the nursing profession.

Sherri Rasmussen-Ruetten was the beloved daughter of Nels and Loretta Rasmussen and the sister of Teresa. Sherri is remembered as very kind, gentle, compassionate, hardworking, and caring.

Summary

In February 1986 John Ruetten returned home and discovered his wife's dead body. She had been beaten and shot. As detectives viewed the crime scene, there appeared to be a terrible struggle. There was broken glass from the sliding glass door, turned-over chairs, a large pool of blood on the floor, and blood spatter on the walls. Rasmussen had been beaten badly and then shot three times, twice in the upper torso area and once in the abdomen. Detectives theorized that Rasmussen had entered her home while two men burglarized the house. There was no solid evidence at the crime scene that tied anyone to this crime: no witnesses, no gun, and no fingerprints.

A few weeks later, a burglary by two men had been reported near Rasmussen's home, which bolstered the detectives' burglary-gone-wrong theory. Police had rough sketches drawn of the two men, whom they considered suspects in the burglaries and Sherri's murder, and distributed them through the neighborhood. But Nels Rasmussen, Sherri's father, offered hearsay evidence that pointed to another motive for the murder.

Nels told detectives that a woman who once dated John Ruetten had been harassing her. He didn't know the name of the woman, but friends and co-workers verified his story and identified the woman as Stephanie Lazarus, a Los Angeles police officer. Ruetten confirmed that he had had an intimate relationship with Lazarus and that he had sex with her after his engagement to Sherri. Despite this information detectives still continued down the road of a botched burglary and never pursued Officer Lazarus as a suspect because there didn't appear to be any evidence to tie her to Rasmussen's murder.

The only conclusive piece of evidence detectives had was a bite mark on Rasmussen's arm they believed occurred during the scuffle and thus belonged to the killer. DNA at the time was not yet a viable forensic tool. Nevertheless, detectives collected the saliva from the bite mark and stored it in the evidence room before closing the case.

Resolution

Because of new DNA technology the LAPD Cold Case Unit quietly re-opened Rasmussen's case in May of 2009. Detectives submitted

12. More Cold Case Success Stories

the saliva to the DNA lab for testing. It revealed a shocking surprise and ruled out the burglary-and-two-killers theory. The DNA belonged to a woman. Immediately, Lazarus became a suspect. But detectives had to be very cautious with their investigation because by this time Lazarus had been promoted to detective. She had a stellar record and had received several police and community awards.

Detectives submitted a request to collect a surreptitious DNA sample from Lazarus, which the LAPD approved. They placed her under surveillance. One day they followed her to a local retail outlet where she discarded a cup and a straw. Detectives collected both items and sent them to the forensic lab for DNA analysis. Lazarus's DNA matched the DNA from the bite mark on Rasmussen's arm. The test indicated that there was a 1.7 sextillion-to-one chance that the DNA belonged to someone other than Lazarus.

The LAPD secretly planned Lazarus's arrest to avoid tipping her off and to orchestrate a plan on how to disarm her before the arrest. Detectives invited Lazarus to join them at the jail to discuss a case. Lazarus followed the detectives to the jail, where, as per policy, she relinquished her firearm before entering the jail. After she walked through the security point, detectives told her they needed to question her about the Rasmussen murder. Lazarus thought it was about an art theft case she had been working on but quickly realized it was about Rasmussen's murder. Although she answered all the questions and admitted to being Ruetten's ex-girlfriend and aware of Rasmussen's murder, she couldn't understand the reason for questioning her about a guy she dated over 20 years prior.

Detectives then pointed out that Sherri's father and friends indicated that she had exchanged words with Rasmussen about Ruetten, which led to several arguments. Lazarus claimed she couldn't recall. Then she shared her disapproval about this line of questioning and walked out of the interrogation room. After she stepped out, detectives arrested her and read the Miranda rights.

As the investigation continued, detectives discovered that two weeks after Rasmussen's murder, Lazarus reported her gun, a 38-caliber Smith & Wesson, stolen to the Santa Monica police. The ballistics tests and gunshot residue indicated that the same type of weapon was used to kill Rasmussen.

Detectives searched Lazarus's home and discovered a diary. In it, she had written a comment about her disappointment and frustration at Ruetten's marriage to Rasmussen. Detectives questioned Ruetten, who testified that he had met with Lazarus and that she had been so upset she cried and begged him not to get married. He also admitted that they had sex that day.

Detectives now found a motive: the love triangle had resulted in a murder. They concluded that Lazarus showed up at the condo armed with her 38 Smith & Wesson revolver. During the argument, an altercation ensued. At some point during the struggle, detectives believe Lazarus bit Rasmussen's arm. After which, Lazarus grabbed her gun and shot Rasmussen three times.

On March 8, 2012, the jury declared Stephanie Lazarus guilty of murder in the first degree of Sherri Rasmussen. Superior Court Judge Robert Perry sentenced Lazarus to a term of 25 years to life.[1]

Cold Case #33: Government of Florida v. Warren—Victim Marlene Warren

About Marlene Warren

Marlene was married at a young age to John Ahrens and had two children with him. Unfortunately, in 1969, John died in a car crash, leaving Marlene a widow and single mother at 19 years old.

Three years later Marlene married Michael Warren in Mount Clemens, Michigan, a suburb of Detroit. The Warrens lived there until 1973 and then moved to Florida, where they began flipping houses. They started buying land and buildings for rental properties, eventually amassing 17 throughout Palm Beach County. Marlene managed and maintained them while Michael built up a business selling and renting used cars.

Marlene was 40 years old at the time of her murder. She left behind a husband, Michael Warren; two sons, John Jr. and Joseph; and two sisters, Debbie and Lee Ann.

Summary

In May of 1990 Marlene Warren answered her door and was greeted by a person dressed as a clown in an orange wig and red bulb nose. The clown handed her flowers and balloons and then shot her twice in the face. Two bullets tore through her teeth and tongue and lodged in the back of her throat. Marlene died two days later in the hospital.

Four days later detectives found an abandoned LeBaron in a Winn-Dixie parking lot and found orange, synthetic fibers and brown strands of hair in the car. Detectives ran the vehicle identification number of the LeBaron and discovered it had been reported stolen by Payless Auto Rental.

Marlene Warren's murder led to an extraordinary and baffling murder investigation that led police through the darkest corners of the Sunshine State. They encountered accusations of infidelity, loan sharking, insurance fraud, chop shops, and stolen cars. This led detectives to consider Michael Warren and Sheila Keen as primary suspects.

As detectives continued to follow leads about Marlene's murder it appeared to be an open-and-shut case. However, none of the evidence detectives found was strong enough to arrest Sheila or Michael. What follows is a list of discoveries homicide detectives collected during their investigation, some of which is hearsay or circumstantial.

After the shooting detectives received an anonymous call from a female who said, "You might want to ask Michael Warren and Sheila Keen a few questions."[2] Then she hung up.

Detectives learned that there had been a connection between the Chrysler LeBaron and Bargain Motors and one of Michael's competitors, Payless Auto Rental. Payless had sued Bargain Motors over a deceptive phone book advertisement. The court ordered Bargain Motors to pay $35,000 in damages.

An employee at Bargain Motors told detectives that Michael stole three cars as payback for the lawsuit and that the LeBaron was one of them.

The employee said he drove Michael and Sheila to Payless and watched Michael get into the LeBaron, take the keys from the sun visor, and drive off. It appeared that Michael and Sheila had possession of the car before the killing. This however, was hearsay.

Hours after the LeBaron was found at the Winn-Dixie grocery store, detectives obtained a search warrant for Sheila Keen's apartment. They collected shoes, t-shirts, and jackets as well as a hairbrush, a bathroom trash bag, and a full vacuum-cleaner bag and found synthetic, orange fibers. Detectives attempted to question Sheila, but she remained silent and requested that a lawyer be present.

Detectives interviewed four people of a costume shop in West Palm Beach and Publix grocery store. The two clerks at the costume shop told them that a woman came into the store the Thursday before the shooting and purchased a clown suit, orange wig, white face paint, and red foam nose. One clerk identified the customer as Sheila Keen from a photo lineup. The other clerk did not.

Two Publix employees told detectives that about two hours before Marlene's murder a woman purchased a Memorial Day arrangement of flowers, with red and white carnations in a white basket and two foil balloons. The Publix employees identified Sheila Keen from a photo lineup.

An attorney, Christopher DeSantis, gave investigators a statement concerning his conversation in 1989 with Michael Warren as they left the courthouse. Michael asked him what the ramifications would be if a husband killed his wife on her estate. DeSantis replied, "If the husband had a friend who did it and they couldn't tie the husband to the friend, he'd get away scot-free."[3]

Michael Warren's friends told police that he "did not act very upset" after his wife's death. Witnesses told detectives that a few months before the murder they observed fights between Marlene and Michael Warren, as well as Marlene confronting Sheila Keen about having an affair with Michael. Relatives and employees said Marlene had been threatening to divorce Michael over numerous affairs and physical abuse. Warren's employees told detectives he said he would never divorce because his wife would get half his assets.

One year after the murder Michael, who was the beneficiary of Marlene's life insurance policy, received a check for $53,359.37 from Northwestern Mutual Life Insurance.

Despite all the circumstantial and hearsay evidence, detectives ruled Michael out as a suspect because he had a good alibi. Friends confirmed he had been with them on his way to the Calder Race Track. Neither did they have enough probable cause to arrest Sheila because of a statement from Jean Pratt, a witness who had been at the house during the shooting. Pratt said she thought the person in the clown suit was a man.

Detectives worked on the case periodically over the next 10 years. Then, in June 2000, Donald Carter, a former employee of Bargain Motors, called and told detectives that shortly after Marlene's death, Michael had given him several guns and told him to take them off the Bargain Motors lot. Carter said he stashed the guns in his parents' attic and believed one of them was the murder weapon, but a subsequent search of the attic turned up no weapons. Despite this information, there still wasn't enough evidence to continue the investigation. The case remained cold until 2014.

Resolution

In 2014, thanks to a $125,000 federal grant, the Palm Beach County Sheriff's Office formed a cold case task force with members of the state attorney's office and the FBI and reactivated Marlene's murder case.

New DNA technology allowed detectives to compare the DNA from the crime scene with Sheila Keen's, which had been collected in June of 1990 per a search warrant. In the reopened investigation, detectives sent Sheila's DNA sample to an FBI crime lab. Her DNA matched some of the fibers collected from the Chrysler LeBaron. This gave detectives probable cause to identify Sheila as a prime suspect.

When detectives tracked Sheila down, they were surprised to hear that Michael and Sheila had married 10 years after Marlene's murder and moved to Abingdon, Virginia. They also owned a fast food restaurant called the Purple Cow. The people in the area, however, didn't know about their past life, their connection to Marlene's murder, and that the Debbie Warren they knew was really Sheila Keen.

As investigators combed through the couple's new life, one former Purple Cow employee told investigators that Sheila, known to them as Debbie, got drunk one night and confessed to buying a clown costume and murdering Marlene Warren because the woman's existence was keeping Michael and her apart. Sheila also told her that she and Michael wanted to get married but had to wait for the attention on the case to die down.

Arrest

On September 26, 2017, law enforcement officials arrested Sheila. At the sheriff's headquarters, Sheila sat in an interview room making small talk about her nickname, "Debbie," and where she lived. But then the conversation turned serious when detectives told her that she was being charged for Marlene's murder.

She placed her head down on a desk, declined to say another word, and asked for a lawyer.

At the arraignment, Sheila pleaded not guilty to first-degree murder. The judge denied bail, and Sheila remains in jail. The state also filed a notice seeking the death penalty[4] against Sheila. As of the publication of this book, Keen is still awaiting trial. Despite Warren's trial, the investigation continues because detectives believe that more evidence might lead to Michael's arrest.

Cold Case #34—Government of California v. Mason—Victim Officer Richard Phillips and Officer Milton Curtis

About Officer Richard Phillips and Officer Milton Curtis

Officer Richard Phillips was 28 years old and had served with the El Segundo Police Department for two years. He was survived by his beloved wife, Carole; three children, Carolyn, Patricia, and Richard "Dick" Phillips, Jr.; his parents, T. Grady Phillips and Ethel Payne Phillips; and his siblings, Charles, Clayton, Eunice, and Marcella Phillips.

Officer Milton Curtis was 25 years old and had served with the El Segundo Police Department for two months. He was survived by his wife, son, daughter, and parents, Gus and Jessie Curtis. To memorialize the lives of Officers Phillips and Curtis, two of the four stars on the El Segundo Police officer uniforms, patrol cars, and City seal honor them.

Summary

On the night of Monday, July 22, 1957, a man approached four teenagers at a local lovers' lane. He pulled out a revolver, forced the two couples to strip down to their underwear and then bound and blindfolded them. Then he raped one of the girls. He left the teens alive and drove off in their 1949 Ford sedan.

After he ran a red light Officers Richard Phillips and Milton Curtis of the El Segundo Police Department pulled him over. Officer Phillips approached the vehicle, ticket book in hand, while Officer Curtis backed him up from the vehicle. As Officer Phillips began to write the driver a citation, the man caught the officers off guard, drew a gun, and shot both of them. He fired a total of six shots. The man fled the scene, dumped the car, and vanished into thin air. Backup units and medical personnel arrived on the scene to find Curtis dead in his patrol car, with Phillips lying mortally wounded on the ground. Both officers had been shot three times.

Police did not find all of the shell casings from the officers' guns and concluded that before their death one of them managed to return fire and wound the killer. When the detectives found the car, they lifted fingerprints from the vehicle but found no match. Despite some promising leads, the case went cold.

Three years later a Manhattan Beach resident called police to report the discovery of two watches and a chrome-plated revolver behind a house. The watches belonged to two of the victims.

Detectives conducted a ballistics report, which identified the gun as a rare, nine-shot, Harrington & Richardson 22 revolver. It had been purchased four days before the killings at a Sears store in Shreveport, Louisiana. The buyer gave the name G. D. Wilson and a fictional Miami address. Without any more solid leads detectives closed the case again.

Resolution

In September of 2002, the El Segundo Police Department received a phone call from a woman who claimed to have information on the death of Officer Phillips and Officer Curtis. She said her uncle bragged about the two murders, got away with it, and showed no remorse.

Detectives conducted a background check on the woman's uncle, Gerald F. Mason. They located Mason in his hometown of Columbia, South Carolina. He lived a quiet life as a gas station owner, husband, father, and grandfather with his family in a suburban neighborhood.

During the investigation, detectives discovered that Mason's fingerprint matched a fingerprint found at the crime scene. They also found the signature on the fake gun registration and YMCA form matched the signature on Mason's 1999 South Carolina driver's license application and on an automobile bill of sale. Detectives had three witnesses who identified Mason from a 1956 photograph as the man they had seen the night of the murders. El Segundo Officers Charles Porter and James Gilbert, who had briefly stopped to assist Curtis and Phillips before the murder, identified him as the man they had seen in the car. And a news reporter identified Mason as the man who asked him for a ride on his way to the murder scene.

On January 29, 2003, armed with a search and arrest warrant, detectives arrived at Mason's home to question him about the double homicide of the two officers. Mason declined to answer any questions and asked for a lawyer. When detectives searched the house, they found in his gun collection another rare Harrington & Richardson nine-shot 22-caliber revolver.

At the police station, detectives noticed a scar that appeared to be a bullet graze on Mason's back. After detectives mentioned the scar and presented the other evidence, Mason confessed to holding up the two couples and raping one of the women and said that he shot both police officers in an attempt to cover up the rape, robbery, and theft of the car.

Mason also told detectives, "I really don't have an explanation for why this happened. I wish I did." When asked why he had raped a 15-year-old girl, Mason responded that he no longer remembered. He cried and apologized for the pain he caused and for his actions on that fateful night.

Sentence

Mason pleaded guilty to the murders and was sentenced to two consecutive life terms. As part of the deal, the rape, robbery, and grand theft charges were dropped. At his sentencing hearing, Mason tearfully apologized to the families of Officers Phillips and Curtis. He said, "It's impossible to express to so many people how sorry I am. I do not understand why I did this. It does not fit in my life. It is not the person I know. I detest these crimes."[5]

The judge, as part of the plea bargain, granted him approval to serve his prison sentence near his family in a South Carolina prison. Mason passed away in prison on January 22, 2017, nine days before his 83rd birthday. He spent 14 years in prison.[6]

Cold Case #35: Government of New York v. Elkins—Victim Reyna Angélica Marroquín

About Reyna Angélica Marroquín

Reyna Angélica Marroquín was born in El Salvador, immigrated to the United States, and settled in New York. She lived at a Catholic home that housed single women and worked at a plastic flower-making company and as a nanny. Friends said she had a beautiful personality, with great love for her family and New York, and aspirations of becoming a United States citizen. She attended fashion school and dreamed of becoming a fashion designer. Her mother and two sisters survived her. Marroquín was buried in El Salvador. A month after Reyna was murdered at age 28, Marroquín's mother died and was buried next to her daughter.

Summary

When Reyna Marroquín suddenly stopped writing home in 1969, her mother in El Salvador feared the worst. Her mother had no other relatives in New York, so she had no one to call to ask to look for her daughter. It appeared that her daughter had simply fallen through the immigration system's cracks.

Around the same time, Marroquín called her friend Kathy Andrade. Marroquín told Andrade she had been having an affair with a married man and that she had called her lover's wife and told her about the affair and the pregnancy that had resulted. She said that the husband called her and that he was angry at her for telling his wife and threatened to kill her. Marroquín never revealed the man's identity.

When Andrade didn't hear from Marroquín for weeks, she decided to visit her, but she wasn't home. Andrade immediately contacted the police and reported her friend missing. Unable to locate Marroquín or find any evidence of foul play, the police closed the case.

Resolution

On September 2, 1999, a homeowner found an old 55-gallon drum in the crawl space of his house located in Jericho, New York. The homeowner called the waste management company to pick it up, but they refused to pick up the steel drum because it was too heavy. The homeowner decided to open the barrel to see what was inside. To his horror, he found the decomposed body of a woman.

He immediately called the police, who transported the drum and body to the local morgue for an examination of the contents in the barrel and an autopsy of the body.

The coroner identified the dead body as a Hispanic female in her late twenties who was pregnant and determined that she died of blunt force trauma to the head, which included 10 different lacerations, some with bloodstains. Items found in the drum included polystyrene pellets, a purse, two rings, one locket, a plastic flower stem, and an address book.

After detectives examined the drum, they discovered the following evidence that identified the dead woman and connected her to Howard B. Elkins, a co-owner of Melrose Plastics, a synthetic flower company.

- The drum had been made in 1965 and used for transporting dye. Detectives contacted the manufacturer, who identified the serial numbers. Their records showed the drum had been shipped to Melrose Plastic, a manufacturer of synthetic flowers, which was partly owned by Elkins.
- Forensic scientists examined the address book with infrared light, which revealed legible handwriting that included an alien card number that identified the dead body to be Reyna Marroquín and two names with phone numbers. One was Kathy Andrade, Marroquín's friend, and the other was Elkins.
- Elkins owned the Jericho house, where detectives found the drum and Marroquín's dead body, until 1972.
- Marroquín worked at Melrose Plastics in 1969.
- In Marroquín's address book, detectives also found notes she had written about her affair with Elkins.

- An anonymous call to investigators noted that the plastic pellets were the basis for making synthetic trees and also that Elkins was having an affair in the 1960s with a woman fitting Marroquín's description.

Detectives located and interviewed Andrade. She shared with them the same information she had given the police 30 years prior and said she had been looking for Marroquín ever since. But this time detectives had the name of Marroquín's lover. It was Elkins.

Armed with this solid evidence, detectives now had probable cause to search for Elkins and question him about Marroquín's death. They found Elkins in Boca Raton, Florida, where he lived with his wife and had raised three children.

When detectives interviewed Elkins, he initially denied knowing Reyna Marroquín but eventually admitted he had an affair with her. When questioned about the drum found at the house he owned in Jericho, he denied knowing anything about it. Nevertheless, detectives confirmed the identity of the dead body and found both a motive for the murder and a prime suspect. But exactly what happened that winter day three decades ago?

Detectives believed that on the day of Marroquín's murder, Elkins killed her because she was a threat to his marriage. He killed her with a blunt instrument and placed her body, along with her purse and address book, in the drum. He planned to put the barrel in his boat and dump it into the ocean. He filled the drum with plastic pellets to ensure it would sink. But he miscalculated the weight of the barrel. It was too heavy for one person to move. He had no option but to roll it into the crawl space of his house.

To gather more evidence to connect Elkins to the murder, detectives asked Elkins to take a DNA swap inside his mouth. When Elkins refused, detectives told him that they intended to obtain an order to take his DNA. But the next day Elkins committed suicide with a shotgun he purchased at Walmart earlier that day.

After his suicide, blood was drawn from Elkins and sent to Labcorp, where DNA testing determined with a 99.93 percent certainty that the unborn baby carried by the victim was his child.[7]

Cold Case #36: Government of Texas v. Davis— Victim Diane Maxwell Jackson

About Diane Maxwell Jackson

Diane Jackson was a 25-year-old phone operator for Southwestern Bell and a single mother. She was survived by her parents, David Malvin and Nora Lee Maxwell; her brother, David Maxwell; and her child.

Summary

In December 1969 a man by the name of William Bell noticed a suspicious man walking away from a shack located behind a service station. When Bell looked in the shack, he found the dead body of Diane Maxwell Jackson and immediately notified police. The autopsy revealed that Jackson had been brutally raped, strangled, and stabbed to death.

Jackson had last been seen parking her car, a Ford Mustang, in the Southwestern Bell company parking lot, which was located near the shack. Houston Police Department (HPD) detectives concluded that the killer had accosted Jackson at her car, forced her into the shack, and then raped and killed her. HPD detectives found three fingerprints and one partial palm print on Jackson's Ford Mustang. A database search on the fingerprints did not find a match. Nevertheless, detectives stored the fingerprints and partial palm print in the evidence locker. With no suspect, HPD closed the case.

In 1989, David Maxwell, Jackson's brother, asked the HPD to look over the original evidence and witness reports, in hopes of finding new leads. HPD ran the latent fingerprints and palm print again but found no match. At the same time, a local newspaper ran an article calling attention to the murder and asking the public for help. Despite the HPD's efforts, they had to close Jackson's case again.

Resolution

In the summer of 2003 Jackson's brother once again asked the Houston Police Department to reactivate his sister's case and conduct another fingerprint search. HPD honored his request, but this time they conducted a fingerprint search with the FBI's Automated Fingerprint Identification System (AFIS), which was established in 1999. The search identified James Ray Davis as a potential suspect. Further investigation revealed that Davis had been arrested for various crimes before and after Diane Maxwell Jackson's murder and had just finished a prison term nine days before the murder. This is why they found his fingerprints in AFIS.

Records showed Davis had been in and out of Texas prisons since 1961 for crimes such as possession of stolen property, vehicle theft, and burglary. After he was released from prison in Huntsville, nine days before Jackson's slaying, records showed he stayed in a Houston hotel near the crime scene.

One month after Jackson was killed, police arrested Davis for auto theft. The court found him guilty, sentenced him, and then released him after he served his time. Police arrested Davis again in 1976 in Waco, Texas, for rape. DNA evidence helped to convict him. But in July of 1992, the court granted him clemency.

Detectives located Davis in Texarkana. When detectives arrived at Davis's home to interview him, he acted friendly with them until they narrowed their questions to his activities in 1969 and 1970. Detectives asked Davis for his fingerprints, palm print, and DNA sample. Davis complied. Detectives did not arrest Davis but kept him under surveillance.

Although detectives had fingerprints to connect Davis to Jackson's car, they had no physical evidence that connected him to the murder scene. Therefore, the only way to prove Davis murdered Jackson was for him to confess. Nevertheless, detectives issued a warrant for his arrest. After detectives showed Davis the forensic evidence and photos of the crime scene, he confessed to killing Jackson. At the arraignment, Davis pled guilty. This is an example of how many cold cases need a confession from the killer to increase the chances of obtaining a conviction.

Sentence

On November 24, 2003, the court convicted Davis of the first-degree murder of Diane Maxwell Jackson and sentenced him to life without parole.[8]

Cold Case #37: Government of North Carolina v. Whitt—Victims Myoung Hwa Cho-Whitt and Robert "Bobby" Adam Whitt

About Myoung Hwa Cho-Whitt and Bobby Whitt

Myoung Hwa Cho-Whitt was born on January 27, 1954. Cho was a loving mother and a hard worker, sometimes holding down two jobs. She always found time for her son, Bobby. She liked music, loved to dance, and enjoyed watching Gloria Estefan's music videos and spending time in the pool during the summertime. One sister, Mina, and one niece, Susan, survived Cho.

A relative described Bobby as a sweet, brilliant, funny boy with a bright smile, gentle heart, and dry sense of humor who loved playing video games and air hockey.

Summary

On May 12, 1998, relatives and friends of Myoung Hwa Cho (44) had not seen Cho or her son Robert "Bobby" Adam Whitt (8). When they shared their concerns with Cho's husband, John Russell Whitt, he told them that she had left him and also taken their son back to South Korea.

After several attempts by Cho's relatives to locate them were unsuccessful, they assumed that her family in South Korea had convinced Cho and Bobby to cut off communication with John and their family in the United States. They eventually accepted John's story and didn't file a missing persons report with the police.

While relatives and friends searched for Cho and Bobby, unbeknownst to them police discovered the nude dead body of an Asian female along the side of a road parallel to Interstate 85 in Spartanburg, South Carolina, on May 13, 1998. It was the day after Cho's relatives and friends expressed their concerns to John Whitt about the disappearance of Cho and Bobby. The victim had been bound at the wrists, with ligature marks present, and the autopsy determined her cause of death was suffocation. South Carolina detectives circulated a postmortem photograph printed on posters, but no one identified her.

Four months later, on September 25, 1998, a landscaping crew discovered the skeletal remains of a young boy under a billboard along Industrial Drive along Interstate 85 and Interstate 40 in Mebane, North Carolina. Because the crime scene didn't show any signs of trauma to the boy's body, detectives determined he had been killed at a different location. Forensic investigators determined the time of death as during the spring or summer of 1998 and identified the boy as Hispanic.

Detectives submitted a composite drawing and bust of what the boy might have looked like to the media. They also sought the assistance of the National Center for Missing and Exploited Children but never found a match in their database.

Detectives didn't make the connection that Cho and Bobby were related because they had not been officially considered as missing persons at the time, detectives discovered the bodies in two different locations 200 miles apart, and there was confusion over the boy's race. Since detectives couldn't identify the two victims, they stored their bodies in the medical examiner's office. Cho and Bobby remained as Jane and John Doe cold case victims for two more decades. Detectives dubbed Bobby "The Boy Under the Billboard."

Resolution

Major Tim Horne, an original investigator of the case, in the early nineties said that he deliberately stored "The Boy Under the Billboard" file under his desk in an inconvenient position so that he didn't forget about the boy's unsolved case.

In 2018 Major Horne reopened the cold case and hired Dr. Barbara Rae-Venter, a genetic genealogy consultant, to perform DNA tests on Bobby's body. Dr. Rae-Venter is known for her work in identifying the Golden State Killer. Originally the forensic department identified the boy's race as Hispanic, but Rae-Venter identified the deceased boy as Robert "Bobby" Adam Whitt, who was Asian. This led Major Horne to a close relative who was able to provide more information on the deceased boy and confirm he was Bobby.

Based on additional information gathered from the family,

investigators determined that a strong possibility existed that the child's mother had also been killed during the same time period. A further DNA search led to a match of Bobby's mother, Myoung Hwa Cho, the Jane Doe police discovered the same year of his disappearance.

Suspicion quickly fell on John Russell Whitt (57). Detectives found Whitt in a Kentucky prison. He had been incarcerated for armed bank larceny charges in which he robbed ATM users and intimidated them with a weapon. During the interview, Whitt confessed to the murder of Bobby and Cho. According to Whitt's indictment, it alleged that he killed Cho in Concord, North Carolina, on May 12, 1998, and dumped her body in Spartanburg, South Carolina, and Bobby on July 29, 1998, and dumped his body in Mebane, North Carolina.

Sentence

In May 2019, a grand jury indicted Whitt on a first-degree murder charge in Bobby's death as well as charges for the concealment of his murder. Whitt and Cho's family cremated their bodies and performed a formal funeral on May 18, 2019. They laid the mother and boy to rest together in Mount Orab, Ohio. In January of 2020, Whitt pleaded guilty to two counts each of second-degree murder and concealing a death. The court sentenced him to 26 to 32 years for each murder, to be served consecutively after he completes a stint in federal prison for robbery in 2037.[9]

Appendix A:
Resources and Support Services

Unless otherwise noted, the information provided below is sourced from each organization's website, which is listed at the end of each entry. If you'd like to support one of the following nonprofit organizations with a donation, feel free to contact their office to learn how. Over the past several years, a plethora of well-intended nonprofit cold case groups and individuals have offered their services. But many of them have never solved a cold case and may become more of a hindrance than a help. Therefore, use caution and make sure to conduct thorough research on an organization's history before deciding whether to invite them to help with the investigation of a cold case.

Organizations

North Carolina Homicide Investigators Association (NCHIA) was formed in 1994. It grew out of a June 1994 working group in Raleigh, North Carolina. It was organized by the North Carolina State Bureau of Investigation (NCSBI) and a number of North Carolina homicide investigators in response to a series of unresolved prostitute homicides. The purpose and objectives of the NCHIA are to (1) provide homicide investigators an opportunity to exchange information relative to homicide investigations; (2) encourage such exchange of information; (3) support and encourage regular training sessions, workshops, and special investigative seminars; (4) share information relating to current and unsolved homicides within the state of North Carolina and the dissemination of such information through regular group meetings and publications; (5) establish a network for other law enforcement agencies across the United States to access information; and (6) promote quality homicide investigations within the state of North Carolina through the training, communication, support, and encouragement of the association's members.

NCHIA is a nonprofit organization whose officers include a president, vice president, treasurer, executive secretary, and a seven-member board of directors, as well as an advisory board of past presidents. The NCHIA makes an effort to ensure that all members have access to quality training by having an autumn training conference in November on the coast and a spring training conference in March in the mountains. The conferences also allow time to network with other investigators and present open cases for assistance from the membership. For more information about NCHIA visit their website at *http://nchia.org/*.

The Carolinas Cold Case Coalition is a volunteer-based, nonprofit, organization comprised of retired local, state, and federal law enforcement officers who have extensive backgrounds and experience with death investigations and violent crimes. The coalition members provide case consultations, case reviews, evaluations, advice, and suggestions free of charge to law enforcement practitioners working cold cases and unsolved violent crimes. Coalition members also provide cold case training and investigative support.

The concept for the Carolinas Cold Case Coalition first emerged in 1999 during meetings at the North Carolina Homicide Investigators Association (NCHIA) annual training conference. All coalition members are keenly familiar with the mechanics of homicide investigation and the components required for solving cold cases.

Quarterly case reviews are conducted in Winston-Salem, North Carolina, and Myrtle Beach, South Carolina, where law enforcement practitioners meet with coalition members and present their cases for investigative ideas and suggestions. Coalition members conduct case reviews throughout the year at the coalition office in Colfax, North Carolina. To request assistance in a quarterly case review visit the website or contact a coalition staff at (336) 813–3299, *www.coldcasecoalition.org*.

The Cold Case Foundation was founded in November 2011. Yellowstone County Sheriff Mike Linder developed the Cold Case

Foundation (CCF) to bring back to life a series of cold homicides that had been dormant for a number of years. Linder felt these cases deserved attention and theorized that even a small law enforcement agency should be able to mobilize the manpower and resources to reopen and re-investigate cases that were still solvable.

CCF's mission is to speak for those who can't speak for themselves by seeking answers and justice for victims and their families. It strives to be the ultimate resource for homicide, missing persons, unidentified bodies, and rape/sexual assault cold cases with serial characteristics through funding, consulting, training, networking, and advocating for the victims and their families. For more information about the Cold Case Foundation visit their website at *http://www.coldcasefoundation.org/*.

The Vidocq Society is a 501c(3) nonprofit organization that offers case assistance to law enforcement at no cost to the investigating agency. Its purpose is to act as a catalyst by offering their opinion on how to help law enforcement investigators, prosecutors, victims' families, and the media solve selected cold cases.

The Vidocq Society meets once a month and hears one case per meeting. Small- and medium-sized police departments apply to be allowed to present to the group. A cold case brought before the Vidocq Society should have at least a body, a crime scene, and some physical evidence. The case must be over two years old and the police department must be willing to cooperate.

Vidocq Society members come from all walks of life and include experienced investigators from federal, state, and local law enforcement agencies and the private sector; internationally renowned forensic experts in the fields of pathology, criminology, dactylography, forensic dentistry, psychology, polygraphy, and anthropological facial reconstruction; and many former federal, state, and local career prosecutors. All share a dedication to the search for truth and justice that binds them together in the tradition of the great detectives past and present.

The Training Committee is headed by Ed Gaughan, a former senior detective in the Philadelphia Police Department who provides pro bono assistance in the form of cold case homicide seminars by forensic and investigative experts to law enforcement agencies, regional cold case associations, and prosecutors' offices. During these seminars, investigators can request that the experts review their entire case file, including evidence available for forensic laboratory analysis. For more information visit their website at *https://www.vidocq.org/*.

The American Investigative Society of Cold Cases (AISOCC) is a nonprofit, volunteer-based organization of professional investigators whose sole mission is to assist in solving cold cases. AISOCC uses crime scene reconstruction, crime scene assessments, inductive/deductive criminal profiling, and reasoning to look towards finding resolutions for cold cases. Collectively, it offers advice and suggestions to law enforcement professionals for furthering their cases. If you are in law enforcement and you have a cold case, contact them for a professional review at *http://www.aisocc.com*.

Forensic Genealogy and DNA Experts

Identifinders International and DNA Doe Project. Colleen Fitzpatrick, PhD, is the founder of Identifinders International (IFI). IFI is comprised of highly skilled genetic and traditional genealogists with expertise in both criminal and other genealogical cases. Dr. Fitzpatrick is a forensic genealogical consultant for major military and civilian organizations and the founder of the DNA Doe Project (DDP). DDP is an exciting new initiative that uses genetic genealogy to identify John and Jane Does. DDP's fund program allows smaller and less-well-funded agencies to take advantage of its services. DDP is an all-volunteer organization that has attracted some of the best genetic genealogists in the industry. To learn more about Dr. Fitzpatrick and how to contact her, visit Identifinders International at *https://identifinders.com* and DNA Doe Project at *https://dnadoeproject.org/*.

Ryan Forensic and Pure Gold Forensics. Suzanna Ryan is the owner of Ryan Forensic. Ryan also serves as a DNA analyst at Pure Gold Forensics, which is a private accredited forensic DNA lab in Southern California. She has over 20 years of experience as a forensic serology and DNA expert. She is a member of the American Academy of Forensic Sciences, the California Association of Criminalists, and is certified as a Diplomate in Molecular Biology by the American Board of Criminalistics.

Ryan has worked for both private and public DNA labs. This includes experience at the Bode Technology Group, the Florida Department of Law Enforcement Crime Lab, the Charlotte-Mecklenburg Police Department Crime Lab, and Crime Scene Technologies. With her 10 years of forensic laboratory experience and 10 additional years of consulting experience, Suzanna has had extensive experience conducting DNA casework and technically reviewing DNA data and case files from a number of different local, county, state, federal, and military DNA laboratories.

For more information about Suzanna Ryan and how to contact her, visit Ryan Forensic at *http://ryanforensicdna.com/* and Pure Gold Forensics at *https://www.puregoldforensics.com/*.

Sexual Assault Kit Initiative (SAKI). SAKI's funding helps link victims to advocates and needed services, assists jurisdictions with implementing best practices and comprehensive reform to bring perpetrators to justice, and increases safety in communities by preventing future sexual assaults.

The SAKI Training and Technical Assistance (TTA) program also offers expertise and assistance to jurisdictions as they establish widespread, evidence-based, sustainable practices for (1) collecting and processing forensic evidence, (2) investigating and prosecuting sexual assault cases from previously unsubmitted sexual assault kits, and (3) supporting survivors of sexual assault.

SAKI continues to make a significant difference by improving the response to sexual assault and identifying and apprehending violent offenders. The impact of SAKI is being felt at the community level both in terms of getting dangerous offenders off the street and empowering victims to come forward. In Fayetteville, North Carolina, victims are more confident to come forward and report to law enforcement because of the victim-centered outreach from the police department and their community partners.

In Wayne County, Michigan, more than 60 sexual assault offenders have been convicted. In Cuyahoga County, Ohio, the Sexual Assault Task Force helped link a serial rapist to seven cases. In Las Vegas, the Metro Police have received 43 CODIS hits and arrested eight offenders.

Other states are also experiencing important changes. For example, for the first time in history, the attorney general of Montana has formed a task force to conduct a census of unsubmitted kits and has identified approximately 1,400 kits across the state, which will be sent for testing.

Since 2015, the program has inventoried 61,134 kits and sent 44,952 for testing. Of the 39,565 kits that could be tested to completion, 13,521 produced a DNA profile of high enough quality that it could be entered into CODIS. When the 13,521 kits were entered into CODIS, 6,366 matched to an entry already there. In 2019, the Bureau of Justice awarded the National Sexual Assault Kit Initiative $40 million to help law enforcement agencies and prosecutors test DNA samples from rape victims that have not been submitted to crime laboratories, As well as an additional $6 million for training and technical assistance.[1] For more information about SAKI and how to submit a grant visit *https://www.sakitta.org/*.

Support Services for Families of Victims

The William Burnham, Jr., Death Scene Awareness Project. Nancy Kreiner created the Death Scene Awareness Project as a result of her son's murder in 2006. It is a nonprofit organization that respectfully humanizes the process of death investigation and gives the victim and his or her family a voice for justice. It accomplishes this by reaching out to support the tireless professionals who carry out death investigations every day in more than 3,000 jurisdictions in the United States.

The Death Scene Awareness Project diligently encourages the death investigation community to elevate the valuable work it requires to properly investigate a homicide crime scene. It provides moving presentations to law enforcement professionals such as first responders, forensic scientists, coroners and pathologists, death investigators, and the pre-hospital emergency medical teams.

The Death Scene Awareness Project also hosts a yearly conference that provides speakers who present cutting-edge information and a forum where death investigation professionals can exchange ideas and network with one another.

The William Burnham, Jr., Death Scene Awareness Project has great empathy and compassion for the families of victims. It encourages communication and involvement with them and provides resource links to reliable organizations they can access with confidence and trust if they find themselves seeking information and assistance. For more information about the Death Scene Awareness Project visit *https://www.deathsceneawareness.org.*

Momma On a Mission, Inc. provides a voice and emotional and community support to help families seek justice and resolution for the murder of their loved ones. It embraces other families with love and services they may need to benefit them during their time of grief and as they make funeral arrangements.

Monique Willis started Momma On a Mission (MOM) after her son Alonzo Thomas IV was shot and killed on April 5, 2014. His case is still unsolved, and Willis continues to seek justice for her son. One of the services MOM offers families is canvassing neighborhoods with flyers and posting information on billboards about lost loved ones. It also hosts monthly group meetings on the third Monday of every month at 7 p.m. For more information about MOM visit their website at *https://mommaonamissioninc.org.*

Project Cold Case is a nonprofit organization born out of a desire to provide hope to families of unsolved homicide victims. It has an ambitious goal of publicizing all unsolved homicides in the United States while linking information, families, and law enforcement, and ultimately, helping to solve cold cases.

Ryan Beckmann founded Project Cold Case after his dad's murder in 2009 and found a passion for helping others as a victim advocate serving other families that had lost loved ones to homicide. Ryan has worked closely with Florida Senator Aaron Bean and his team in an attempt to draft meaningful cold case legislation that will make Florida a safer place and inspire other states to do the same.

Project Cold Case's work has led to a significant number of cold case arrests, particularly with the technological advances of DNA testing. It also features more than 150 cold cases on its Case Spotlights Page and thousands more in its Cold Case Database Page. For more information about Project Cold Case visit *https://www.projectcoldcase.org/.*

Appendix B:
List of Cases in Order of Appearance in This Book

1. Government of South Carolina v. Gardner—Victim Melissa McLauchlin—Homicide Case
2. Cold Case #1—Government of Virgin Islands v. Petersen—Victim Dana Bartlett
3. Unsolved Cold Case—Government of North Carolina v. Pope—Victim Nancy Pope
4. Cold Case #2—Government of South Carolina v. Paalan—Victim Annie Tahan
5. Cold Case #3—Government of North Carolina v. Smith—Victim Alanda Jean Yusko
6. Cold Case #4—Government of Florida v. Johnstone—Victim Anita Mae Carter Lukander
7. Cold Case #5—Government of Virginia v. Whittle—Victim Pamela Ann Kimbrue
8. Cold Case #6—Government of Virginia v. Deshazo—Victim Allen McClendon
9. Cold Case #7—Government of Florida v. Hinton—Victim Shannon Melendi
10. Cold Case #8—Government of North Carolina v. Crumitie—Victims Michael Gretsinger, Sharon Cook Crumitie, and James Luther Blanks
11. Cold Case #9—Government of Virginia v. Coleman—Victim Steven S. November

List of Cases in Order of Appearance in This Book 319

12. Cold Case #10—Government of Texas v. Smith and Hamilton—Victim Scott Dunn

13. Cold Case #11—Government of Philadelphia v. Dickson—Victim Deborah Wilson

14. Cold Case #12—Government of North Carolina v. Alvarez—Victims Troy and LaDonna French

15. Cold Case #13—Government of Florida v. Kuenn—Victim Carol Hutto

16. Cold Case #14—Government of Ohio v. Elkins—Victim Judy Johnson

17. Cold Case #15—Government of New Jersey v. List—Victims Helen List, Alma List, Patricia List, John List, Jr., and Frederick List

18. Cold Case #16—Government of Pennsylvania v. Rorrer—Victim Joann Katrinak (Case featured in *Wrong Man* Season 2)

19. Cold Case #17—Government of Florida v. Brown—Victim Identities Not Revealed

20. Cold Case #18—Government of North Carolina v. Lawing—Victim Lacoy McQueen

21. Cold Case #19—Government of California v. Kenneth Clair—Victim Linda Faye Rodgers (Case featured in *Wrong Man* Season 2)

22. Cold Case #20—Government of California v. Laudenberg—Victims Lois Petrie, Catherine Medina, Anna Felch, Irene Hind, Maude Burgess, and Leah Griffin

23. Cold Case #21—Government of Florida v. Hartley—Victim Lieutenant Verle Lee Hartley

24. Cold Case #22—Government of Mississippi v. Flowers—Victims Bertha Tardy, Carmen Rigby, Robert Golden, and Derrick "Bobo" Stewart (Case featured in *Wrong Man* Season 1)

25. Cold Case # 23—Government of Washington v. Evaristo Salas—Victim Jose Arreola (Case featured in *Wrong Man* Season 1)

26. Cold Case #24—Government of Tennessee v. Smith—Victim Jessie Nicole Morrison (Case featured in *Wrong Man* Season 2)

27. Cold Case #25—Government of Washington v. Talbott—Victims Jay Cook and Tanya Van Cuylenborg

28. Cold Case #26—Government of Idaho v. Tapp and Dripps—

Victim Angie Raye Dodge (Wrongful conviction to cold case to solved case featured in *Wrong Man* Season 1)

29. Cold Case #27—Government of California v. Davis and Green—Victim Jane Hylton

30. Cold Case #28—Government of Arizona v. Miller—Victims Angela Brosso and Melanie Bernas

31. Cold Case #29—Government of Washington v. Nicholas—Victim Sarah Yarborough

32. Cold Case #30—Government of Iowa v. Burns—Victim Michelle Martinko

33. DNA Doe Project Alias Case #1—Lyle Stevik

34. DNA Doe Project Alias Case #2—Victim confidential

35. DNA Doe Project Alias Case #3—Tracey Coreen Hobson

36. Cold Case #31—Government of California v. Curry—Victim Mary Edith Salvani

37. Unsolved Cold Case #1—Orange Socks—Victim Debra Jackson

38. Unsolved Cold Case #2—Victim Officer Jason Ellis

39. Unsolved Cold Case #3—Government of Iowa v. Carter—Victim Shirley Carter

40. Unsolved Cold Case #4—Government of Pennsylvania v. Weigel—Victim William Burnham, Jr.

41. Unsolved Cold Case #5—Victim Elizabeth Hills Grant

42. Unsolved Cold Case #6—Victim Officer Kevin Brame

43. Cold Case #32—Government of California v. Lazarus—Victim Sherri Rasmussen

44. Cold Case #33—Government of Florida v. Warren—Victim Marlene Warren

45. Cold Case #34—Government of California v. Mason—Victims Officer Richard Phillips and Officer Milton Curtis

46. Cold Case #35—Government of New York v. Elkins—Victim Reyna Angélica Marroquín

47. Cold Case #36—Government of Texas v. Davis—Victim Diane Maxwell Jackson

48. Cold Case #37—Government of North Carolina v. Whitt—Victims Myoung Hwa Cho-Whitt and Robert "Bobby" Adam Whitt

Chapter Notes

Preface

1. "It's Not Just Chicago: Murder Clearance Rate As a 'National Disaster,'" Firearms Owners Against Crime, September 9, 2018, https://foac-pac.org/Its-Not-Just-Chicago-Murder-Clearance-Rate-Is-A-national-Disaster/News-Item/8687.

Introduction

1. Mike Mount, "Philippine Blast 'Suicide Attack,'" CNN, Thursday, October 3, 2002, https://edition.cnn.com/2002/WORLD/asiapcf/southeast/10/02/philippines.blast/index.html.
2. Ibid.
3. Martin Kaste, "Open Cases: Why One-Third of Murders in America Go Unresolved," NPR, March 30, 2015, https://www.npr.org/2015/03/30/395069137/open-cases-why-one-third-of-murders-in-america-go-unresolved.
4. Eric Martin, Elizabeth Dawn Schwarting, and Ruby J. Chase, "Serial Killer Connections Through Cold Cases," *National Institute of Justice Journal*, June 15, 2020, https://nij.ojp.gov/topics/articles/serial-killer-connections-through-cold-cases; "NIJ Journal 282: Serial Killer Connections Through Cold Cases," Before It's News, January 28, 2021, https://beforeitsnews.com/crime-all-stars/2021/01/nij-journal-282-serial-killer-connections-through-cold-cases-2486450.html.
5. NCIS-3 Chapter 6: Investigative Theory and Procedures, POC: Code 23C, December 6, 2020, https://www.ncis.navy.mil/Portals/25/Documents/Reading%20Room/Operational%20Records/NCIS%203%20release.pdf?ver=2020-05-28-151815-053.
6. "NCIS Did Not Forget Them," *NCIS Bulletin*, Volume II, Edition 6, October 1998, https://ncisahistory.org/wp-content/uploads/2017/06/NCIS-Bulletin-Vol-II-Edition-6-October-1998.pdf.
7. Fleming Smith, "40 Years Later, NCIS Works to Solve Murder of 21-Year-Old at Charleston Naval Base," *The Post and Courier*, December 31, 2019, https://www.postandcourier.com/news/40-years-later-ncis-works-to-solve-murder-of-21-year-old-at-charleston-naval/article_4d973cdc-21b3-11ea-9517-d7a5b519fe65.html.
8. U.S. District Court for the District of the U.S. Virgin Islands—19 F.Supp 2d 430 (D.V.I. 1998), August 28, 1998, https://law.justia.com/cases/federal/district-courts/FSupp2/19/430/2530348/.
9. Thomas J. Leeper, "Means, Motive, and Opportunity: Addressing Gun Violence Requires Moving Beyond the Usual Frames," *Psychology Today*, December 15, 2012, https://www.psychologytoday.com/us/blog/polarized/201212/means-motive-and-opportunity.
10. "Violent Crime Scene Analysis: Modus Operandi, Signature, and Staging," *Criminal Profiling*, August 9, 2001, https://criminalprofiling.com/violent-crime-scene-analysis-modus-operandi-signature-and-staging/.
11. Daryl Clemens, "Violent Crime Scene Analysis: Modus Operandi, Signature, and Staging," *Criminal Profiling*, January 26, 2013, https://crimeandclues.com/2013/01/26/violent-crime-scene-analysis-modus-operandi-signature-and-staging/.

12. A. Minello and G. Dallas-Zuanna, "A Gender Geography of Intentional Homicide Within and Outside of the Family: Male and Female Murders in Europe, the U.S. and Canada (2003–15)," *Sage Journal*, November 11, 2019, https://journals.sagepub.com/doi/full/10.1177/1477370819884251.

13. "Serving Survivors of Homicide Victims During Cold Case Investigations: A Guide for Developing a Law Enforcement Protocol," National Sheriffs' Association, August 2011, https://www.sheriffs.org/sites/default/files/uploads/guidefordevelopingalawenforcementprotocolaugust172011.pdf.

14. "The FBI's Combined DNA Index System (CODIS) Hits Major Milestone," *FBI News*, April 21, 2021, https://www.fbi.gov/news/pressrel/press-releases/the-fbis-combined-dna-index-system-codis-hits-major-milestone.

15. Bruce Budowle, "This New Advancement in Interpreting DNA Evidence Could be a Game Changer," Route Fifty, February 24, 2021, https://www.routefifty.com/public-safety/2021/02/new-advancement-dna-evidence/172276/.

16. "National Integrated Ballistic Information Network (NIBIN)," ATF, December 6, 2021, https://www.atf.gov/firearms/national-integrated-ballistic-information-network-nibin.

17. Jory Heckman, "Automated Fingerprint Matching at FBI Allows Employees to Shift to Higher-value Work," Federal News Network, February 17, 2020, https://federalnewsnetwork.com/automation/2020/02/automated-fingerprint-matching-at-fbi-allows-employees-to-shift-to-higher-value-work/.

18. Chris Burt, "NGI Delivers Faster Results from More Biometric Modalities with No Shopping Mall Storage," September 20, 2021, https://www.biometricupdate.com/202109/ngi-delivers-faster-results-from-more-biometric-modalities-with-no-shopping-mall-storage.

19. Raffi Khatchadourian, "How Your Family Tree Could Catch a Killer," *The New Yorker*, November 22, 2021, https://www.newyorker.com/magazine/2021/11/22how-your-family-tree-could-catch-a-killer.

20. James M. Adcock and Sarah Stein, *Cold Cases: An Evaluation Model with Follow-up Strategies for Investigators* (Boca Raton, FL: CRC Press, 2017).

21. Melinda Beck, "How a Group of Active and Retired Homicide Investigators Anonymously Solve Cold Cases," A&E True Crime Blog, April 9, 2021, https://www.aetv.com/real-crime/solving-cold-cases-anonymously.

22. https://www.wikiwand.com/en/Grapevine_(gossip).

Chapter 1

1. Daniel Adeniji, "Criminal Justice, Law Enforcement," NPR, RSA Conference, Learning in the Open, May 21, 2018, https://learningintheopen.org/2018/05/21/vidocq-society/.

2. https://www.vidocq.org.

3. Graham Kates, "Murder on the Menu," *Salon*, November 22, 2012, https://www.salon.com/2012/11/22/murder_on_the_menu/.

4. Fleming Smith, "40 Years Later, NCIS Works to Solve Murder of 21-Year-Old at Charleston Naval Base," *The Post and Courier*, December 31, 2019, https://www.postandcourier.com/news/40-years-later-ncis-works-to-solve-murder-of-21-year-old-at-charleston-naval/article_4d973cdc-21b3-11ea-9557-d7a5b519fe65.html.

5. Selwyn Raab, "26 Months in a Prison, Wrongly," *The New York Times*, December 16, 1987, https://www.nytimes.com/1987/12/16/nyregion/26-months-in-a-prison-wrongly.html.

6. Ricki Lewis, "RIP Kary Mullis, Father of PCR," DNA Science, August 15, 2019, https://dnascience.plos.org/2019/08/15/rip-kary-mullis-father-of-pcr/.

7. Monivette Cordiero, "Judge Grants Release to Orlando Serial Rapist Tommie Lee Andrews from Sex Offender Facility," *Orlando Sentinel*, August 27, 2021, https://www.orlandosentinel.com/news/crime/os-ne-tommie-lee-andrews-release-20210828-isgb5pjtvjetdauun5tsrqvm3a-story.html; "Serial Rapist and First Person Convicted with DNA Evidence Seeks Freedom," WESH 2 News, June 28, 2017, https://www.wesh.com/article/serial-rapist-and-first-person-convicted-with-dna-evidence-seeks-freedom/10231181.

8. Sandra E. Garcia, "DNA Evidence

Exonerates a Man of Murder After 20 Years in Prison," *The New York Times*, October 16, 2018, https://www.nytimes.com/2018/10/16/us/20-years-exonerated-dna-prison.html; Robert Warden, "First DNA Exoneration, Gary Dotson, The Rape That Wasn't—The Nation's First DNA Exoneration," Northwestern Pritzker School of Law, August 2019, https://www.law.northwestern.edu/legalclinic/wrongfulconvictions/exonerations/il/gary-dotson.html.

9. Justin Rohrlich, "Why Are There Up to 120,000 Innocent People in U.S. Prisons?" VICE News, November 10, 2014, https://www.vice.com/en/article/9kvj3d/why-are-there-up-to-120000-innocent-people-in-us-prisons.

10. "Exonerate the Innocent," Innocence Project, February 2022, https://innocenceproject.org/exonerate/.

11. Deanna Boyd, "Investigators in Fort Worth Review Hundreds of Cold Cases," *Associated Press*, September 20, 2017, https://apnews.com/article/b11a648518e142b2aff644f1b7659bfe.

12. Laura Barcella, "Why Did Nashville Become a Serial-Killer Haven in the 1970s?" A&E, October 16, 2018, https://www.aetv.com/real-crime/nashville-serial-killer-paul-dennis-reid.

13. *Ibid.*

14. Tom Jackman, "More Than Half of All Wrongful Criminal Convictions Are Caused by Government Misconduct, Study Finds," *Washington Post*, September 16, 2020, https://www.washingtonpost.com/crime-law/2020/09/16/more-than-half-all-wrongful-criminal-convictions-caused-by-government-misconduct-study-finds/.

15. Kory Grow, "'Paradise Lost' at 20: How West Memphis Three Doc Influenced the True-Crime Boom," *Rolling Stone*, December 14, 2016, https://www.rollingstone.com/movies/movie-features/paradise-lost-at-20-how-west-memphis-three-doc-influenced-the-true-crime-boom-122606/.

16. Dan Schindel, "Paradise Lost Trilogy," *Paste*, November 15, 2012, https://www.pastemagazine.com/movies/paradise-lost-trilogy/; Kory Grow, "'Paradise Lost' at 20: How West Memphis Three Doc Influenced the True-Crime Boom," *Rolling Stone*, December 14, 2016, https://www.rollingstone.com/movies/movie-features/paradise-lost-at-20-how-west-memphis-three-doc-influenced-the-true-crime-boom-122606/.

17. Campbell Robertson, "Deal Frees 'West Memphis Three' in Arkansas," *The New York Times*, August 19, 2011, https://www.nytimes.com/2011/08/20/us/20arkansas.html; Patrick Doyle, "How Rockers Helped Free the West Memphis Three," *Rolling Stone*, September 1, 2011.

18. "Emotions Run High Among Parents of Slain Arkansas Boys," CNN, August 20, 2011, http://www.cnn.com/2011/CRIME/08/19/arkansas.release.families/index.html.

19. Maria Ricapito, "What Makes a Good Homicide Investigator?" A&E, May 25, 2017, https://www.aetv.com/real-crime/what-makes-a-good-homicide-investigator.

20. *Ibid.*

21. Rebecca Boswell, "Oxygen Media Renews 'Cold Justice' and 'Criminal Confessions' From Executive Producer Dick Wolfe," Oxygen Media, April 23, 2018, https://www.nbcuniversal.com/press-release/oxygen-media-renews-cold-justice-and-criminal-confessions-executive-producer-dick.

22. "The Real Story of 'Three Billboards Outside Ebbing, Missouri,'" The True Crime, May 26, 2021, https://www.truecrimeedition.com/post/kathy-page.

23. Harriet Ryan, "Case of the Missing Heiress: Who killed Jacqueline Levitz?" CNN, November 11, 2002, https://edition.cnn.com/2002/LAW/11/11/ctv.levitz/.

24. Mosi Reeves, "8 Ways Tupac Shakur Changed the World," *Rolling Stone*, September 13, 2016, https://www.rollingstone.com/music/music-news/8-ways-tupac-shakur-changed-the-world-128421/.

25. Curt Anderson, "U.S. to Pay $2.5M in Tabloid Photo Editor Robert Steven 2001 Anthrax Death," *Lawrence Journal World*, November 29, 2011, https://www2.ljworld.com/news/2011/nov/29/us-pay-25m-tabloid-photo-editor-robert-stevens-200/.

26. David Wright, Katie Kindelan, and Kelly McCarthy, "Former Rep. Gary Condit Breaks Silence 15 Years After Chandra Levy Murder Scandal," ABC News, October 25, 2016, https://abcnews.go.com/US/rep-gary-condit-

breaks-silence-15-years-chandra/story?id=43034319.

27. Terence Chea, "Couple Found Shot to Death on Beach," *The Spokesman-Review*, August 21, 2004, https://www.spokesman.com/stories/2004/aug/21/couple-found-shot-to-death-on-beach/.

28. Stephanie Butzer, "25 Years Later: Boulder's Investigation into JonBenét Ramsey's Murder Continues," *The Denver Channel*, December 27, 2021, https://www.thedenverchannel.com/news/local-news/25-years-later-boulders-investigation-into-jonbenet-ramseys-murder-continues.

29. Ray Richmond, "Have You Seen Andy?" *The Hollywood Reporter*, June 10, 2007, https://www.hollywoodreporter.com/movies/movie-reviews/have-you-seen-andy-158225/.

30. "PEOPLE's True Crime TV Show Uncovers Shocking Twists in Infamous Cases," *People*, October 14, 2016, https://people.com/crime/trailer-people-investigates-people-magazine-tv-series/; "First Look at PEOPLE's True Crime TV Series on Investigation Discovery," *People*, November 7, 2016, https://people.com/crime/people-magazines-launches-tv-series-people-investigates-investigation-discovery/.

31. Kyle Hemmert, "Joe Berlinger's Documentary Series *Wrong Man* Debuting June 3 on Starz," *ComingSoon*, March 28, 2018, https://www.comingsoon.net/tv/news/933659-joe-berlingers-documentary-series-wrong-man-debuting-june-3-on-starz.

32. Ken Otterbourg, "Christopher Tapp," National Registry of Exonerations, August 1, 2019, https://www.law.umich.edu/special/exoneration/Pages/casedetail.aspx?caseid=5592.

33. Carissa Pavlica, "*Wrong Man* Season 2 Review: Joe Berlinger's Dream Team Tries Changing Three More Lives," *TV Fanatic*, February 8, 2020, https://www.tvfanatic.com/2020/02/wrong-man-season-2-review-joe-berlingers-dream-team-tries-changi/.

34. "Best 15 Voltaire Quotes," Humble Pics, January 11, 2021, https://humblepics.com/best-15-voltaire-quotes/.

35. "Man Will Die for 1992 Rape, Killing Motivated by Race," *American Renaissance*, November 18, 2008, https://www.amren.com/news/2008/11/man_will_die_fo/.

36. Government of Virgin Islands v. Petersen, 19 F. Supp. 2d 430 (D.V.I. 1998), U.S. District Court for the District of the U.S. Virgin Islands—19 F. Supp. 2d 430 (D.V.I. 1998), Justia U.S. Law, August 28, 1998, https://law.justia.com/cases/federal/district-courts/FSupp2/19/430/2530348/.

37. "NCIS Did Not Forget Them," *NCIS Bulletin*, October 1998, Volume III, Edition 6, https://ncisahistory.org/wp-content/uploads/2017/06/NCIS-Bulletin-Vol-II-Edition-6-October-1998.pdf.

Chapter 2

1. Jamil Zaki, "Six Things We Get Wrong About Empathy," Powell's City of Books, June 10, 2019, https://www.powells.com/post/lists/six-things-we-get-wrong-about-empathy.

2. Claire Cain Miller, "How to be More Empathetic," *The New York Times*, August 6, 2019, https://www.nytimes.com/guides/year-of-living-better/how-to-be-more-empathetic.

3. Eric Schlosser, "A Grief Like No Other," *The Atlantic*, September 1, 1997, https://www.theatlantic.com/magazine/archive/1997/09/a-grief-like-no-other/376944/.

4. German Lopez, "Examining the Spikes in Murders," *The New York Times*, January 18, 2022, https://www.nytimes.com/2022/01/18/briefing/crime-surge-homicides-us.html.

5. Dean G. Kilpatrick, Heidi Zinzow, Alyssa A. Rheingold, Alesia Hawkins, and Benjamin E. Saunders, "Losing a Loved One to Homicide: Prevalence and Mental Health Correlates in a National Sample of Young Adults," *Journal of Traumatic Stress*, February 22, 2009, https://www.ncbi.nlm.nih.gov/pmc/articles/PMC2829865/; Eric Schlosser, "A Grief Like No Other," *The Atlantic*, September 1, 1997, https://www.theatlantic.com/magazine/archive/1997/09/a-grief-like-no-other/376944/.

6. Jennifer Levitz, "Florida Yoga Studio Shooter Had History of Allegedly Harassing Women, Authorities Say," *The Wall Street Journal*, November 4, 2018,

https://www.wsj.com/articles/florida-yoga-studio-shooter-had-history-of-allegedly-harassing-women-authorities-say-1541367874.

7. Mihir Zaveri, Julia Jacobs, and Sarah Mervosh, "Gunman in Yoga Studio Shooting Recorded Misogynistic Videos and Faced Battery Charges," *The New York Times*, November 3, 2018, https://www.nytimes.com/2018/11/03/us/yoga-studio-shooting-florida.html.

8. Gary Fineout, "Yoga Shooter Appeared to Have Made Misogynistic Videos," *AP News*, November 3, 2018, https://apnews.com/article/tallahassee-north-america-us-news-ap-top-news-shootings-dea39b8b45d2471a8c0df817cb9656d0.

9. Brendan O'Brien and Alex Dobuzinskis, "Gunman at Florida Yoga Studio Had Been Accused of Harassment," *Reuters*, November 3, 2018, https://www.reuters.com/article/us-florida-shooting/gunman-at-florida-yoga-studio-had-been-accused-of-harassment-idUSKCN1N80BS.

10. Matt Hamilton, James Queally, and Richard Winton, "'I hope people call me insane': Social Media Posts, Former Teachers Reveal Alarming Mind-Set of Thousand Oaks Gunman," *Los Angeles Times*, November 9, 2018, https://www.latimes.com/local/lanow/la-me-ln-thousand-oaks-shooting-20181109-story.html.

11. Alejandro De La Garza, "69 People Have Been Killed in Mass Shootings in 2019 Alone," *Time*, August 4, 2019, https://time.com/5643553/2019 mass-shootings-list/.

12. Eric Schlosser, "A Grief Like No Other," *The Atlantic*, September 1, 1997, https://www.theatlantic.com/magazine/archive/1997/09/a-grief-like-no-other/376944/.

13. Ibid.

14. Crime Victims' Rights Act: A Summary and Legal Analysis of 18 U.S.C. § 3771, RL33679, EveryCRSReport, September 29, 2006–June 8, 2021, https://www.everycrsreport.com/reports/RL33679.html.

15. Wesley Spears Newsome, "The Year Clichés Stopped Making Sense," *Baptist News Global*, August 23, 2016, https://baptistnews.com/article/where-is-god-in-2016/#.YgzKVi-B23U; Eric Schlosser, "A Grief Like No Other," *The Atlantic*, September 1, 1997, https://www.theatlantic.com/magazine/archive/1997/09/a-grief-like-no-other/376944/.

16. Eric Schlosser, "A Grief Like No Other," *The Atlantic*, September 1, 1997, https://www.theatlantic.com/magazine/archive/1997/09/a-grief-like-no-other/376944/.

17. Hilary Shenfeld, "Cold Cases Aren't Closed Cases," A&E, November 9, 2017, https://www.aetv.com/real-crime/who-decides-to-reopen-a-cold-case-dormant-files-can-heat-up-with-just-one-small-clue.

18. Luke Barr, "Record Number of Law Enforcement Officers Killed in Line of Duty in 2021, Most from COVID: Report," ABC News, January 12, 2022, https://abcnews.go.com/Politics/record-number-law-enforcement-officers-killed-line-duty/story?id=82219737.

19. Pamela Kulbarsh, "Police Suicides in 2016," Officer.com, January 11, 2017, https://www.officer.com/training-careers/article/12293261/police-suicides-in-2016; Bob Price, "2016 Closes with 140 Cops Being Killed in the Line of Duty," *Breitbart*, January 2017, https://www.breitbart.com/border/2017/01/01/2016-closes-140-cops-killed-line-duty/.

20. Francesca Mirabile, "When Police Fail to Solve Homicides, Families Carry the Weight," *The Trace*, December 16, 2016, https://www.thetrace.org/2017/06/police-fail-solve-homicides-families-carry-weight/.

21. People V. Simpson, [Crim. No. 5547. In Bank. Oct. 26, 1954.] The People, Respondent, v. Henry C. Simpson, Appellant, https://law.justia.com/cases/california/supreme-court/2d/43/553.html.

22. Lara Brenckle, "Acquittal in Slaying Case Stuns Prosecutor," *The Patriot-News*, May 11, 2007, https://www.pennlive.com/patriotnews/2007/05/acquittal_in_slaying_case_stun.html.

23. Gerrad Hall, "*Cold Justice* Digs into 27-Year-Old Murder Case That Inspired *Three Billboards Outside Ebbing, Missouri*," *Entertainment*, October 6, 2018, https://ew.com/tv/2018/10/06/cold-justice-finale-murder-case-inspired-three-billboards/.

24. Jonathan Leach, "48 Hours: NCIS: Body of Evidence," CBS News, June 6, 2017, https://www.cbsnews.com/news/48-hours-ncis-annie-tahan-disappearance-murder-body-of-evidence/.

25. *Ibid.*
26. *Ibid.*
27. Sarah Bowman, "Victim's Family Stunned by Murder's Release," *The Beaufort Gazette*, August 19, 2013, https://www.islandpacket.com/news/local/community/beaufort-news/article33527865.html.
28. Keith Herbert, "Man Held in Death of Area Woman in '82. Suspect Is Arrested in North Carolina Slaying of Slatington Resident," *The Morning Call*, June 19, 2002, https://www.mcall.com/news/mc-xpm-2002-06-19-3402444-story.html.
29. *Ibid.*
30. Alice de Sturler, "Anita Mae Carter Lukander," Defrosting Cold Cases, August 18, 2019, https://defrostingcoldcases.com/anita-mae-carter-lukander-oct-21-1965-march-18-1988/.

Chapter 3

1. Lynn Waltz, "15 Years After Murder, Family Has Day in Court," *The Virginian-Pilot*, January 29, 1997, https://scholar.lib.vt.edu/VA-news/VA-Pilot/issues/1997/vp970129/01290461.htm; Efrain Hernandez, "Palmdale Man Charged with 1982 Murder," *Los Angeles Times*, June 28, 1996, https://www.latimes.com/archives/la-xpm-1996-06-28-me-19395-story.html.
2. Sean Glatch, "Character Development Definition: A Look at 40 Character Traits," Writers.com, October 26, 2021, https://writers.com/character-development-definition.
3. Don J. Read, "Detection of Fs in a Single Statement: The Role of Phonetic Recoding," *Memory and Cognition*, vol. 11, no. 4 (1983), 390-399, https://link.springer.com/content/pdf/10.3758/BF03202454.pdf.
4. "Episode Review: Columbo An Exercise in Fatality," Columbophile, May 27, 2018, https://columbophile.com/about/.
5. IMDb, "An Exercise in Fatality," IMDb, September 15, 1974, https://www.imdb.com/title/tt0072802/characters/nm0000393.
6. "My Cousin Vinny, Defense Council Vincent Gambini Cross Examines Mr. Tipton," American Rhetoric: Movie Speech, March 13, 1992, https://www.americanrhetoric.com/MovieSpeeches/moviespeechmycousinvinny3.html.

7. Michael Gordon, "People Close to This Ex-pastor Keep Dying Violently. Now He's on Trial—Again," *Miami Herald*, February 12, 2018, https://www.miamiherald.com/news/nation-world/national/article199694909.html.
8. Maria Ricapito, "What Makes a Good Homicide Investigator?" A&E, May 25, 2017, https://www.aetv.com/real-crime/what-makes-a-good-homicide-investigator.
9. Ronald Roach, "Drugfire and IBIS Help Lawmen Fight the Bad Guys," *The Washington Business Journal*, May 19,1997, https://www.bizjournals.com/washington/stories/1997/05/19/focus6.html.
10. Dipti Garpade, "Comparison of IBIS and NBIS," Legal Desire, June 1, 2021, https://legaldesire.com/comparison-of-ibis-and-nbis/.
11. Ronald E. Bowers, "Tenacity Solved Murder," January 28, 2019, https://www.barnesandnoble.com/w/tenacity-solved-murder-ronald-e-bowers/1130409825.
12. Laurence Miller, "Dealing with the Stress of Criminal Investigation: 'It gets to you,'" Police 1, March 6, 2008, https://www.police1.com/archive/articles/dealing-with-the-stress-of-criminal-investigation-it-gets-to-you-9x2ECzkR87DVrzdu/.
13. Louis N. Eliopulos, *Death Investigator's Handbook: A Field Guide to Crime Scene Processing, Forensic Evaluations, and Investigative Techniques* (Boulder, CO: Paladin Press, 1993).
14. Jon Frank, "Man Convicted of Murdering Housemate, Eight Years Later," *The Virginian-Pilot*, September 30, 2000, https://groups.google.com/g/alt.true-crime/c/_jyaEC2uH2o.
15. Caroline Warnock, "Shannon Melendi: Teen Was Abducted and Killed by Convicted Sexual Predator," *Heavy*, February 6, 2021, https://heavy.com/news/shannon-melendi-murder/.

Chapter 4

1. "Serving Survivors of Homicide Victims During Cold Case Investigations: A Guide for Developing a Law Enforcement Protocol," National Sheriffs' Association, August 2022, https://www.sheriffs.org/sites/default/files/uploads/guidefor

developingalawenforcementprotocolaugust172011.pdf.

2. Raymond Keene, "The Touchstone of Intellect," The Article, July 4, 2020, https://www.thearticle.com/the-touchstone-of-intellect.

3. "Chess and Checkers," The Huffington Post Growing Leaders, October 12, 2012, https://growingleaders.com/blog/chess-and-checkers/.

4. "The Psychology of Chess: Strategies, and Tactics Will Only Get You So Far—to Really Master Chess, You Need to Understand the Psychology Behind It," Chess Site, September 8, 2017, https://www.chess-site.com/articles/the-psychology-of-chess/.

5. "Tool 5.2 Snapshot of Investigative methodologies," United Nations Office on Drugs and Crime, May 8, 2003, https://www.unodc.org/documents/human-trafficking/HT_Toolkit08_English.pdf.

6. Bruce Gerencser, "Updated: Black Collar Crime: Pastor Tim Crumitie Convicted of Murder, Now Facing More Murder Charges," The Life and Times of Bruce Gerencser, December 31, 2021, https://brucegerencser.net/2021/12/black-collar-crime-pastor-tim-crumitie-accused-murder/; "He Tried to Kill a Charlotte Woman. She Survived and Helped Convict Him of Murder," WBTV 3, February 22, 2018, https://www.wbtv.com/story/37564714/he-tried-to-kill-a-charlotte-woman-she-survived-and-helped-convict-him-of-murder/.

7. Kevin Bonsor, "How Witness Protection Works," How Stuff Works, March 30, 2021, https://people.howstuffworks.com/witness-protection.htm.

8. Ronald K. Fitten, "Man Guilty of Killing 2 Women in Shoreline—Jurors Will Consider Death or Life in Prison in Next Phase of Trial," *Seattle Times*, February 25, 1999, https://archive.seattletimes.com/archive/?date=19990225&slug=2946172; Ronald K. Fitten, "Parker Won't Get the Death Penalty," *Seattle Times*, March 8, 1999, https://archive.seattletimes.com/archive/?date=19990308&slug=2948281.

9. "How Long Does It Take to Get DNA Paternity Test Results?" DNA Diagnostic Center Blog, May 22, 2018, https://dnacenter.com/blog/long-take-get-dna-paternity-test-results/.

10. Kevin Johnson and Kristine Phillips, "'Perfect Storm': Defund the Police, COVID-19 Lead to Biggest Police Budget Cuts in Decade," *USA Today*, July 31, 2020, https://www.usatoday.com/story/news/politics/2020/07/31/defund-police-covid-19-force-deepest-cop-budget-cuts-decade/5538397002/.

11. "ISU Team Calculates Societal Costs of Five Major Crimes; Finds Murder at $17.25 Million," Iowa State University, September 27, 2010, https://www.news.iastate.edu/news/2010/sep/costofcrime; Laura Strachan, "Average Homicide Cost Is $17.25M, Study Concludes," Find Law, October 19, 2010, https://www.findlaw.com/legalblogs/criminal-defense/average-homicide-cost-is-1725m-study-concludes/.

12. "Sexual Assault Kit Initiative," Bureau of Justice Assistance, February 8, 2022, https://bja.ojp.gov/program/sexual-assault-kit-initiative-saki/overview.

13. Bureau of Justice Assistance, U.S. Department of Justice, "National Sexual Assault Kit Initiative (SAKI): Overview," https://bja.ojp.gov/program/national-sexual-assault-kit-initiative-saki/overview.

14. Alice de Sturler, "What Are the Costs of Touch DNA Testing?" Defrosting Cold Cases, August 19, 2014, https://defrostingcoldcases.com/costs-touch-dna-testing/.

15. "Parabon Continues Cold Case Crime-Solving Spree in 2020," Paragon NanoLabs, January 12, 2020, https://parabon-nanolabs.com/news-events/2021/01/parabon-continues-cold-case-crime-solving-spree-in-2020.html.

16. Aaron Mak, "Genetic Genealogy's Less Reliable Cousin: DNA Phenotyping Promises to Tell Law Enforcement What a Suspect Looks Like. Does It Work?" *Slate*, July 25, 2019, https://slate.com/technology/2019/07/parabon-nanolabs-genetic-genealogy-phenotyping.html.

17. Michelle Taylor, "FBI Study: M-Vac System Collects More DNA Swabbing," *Forensic Magazine*, August 3, 2020, https://www.forensicmag.com/566802-FBI-Study-M-Vac-System-Collects-More-DNA-Than-Swabbing/.

18. Martin Kaste, "Open Cases: Why One-Third Of Murders in America Go

Unresolved," Nevada Public Radio, March 30, 2015, https://knpr.org/npr/2015-03/open-cases-why-one-third-murders-america-go-unresolved.

19. "A Beloved Miami College Student Vanished 25 Years Ago. There Was a Murder, but No Closure," *Miami Herald*, March 11, 2019, https://www.miamiherald.com/news/local/community/miami-dade/article227379809.html.

20. Michael McNutt, "Perry Man Gets Life Sentence for Wife's Poisoning," *The Oklahoman*, April 4, 1998, https://www.oklahoman.com/article/2608309/perry-man-gets-life-sentence-for-wifes-poisoning.

21. Warren Sonne, "Meet Mr. Murder," *PI Magazine*, Date N/A, https://www.practicalhomicide.com/articles/PIMag0305.htm.

22. Larry McShane, "Sliwa Forever a Guardian Angel," *Associated Press*, May 16, 1999, https://apnews.com/article/a70c0902214da9aea7f039bdcf819a59; Rebecca Rosenberg and Jamie Schram, "Lawyer Says Hells Angels Shooter 'Tried to Defend Himself,'" *New York Post*, December 21, 2016, https://nypost.com/2016/12/21/lawyer-says-hells-angels-shooter-tried-to-defend-himself/; Dan Mangan, "Kuby's Testimony Radio-Active-Jr. Said He Was Leaving Mob," *New York Post*, March 7, 2006, https://nypost.com/2006/03/07/kubys-testimony-radio-active-jr-said-he-was-leaving-mob/; Tony Sokol, "*Wrong Man*'s NCIS and Homicide Cop Joe Kennedy Talks Blue," Den of Geek, June 1, 2018, https://www.denofgeek.com/tv/wrong-man-s-ncis-and-homicide-cop-joe-kennedy-talks-blue/.

23. Barry Evans, "Lies, Damned Lies and Statistics," *North Coast Journal of Politics*, May 8, 2014, https://www.northcoastjournal.com/humboldt/lies-damned-lies-and-statistics/Content?oid=2555940.

24. Eryk Pruitt, "Pat and Jesse," The Long Dance Podcast, July 1, 2018, https://thelongdancepodcast.com; Adam Powell, "Possible Break in 47-Year-Old Cold Case: Orange County Authorities Seek Closure in 1971 Double Murder," *The News of Orange County*, April 3, 2018, https://www.newsoforange.com/news/article_b9e5fb30-377c-11e8-89de-2f9c73bd334f.html.

25. Cindy Lash, "Brothers Guilty in Killing of 11-Year-Old Girl," *Post Gazette*, October 26, 2005, https://www.post-gazette.com/uncategorized/2005/10/27/Brothers-guilty-in-killing-of-11-year-old-girl/stories/200510270354.

26. Stephen Dark, "The Ice Man Cometh: Salt Lake County Detective Todd Park Lives to See Cold Cases Thawed," *City Weekly*, February 9, 2006, https://www.cityweekly.net/utah/the-ice-man-cometh/Content?oid=2128890; "Maximum Sentence Is Imposed in '91 Slaying," *Deseret News*, April 17, 2007, https://www.deseret.com/2007/4/17/20013536/maximum-sentence-is-imposed-in-91-slaying.

27. Paul Mendelle, "Why Juries Work Best," *The Guardian*, February 21, 2010, https://www.theguardian.com/commentisfree/2010/feb/21/juries-work-best-research; "14 Important Pros and Cons of the Jury System," Connect Us, November 18, 2019, https://connectusfund.org/14-important-pros-and-cons-of-the-jury-system.

28. United States v. Hector A. Coleman Airman Apprentice (E-2), U.S. Navy, In the U.S. Navy-Marine Corps Court of Criminal Appeals Washington Navy Yard, Washington D.C., NMCCA 200101009, February 10, 2006, https://www.jag.navy.mil/courts/documents/archive/2006/COLEMAN%20H.A.%20200101009%20unpub.pdf.

29. Ana Writes, "24-Year-Old Scott Dunn Was Killed by His Girlfriend," Medium, October 19, 2021, https://medium.com/the-criminalist/vengeful-girlfriend-kills-boyfriend-after-finding-out-about-his-fiancée-f551e73b2b7d.

Chapter 5

1. John Kerr, "Libertyville's Riley Lees Makes Up for Late Mistake with Winning Touchdown," *Chicago Tribune*, November 22, 2015, https://www.chicagotribune.com/suburbs/libertyville/sports/ct-lbr-libertyville-football-state-preview-tl-1126-20151122-story.html.

2. Victoria Kim, "Coroner's Long-forgotten Evidence Unlocks Old Mysteries," *Los Angles Times*, June 2, 1011, https://www.latimes.com/local/la-xpm-2011-jun-

02-la-me-coroner-evidence-20110602-story.html.

3. Meredith Kile, "Need to Know: Identifying a Killer Using Just Eight Skin Cells," *Aljazeera America*, February 19, 2014, http://america.aljazeera.com/watch/shows/techknow/blog/2014/2/19/need-to-know-identifyingakillerusingjusteightskincells.html.

4. Rich Press, "DNA Mixtures: A Forensic Science Explainer What Are DNA Mixtures? And Why Are They Sometimes So Difficult to Interpret?" National Institute of Standards and Technology, April 3, 2019, https://www.nist.gov/feature-stories/dna-mixtures-forensic-science-explainer.

5. Andrey Peter Smith, "When DNA Implicates the Innocent: The Criminal Justice System's Reliance on DNA Evidence, Often Treated as Infallible, Carries Significant Risks," *Scientific American*, June 1, 2016, https://www.scientificamerican.com/article/when-dna-implicates-the-innocent/.

6. Matthew Shaer, "The False Promise of DNA Testing: The Forensic Technique Is Becoming Ever More Common—and Ever Less Reliable," *The Atlantic*, June 15, 2016, https://www.theatlantic.com/magazine/archive/2016/06/a-reasonable-doubt/480747/.

7. Roma Khanna and Mike Glen, "HPD Makes Arrest in Iconic DNA Case," *Chronicle*, June 22, 2006, https://www.chron.com/news/houston-texas/article/HPD-makes-arrest-in-iconic-DNA-case-1581308.php.

8. Peter Andrey Smith, "When DNA Implicates the Innocent," *Scientific American*, June 1, 2016, https://www.scientificamerican.com/article/when-dna-implicates-the-innocent/.

9. Katie Worth, "Framed for Murder by His Own DNA," The Marshall Project, April 19, 2018, https://www.themarshallproject.org/2018/04/19/framed-for-murder-by-his-own-dna.

10. Tracey Kaplan, "Monte Sereno Murder Case Casts Doubts on DNA Evidence," *The Mercury News*, June 28, 2014, https://www.mercurynews.com/2014/06/28/monte-sereno-murder-case-casts-doubts-on-dna-evidence/.

11. Myles Zernik-Traxler, "The Unbelievable Story of What Happened to Candice," Forensic Myles, May 12, 2020, https://www.forensicmyles.com/blogs/forensic-myles/the-unbelievable-story-of-what-happened-to-candice.

12. Rebecca Reisner, "What Happened to Doctor John Schneeberg?" Forensic Files Now, November 1, 2008, https://forensicfilesnow.com/index.php/tag/candice-fonagy/; Myles Zernik-Traxler, "The Unbelievable Story of What Happened to Candice," Forensic Myles, May 12, 2020, https://www.forensicmyles.com/blogs/forensic-myles/the-unbelievable-story-of-what-happened-to-candice.

13. "Authorities Covering Brushfires Too Reliant on DNA," Swinburne University of Technology, November 4, 2010, https://phys.org/news/2010-11-authorities-brushfires-reliant-dna.html.

14. "An Over-reliance on Forensics," Science Alert, November 5, 2010, https://gfmc.online/media/2010/11-2010/news_20101105_au.html.

15. Douglas Starr, "What Your Cell Phone Can't Tell the Police," *The New Yorker*, June 26, 2014, https://www.newyorker.com/news/news-desk/what-your-cell-phone-cant-tell-the-police.

16. *Ibid.*; Talullah Plummer-Blanco, "This Portland Woman Spent 12 Years in Prison—for a Murder She Didn't Commit," *Portland Monthly*, June 8, 2018, https://www.pdxmonthly.com/arts-and-culture/2018/06/this-portland-woman-spent-12-years-in-prison-for-a-murder-she-didnt-commit

17. Lewis Beale, "To Catch a Killer: A Bunch of Cops and Attorneys Get Together Once a Month to Try to Crack Unsolved Cases," *Los Angeles Times*, May 13, 1992, https://www.latimes.com/archives/la-xpm-1992-05-13-vw-1584-story.html.

18. Rob Wallace, Lauren Putrino, and Tom McCarthy, "Cold Case Squad: Modern-Day 'Sherlock Holmes' Team Takes on Oregon Slaying," ABC News, August 11, 2010. https://abcnews.go.com/2020/leah-freeman-oregon-teen-murder-vidocq-society/story?id=11374958.

19. "Army Reservist & Drexel University Security Guard David Dickson Murdered Deborah Wilson on Campus; Sentenced to Life in Prison," Military Justice For All, November

30, 1984, https://militaryjusticeforall. com/1984/11/30/army-recruiter-drexel-university-security-guard-david-dickson-murdered-student-deborah-wilson-stole-her-sneakers-sentenced-to-life-in-prison-1984/.

20. "Foot Fetishist Convicted of Murdering Barefoot Student," *Associated Press*, December 2, 1995, https://apnews.com/article/b5d2113df4bbdfe03c1a2369f23c409c.

21. "Former Guard at Drexel U. Convicted of Student's Murder," *The Chronicle*, December 15, 1995, https://www.chronicle.com/article/former-guard-at-drexel-u-convicted-of-students-murder/.

22. Connor Raikes, "The 'Howcatchem' Hero: Why Columbo's Innovative Plot Structure Makes You Love the Character More," Connor Raises Blog, No Date, https://www.connorraikes.com/scriptstudies/howcatchem-hero-columbo.

23. Debra Cassens Weiss, "The Best Way to Interrogate: Think Columbo," *American Bar Association Journal*, May 12 2009, https://www.abajournal.com/news/article/the_best_way_to_interrogate_think_columbo.

24. Mark Griffiths, "'Just one more thing': The Psychology of Columbo," Dr. Mark Griffiths, August 8, 2016, https://drmarkgriffiths.wordpress.com/2016/08/08/just-one-more-thing-the-psychology-of-columbo/.

25. Benedict Carey, "Judging Honesty by Words, Not Fidgets," *The New York Times*, May 11, 2009, https://www.nytimes.com/2009/05/12/science/12lying.html.

26. George Schiro, "Collection and Preservation of Evidence," Crime Scene Investigator LSU, https://www.crime-scene-investigator.net/evidenc3.html.

27. Hailey Branson-Potts, "After Oklahoma City Bombing, McVeigh's Arrest Almost Went Unnoticed," *Los Angeles Times*, April 19, 2015, https://www.latimes.com/nation/la-na-oklahoma-city-bombing-20150419-story.html; Terry Lynn Nichols, Petitioner, v. Wayne E. Alley, District Judge, Respondent. United States of America, Real Party in Interest, No. 95-6341. United States Court of Appeals, Tenth Circuit, December 1, 1995, https://openjurist.org/71/f3d/347/nichols-v-e-alley.

28. Dan Nosowitz, "Private Eyes Tell Us About Digging Through People's Trash," *Atlas Obscura*, March 18, 2016, https://www.atlasobscura.com/articles/private-eyes-tells-us-about-digging-through-peoples-trash.

29. David E. Hoffman, "Circle of Treason: A CIA Account of Traitor Aldrich Ames and the Men He Betrayed," *The Washington Post*, November 30, 2012, https://www.washingtonpost.com/opinions/circle-of-treason-a-cia-account-of-traitor-aldrich-ames-and-the-men-he-betrayed-by-sandra-grimes-and-jeanne-vertefeuille/2012/11/30/f164853c-3402-11e2-bb9b-288a310849ee_story.html.

30. Legal Information Institute, "39 CFR § 233.3-Mail Covers," https://www.law.cornell.edu/cfr/text/39/233.3.

31. Julie Rooney, "Going Postal: Analyzing the Abuse of Mail Covers Under the Fourth Amendment," Vanderbilt Law, September 25, 2017, https://scholarship.law.vanderbilt.edu/vlr/vol70/iss5/5/.

32. Legal Information Institute, "39 CFR § 233.3-Mail Covers," https://www.law.cornell.edu/cfr/text/39/233.3.

33. Ron Nixon, "U.S. Postal Service Logging All Mail for Law Enforcement," *The New York Times*, July 3, 2013, https://www.nytimes.com/2013/07/04/us/monitoring-of-snail-mail.html.

34. Joni E. Johnston, "Dark Ambitions: Recent Research Traces the Path from Aspiring Serial Killer to the Real Deal," *Psychology Today*, April 24, 2019, https://www.psychologytoday.com/us/blog/the-human-equation/201904/dark-ambitions.

35. "The French Homicides," Parabon NanoLabs, July 8, 2016, https://snapshot.parabon-nanolabs.com/snapshot-case-summary-rockingham-nc-french-homicides.html.

36. Sarah Newell Williamson, "Judge Says Jose Alvarez Will 'Die in Prison' in French Double Homicide Sentencing," *Greensboro News and Record*, July 8, 2016, https://greensboro.com/news/crime/judge-says-jose-alvarez-will-die-in-prison-in-french-double-homicide-sentencing/article_23c2f468-3726-5a59-ab6a-933f91159338.html.

Chapter 6

1. Austin Cline, "Deductive and Inductive Logic in Arguments," Learn

Religions, January 25, 2019, https://www.learnreligions.com/deductive-and-inductive-arguments-249754; Sohail Ansari, "Deductive Reasoning," Brain Quoutes an Logical Thinking, February 7, 2017, http://brainqoutesandlogicalthinking.blogspot.com/2017/02/deductive-reasoning.html.

2. Sydney Goldstein, "Criminal Statutes of Limitations: Time Limits for State Charges," LawInfo, February 18, 2021, https://www.lawinfo.com/resources/criminal-defense/criminal-statute-limitations-time-limits.html.

3. David Perez, "11 Ways to Save Stuff in Evernote," Evernote, July 3, 2019, https://evernote.com/blog/11-ways-save-stuff-evernote/; Michael Kissiah, "Evernote for Recording Case Notes," E-Investigator, December 28, 2021, https://www.einvestigator.com/evernote-app-record-case-notes/.

4. Stephanie Wilkins, "CaseMapCloud: Superior Case Management, Available Any Time, Anywhere," Above the Law, December 13, 2021, https://abovethelaw.com/2021/12/casemap-cloud-superior-case-management-available-any-time-anywhere/.

5. Eric Stirgus, "The Victim's Mother Lectures the Killer, Sentenced to Life 'You took that away,'" *Tampa Bay Times*, February 16, 2000, https://www.tampabay.com/archive/2000/02/16/the-victim-s-mother-lectures-the-killer-sentenced-to-life-you-took-that-away/.

6. John E. Smialek, Charlotte Word, and Arthur J. Westveer, "Microscopic Slide: A Potential DNA Reservoir," *FBI Law Enforcement Bulletin*, vol. 69, issue 11 (2000), 822, NCJ Number 185831, https://www.ojp.gov/ncjrs/virtual-library/abstracts/microscopic-slide-potential-dna-reservoir.

7. "When Off-Line Is Better: Another Way to Search Crime Records," FBI, January 4, 2010, https://archives.fbi.gov/archives/news/stories/2010/january/ncic_010410.

8. Dr. Kartikey, "Grapevine: The Informal Transmission of Information," *Notions*, Vol. 8, No. 2 (2017): 56–60.

9. "History," M–Vac Systems, Inc., https://www.m-vac.com/history.

10. Alice de Sturler, "Victims and Investigators Deserve This Technology," Defrosting Cold Cases, April 4, 2016, https://defrostingcoldcases.com/victims-and-investigators-deserve-this-technology/; "How Does the M-Vac Work?" M-Vac Systems, Inc., https://www.m-vac.com/why-mvac/how-it-works.

11. "Rule 4. Arrest Warrant or Summons on a Complaint," Cornell Law School, No Date, https://www.law.cornell.edu/rules/frcrmp/rule_4.

12. Gary Delshon, "Cracking an Unsolved Rape Case Makes History," The Alicia Patterson Foundation Blog, May 4, 2011, https://aliciapatterson.org/stories/cracking-unsolved-rape-case-makes-history; Court of Appeals Wisconsin, State of Wisconsin, Respondent, Bobby R. Dabney, Appellant, Case No: 02-2445-CR, April 29, 2003, https://www.wicourts.gov/html/ca/02/02-2445.htm.

13. Sara James, "Killer Instinct," NBC News, January 2, 2009, https://www.nbcnews.com/id/wbna28471722; Matt Young, "Incredible Story of the Murder of Judith Johnson, and How Her Daughter Found Her Killer," *New Zealand Herald*, May 19, 2017, https://www.nzherald.co.nz/world/incredible-story-of-the-murder-of-judith-johnson-and-how-her-daughter-found-her-killer/MBWFX5W7X65YX74IPR5UFWKMFQ/; "Wrongly Convicted Ohio Man Snags Another Man's Cigarette Butt to Clear His Name," True Crime Daily, June 5, 2017, https://truecrimedaily.com/2017/06/05/wrongly-convicted-ohio-man-snags-other-inmates-cigarette-butt-to-clear-his-name/.

14. All That's Interesting, "John List, the Mass Murderer Who Killed His Family So He'd See Them in Heaven," https://allthatsinteresting.com/john-list.

15. Cole Waterman, "America's Most Wanted Killer John List Remains Infamous Bogeyman in His Michigan Hometown," MLive, November 9, 2021, https://www.mlive.com/news/2021/11/americas-most-wanted-killer-john-list-remains-infamous-bogeyman-in-his-michigan-hometown.html; Katie Serena, "John List, the Mass Murderer Who Killed His Family so He'd See Them in Heaven," All That's Interesting, November 16, 2021, https://allthatsinteresting.com/john-list.

16. John Temple, "Longtime Suspect Charged in Murders," *News & Record*, June 25, 1997, https://greensboro.

com/longtime-suspect-charged-in-murders/article_d7f1cb67-8f81-560b-a67c-fabcbde6a99b.html; Rebecca Reisner, "Joann Katrinak's Killer Still Has Innocence Advocates," Forensic Files, September 26, 2020, https://forensicfilesnow.com/index.php/2020/09/26/patricia-rorrer-an-update/comment-page-1/; Chris Harris, "WATCH: ID Examines Controversial 1994 Case of Woman Convicted of Murdering Ex-Boyfriend's Wife and Son," *People*, March 2, 2017, https://people.com/crime/murder-lehigh-valley-controversial-patricia-rorrer-conviction/.

Chapter 7

1. Eric Lichtblau and William M. Arkin, "More Federal Agencies Are Using Undercover Operations," *The New York Times*, November 15, 2014, https://www.nytimes.com/2014/11/16/us/more-federal-agencies-are-using-undercover-operations.html.
2. Dale Marshall, "How to Get a Job as a Deep Undercover Cop," *Chronicle*, May 29, 2016, https://work.chron.com/job-deep-undercover-cop-24544.html; Don Jacobson, "Still in Seclusion, FBI Agent Who Was Real 'Donnie Brasco' Glad He Took Down Mafia 40 Years Ago," *United Press International*, July 27, 2021, https://www.upi.com/Top_News/US/2021/07/27/joe-pistone-donnie-brasco-fbi/9661621900329/.
3. Joseph L. Martell, "Critical Review of the Literature in Support of Intended Dissertation Topic: Identifying the Dangers of Shallow Alias Cover Personas and Offering Methods to Strengthen Undercover Law Enforcement Operations," October 2021, DOI:10.13140/RG.2.2.24957.69608; Emily Bryson York, "What It Takes to Be an 'Undercover Boss,'" *Business Insider*, February 15, 2010, https://www.businessinsider.com/what-it-takes-to-be-an-undercover-boss-2010-2.
4. "48 Hours: NCIS: Can Agents Stop a Ruthless Attacker Preying on Marine Wives?" 48 Hours, CBS News, May 22, 2018, https://www.cbsnews.com/news/48-hours-ncis-can-agents-stop-a-ruthless-attacker-preying-on-marine-wives/; North Carolina Court of Appeals, State of North Carolina v. Willie Abner Brown, Defendant, No. COA14-814, Onslow County, Nos. 12 CRS 5633-36, 56338-39, 13 CRS 52796-84, 13 CRS 52807, Justia U.S. Law, December 16, 2014, https://law.justia.com/cases/north-carolina/court-of-appeals/2014/14-814.html.
5. State v. Lawing, In the Court of Appeals of North Carolina, No. COA17-231, Justia Law, June 5, 2018, No. 14CRS 007299, https://law.justia.com/cases/north-carolina/court-of-appeals/2018/17-231.html.
6. The People, Plaintiff and Respondent, v. Kenneth Clair, Defendant and Appellant, Supreme Court of California, In Bank, FindLaw, No. S004789, May 07, 1992, https://caselaw.findlaw.com/ca-supreme-court/1774317.html; Nancy Wride, "Santa Ana Man Held in Torture and Murder of Disabled Baby Sitter," *Los Angeles Times*, January 25, 1985, https://www.latimes.com/archives/la-xpm-1985-01-25-me-9402-story.html.

Chapter 8

1. Debra Cassens Weiss, "Study Finds Memories Can Change with Each Recall; Researcher Sees Criminal Justice Implications," *American Bar Association Journal*, September 24, 2012, https://www.abajournal.com/news/article/study_finds_memories_can_change_with_each_recall.
2. Ibid.
3. Ari Zoldan, "7 Ways to Turn a Toxic Co-Worker Into an Ally," *Inc.*, August 1, 2017, https://www.inc.com/ari-zoldan/7-simple-tips-to-help-you-get-along-with-your-diff.html.
4. Ibid.; "The Power of Choice: Freedom Over Circumstances," Mind for Life, August 23, 2017, http://www.mindforlife.org/power-of-choice-freedom-over-circumstances/.
5. Charles Swindoll, "The Importance of Attitude," Insight for Today, July 20, 2015, https://www.insight.org/resources/daily-devotional/individual/the-importance-of-attitude.
6. Molly St. Louis, "How to Spot Visual, Auditory, and Kinesthetic-Learning Executives," *Inc.*, April 1, 2017, https://www.inc.com/molly-reynolds/how-to-spot-visual-auditory-and-kinesthetic-learni.html; Matt Strader, "Kinesthetic, Visual, Auditory, Tactile, Oh My! What Are

Learning Modalities and How Can You Incorporate Them in the Classroom?" Edmentum, Thursday, March 11, 2021, https://blog.edmentum.com/kinesthetic-visual-auditory-tactile-oh-my-what-are-learning-modalities-and-how-can-you-incorporate.

7. Vincent A. Sandoval, "Subtle Skills for Building Rapport: Using Neuro-Linguistic Programming in the Interview Room," Spying for Lying, August 27, 2009, https://spyingforlying.blogspot.com/2009/08/subtle-skills-for-building-rapport.html.

8. *Ibid.*

9. Alan Chapman and Sandra McCarthy, "Reading Body Language Signs and Communications: Why Is Body Language Relevant?" Business Balls, January 7, 2017, https://www.businessballs.com/self-awareness/body-language/; Ashish Arora, "What Is Paralanguage? And How Can You Use It to Give Better Presentations?" July 17, 2017, https://visme.co/blog/what-is-paralanguage/.

10. Maryn Liles, "What Your Sibling Birth Order Reveals About Your Personality Traits (Even If You're an Only Child)," *Parade*, February 18, 2021, https://parade.com/1129516/marynliles/birth-order-personality-traits/.

11. Pamela Prindle Fierro, "Does Birth Order Affect Twins?" Very Well Family, May 16, 2020, https://www.verywellfamily.com/birth-order-and-twins-2446666.

12. Ryan Fan, "The Santa Strangler Was Caught Almost 30 Years After His Murders," Newsbreak, January 11, 2021, https://original.newsbreak.com/@ryan-fan-561172/2141931294255-the-santa-strangler-was-caught-almost-30-years-after-his-murders; Jaxon Van Derbeken, "How Alleged Serial Killer Fell into Trap/Man's Loose Lips Led to Ruse to get DNA," *SFGATE*, September 21, 2003, https://www.sfgate.com/news/article/How-alleged-serial-killer-fell-into-trap-Man-s-2556309.php.

13. "Navy Spouse Pamela Hartley Pleaded Guilty to the 2nd Degree Murder of Lt. Verle Lee Hartley in Florida State Court," Military Justice for All, October 16, 1996, https://militaryjusticeforall.com/tag/pam-hartley/; Jason Hughes, "Unusual Suspects: Navy Man Poisoned by Wife's Care Packages," *Huffington Post*, December 10, 2012, https://www.huffpost.com/entry/unusual-suspects-care-package-poison-video_n_2269822.

14. The Supreme Court of Mississippi. Curtis Giovanni Flowers v. State of Mississippi, FindLaw, No. 1999-DP-01369-SCT, Decided: April 03, 2003, https://caselaw.findlaw.com/ms-supreme-court/1439558.html; Emily Wagster Pettus and Jeff Amy, "No 7th Trial for Mississippi Man Freed from Prison in 2019," WCTI, September 4, 2020, https://wcti12.com/news/nation-world/no-7th-trial-for-mississippi-man-freed-from-prison-in-2019; "Mississippi Judge Frees Curtis Flowers on Bail After Six Trials and 23 Years in Jail," Death Penalty Information Center, December 16, 2019, https://deathpenaltyinfo.org/news/mississippi-judge-frees-curtis-flowers-on-bail-after-six-trials-and-23-years-in-jail.

15. Phil Ferolito, "Family, Friends Rally in Hopes of a New Trial for Evaristo Salas in 1995 Sunnyside Murder," *Yakima Herald-Republic*, August 22, 2021, https://www.spokesman.com/stories/2021/aug/22/family-friends-rally-in-hopes-of-a-new-trial-for-e/; Phil Ferolito, "Judge Denies New Trial for Salas, Who Aims to Clear His Name in '96 Sunnyside Murder Conviction," *Yakima Herald-Republic*, November 1, 2021, https://www.yakimaherald.com/news/local/judge-denies-new-trial-for-salas-who-aims-to-clear-his-name-in-96-sunnyside/article_5ad775d7-b98e-5a5b-91cc-10884dbca56e.html.

16. Akshay Pai, "Grandmother Jailed for Brutally Murdering Pregnant Woman and Her Unborn Child Could Be Innocent, Docu Claims," Media Entertainment Arts WorldWide, February 7, 2020, https://meaww.com/wrong-man-51-year-old-grandmother-convicted-killing-pregnant-woman-believed-to-be-innocent; Ken Little, "Convictions Affirmed by Appeals Court," *The Greenville Sun*, February 25, 2021, https://www.greenevillesun.com/news/local_news/vonda-star-smith-murder-convictions-affirmed-by-appeals-court/article_35bf375f-b3a5-5764-bfc7-9f27a6d8ea4e.html.

Chapter 9

1. Paige St. John, "The Untold Story of How the Golden State Killer Was Found:

A Covert Operation and Private DNA," *Los Angeles Times*, December 8, 2020, https://www.latimes.com/california/story/2020-12-08/man-in-the-window.

2. Heather Murphy, "Genealogy Sites Have Helped Identify Suspects. Now They've Helped Convict One," *The New York Times*, July 1, 2019, https://www.nytimes.com/2019/07/01/us/dna-genetic-genealogy-trial.html.

3. Emily Shapiro, "Signaling a 'New Era' in Forensic Investigation, a Man Caught Through Genetic Genealogy Gets Life in Prison for 1987 Double Murder," ABC News, July 24, 2019, https://abcnews.go.com/U.S./signaling-era-forensic-investigation-man-caught-genetic-genealogy/story?id=64540673; Neil Vigdor, "An Innocent Man Went to Prison for Murder. Now, It's the Real Killer's Turn," *The New York Times*, June 8, 2021, https://www.nytimes.com/2021/06/08/us/angie-dodge-murder.html.

4. David H. Bayley and Christine Nixon, "Changing Environment for Policing, 1985–2008," National Institute of Justice, *NCJ* Number 230576, September 2010, https://nij.ojp.gov/library/publications/changing-environment-policing-1985-2008.

5. Tony Feder, "Q&A: Colleen Fitzpatrick, a Physicist Who Cracks Cold Murder Cases," *Physics Today*, April 9, 2020, https://physicstoday.scitation.org/do/10.1063/PT.6.4.20200409a/full/.

6. Megan Molteni, "The First Murder Case to Use Family Tree Forensics Goes to Trial," *Wired*, June 18, 2019, https://www.wired.com/story/the-first-murder-case-to-use-family-tree-forensics-goes-to-trial/; Caleb Hutton, "Life in Prison for 1987 Killer of Young Canadian Couple," *Seattle Weekly*, July 23, 2019, https://www.seattleweekly.com/news/life-in-prison-for-1987-killer-of-young-canadian-couple/.

7. Boaz Halaban, Marc Dorian, Sandy Evans, Carrie Cook, and Haley Yamada, "Mom Overturns Wrongful Convictions, Catches True Killer in Daughter's Murder 25 Years Later," ABC News, March 13, 2021, https://abc7chicago.com/angie-dodge-killed-mom-solves-daughters-murder-carol-abc-2020/10413871/.

8. "Snapshot Kinship Inference," https://snapshot.parabon-nanolabs.com/kinship.

9. Peter Aldhous, "Genetic Genealogy Helped Finally Crack the 1996 Murder of 18-Year-Old Angie Dodge," *BuzzFeed News*, May 16, 2019, https://www.buzzfeednews.com/article/peteraldhous/angie-dodge-cold-case-murder-genetic-genealogy-parabon.

10. Danny R. Smith, "The Unsolved Murder of Angie Dodge," The Murder Memo, June 13, 2018, https://dickiefloydnovels.com/angie-dodge-murder/; Ken Otterbourg, "Christopher Tapp: Time Served: 21 Years," Innocence Project, July 17, 2019, https://innocenceproject.org/cases/christopher-tapp-has-murder-conviction-vacated-after-serving-21-years/; Peter Aldhous, "Genetic Genealogy Helped Finally Crack the 1996 Murder of 18-Year-Old Angie Dodge," *BuzzFeed*, May 16, 2019, https://www.buzzfeednews.com/article/peteraldhous/angie-dodge-cold-case-murder-genetic-genealogy-parabon.

11. Crystal Bonvillian, "Man Cleared of Murder by Genetic Genealogy After 15 Years in Prison, New Suspect Charged," CBS 47 Action News Jax, February 19, 2020, https://www.actionnewsjax.com/news/trending/california-man-cleared-murder-by-genetic-genealogy-after-15-years-prison-new-suspect-charged/IAOFAYHAQJCZZALDPX5BZDZ4YU/; Anna Giles, "New DNA Evidence Exonerates Man Convicted in 1985 El Dorado Hills Murder; New Suspect Arrested," CBS Sacramento, February 13, 2020, https://sacramento.cbslocal.com/2020/02/13/ricky-davis-exonerated-jane-hylton-1985-murder-genetic-genealogy/.

12. Brenda Kellow, "Tracing Our Roots: Award-Winning Forensic Researcher to Speak to Genealogy Friends in September," *Star Local Media*, May 22, 2018, https://starlocalmedia.com/opinion/blogs/blog_7/tracing-our-roots-award-winning-forensic-researcher-to-speak-to-genealogy-friends-in-september/article_d2fc25ec-5de0-11e8-b1ad-5f11d07c5106.html; Jessica Testa, "Nobody Was Going to Solve These Cold Cases. Then Came the DNA Crime Solvers," *BuzzFeed News*, September 22, 2018, https://www.buzzfeednews.com/article/jtes/dna-cold-case-crime-doe-project-genealogy.

13. "Case Study: Stopping a Dangerous Predator," Identifinders International,

May 27, 2021, https://identifinders.com/case-study-phoenix-canal-killer/.

14.

15. Sarah Jean Green, "Arrest Made in Death of Federal Way Teen Nearly 30 Years After Her Body Was Found," *The Seattle Times*, October 3, 2019, https://www.seattletimes.com/seattle-news/law-justice/arrest-made-in-death-of-federal-way-teen-after-nearly-28-years/; Jessica Testa, "Nobody Was Going to Solve These Cold Cases. Then Came the DNA Crime Solvers," *BuzzFeed News*, September 22, 2018, https://www.buzzfeednews.com/article/jtes/dna-cold-case-crime-doe-project-genealogy.

16. Anna Spoerre, "DNA on a Straw Helps Jury Convict Man of Murder in 1979 Slaying of Iowa Teen," *USA Today*, February 25, 2020, https://www.usatoday.com/story/news/nation/2020/02/25/jerry-lynn-burns-trial-michelle-martinko-murder-iowa-cold-case/4866603002/.

17. Tresa Baldas, "DNA Reveals Identity of Woman Killed in Nevada in 1982—She Was from Detroit," *Detroit Free Press*, May 9, 2019, https://www.freep.com/story/news/local/michigan/2019/05/09/sheeps-flat-jane-doe-detroit-nevada/1141658001/.

18. Tresa Baldas, "She Was Killed 37 Years Ago—and Her Friends Just Found Out: 'She was my bridesmaid,'" *Detroit Free Press*, June 7, 2019, https://www.freep.com/story/news/local/michigan/detroit/2019/06/07/jane-doe-dna-sheeps-flat-lake-tahoe-mary-savlla/1361068001/.

19. Sami Edge, "Internet Sleuths, DNA Link John Doe to Northern New Mexico," *The New Mexican*, March 31, 2018, https://www.santafenewmexican.com/news/local_news/internet-sleuths-dna-link-john-doe-to-northern-new-mexico/article_3e26622a-6ecc-5f64-94a7-922eff538382.html; Stephanie Dube Dwilson, "Lyle Stevik: 5 Fast Facts You Need to Know," Heavy.com, May 9, 2018, https://heavy.com/news/2018/05/lyle-stevik/.

20. Ashley Ludwig, "Cold Case Homicide Victim ID'd 30 Years Later," Patch, January 17, 2019, https://patch.com/california/orange-county/cold-case-homicide-victim-idd-30-years-later; "Anaheim Jane Doe Identified 31 Years Later," ABC News, Friday, January 18, 2019, https://abc7.com/jane-doe-orange-county-tracey-coreen-hobson/5096848/.

21. Andrea Reiher, "CeCe Moore, the Genetic Detective: 5 Fast Facts You Need to Know," Heavy.com, https://heavy.com/entertainment/2020/05/cece-moore-genetic-detective/.

22. KC Baker, "Forensic DNA Expert CeCe Moore Solves Decades-Old Cold Cases in ABC's *The Genetic Detective*," *People*, May 26, 2020, https://people.com/crime/forensic-dna-expert-cece-cold-cases-genetic-detective/.

Chapter 10

1. John Gramlich, "What We Know About the Increase in U.S. Murders in 2020," Pew Research Center, October 27, 2021, https://www.pewresearch.org/fact-tank/2021/10/27/what-we-know-about-the-increase-in-u-s-murders-in-2020/.

Chapter 11

1. Claire Osborn, "40 Years Later, 'Orange Socks' Homicide Victim Identified," *Statesman*, August 7, 2019, https://www.statesman.com/story/news/crime/2019/08/07/40-years-after-her-death-debra-jackson-of-abilene-identified-as-orange-socks/4508268007/.

2. Travis Ragsdale, "Seventh Anniversary of Bardstown Police Officer's Murder Brings Renewed Effort for Tips," WDRB, May 25, 2020, https://www.wdrb.com/news/seventh-anniversary-of-bardstown-police-officers-murder-brings-renewed-effort-for-tips/article_6b8eeec6-9ebb-11ea-9837-e3f3b288cb20.html.

3. Matthew Glowicki, "Who Killed Bardstown Officer Jason Ellis? 5 Years Later, Nobody Knows," *Courier Journal*, May 24, 2018, https://www.courier-journal.com/story/news/crime/2018/05/22/bardstown-police-officer-jason-ellis-ambush-murder-investigation-mystery/612709002/; Travis Ragsdale, "Seventh Anniversary of Bardstown Police Officer's Murder Brings Renewed Effort for Tips," WDRB, May 25, 2020, https://www.wdrb.com/news/seventh-anniversary-of-bardstown-police-officers-murder-brings-renewed-effort-for-tips/article_6b8eeec6-9ebb-11ea-9837-e3f3b288cb20.html.

4. Charles Flesher, "A&E Documentary Premiering Tuesday Follows Trial of Iowa

Farmer Accused of Killing His Mother," *Des Moines Register*, May 24, 2020, https://www.desmoinesregister.com/story/news/2020/05/24/ae-tv-accused-guilty-innocent-crime-documentary-jason-carter-iowa-farmer-murder-trial-killing-mother/5252240002/; William Morris, "Federal Appeals Court Revives Jason Carter's Lawsuit Against Father, Iowa Investigators Over His Mother's Killing," *Des Moines Register*, July 21, 2021, https://www.desmoinesregister.com/story/news/crime-and-courts/2021/07/21/jason-carter-lawsuit-against-investigators-revived-appeals-court-murder-shirley-carter/8044655002/.

5. Lara Brenckle, "Acquittal in Slaying Case Stuns Prosecutor," *The Patriot News*, May 11, 2007, https://www.pennlive.com/patriotnews/2007/05/acquittal_in_slaying_case_stun.html.

6. Jenny Drabble, "Granddaughter of Woman Stabbed 54 Times on Robinhood Road in 1969 Still Searching for Answers," *Winston Salem Journal*, https://journalnow.com/news/local/granddaughter-of-woman-stabbed-54-times-on-robinhood-road-in-1969-still-searching-for-answers/article_ad176219-e261-5a0c-a001-21b68998cda2.html.

7. Jackie Montalvo, "Dayton Police Officer Kevin Brame's Murder Remains Unsolved After 18 Years," NBC News, November 4, 2017, https://www.nbcnews.com/feature/cold-case-spotlight/dayton-police-officer-kevin-brame-s-murder-remains-unsolved-after-n817476; Cornelius Frolik, "20 Years Later: DPD Officer's Unsolved Murder Still Painful," *Dayton Daily News*, November 29, 2019, https://www.daytondailynews.com/news/local/years-later-dpd-officer-unsolved-murder-still-painful/vVQH3976nbcLyGE38fxktN/.

Chapter 12

1. Mark Bowden, "A Case So Cold It Was Blue," *Vanity Fair*, June 14, 2012, https://www.vanityfair.com/culture/2012/07/lapd-lazurus-murder-mystery-killer.

2. Marc Freeman, "New Details in Notorious 'Killer Clown' Case Show Why Prosecutors Are So Sure Who Was Under the Wig," *South Florida Sun-Sentinel*, November 21, 2020, https://www.sun-sentinel.com/local/palm-beach/fl-ne-killer-clown-case-prosecution-evidence-20201120-jxl2py44t5dgrfypeabrh2nyfa-story.html.

3. Marc Freeman and Paula McMahon, "Used DNA from Hair Samples to Make Cold Case Arrest," *South Florida Sun-Sentinel*, April 12, 2018, https://www.sun-sentinel.com/local/palm-beach/fl-pn-clown-murder-case-evidence-20180412-story.html.

4. Jenner Smith, Lauren Effron, and Ed Lopez, "Killer Clown Suspect's Husband Insists She's 'Falsely Accused' of Shooting His 1st Wife," ABC News, October 19, 2017, https://abcnews.go.com/U.S./killer-clown-suspects-husband-insists-shes-falsely-accused/story?id=50536783; Merris Badcock, "Killer Clown Case: Breakthrough Witness Claims to Know Where Gun, Clown Costume Were Dumped," WPTV, November 14, 2018, https://www.wptv.com/news/region-c-palm-beach-county/wellington/killer-clown-case-breakthrough-witness-claims-to-know-where-gun-clown-costume-were-dumped.

5. "The Ghosts of El Segundo," CBS News, July 5, 2005, https://www.cbsnews.com/news/the-ghosts-of-el-segundo-05-07-2005/.

6. Richard Winton and Steve Berry, "Man Sentenced to Life in Two 1957 Police Murders," *Los Angeles Times*, March 25, 2003, https://www.latimes.com/archives/la-xpm-2003-mar-25-me-segundo25-story.html.

7. "The Clue in the Drum," CBS News, March 8, 2000, https://www.cbsnews.com/news/the-clue-in-the-drum/; Traciy Curry-Reyes, "Reyna Marroquin, Howard Elkins: 'Grave Secrets'--Drum Barrel Murder of Missing Pregnant Immigrant from El Salvador Found Mummified in Jericho, New York Home on ID," TV Crime Sky, April 15, 2012, https://tvcrimesky.com/2017/11/13/reyna-marroquin-howard-elkins-grave-secrets-drum-barrel-murder-of-missing-pregnant-immigrant-from-el-salvador-found-mummified-in-jericho-new-york-home-on-id/889.

8. Peggy O'Hare, "Fingerprints Lead to

Arrest in 1969 Slaying," *Chronicle*, August 27, 2003, https://www.chron.com/news/houston-texas/article/Fingerprints-lead-to-arrest-in-1969-slaying-2129782.php.

9. "Man Gets Life for Rape and Murder 34 Years Ago," *Chronicle*, January 15, 2004, https://www.chron.com/news/houston-texas/article/Man-gets-life-for-rape-and-murder-34-years-ago-1519549.php; Kyle Swenson, "He Said His Wife and Son Moved to South Korea. Decades Later, a Detective Learned the Truth," *The Washington Post*, February 6, 2019, https://www.washingtonpost.com/nation/2019/02/06/he-said-his-wife-son-moved-south-korea-decades-later-detective-learned-truth/.

Appendix A

1. "Justice Department Announces More Than $376 Million in Awards to Promote Public Safety," The United States Department of Justice Newsletter, December 4, 2019. https://www.justice.gov/opa/pr/justice-department-announces-more-376-million-awards-promote-public-safety.

Bibliography

Cold Cases

Cold Case #1—Victim Dana Bartlett
Government of Virgin Islands v. Petersen, 19 F. Supp. 2d 430 (D.V.I. 1998), U.S. District Court for the District of the U.S. Virgin Islands—19 F. Supp. 2d 430 (D.V.I. 1998), Justia U.S. Law, August 28, 1998, https://law.justia.com/cases/federal/district-courts/FSupp2/19/430/2530348/.

Cold Case #2—Victim Annie Tahan
Bowman, Sarah. "Victim's Family Stunned by Murder's Release," *The Beaufort Gazette*, August 19, 2013, https://www.islandpacket.com/news/local/community/beaufort-news/article33527865.html.
Heffernan, Erin. "Lowcountry Homicide Featured on 48 Hours: NCIS," *The State*, June 8, 2017, https://www.thestate.com/entertainment/tv/article155085524.html.
Leach, Jonathan. "48 Hours: NCIS: Body of Evidence." CBS 48 Hours, June 6, 2017. https://www.cbsnews.com/news/48-hours-ncis-annie-tahan-disappearance-murder-body-of-evidence/.

Cold Case #3—Victim Alanda Jean Yusko
"Break in 20-Year-Old Murder," *New Bern Sun Journal*, June 14, 2002, Page 1, https://newspaperarchive.com/new-bern-sun-journal-jun-14-2002-p-1/.
Herbert, Keith. "Man Held in Death of Area Woman in '82: Suspect Is Arrested in North Carolina Slaying of Slatington Resident." *The Morning Call*, June 19, 2002, https://www.mcall.com/news/mc-xpm-2002-06-19-3402444-story.html.

Cold Case #4—Victim Anita Mae Carter Lukander
De Sturler, Alice. "Anita Mae Carter Lukander (Oct 21, 1965–March 18, 1988)," Defrosting Cold Cases, April 18, 2019, https://defrostingcoldcases.com/anita-mae-carter-lukander-oct-21-1965-march-18-1988/.
"FBI Investigating Slaying of Navy Airman," *Associated Press*, March 29, 1988, https://apnews.com/article/27ad508c3502aed4e7ea13b5cee99f47.

Cold Case #5—Victim Pamela Ann Kimbrue
Hernandez, Efrain. "Palmdale Man Charged with 1982 Murder," *Los Angeles Times*, June 28, 1996, https://www.latimes.com/archives/la-xpm-1996-06-28-me-19395-story.html.
Waltz, Lynn. "Californian Man Pleads Guilty to '82 Murder," *The Virginian Pilot*, September 19, 1996, https://scholar.lib.vt.edu/VA-news/VA-Pilot/issues/1996/vp960919/09190346.htm.
Waltz, Lynn. "15 Years After Murder, Family Has Day in Court," *Virginian Pilot*, January

29, 1997, https://scholar.lib.vt.edu/VA-news/VA-Pilot/issues/1997/vp970129/01290461.htm.

Cold Case #6—Victim Allen McClendon

"Former Navy Serviceman Charged In 1992 Murder," *Greensboro News and Record*, July 9, 1998, https://greensboro.com/former-navy-serviceman-charged-in-1992-murder/article_fec0d486-5a6e-5ee3-94cf-c078fe0e5624.html.

Frank, John. "Man Convicted of Murdering Housemate, Eight Years Later," *The Virginian Pilot*, September 30, 2000, https://groups.google.com/g/alt.true-crime/c/_jyaEC2uH2o.

"Police Arrest Woman in Connection with Sailor's 1992 Killing," *Greensboro News and Record*, August 17, 1998, https://greensboro.com/police-arrest-woman-in-connection-with-sailors-1992-killing/article_1a352d7b-40c8-5778-881b-cdf0d3be1afc.html.

Cold Case #7—Victim Shannon Melendi

Aldridge, Donesha, Maddie Ray, and Jon Shirek. "Man Convicted of Killing Emory Student Up for Parole," *First Coast News*, February 20, 2020, https://www.firstcoastnews.com/article/news/crime/melendi-files-hinton-parole-eligible/85-68b849e5-61e9-42b4-9e14-92464114852c.

"A Beloved Miami College Student Vanished 25 Years Ago. There Was a Murder, But No Closure," *Miami Herald*, March 10, 2019, https://www.miamiherald.com/news/local/community/miami-dade/article227379809.html.

Brock, Ed. "Clayton Man Arrested in Killing," *Clayton News Daily*, August 30, 2004, https://www.news-daily.com/news/clayton-man-arrested-in-killing/article_b7a3ae59-45df-508b-a12e-86df9adbcac6.html.

Warnock, Caroline. "Shannon Melendi: Teen Was Abducted and Killed by Convicted Sexual Predator," Heavy, February 6, 2021, https://heavy.com/news/shannon-melendi-murder/.

Cold Case #8—Victims Michael Gretsinger, Sharon Cook Crumitie, and James Luther Blanks

Beach, Marvin, and Justin Pryor. "Former Concord Pastor Convicted Of 2016 Murder, Attempted Murder, WCCB Charlotte, February 21, 2018, https://www.wccbcharlotte.com/2018/02/21/victims-mother-concord-pastor-accused-in-shooting-should-have-been-in-jail/.

"Former Kannapolis Pastor on Trial for Murder," *Independent Tribune*, February 5, 2018, https://independenttribune.com/news/former-kannapolis-pastor-on-trial-for-murder/article_017c86d0-0a91-11e8-a031-ff10eb7b80e6.html.

Kidd, Erin. "Crumitie's Charge Upgraded to Murder," *Independent Tribune*, August 23, 2016, https://independenttribune.com/news/crumities-charge-upgraded-to-murder/article_8b4ed244-6972-11e6-8963-7319eee6c38e.html.

"Man Serving Life Sentence Charged in Murder of Woman Found Near Mooresville Last January," *Statesville*, January 23, 2020, https://statesville.com/news/crime/man-serving-life-sentence-charged-in-murder-of-woman-found-near-mooresville-last-january/article_4538d245-d843-5362-befa-c4060389e344.html

Marusk, Joe. "Former NC Pastor Charged with Murder of Missing Woman. Police Say He's Killed Before," *Charlotte Observer*, January 23, 2020, https://www.charlotteobserver.com/news/state/north-carolina/article239561193.html

State of North Carolina v. Timothy Lavaun Crumitie, Justia US Law, No. COA18–781, 16 July 2019, Mecklenburg County, Nos. 16 CRS 230974–75, 23322, 229841–42, https://law.justia.com/cases/north-carolina/court-of-appeals/2019/18-781.html

Cold Case #9—Victim Steven S. November

"2 Carrier Sailors Accused of Murder," *Daily Press*, May 30, 1998, https://www.dailypress.com.

United States v. Hector A. Coleman Airman Apprentice, *U.S. Navy Judge Advocate General's Corps* (E-2), U. S. Navy in the U.S. Navy Marine Corps Court of Criminal Appeals Washington Navy Yard, Washington D.C., Charles Wm. DORMAN, NMCCA 200101009, February 10, 2006 https://www.jag.navy.mil/courts/documents/archive/2006/COLEMAN%20H.A.%20200101009%20unpub.pdf.

Cold Case #10—Victim Scott Dunn

Coryell, Lisa. "Former Yardley, PA. Man Was Able to Bury His Son, More Than Decade After His Murder," NJ Com, True New Jersey, March 30, 2019, https://www.nj.com/mercer/2012/10/former_yardley_pa_man_is_final.html.

Logan, Nicki Bruce. "Family May Finally Get Answer in 1991 Disappearance," *My Plainview*, May 21, 2012, https://www.myplainview.com/news/article/Family-may-finally-get-answer-in-1991-8416196.php.

"Medical Examiner Concludes Human Remains Are Scott Dunn," KCBD News, October 17, 2016, https://www.kcbd.com/story/18604205/medical-examiner-concludes-human-remains-are-scott-dunn/.

Sinclair, Andrea. "Dunn's Remains Preserved by Killers' Wrapping Method," *Lubbock Avalanche-Journal*, May 23, 2012, https://www.lubbockonline.com/article/20120523/NEWS/305239780.

Writes, Ana. "24-Year-Old Scott Dunn Was Killed by His Girlfriend," Medium, October 19, 2021, https://medium.com/the-criminalist/vengeful-girlfriend-kills-boyfriend-after-finding-out-about-his-fiancée-f551e73b2b7d.

Cold Case #11—Victim Deborah Wilson

"Army Reservist and Drexel University Security Guard David Dickson Murdered Deborah Wilson on Campus; Sentenced to Life in Prison," Military Justice for All, November 30, 1984, https://militaryjusticeforall.com/1984/11/30/army-recruiter-drexel-university-security-guard-david-dickson-murdered-student-deborah-wilson-stole-her-sneakers-sentenced-to-life-in-prison-1984/.

Beale, Lewis. "To Catch a Killer: A Bunch of Cops and Attorneys Get Together Once a Month to Try to Crack Unsolved Cases," *Los Angeles Times*, May 13, 1992, https://www.latimes.com/archives/la-xpm-1992-05-13-vw-1584-story.html.

"Foot Fetishist Convicted of Murdering Barefoot Student," *Associated Press*, December 2, 1995, https://apnews.com/article/b5d2113df4bbdfe03c1a2369f23c409c.

"Former Guard at Drexel U. Convicted of Student's Murder," *Chronicle*, December 15, 1995, https://www.chronicle.com/article/former-guard-at-drexel-u-convicted-of-students-murder/.

"Lurid Tapes Figure in Death Case," *Orlando Sentinel*, July 3, 1993, https://www.orlandosentinel.com/news/os-xpm-1993-07-03-9307030398-story.html.

"Unusual Suspects Premiered 'Barefoot Homicide' on ID: Drexel University Student Deborah Wilson Found Murdered on Campus," Military Justice for All, April 5, 2015. https://militaryjusticeforall.com/tag/david-dickson/.

Wallace, Rob, Lauren Putrino, and Tom McCarthy. "Cold Case Squad: Modern-Day 'Sherlock Holmes' Team Takes on Oregon Slaying," ABC News, August 11, 2010. https://abcnews.go.com/2020/leah-freeman-oregon-teen-murder-vidocq-society/story?id=11374958.

Cold Case #12—Victims Troy and LaDonna French

Battaglia, Danielle. "Newly Released 911 Audio from French Killings Filled with Terror, Despair," *Greensboro Rockingham Now*, July 18, 2017, https://greensboro.com/rockingham_now/news/newly-released-911-audio-from-french-killings-filled-with-terror-despair/article_9e5f4939-a05d-56be-afc8-718542d01a0d.html.

Williamson, Sarah Newell. "Judge Says Jose Alvarez Will 'Die in Prison' in French Double Homicide Sentencing," *Greensboro News & Record*, July 8, 2016, https://journalnow.

com/news/local/judge-says-jose-alvarez-will-die-in-prison-in-french-double-homicide-sentencing/article_8c21e8c1-4b1a-5183-9651-31281ee82b28.html.

Cold Case #13—Victim Carol Hutto

"HS Student Carol Hutto Found Dead in Largo, Florida Pond; Boyfriend and Navy P.O. James Kuenn Sentenced to Life in Prison Two Decades Later (1976)," *Military Justice for All*, February 11, 2000, https://militaryjusticeforall.com/1976/12/13/carol-hutto-largo-florida-1976/.

"Man Convicted of 1976 Murder," *Associated Press*, February 9, 2000, https://apnews.com/article/c80519dc671a9ec738cb9ec7f531f9d1.

Stirgus, Eric. "After 24 Years, He's Found Guilty," *Tampa Bay Times*, September 26, 2005, https://www.tampabay.com/archive/2000/02/10/after-24-years-he-s-found-guilty/.

Stirgus, Eric. "The Victim's Mother Lectures the Killer, Sentenced to Life 'You took that away,'" *Tamp Bay Times*, February 16, 2000, https://www.tampabay.com/archive/2000/02/16/the-victim-s-mother-lectures-the-killer-sentenced-to-life-you-took-that-away/.

Cold Case #14—Victim Judy Johnson

James, Sara. "Killer Instinct," NBC News, January 2, 2009, https://www.nbcnews.com/id/wbna28471722.

U.S. Supreme Court, Elkins v. United States, 364 U.S. 206 (1960), No. 126, Argued March 28–29, 1960, Decided June 27, 1960, 364 U.S. 206, Justia US Law, https://supreme.justia.com/cases/federal/us/364/206/.

"Wrongly Convicted Ohio Man Snags Another Man's Cigarette Butt to Clear His Name," *True Crime Daily*, June 5, 2017, https://truecrimedaily.com/2017/06/05/wrongly-convicted-ohio-man-snags-other-inmates-cigarette-butt-to-clear-his-name/.

Young, Matt. "Incredible Story of the Murder of Judith Johnson, and How Her Daughter Found Her Killer," *New Zealand Herald*, May 19, 2017, https://www.nzherald.co.nz/world/incredible-story-of-the-murder-of-judith-johnson-and-how-her-daughter-found-her-killer/MBWFX5W7X65YX74IPR5UFWKMFQ/.

Cold Case #15—Victims Helen List, Patricia List, John List, Jr., and Frederick List

Bridget Lusky. "Was John List the Nastiest Mass Murderer of All Time?" *Film Daily*, March 16, 2020, https://filmdaily.co/news/john-list-mass-murderer/.

"1971 Family Killer Breaks Silence," ABC News, January 5, 2006, https://abcnews.go.com/2020/story?id=132646&page=1.

Serena, Katie. "John List, the Mass Murderer Who Killed His Family so He'd See Them in Heaven," *All That's Interesting*, November 16, 2021, https://allthatsinteresting.com/john-list.

State v. List, 270 N.J. Super. 169 (1993), 636 A.2d 1054, State of New Jersey, Plaintiff-Respondent v. John E. List, Defendant-Appellant, Superior Court of New Jersey, Appellate Division, Argued April 27, 1993, Decided June 21, 1993, 171 Before Judges PRESSLER, R.S. COHEN and KESTIN, Justia US Law, https://law.justia.com/cases/new-jersey/appellate-division-published/1993/270-n-j-super-169-1.html.

Waterman, Cole. "America's Most Wanted Killer John List Remains Infamous Bogeyman in His Michigan Hometown," Mlive, November 09, 2021, https://www.mlive.com/news/2021/11/americas-most-wanted-killer-john-list-remains-infamous-bogeyman-in-his-michigan-hometown.html.

Cold Case #16—Victim Joann Katrinak

Harris, Chris. "WATCH: ID Examines Controversial 1994 Case of Woman Convicted of Murdering Ex-Boyfriend's Wife and Son," *People*, March 2, 2017, https://people.com/crime/murder-lehigh-valley-controversial-patricia-rorrer-conviction/.

Reisner, Rebecca. "Joann Katrinak's Killer Still Has Innocence Advocates," Forensic Files, September 26, 2020, https://forensicfilesnow.com/index.php/2020/09/26/patricia-rorrer-an-update/comment-page-1/.
Temple, John. "Longtime Suspect Charged in Murders," *News & Record*, June 25, 1997, https://greensboro.com/longtime-suspect-charged-in-murders/article_d7f1cb67-8f81-560b-a67c-fabcbde6a99b.html.

Cold Case #17—Victim Identities Not Revealed
Basak, Asena. "48 Hours: NCIS: Can Agents Stop a Ruthless Attacker Preying on Marine Wives?" CBS 48 Hours, May 22, 2018, https://www.cbsnews.com/news/48-hours-ncis-can-agents-stop-a-ruthless-attacker-preying-on-marine-wives/.
"48 Hours NCIS Premiered 'Ruthless' on CBS: The True Crime Story of Serial Rapist and Camp Lejeune Janitor Willie Abner Brown," Military Justice for All, May 26, 2018, https://militaryjusticeforall.com/tag/willie-abner-brown/.
"Man Accused of Multiple Rapes," *The Daily News* (Jacksonville, NC), May 1, 2013, https://www.jdnews.com/article/20130501/News/305019924.
North Carolina Court of Appeals, State of North Carolina v. Willie Abner Brown, Defendant, No. COA14-814, Onslow County, Nos. 12 CRS 5633-36, 56338-39, 13 CRS 52796-84, 13 CRS 52807, Justia U.S. Law, December 16, 2014, https://law.justia.com/cases/north-carolina/court-of-appeals/2014/14-814.html.
Todd, Michael. "Convicted Serial Rapist Re-Sentenced," *The Daily News* (Jacksonville, NC), January 27, 2015, https://www.jdnews.com/article/20150127/News/301279877.

Cold Case #18—Victim Lacoy McQueen
Blythe, Amy. "Man Gets Life Sentence in 20-Year-Old Raleigh Murder Case," *The News & Observer*, February 29, 2016, https://www.newsobserver.com/news/local/crime/article63157462.html.
"Concord Man Charged with Murder in 1996 Killing," *Independent Tribune*, December 18, 2014 Updated Apr 7, 2019, https://independenttribune.com/news/concord-man-charged-with-murder-in-1996-killing/article_60c16dda-86f6-11e4-808a-0f7e25450538.html.
State v. Lawing, In the Court of Appeals of North Carolina, No. COA17-231, Justia Law, June 5, 2018, No. 14CRS007299, https://law.justia.com/cases/north-carolina/court-of-appeals/2018/17-231.html.
State v. Lawing, Justia US Law, October 20, 2015, COA14–1288, Mecklenberg County, No. 12 CRS 246991, https://law.justia.com/cases/north-carolina/court-of-appeals/2015/14-1288.html.

Cold Case #19—Victim Linda Faye Rodgers
The People, Plaintiff and Respondent, v. Kenneth Clair, Defendant and Appellant, Supreme Court of California, In Bank, FindLaw, No. S004789, May 07, 1992, https://caselaw.findlaw.com/ca-supreme-court/1774317.html.
People v. Clair [No. S004789. Crim. No. 26423. May 7, 1992.] The People, Plaintiff and Respondent, v. Kenneth Clair, Defendant and Appellant, Justia US Law, https://law.justia.com/cases/california/supreme-court/4th/2/629.html.
"Tony Saavedra, DA Explains Why DNA Doesn't Exonerate Convicted Murderer Kenneth Clair," *Orange County Register*, June 13, 2016, https://www.ocregister.com/2016/01/14/da-explains-why-dna-doesnt-exonerate-convicted-murderer-kenneth-clair/.
Wride, Nancy. "Santa Ana Man Held in Torture and Murder of Disabled Baby Sitter," *Los Angeles Times*, January 25, 1985, https://www.latimes.com/archives/la-xpm-1985-01-25-me-9402-story.html.

Cold Case #20—Victims Lois Petrie, Catherine Medina, Anna Felch, Irene Hind, Maude Burgess and Leah Griffin

Blankstein, Andrew, and Richard Winton. "Man Is Charged in 1972 Murder," *Los Angeles Times*, September 10, 2003, https://www.latimes.com/archives/la-xpm-2003-sep-10-me-kill10-story.html.

Fan, Ryan. "The Santa Strangler Was Caught Almost 30 Years After His Murders," Newsbreak, January 11, 2021, https://original.newsbreak.com/@ryan-fan-561172/2141931294255-the-santa-strangler-was-caught-almost-30-years-after-his-murders.

"Octogenarian Convicted of Woman's Christmas Eve 1972 Slaying," *San Diego Union-Tribune*, November 21, 2006, https://www.sandiegouniontribune.com/sdut-octogenarian-convicted-of-womans-christmas-eve-2006nov21-story.html.

Van Derbeken, Jaxon. "How Alleged Serial Killer Fell into Trap/ Man's Loose Lips Led to Ruse to get DNA," *San Francisco Gate*, September 21, 2003, https://www.sfgate.com/news/article/How-alleged-serial-killer-fell-into-trap-Man-s-2556309.php.

Cold Case #21—Victim Verle Lee Hartley

Brown, Jerry. "Navy Lt. Lee Hartley Was Murdered by His Wife Pamela Hartley: 48 Hours on ID: NCIS Investigates," Monsters and Critics, July 17, 2020, https://www.monstersandcritics.com/tv/true-crime/navy-lt-lee-hartley-was-murdered-by-his-wife-pamela-hartley/.

Hughes, Jason. "Unusual Suspects: Navy Man Poisoned by Wife's Care Packages," Huffington Post, December 10, 2012, https://www.huffpost.com/entry/unusual-suspects-care-package-poison-video_n_2269822.

Leach, Jonathan. "Mysterious Poisoning of a Navy Lieutenant Leads to One of NCIS' Most Notorious Cold Cases," CBS News, May 29, 2019, https://www.cbsnews.com/news/mysterious-poisoning-death-of-a-navy-lieutenant-leads-to-one-of-ncis-most-notorious-cold-case-investigations/.

"Navy Lt. Verle Lee Hartley Died of Arsenic Poisoning in 1982; NCIS Cold Case Squad Solved Murder 13 Years Later; Wife Pamela Served 16 of 40 Years in Prison, Paroled (November 18, 1982)," Military Justice for All, May 29, 2019, https://militaryjusticeforall.com/1982/11/18/lt-verle-lee-hartley-us-navy-1982/.

"Navy Spouse Pamela Hartley Pleaded Guilty to the 2nd Degree Murder of Lt. Verle Lee Hartley in Florida State Court," Military Justice, October 16, 1996, https://militaryjusticeforall.com/tag/pam-hartley/.

Cold Case #22—Victims Bertha Tardy, Carmen Rigby, Robert Golden and Derrick "Bobo" Stewart

Flowers v. Mississippi, 136 S. Ct. 2157, NO. 2010-DP-01348-SCT (2016), Justia US Law, June 19, 2010, https://law.justia.com/cases/mississippi/supreme-court/2017/2010-dp-01348-sct.html.

McLaughlin, Elliott C. "Mississippi Prosecutor Who Tried Curtis Flowers on Murder Charges Six Times Steps Down," CNN, January 8, 2020, https://www.cnn.com/2020/01/07/us/mississippi-curtis-flowers-prosecutor-recuses/index.html.

"Mississippi Judge Frees Curtis Flowers on Bail After Six Trials and 23 Years in Jail," Death Penalty Information Center, December 16, 2019, https://deathpenaltyinfo.org/news/mississippi-judge-frees-curtis-flowers-on-bail-after-six-trials-and-23-years-in-jail.

Pettus, Emily Wagster, and Jeff Amy. "No 7th Trial for Mississippi Man Freed from Prison in 2019," WCTI, September 4, 2020, https://wcti12.com/news/nation-world/no-7th-trial-for-mississippi-man-freed-from-prison-in-2019.

Zhu, Alissa. "Curtis Flowers: What You Need to Know About the Winona Furniture Store Quadruple Homicides," *Mississippi Clarion Ledger*, March 18, 2019, https://www.clarionledger.com/story/news/2019/03/18/curtis-flowers-what-you-need-know-quadruple-homicide/3128793002/.

Cold Case #23—Victim Jose Arreola
"Evaristo Salas Junior Salas Washington," Actual Innocent Prisoners, April 19, 2020, https://actualinnocentprisoners.com/evaristo-salas-jr.
Ferlolito, Phil. "An Alibi, a Sanitized Murder Scene and an Informant Who Says He Lied. Is the Wrong Man in a Spokane-area Jail for This Sunnyside Slaying?" *The Spokesman Review*, June 24, 2018, https://www.spokesman.com/stories/2018/jun/24/an-alibi-a-sanitized-murder-scene-and-an-informant/.
Ferlolito, Phil. "Evaristo Salas Still Claims He Was Wrongfully Convicted in a 1995 Murder," *Yakima Herald-Republic*, July 12, 2020, https://www.yakimaherald.com/news/crime_and_courts/evaristo-salas-still-claims-he-was-wrongfully-convicted-in-a-1995-murder-he-may-get/article_e3f33f67-91bd-59af-84a8-573ea724909f.html.
Ferolito, Phil. "Family, Friends Rally in Hopes of a New Trial for Evaristo Salas in 1995 Sunnyside Murder," *Yakima Herald-Republic*, August 22, 2021, https://www.spokesman.com/stories/2021/aug/22/family-friends-rally-in-hopes-of-a-new-trial-for-e/.
Ferolito, Phil. "Judge Denies New Trial for Salas, Who Aims to Clear His Name in '96 Sunnyside Murder Conviction," *Yakima Herald-Republic*, November 1, 2021, https://www.yakimaherald.com/news/local/judge-denies-new-trial-for-salas-who-aims-to-clear-his-name-in-96-sunnyside/article_5ad775d7-b98e-5a5b-91ee-10884dbca56e.html.

Cold Case #24—Victim Jessie Nicole Morrison
Akshay, Pai. "Grandmother Jailed for Brutally Murdering Pregnant Woman and Her Unborn Child Could Be Innocent, Docu Claims," Media Entertainment Arts World-Wide, February 7, 2020, https://meaww.com/wrong-man-51-year-old-grandmother-convicted-killing-pregnant-woman-believed-to-be-innocent.
Little, Ken. "Convictions Affirmed by Appeals Court," *The Greenville Sun*, February 25, 2021, https://www.greenevillesun.com/news/local_news/vonda-star-smith-murder-convictions-affirmed-by-appeals-court/article_35bf375f-b3a5-5764-bfc7-9f27a6d8ea4e.html.

Cold Case #25—Victims Jay Cook and Tonya Van Cuylenborg
Hutton, Caleb. "Jurors Share Why They Found Talbott Guilty of Double Murder," *Herald*, July 7, 2019, https://www.heraldnet.com/news/jurors-share-why-they-found-talbott-guilty-of-double-murder/.
Hutton, Caleb. "Life in Prison for 1987 Killer of Young Canadian Couple," *Seattle Weekly*, July 23, 2019, https://www.seattleweekly.com/news/life-in-prison for 1987 killer of young canadian-couple/.
Hutton, Caleb. "Talbott Trial Testimony Retraces a 30-year Murder Mystery," *Herald*, June 25, 2019, https://www.heraldnet.com/news/talbott-trial-testimony-retraces-a-30-year-murder-mystery/.
Molteni, Megan. "The First Murder Case to Use Family Tree Forensics Goes to Trial," Wired, June 18, 2019, https://www.wired.com/story/the-first-murder-case-to-use-family-tree-forensics-goes-to-trial/.
"SeaTac Man Convicted of 1987 Murders of Canadian Couple after DNA Evidence Linked Him to Case," *Seattle Times*, June 28, 2019, https://www.seattletimes.com/seattle-news/crime/seatac-man-convicted-of-1987-murders-of-canadian-couple-after-dna-evidence-linked-him-to-case/.

Cold Case #26—Victim Angie Raye Dodge
Aldhous, Peter. "Genetic Genealogy Helped Finally Crack the 1996 Murder of 18-Year-Old Angie Dodge," Buzz Feed News, May 16, 2019, https://www.buzzfeednews.com/article/peteraldhous/angie-dodge-cold-case-murder-genetic-genealogy-parabon.
Bishop, Shane. "Police Arrest Idaho Man in 23-Year-Old Cold Case Murder of Angie Dodge," NBC News, May 16, 2019, https://www.nbcnews.com/dateline/police-arrest-idaho-man-23-year-old-cold-case-murder-n1006720.

"DNA Testing Identifies Actual Perpetrator in 1996 Idaho Falls Rape and Murder, Confirming Christopher Tapp's Innocence," Innocence Project, July 17, 2019, https://innocenceproject.org/christopher-tapp-exoneration/.

Eaton, Nate. "The Angie Dodge Case From 1996 Until Today. What's Happened, Why and What's Next," *East Idaho News*, July 17, 2019, https://www.eastidahonews.com/2019/07/the-angie-dodge-case-from-1996-until-today-whats-happened-why-and-whats-next/.

Halaban, Boaz, Marc Dorian, Sandy Evans, Carrie Cook, and Haley Yamada. "Mom Overturns Wrongful Convictions, Catches True Killer in Daughter's Murder 25 Years Later," ABC News, March 13, 2021, https://abc7chicago.com/angie-dodge-killed-mom-solves-daughters-murder-carol-abc-2020/10413871/.

Otterbourg, Ken. "Christopher Tapp: Time Served: 21 Years," Innocence Project, July 17, 2019, https://innocenceproject.org/cases/christopher-tapp-has-murder-conviction-vacated-after-serving-21-years/.

Smith, Danny R. "The Unsolved Murder of Angie Dodge," The Murder Memo, June 13, 2018, https://dickiefloydnovels.com/angie-dodge-murder/.

State of Idaho, Plaintiff-Respondent, v. Christopher C. Tapp, Defendant-Appellant., No. 25295, Decided: Find Law, July 20, 2001, https://caselaw.findlaw.com/id-court-of-appeals/1368675.html.

Cold Case #27—Victim Jane Hylton

Bonvillian, Crystal. "Man Cleared of Murder by Genetic Genealogy After 15 Years in Prison, New Suspect Charged," Boston 25 News, February 19, 2020, https://www.boston25news.com/news/trending/california-man-cleared-murder-by-genetic-genealogy-after-15-years-prison-new-suspect-charged/IAOFAYHAQJCZZALDPX5BZDZ4YU/.

"DNA Clears Imprisoned Man in 1985 Murder as New Suspect Is Identified," *Los Angeles Times*, February 13, 2020, https://www.latimes.com/california/story/2020-02-13/a-man-was-found-innocent-after-15-years-in-custody-and-a-new-suspect-was-identified-in-the-decades-old-crime.

Giles, Anna. "New DNA Evidence Exonerates Man Convicted in 1985 El Dorado Hills Murder; New Suspect Arrested," CBS Sacramento, February 13, 2020, https://sacramento.cbslocal.com/2020/02/13/ricky-davis-exonerated-jane-hylton-1985-murder-genetic-genealogy/.

Cold Case #28—Victims Angela Brosso and Melanie Bernas

Billeaud, Jaques. "Bid to Toss DNA Evidenced in Phoenix Canal Killings Rejected," *Times Union*, February 3, 2021.

Casey, Matthew. "Canal Murder Suspect Felt Chills After '89 Stabbing," *The Republic AZ Central*, January 23, 2015, https://www.azcentral.com/story/news/local/phoenix/2015/01/23/phoenix-bryan-patrick-miller-canal-murders-juvenile-records/22230819/.

Cassidy, Megan. "How Forensic Genealogy Led to an Arrest in the Phoenix 'Canal Killer' Case," *The Republic AZ Central*, November 30, 2016, https://www.azcentral.com/story/news/local/phoenix/2016/11/30/how-forensic-genealogy-led-arrest-phoenix-canal-killer-case-bryan-patrick-miller-dna/94565410/.

Cassidy, Megan. "Prosecutors Seek Death Penalty in Canal Murders," *The Republic AZ Central*, June 5, 2015, https://www.azcentral.com/story/news/local/phoenix/2015/06/05/miller-death-penalty-abrk/28557259/.

Costantino, Ann. "Pretrial Hearings Underway for 'Zombie Hunter' Accused in Heinous Murder of Camp Hill, Pennsylvania Woman Killed in Arizona," *The Gunpowder Gazette*, October 27, 2019, https://gunpowdergazette.com/2019/10/27/pretrial-hearings-underway-for-heinous-murder-of-camp-hill-pennsylvania-woman-murdered-in-arizona/.

Cold Case #29—Victim Sarah Yarborough

Green, Sarah Jean. "Arrest Made in Death of Federal Way Teen Nearly 30 Years After Her Body Was Found," *The Seattle Times*, October 3, 2019, https://www.seattletimes.com/seattle-news/crime/arrest-made-in-death-of-federal-way-teen-after-nearly-28-years/.

Halverson, Alex. "55-year-old Charged with 1991 Murder of Federal Way Teen; DNA Evidence Led to Arrest," *Seattle P-I*, October. 3, 2019, https://www.seattlepi.com/local/crime/article/55-year-old-arrested-in-connection-with-1991-14490324.php.

Shapiro, Emily. "Man Arrested in 1991 Cold Case Killing of 16-Year-Old Girl After He's Linked by DNA: Sheriff," ABC News, October 4, 2019, https://abcnews.go.com/US/man-arrested-1991-cold-case-killing-16-year/story?id=66057562.

Sullivan, Olivia. "Covington Man Arrested for 1991 Cold Case Murder of 16-Year-Old Federal Way Girl," *Seattle Weekly*, October 4, 2019, https://www.seattleweekly.com/news/covington-man-arrested-for-1991-cold-case-murder-of-16-year-old-federal-way-girl/.

Testa, Jessica. "Nobody Was Going to Solve These Cold Cases. Then Came the DNA Crime Solvers," Buzz Feed News, September 22, 2018, https://www.buzzfeednews.com/article/jtes/dna-cold-case-crime-doe-project-genealogy.

Cold Case #30—Victim Michelle Martinko

Mehaffey, Trish. "Jerry Burns Found Guilty in 1979 Killing of High School Student," *The Courier*, February 25, 2020, https://wcfcourier.com/news/local/crime-and-courts/update-new-details-jerry-burns-found-guilty-in-1979-killing-of-high-school-student/article_735cf464-5ebc-5c31-a3d0-965486834236.html.

Moulton, Jan. "Michelle Martinko's Murder 'Haunted' the Cedar Rapids Community for 40 Years. Now Her Suspected Killer Is Set to Go on Trial," *Little Village Magazine*, October 2, 2019, https://littlevillagemag.com/michelle-martinko-murder-trial/.

Payne, Kate. "Burns Sentenced to Life in Prison for Martinko Murder, Plans to Appeal," Iowa Public Radio News, August 7, 2020, https://www.iowapublicradio.org/ipr-news/2020-08-07/burns-sentenced-to-life-in-prison-for-martinko-murder-plans-to-appeal.

Sides, Sam. "Timeline: What Led to the Arrest, Trial and Conviction of Jerry Burns," We Are Iowa, February 24, 2020, https://www.weareiowa.com/article/news/local/jerry-burns-murder-michelle-martinko-trial-guilty-timeline/524-88e06942-6134-4506-837d-953433e24218.

Spoerre, Anna. "DNA on a Straw Helps Jury Convict Man of Murder in 1979 Slaying of Iowa Teen," *The Des Moines Register*, February 25, 2020, https://www.usatoday.com/story/news/nation/2020/02/25/jerry-lynn-burns-trial-michelle-martinko-murder-iowa-cold-case/4866603002/.

Cold Case #31—Victim Mary Edith Salvani

Baldas, Tresa. "DNA Reveals Identity of Woman Killed in Nevada in 1982—She Was from Detroit," *Detroit Free Press*, May 9, 2019, https://www.freep.com/story/news/local/michigan/2019/05/09/sheeps-flat-jane-doe-detroit-nevada/1141658001/.

Baldas, Tresa. "She Was Killed 37 Years Ago—and Her Friends Just Found Out: 'She was my bridesmaid,'" *Detroit Free Press*, June 7, 2019, https://www.freep.com/story/news/local/michigan/detroit/2019/06/07/jane-doe-dna-sheeps-flat-lake-tahoe-mary-savila/1361068001/.

Gomez, Mark. "Cold Case: DNA Links Suspected South Bay Killer to 1982 Tahoe Murder," *Mercury News*, May 8, 2019. https://www.mercurynews.com/2019/05/08/cold-case-dna-links-south-bay-killer-to-1982-nevada-murder/.

Hernandez, Lauren. "Suspect in 37-Year-Old Unsolved Lake Tahoe Homicide Linked to Bay Area," *San Francisco Chronicle*, May 8, 2019, https://www.sfchronicle.com/crime/article/Suspect-in-37-year-old-unsolved-Lake-Tahoe-13827776.php.

Cold Case #32—Victim Sheri Rasmussen

Bowden, Mark. "A Case So Cold It Was Blue," *Vanity Fair*, June 14, 2012, https://www.vanityfair.com/culture/2012/07/lapd-lazarus-murder-mystery-killer.

"Matthew McGough on How an LAPD Officer Hid a Murder for Nearly 30 Years," *Los Angeles Times*, May 3, 2019, https://www.latimes.com/books/la-et-jc-matthew-mcgough-interview-20190503-story.html.

McGough, Matthew. "The Lazarus File," *The Atlantic*, June 2011, https://www.theatlantic.com/magazine/archive/2011/06/the-lazarus-file/308499/.

Mikulan, Steven. "In Plain Sight," *Los Angeles Magazine*, September 1, 2012, https://www.lamag.com/citythinkblog/in-plain-sight1/.

State of California, Second Appellate District. Division Four. The People, Plaintiff and Respondent,v. Stephanie Ilene Lazarus, B241172, Los Angeles County Super. Ct. No. BA357423, Justia US Law, July 13, 2015, https://law.justia.com/cases/california/court-of-appeal/2015/b241172.html.

Cold Case #33—Victim Marlene Warren

Badcock, Merris. "Killer Clown Case: Breakthrough Witness Claims to Know Where Gun, Clown Costume Were Dumped," WPTV, November 14, 2018, https://www.wptv.com/news/region-c-palm-beach-county/wellington/killer-clown-case-breakthrough-witness-claims-to-know-where-gun-clown-costume-were-dumped.

Freeman, Marc. "New Details in Notorious 1990 'Killer Clown' Case Show Why Prosecutors Are So Sure Who Was Under the Wig," *Sun Sentinel*, November 20, 2021, https://www.sun-sentinel.com/local/palm-beach/fl-ne-killer-clown-case-prosecution-evidence-20201120-jxl2py44t5dgrfypeabrh2nyfa-story.html.

Freeman, Marc, and Paula McMahon. "Used DNA from Hair Samples to Make Cold Case Arrest," *South Florida Sun-Sentinel*, April 12, 2018, https://www.sun-sentinel.com/local/palm-beach/fl-pn-clown-murder-case-evidence-20180412-story.html.

"Killer-Clown Cold Case Leads to Arrest of Woman at Center of Florida Love Triangle," NBC News, September 27, 2017, https://www.wrcbtv.com/story/36465083/killer-clown-cold-case-leads-to-arrest-of-woman-at-center-of-florida-love-triangle.

Luscombe, Richard. "Florida Case of Clown Who Killed Woman Solved, Police Say—27 Years Later," *The Guardian*, September 28, 2017, https://www.theguardian.com/us-news/2017/sep/28/florida-clown-killing-marlene-warren-sheila-keen.

Smith, Jennifer, and Lauren Effron. "Killer Clown Suspect's Husband Insists She's 'Falsely Accused' of Shooting His 1st Wife," ABC News, October 19, 2017, https://abcnews.go.com/U.S./killer-clown-suspects-husband-insists-shes-falsely-accused/story?id=50536783.

Sorrell, Robert. "COVID-19 Delays Clown Murder Trial in Florida," *Herald Courier*, May 14, 2020, https://heraldcourier.com/news/covid-19-delays-clown-murder-trial-in-florida/article_f16a49b9-e19c-54f1-9db4-8b59a3ea0709.html,

Cold Case #34—Victims Richard Phillips and Milton Curtis

"El Segundo Cop Killing Cold Case," Criminally Intrigued, July 29, 2017, https://www.criminallyintrigued.com/blog/2017/7/18/el-segundo-cop-killing-cold-case.

"The Ghosts of El Segundo," CBS News, July 5, 2005, https://www.cbsnews.com/news/the-ghosts-of-el-segundo-05-07-2005/.

"Men Sentenced to Life in Two 1957 Police Murders," *Los Angeles Times*, March 25, 2003, https://www.latimes.com/archives/la-xpm-2003-mar-25-me-segundo25-story.html.

Rees, Chris. "Columbia Man Accused of 1957 Murders Enters Guilty Pleas," *WIS News*, March 24, 2003, https://www.wistv.com/story/1195607/columbia-man-accused-of-1957-murders-enters-guilty-pleas/.

Winton, Richard, and Steve Berry. "Man Sentenced to Life in Two 1957 Police Murders," *The Los Angeles Times*, March 25, 2003, https://www.latimes.com/archives/la-xpm-2003-mar-25-me-segundo25-story.html.

Cold Case #35—Victim Reyan Angelica Marroguin

"The Clue in the Drum," CBS News 48 Hours, March 8, 2000, https://www.cbsnews.com/news/the-clue-in-the-drum/.

Curry, Traciy Reyes. "Reyna Marroquin, Howard Elkins: 'Grave Secrets'--Drum Barrel Murder of Missing Pregnant Immigrant from El Salvador Found Mummified in Jericho, New York Home on ID," TV Crime Sky, April 15, 2012, https://tvcrimesky.com/2017/11/13/reyna-marroquin-howard-elkins-grave-secrets-drum-barrel-murder-of-missing-pregnant-immigrant-from-el-salvador-found-mummified-in-jericho-new-york-home-on-id/889.

Jin, Liz. "The Murder of a 9-Month Pregnant Woman Whose Body Was Found in a Barrel," Medium, November 3, 2020, https://medium.com/chameleon/the-murder-of-a-9-month-pregnant-woman-whose-body-was-found-in-a-barrel-35604dd57cf2.

"The Reyna Marroquin Story Unsealed," Forensic Files Now, February 23, 2017, https://forensicfilesnow.com/index.php/tag/reyna-marroquin/.

Cold Case #36—Victim Dianne Maxwell Jackson

"Houston Cold Case Solved Forensics Personnel Honored by FBI," *FBI News*, October 14, 2011, https://www.fbi.gov/news/stories/houston-cold-case-solved.

"Man Gets Life for Rape and Murder 34 Years Ago," *Chronicle* (Houston, TX), January 15, 2004, https://www.chron.com/news/houston-texas/article/Man-gets-life-for-rape-and-murder-34-years-ago-1519549.php.

O'Hare, Peggy. "Fingerprints Lead to Arrest in 1969 Slaying," *Chronicle* (Houston, TX), August 27, 2003, https://www.chron.com/news/houston-texas/article/Fingerprints-lead-to-arrest-in-1969-slaying-2129782.php.

Cold Case #37—Victims Myoung Hwa Cho-Whitt and Robert "Bobby" Adam Whitt

Betz, Bradford. "20-Year-Old Cold Case Solved After Murdered Mom and Son ID'd by DNA," *New York Post*, February 6, 2019, https://nypost.com/2019/02/06/20-year-old-cold-case-solved-after-murdered-mom-and-son-idd-by-dna/.

Croxton, Katie. "20 Years Later, Gap Remains for Family of Slain Mother, Boy," *The Times News*, February 8, 2019, https://www.thetimesnews.com/news/20190208/20-years-later-gap-remains-for-family-of-slain-mother-boy.

Fruen, Lauren. "Father Faces Charges for Murdering Wife and Young Son," *Daily Mail*, May 14, 2019, https://www.dailymail.co.uk/news/article-7027579/Man-charged-sons-death-20-years-remains-found.html.

"Man Gets Life for Rape and Murder 34 Years Ago," *Chronicle* (Houston, TX), January 15, 2004, https://www.chron.com/news/houston-texas/article/Man gets life for rape and murder-34-years-ago-1519549.php.

Swenson, Kyle. "He Said His Wife and Son Moved to South Korea. Decades later, A Detective Learned the Truth," *The Washington Post*, February 6, 2019, https://www.washingtonpost.com/nation/2019/02/06/he-said-his-wife-son-moved-south-korea-decades-later-detective-learned-truth/.

Unsolved Cold Cases

Unsolved Cold Case #1—Victim Debra Jackson

Falcon, Russel, and Will Dupree. "Williamson County Names Victim in 40-Year-Old 'Orange Socks' Cold Case," KXAN News, August 6, 2019, https://www.kxan.com/news/local/williamson-county/breaking-a-40-year-old-williamson-county-cold-case-victim-has-been-identified/.

Gutschke, Laura. "Investigators Seek Tips on Orange Socks Victim Now Identified as Debra Jackson of Abilene," *Abilene Reporter News*, September 3, 2019, https://www.reporternews.com/story/news/crime/2019/09/03/investigators-seek-help-orange-socks-murder-cold-case-abilene-woman-debra-jackson/2199234001/.

Kunkel, Kayla. "Unsolved: Who Killed Debra 'Orange Socks' Jackson?" *The Western Journal*,

October 30, 2019, https://www.westernjournal.com/unsolved-killed-debra-orange-socks-jackson/.

Osborn, Claire. "40 Years Later, 'Orange Socks' Homicide Victim Identified," *Statesman*, August 7, 2019, https://www.statesman.com/news/20190807/40-years-after-her-death-debra-jackson-of-abilene-identified-as-orange-socks.

Unsolved Cold Case #2—Victim Jason Ellis

Glowicki, Matthew. "Who Killed Bardstown Officer Jason Ellis? 5 Years Later, Nobody Knows," *Courier Journal*, May 22, 2018, https://www.courier-journal.com/story/news/crime/2018/05/22/bardstown-police-officer-jason-ellis-ambush-murder-investigation-mystery/612709002/.

"Police Officer Jason S. Ellis| Bardstown (KY) Police Department," Greater Cincinnati Police Museum, https://police-museum.org/line-of-duty/21th-century/police-officer-jason-s-ellis-bardstown-ky-police-department/.

Ragsdale, Travis. "Seventh Anniversary of Bardstown Police Officer's Murder Brings Renewed Effort for Tips," WDRB News, May 25, 2020, https://www.wdrb.com/news/seventh-anniversary-of-bardstown-police-officers-murder-brings-renewed-effort-for-tips/article_6b8eeec6-9ebb-11ea-9837-e3f3b288cb20.html.

Unsolved Cold Case #3—Victim Shirley Carter

Flesher, Charles. "A&E Documentary Premiering Tuesday Follows Trial of Iowa Farmer Accused of Killing His Mother," *Des Moines Register*, May 24, 2020, https://www.desmoinesregister.com/story/news/2020/05/24/ae-tv-accused-guilty-innocent-crime-documentary-jason-carter-iowa-farmer-murder-trial-killing-mother/5252240002/.

"Jury Finds Jason Carter Not Guilty," Iowa Cold Cases, March 21, 2019, https://iowacoldcases.org/case-summaries/shirley-carter/.

Morris, William. "Federal Appeals Court Revives Jason Carter's Lawsuit Against Father, Iowa Investigators Over His Mother's Killing," *Des Moines Register*, July 21, 2021, https://www.desmoinesregister.com/story/news/crime-and-courts/2021/07/21/jason-carter-lawsuit-against-investigators-revived-appeals-court-murder-shirley-carter/8044655002/.

Nozicka, Luke. "Jason Carter Found Civilly Responsible in Mother's Death, Acquitted of Murder," *The Des Moines Register*, March 21, 2019, https://www.desmoinesregister.com/story/news/crime-and-courts/2019/03/21/jason-carter-bill-shirley-murder-trial-lacona-iowa-knoxville-dateline-nbc-crime-farm-marion-shooting/3232192002/.

Richy, Maria Jacob. "Shirley Carter's Murder: How Did She Die? Who Killed Her?" The Cinemaholic, May 26, 2020, https://www.thecinemaholic.com/shirley-carters-death/.

Unsolved Cold Case #4—Victim William Burnham, Jr.

Brenckle, Lara. "Acquittal in Slaying Case Stuns Prosecutor," *The Patriot News*, May 11, 2007, https://www.pennlive.com/patriotnews/2007/05/acquittal_in_slaying_case_stun.html.

Brenckle, Lara. "Wife Describes Fight Between Lover and Husband," *The Patriot News*, May 9, 2007, https://www.pennlive.com/patriotnews/2007/05/accused_killers_wife_describes.html.

Unsolved Cold Case #5—Victim Elizabeth Hills Grant

Drabble, Jenny Drabble. "Forsyth County Homicide Remains a Secret 47 Years Later," *The Washington Times*, December 4, 2016, https://www.washingtontimes.com/news/2016/dec/4/forsyth-county-homicide-remains-a-secret-47-years-/.

Drabble, Jenny. "47 Years Later, Forsyth County Homicide Remains a Mystery," *The Times News*, December 4, 2016, https://www.thetimesnews.com/news/20161204/47-years-later-forsyth-county-homicide-remains-mystery?fbclid=IwAR2NeWfPv6voFkExUAxH1Edi PcZlVmdO3tW4yaDEH3E1npGKIC5HzXdwFD8.

Drabble, Jenny. "Granddaughter of Woman Stabbed 54 times on Robinhood Road in 1969 Still Searching for Answers," *Winston-Salem Journal,* May 12, 2018, https://journalnow.com/z-no-digital/granddaughter-of-woman-stabbed-54-times-on-robinhood-road-in-1969-still-searching-for-answers/article_6fd6249f-ee95-5d4d-ba78-670d05c29540.html.

Unsolved Cold Case #6—Victim Kevin Brame

Frolik, Cornelius. "20 Years Later: DPD Officer's Unsolved Murder Still Painful," *Dayton Daily News,* November 29, 2019, https://www.daytondailynews.com/news/local/years-later-dpd-officer-unsolved-murder-still-painful/vVQH3976nbcLyGE38fxktN/.

Montalvo, Jackie. "Dayton Police Officer Kevin Brame's Murder Remains Unsolved After 18 Years," *NBC News,* November 4, 2017, https://www.nbcnews.com/feature/cold-case-spotlight/dayton-police-officer-kevin-brame-s-murder-remains-unsolved-after-n817476

Other Sources

Bennette, Margo, and John E. Hess. "Cognitive Interviewing," *FBI Law Enforcement Bulletin,* March 1991: 8–11.

Bettinger, Blaine T. *The Family Tree Guide to DNA Testing and Genetic Genealogy.* Cincinnati, OH: Family Tree Books, 2019.

Chancellor, Arthur S., and Grant D. Graham. *Crime Scene Staging: Investigating Suspect Misdirection of the Crime Scene.* Springfield, IL: Charles C. Thomas, 2017.

Douglas, John E., Ann Burgess, Allen G. Burgess, and Robert K. Ressler. *Crime Classification Manual.* San Francisco, CA: Jossey Bass, 1992.

Douglas, John E., and Corinne Munn. "Violent Crime Scene Analysis, Modus Operandi, Signature, and Staging," *FBI Law Enforcement Bulletin,* February 1992: 1–10.

Eliopulos, Louis N. *Death Investigator's Handbook: A Field Guide to Crime Scene Processing, Forensic Evaluations, and Investigative Techniques.* Boulder, CO: Paladin Press, 1993.

Eliopulos, Louis N. *Death Investigator's Handbook: Expanded and Updated Edition.* Boulder, CO: Paladin Press, 2003.

Fitzpatrick, Colleen, and Andrew Yeiser. *Forensic Genealogy: Revised Edition.* Fountain Valley, CA: Rice Book Press, 2031.

Geberth, Vernon J. *Practical Homicide Investigation: Tactics, Procedures, and Forensic Techniques, Third Edition.* Boca Raton, F: CRC Press, 1996.

Geberth, Vernon J. *Sex-Related Homicide and Death Investigation: Practical and Clinical Perspectives, Second Edition.* Boca Raton, FL: CRC Press, 2010.

Giacalone, Joseph L. *The Criminal Investigative Function: A Guide for New Investigators, Second Edition.* Flushing, NY: Looseleaf Law Publications, 2015.

Kennedy, Joe D. *NCIS Cold Case Squad Outline, Methodology and Protocol for Cold Cases.* September 1996: 1–13.

Nordby, Jon J. *Dead Reckoning: The Art of Forensic Detection.* Boca Raton, FL: CRC Press, 2000.

"The Off-Line Search," *FBI Law Enforcement Bulletin,* March 2005.

O'Hara, Charles E., and Gregory L. O'Hara. *Fundamentals of Criminal Investigation, Fifth Edition, Second Printing.* Springfield, IL: Charles C. Thomas, 1980.

Ressler, Robert K., Ann W. Burgess, and John E. Douglas. *Sexual Homicide Patterns and Motives.* New York: The Free Press, 1992.

Rossmo, D. Kim. *Criminal Investigative Failures.* Boca Raton, FL: CRC Press, Taylor and Francis Group, 2009.

Rossmo, D. Kim. *Geographic Profiling.* Boca Raton, FL: CRC Press, 2000.

Sandoval, Vincent A., and Susan H. Adams. "Subtle Skills for Building Rapport Using Neuro-Linguistic Programming in the Interview Room," *FBI Law Enforcement Bulletin,* August 2011: 1–5.

Smialek, John E., Charlotte Word, and Arthur E. Westveer. "The Microscopic Slide, a Potential DNA Reservoir," *FBI Law Enforcement Bulletin,* November 2000: 18–21.
Snow, Robert L. *Murder 101: Homicide and Its Investigation.* Westport, CT: Praeger, 2005.
Snow, Robert L. *Sex Crimes Investigation: Catching and Prosecuting the Perpetrators.* Westport, CT: Praeger, 2006.
Soderman, Harry, and John J. O'Connell. *Modern Criminal Investigation.* New York: Funk and Wagnalls, 1962.

Media and Organizations

The Carolina Cold Case Coalition, www.coldcasecoalition.org.
The Cold Case Campaign, www.coldcasecampaign.com.
The Cold Case Foundation, http://www.coldcasefoundation.org.
Crime Con, https://www.crimecon.com.
Iowa Cold Cases, https://iowacoldcases.org.
Mid-South Cold Case Initiative, https://www.ms-coldcaseinitiative.com.
National Sexual Assault Kit Initiative, https://www.sakitta.org.
North Carolina Homicide Investigator's Association, http://nchia.org.
Practical Homicide, http://www.practicalhomicide.com.
Project Cold Case, https://www.projectcoldcase.org.
Vidocq Society, https://www.vidocq.org.
The William Burnham, Jr., Death Scene Awareness Project, http://www.deathsceneawareness.org/index.html.
Wrong Man Television Series, https://www.imdb.com/title/tt7708956/.

Law Enforcement Magazines

American Cop Magazine, https://americancopmagazine.com.
American Police Beat, https://apbweb.com.
Blue Line Magazine, https://www.blueline.ca.
California Police Chief Magazine, https://www.californiapolicechiefs.org/california-police-chief-magazine.
Chief of Police Magazine, https://nacoponline.org/index.html.
Crime Magazine, http://crimemagazine.com.
Law Officer Magazine, https://www.policeone.com.
National Sherriff's Association, https://www.sheriffs.org.
Police Chief, http://www.policechiefmagazine.org.
Police Magazine, https://www.policemag.com.
Women Police Magazine, https://iawp.wildapricot.org.

True Crime Podcasts and Blogs

Canadian True Crime, https://canadiantruecrime.ca.
Case File, https://casefilepodcast.com.
Cold, https://thecoldpodcast.com.
Crime Junkie, https://crimejunkiepodcast.com.
Crime Town, https://www.crimetownshow.com.
Crime Writers On, http://www.crimewriterson.com.
Criminal, https://thisiscriminal.com.
The Generation Why, https://genwhypod.com.
The Gumshoe Diary, https://www.thegumshoediary.com.
In the Dark, https://features.apmreports.org/in-the-dark/.
Jenson and Holes the Murder Squad, http://themurdersquad.com.
Real Crime Profile, https://www.realcrimeprofile.com.

Serial, https://serialpodcast.org.
Someone Knows Something, https://www.cbc.ca/radio/sks.
Sword and Scale, http://swordandscale.com.
Trail Went Cold, http://trailwentcold.com.
True Crime Garage, https://www.truecrimegarage.com.
UK True Crime, https://www.uktruecrime.com.
Undisclosed, https://undisclosed-podcast.com.
Unsolved Murders—Parcast, https://www.parcast.com.
The Vanished, http://www.thevanishedpodcast.com.
Your Own Backyard, https://www.yourownbackyardpodcast.com.

Index

A&E 46
acquaintances 24, 30, 36, 274
Adams, Gregory 135
Addock, Jim 5
AFIS 273, 307
Ahrens, John 296
aircraft carrier 235
Alachua County, Florida 69
alibi 89, 173
Alford plea 45
Allen, Jason 48
Al-Qaeda 12
alternate light source (ALS) 28, 169, 276
Alvarez, John 157
American Academy of Forensic Sciences 137, 266
American Bar Association Journal 148
American Investigative Society of Cold Cases 314
America's Most Wanted 46, 52, 188
Ames, Aldrich Hazen 154
analysis 14
AncestryDNA 271
Anderson, Lukis 137
Andrade, Kathy 303
Andrews, Tommy Lee 41
Annie 73
architect 20
Arouet, Francois-Marie 50
Arreola, Jose 49, 238
arrest 15, 34
arsenic 235
Ashley Phosphate Road 18
Asimos, Tom 172
associates 24, 30, 36, 274
attacker 290
auditory 224
Automated Fingerprint Identification System 95
autopsy 30, 164, 290
AWOL 52

baby 74
background check 32, 247
The Badge of Life 68

Bainbridge Avenue 40
Baldonado, Dennis 12, 25
Baldwin, Jason 44
ballistics test 295
bank 124
Bartlett, Dana 4, 10, 20, 53
Bartlett, John 68
bed 18
behavioral clues 11 17, 18, 23
Bell, William 306
Bender, Frank 39, 188
Berkley County Sheriff's Office 73
Berlinger, Joe 44
Bernas, Melanie 259
Bible 6
binders 166
biologists 81
biometrics 94
Blanks, James 91, 107
bleach 53
blood evidence 88
bloodstains 211
Blue Line Training Group 5
Boca Raton, Florida 48
bomb 12
Boon, Rob 22
Boston Cold Case Squad 10, 11, 21, 22
Bradley, Crystal 120
Bradley, Dale 120
Brame, Carla 291
Brame, Kevin 291
Branch, Steven, Sr. 45
Brandt, Oliver 6
Breeze, Dawn 72, 74, 76, 105
Bridge, Donna 218
Brosso, Angela 259
brothers 119
Brown, Wayne 58
Brown, Willie Abner 201, 202
brownies 58
USS *Brumby* 71, 72
Brussel, James A. 290
building blocks 24
Bundy, Ted 65
burglary 294

355

Index

Burnham, William, Jr. 287
Busby, Russell 115
business partner 6
Byers, John Mark 45
bystander 70, 88, 118

Cale, Cynthia M. 136
Camaro 120
Candice 138, 139
canvass 19, 31
Carballo, Alan 21
Cardozo School of Law 40
Carlock, Derrick 40
Carolina Cold Cases Coalition 291, 312
Carter, Bill 285
Carter, Jason 285
Carter, Shirley 285
case file 27
case notes 166
CaseMap 28, 167
cases 12
Cassidy, Dr. James 116
cat and mouse 30
cells 134
Center on Wrongful Convictions at Northwestern University of Law 43
Central Intelligence Agency 153
Chambers, Alice Grant 289
chance meeting 59
changing relationship 35, 36, 170
Charleston, South Carolina 19, 71
checklist 11
checkers 103
Cherry, Kimberley 107
Cherry, Michael 143
Cherry Biometrics 143
chess 13, 103
Chevy Impala 122
Cielto, Ansel Eli 4, 56
cigarette butt 29, 87
Cinemax 48
circumstantial evidence 216
civil suit 140
Clair, Kenneth 44, 50, 144, 215
Clark Alison 144
Clark, Robert 188
CNN 216
Coakley, Marion 40
CODIS 25, 130, 131, 132, 136, 138, 260, 316
cognitive interviewing 37
cognitive technique 222
Cold Case Files 46
Cold Case Foundation 312
cold case homicide unit 3
Cold Justice 47, 70
Coleman, Hector 124
Columbia, South Carolina 301
Columbo 6, 89
common ancestors 273
compassion 5

composite sketch 263
conclusively identified 13, 272
Condit, Gary 48
confession 15
confidential informants 10
Constatino, Virgina 77
Cook, Jay 245
core team expert 2
coroner 131
correlation charts 166
court orders 36
covert meeting 59
coworkers 24, 30, 36, 63, 273
Cox, Huey 40
credit histories 36
crime experts 9
crime scene 23, 30, 168; photos 11, 29
Crime Stoppers 27
Criminal Investigations Division (Code 23) 20
criminalists 276
criminals 278; backgrounds 16
criminologists 13
criminology professor 135
Crumitie, Sharon Cook 107
Crumitie, Timothy 81, 106, 108
CSI 47
Cuba 79
Curry, James Richard 267
Curtis, Officer Milton 300
Cutchall, Lindsay 48
Cuylenborg, Tanya Van 245

Dabney, Bobby 180
dad 4
database 103
Dateline 250
Davis, James Ray 307
Davis, Ricky 252
Dayton Police Department 291
death desk 20
death row stories 216
Death Scene Awareness Project 316
defense attorneys 123
DeLisi, Matt 112
Delta Airlines 100
dental records 211
DeSantis, Christopher 298
Deshazo, David Allan 96, 97
detective 9, 14, 30, 55, 68, 110, 138, 295
Detroit 42
diaries 156, 296
Dickson, David 145
DNA 9, 15, 16, 22, 25, 35, 41, 94, 111, 120, 131, 137, 138, 140, 237, 241; phenotyping 114
DNA Doe Project 258, 266, 282, 314
Docketry, Ivan 125
doctor 172
documentation Dissection 81, 82, 85, 88, 90
Dodge, Angie 49, 244, 248

Dodge, Carol 49, 249
Doe, Jane 265
Doe Fund Me 269
Dripps, Brian Leigh 244, 252
Drizin, Steven 252
duct tape 127
DUI 34, 276
Dunn, Scott 127
DWI 34, 276

Ealey, Gary 240
Ealey, J.D. 240
Early, David 172
Echols, Damien 44
El Dorado County Sheriff's Office 254
El Salvador 303
El Segundo Police Department 300
element of surprise 35, 105
Elkins, Howard B. 304
Ellington, Scott 45
Ellis, Jason 283
Emory University 98
emotional intelligence 60
empathy 5, 30, 61, 62, 68
English, Tal 126
enlisted club 19, 40
ethylene glycol 116
evaluation 14
Evans, Doug 238
Evernote 166
evidence-based investigation 17, 279
evidence custodian 28
evidentiary items 166
ex-boyfriend 24, 110
ex-girlfriends 24
ex-husbands 24
ex-wives 24
eyewitnesses 237

Facebook 28
facts 12, 14
family 24, 30, 35, 36, 62, 273; DNA 159, 255, 271
Family Finder 271
Farrow, David 115
Faulk, Jerry 212
FBI 4, 13, 52, 132, 172, 268, 273
Federal Law Enforcement Training 22
fellowship halls 31
field notes 33, 275
file 27, 103
final crime theory 168
Finding Your Roots 271
fingerprints 15, 110
fire 34
The First 48 Hours 46, 47
Fischer, Bobby 103
fitness trackers 274
Fitzpatrick, Dr. Colleen 244, 256
Fleisher, William 39

Flowers, Curtis 49, 236
foot fetish 146
foot pornography 146
footprints 266
Ford Mustang 306
Forensic Files 182
forensic genealogy 9, 12, 20, 25, 29, 127, 188, 209, 234, 235, 243, 256, 268, 273, 282
USS *Forrestal* 235
Fort Worth 42
four phases 14
Frankl, Victor 221
French, Kathi 72
French, LaDonna Moseley 157
French, Troy 157
Friedman, Lucy N. 67
friends 24, 30, 36, 63, 273
frog 81, 82
Fulton, James 47

Gahn, Norman 179
Gambini, Vinny 91
Gardner, Joseph Martin Luther 52, 53
Garyantes, Mike 284
Geberth, Vernon 116
GedMatch 243, 246, 264, 269, 282
genealogist 9
Genetic Detective 271
genetic genealogy 130
George Washington University 20
Georgetown, Texas 280
Getsinger, Michael 107
ghost suspect 28, 273, 276
Godsey, Mark 183
Golden, Robert 236
Golden State Killer 35, 172, 243
Goose Creek, South Carolina 73
Graff, Bill 288
Grant, Elizabeth 289
grapevine effect 173
Grebas, Jim 73
Green, Michael 255
Green Berets 25
Grinder, John 223
Grodi, Detective Norman 210
gumshoe 110, 147, 155
gunshot residue 295

hair 111 Hawaii 73
half-truths 173
Hamilton, Leisha 127
Hampikian, Greg 249
Hanna, Heather 213
Hartley, Pamela 235
Hartley, Verle Lee 235
Have You Seen Andy? 48
Hellar, Carol Ann 115
Hellar, Dennis 115
Hemphill, Eddie 9, 31
Henderson, Nevada 57

358 Index

Henerey, Detective C.W. "Butch" 10, 19
High Point 1
Hillger, Jason 211
Hinton, Butch 98, 100, 115
Hobson, Tracey Coreen 270
Holes, Paul 243
Holland Street 40
Holmes, Sherlock 89
homicide detective 22
The Homicide Project 5
Horne, Tim 309
hotel rooms 31
Houston Police Department 306
howcatchem 147
Howe, Shauna 119
Hughes, Pete 73
Hunt, Alexa 213
Hunter 157
Hutto, Carol 170
hydrogen peroxide 53
Hylton, Jane 253
hypnosis 263

IAFIS 25, 273
IBIS 95
Idaho Falls 248
Idaho Falls Police Department 250
Idaho Innocence Project 249
Identifinders 257
Identifinders International 258, 260, 314
indirect assessment 174
indoors 16
informants 36, 55
Innocence Project 40, 41, 42
Instagram 28
Integrated Ballistics Identification System 95
International Association of Chiefs of Police 11, 22
International Symposium on Human Identification 259
interrogator 4, 31
Interstate 26 18
Interstate 95 18
interviewer 4
Investigation Discovery 48
investigative files 9
investigators 12, 23, 32, 86
Iowa Division of Criminal Investigation 287
Iowa State University 112

Jackson, Debra 282
Jackson, Diane 306
Jackson, Mark 12, 25, 26
Jade 74, 75
jailhouse informants 36
Janus, Milo 89
Japan National Police 11, 22
Jasper County, South Carolina 73
Jefferys, Alec 94

Jeffries, Stephanie 210
Jenkins, Edna Lee 52, 53
Jericho, New York 304
Jesus Christ 6
Jimmy Ryce Act 41
John Doe Warrant 180
Johnson, Danny Kaye 107
Johnson, Judy 181
Johnstone, Peter 79
journals 156
judges 144
Judges for Justice 249
judicial system 106
jury 69, 123, 144
justice system 66

K-9 unit 120
Kannapolis 107
Katrinak, Andy 189
Katrinak, Joann 189
Keen, Sheila 297
Kelley Point Park 144
Kelly, Elaine 9, 19
Kennecott Mine 120
Kentucky State Police 284
killer 10, 11, 45, 62, 82, 234
Kimbrue, Pamela 35, 85
kinesthetic 224
Kilpatrick, Dean G. 63
knife 18
Korea 146
Krakowiecki, Joseph 259
Kreiner, Nancy 71, 316
Kuby, Ron 117
Kuenn, James Brian 170
Kumra, Raveesh 137

Lacona, Iowa 285
Lain, Jana 285
Largo High School 170
Larison, Doug 264
Las Vegas Metro Police 47
Laser, David Judge 45
Laudenberg, Adolph Theodore 229
Law and Order 47
Lawing, Edwin Christopher 210
Lawrence, Johnny 242
Lazarus, Stephanie 294
Legal Aid Society 41
Lemmon, Richard, Jr. 268
lethal injection 53
letters 156
Levitz, Jacqueline 48
Levy, Chandra 48
LexisNexis 28
libraries 31, 164
lie detector test 286
lies 118
List, Helen 186
List, John 186, 187

Index

list of inconsistencies 34, 86, 90, 167
Long Beach Naval Station 76
Los Angeles Police Department 131, 228, 295
Los Angeles Times 64
Low County serial rapist 10, 19
Lubbock, Texas 126
Lubbock County 68
Lucas, Henry Lee 280
Lukander, Anita Mae Carter 79
Lukander, Bill 79
luminol testing 211
The Long Dance 119, 176

Mack, Matthew 52, 53
magnifying glass 87
mail covers 36, 149
Maine 72
Mann, Patricia Ann 118
Man's Search for Meaning 221
Marine Corps 3, 56, 58
Marion County Sheriff's Office 287
M-Vac 12, 114, 178, 251
Marroquin, Reyna Angelica 303
Marshall, Marcus 160
Marshall University 160
Martinko, Michelle 262
masking tape 100
Mason, Gerald F. 301
McBane, Jesse Allen 118
McCall, Danny DeWayne 52, 53
McClendon, Jerry Allen 96
McCoy, C.D. 292
McDaniel, Mike 99
McLachlin Homicide Task Force
McLauchlin, Melissa 51
McQueen, Lacoy 210
McVeigh, Timothy 150
Meaders, Anastasia 107
means 23, 194
Mebane, North Carolina 309
medical examiner 9, 35, 79, 131, 132, 172, 263
Medical University of South Carolina 63
Melendi, Shannon 98, 115
mentor 10
methodology 9, 10, 22
Metro-Dade Miami Cold Case Unit 10, 11, 21
Miami 98
Miami Dade County 122
Michigan State University of College Law 43
microscopic slides 228
Mid-South Cold Case Initiative 5
Miller, Bryan Patrick 258, 260
minor 4
Misaya, Alhabsy 12
missing persons cases 16
Misskelley, Jessie, Jr. 44
Missy McLauchlin Investigative Task Force 10, 19, 20
modus operandi 23, 201, 277
Momma on a Mission 317

Moore, CeCe 244, 251
Mooresville 107
USS *Moosbrugger* 40
morgue personnel 34
Morrison, Jessie Nicole 240
Morrison, Tammy 240
motive 17, 23, 194
motor scooter 12
Mr. Tipton 91
Mullis, Kary 40
murder 23
murderer 32, 65, 66
Murphy, Erin E. 134
Murphy, Stephen 11, 22
Murray, Tim 11, 21
Murry, Natalie 282
My Cousin Vinny 91

Nance, Gerald 21
Nance, Jerry 53
National Center for Bio-technology Information 63
National Center for Missing and Exploited Children 281, 309
National Crime Information Center 28, 149
National Crime Victims Research and Treatment Center 63
National Institute of Justice 42
National Insurance Crime Bureau 169
National Registry of Exonerations 43
National Sheriffs' Association 11, 22
Naval Criminal Investigative Service 3, 9, 18, 20, 22, 35, 47, 73
Naval Station Mayport 76
Naval Weapons Station in Goose Creek, South Carolina 18
Navy 55
Navy Communications Center 85
NCIC off-line 36, 118, 124, 149
Nedrow, Roy 21, 53
Neufeld, Peter 40
neuro-linguistic programing 223
New Bern, North Carolina 77
New England Patriots 131
New Genetics and Society 141
New York City 67, 125
Next Generation Identification Fingerprint 25, 94, 95
NIBIN 25, 95
Nicholas, Patrick 262
nightmares 104
911 calls 32
Nobel Prize 41
Norfolk Naval Air Station 85
Norman, Oklahoma 68
North Carolina Geological Survey 213
North Carolina Homicide Investigation Association 5, 311
North Carolina State Bureau of Investigation 11, 311

North Carolina State University 210
North Charleston Police Department 10, 18, 21
Northern California Innocence Project 254
November, Steve S. 124

Ofelia 238
office manager 9
Officer Down Memorial Page 69
Ohio Innocence Project 183
Olson, John 243
opportunity 23, 194
Orange County Sheriff's Department 270
"Orange Socks" 289
original crime theory 168
original investigator 34, 168
outdoors 16
Oxygen 47

Paalan, Michael 71, 75, 105
pacemakers 274
Page, Kathy 47, 69, 70
Parabon NanoLabs 114, 160, 246, 271
Paradise Lost 44
paralanguage 226
paramedics 83
Parham, Deborah 18, 19
Parham, Ronald L. 18
park benches 31
parks 31
Parks, Jim 68
passive blood flow 29, 88
passive listening posts 36
pastor 106
pattern of life 33
Pearl Harbor Naval Station 73
Pennsylvania 52
People Magazine 48
perfectionist 4
peripheral witness 36, 173
Perkins, Melanie 48
perpetrator 23, 24, 55
perpetual calendar 179
Perry, Jon Special Agent 11, 22
Perry, Oklahoma 115
Petersen, Nefta 4, 55, 104
Petro, Jim 185
Petry, John 99
Pfeiffer College 1
phenotyping 156, 160, 264
Philippines 11, 12, 22, 25
Phillips, Officer Richard 300
Phoenix Police Department 257
photographs 9, 29, 83, 87; lineup 298
physical evidence 15
pier 20
Pierce, Roger 18
pillow 18
playing cards 246

podcast 119
poison 236
Pokorny, John 281
police 34, 37, 71, 111
polygraph 33, 171, 176, 278
polymerase chain reaction 40
Pope, Nancy 57, 58, 67
Pope, William 56, 104
Portland, Maine 71
post offense behavior 33, 176, 275
Postiglione, Pat 43
pre-event stressors 273
Press, Margaret 258
prison staff 36
private investigator 140
private residence 16
program manager 20
programming 14
Project Cold Case 317
property room 165
prosecutor 9, 28, 66, 110, 123, 165
protocol 22
Pruitt, Eryk 119
PTSD 69
Puglisi, Andy 48
Pure Gold Forensics 314

Rae-Venter, Dr. Barbara 309
Raleigh Police Department 210
Ramirez, Melissa-Ruiz 260
Ramsey, JonBenet 48
rapists 45
rapport 223
Rasmussen, Nels 294
Rasmussen, Sherri 293
Raziq, David 135
relatives 63
rescue squad 34
resolution 234
restaurant 12
Rigby, Carmen 236
River Bend 77
Rivers, David 11, 21
Roberts, Lisa Marie 143
Robinson, Sue Ann 49
rock analysis 209
Rodgers, Linda Faye 215
Rogers, Curtis 243
Rorrer, Patricia 44, 50, 189
Rowan County 107, 108
Ruby, Ronald 49
Rueben, John 293
Ruff, Bryan 120
ruse 195
Ryan, Suzanna 144, 217

Sacramento County Crime Lab 255
St. Thomas, Virgin Islands 53
Salas, Evaristo 49, 239
Saldana, Carlos, Jr. 124

Index

saliva 169
Santa Monica police 295
Santa Strangler 228
Sayyaf, Abu 12, 26
Scheck, Barry 40
Schneeberger, Dr. John 139
screwdriver 57
Seat, Michael 247
semen 169, 228, 261
Sentell, Jean Marie 20
serial murderers 45
sexual assault kit 113, 315
Shakur, Tupac 48
Shatzkes, Art 221
Shaw University 210
Shepherd, Dr. Richard 128
Siegler, Kelly 47, '70
signature 23, 277
Silvani, Mary Edith 267
Simmons, Indira 52
single perpetrator 278
sister 58
ski mask 85, 86, 201
Smaldone, Ed 160
Smith, Carlton Tyrone 78
Smith, Tim 127
Smith, Vonda 44, 50, 239, 240
Snapchat 28
snapshot kinship inference 251
Snohomish County Sheriff's Office 246
SNP 257
social media 36
sociologist 112
solvability factors 16, 164
Sorenson Forensics 282
special agent 22
Special Operations Division 20
Stafford, Gene 89
staging 23, 277
Starz 50
statement analysis 34, 92
statement time-check charts 166
steak knife 136
Stevens, Bob 48
Stevik, Lyle 268
Stewart, Derrick Bobo 236
STR-mix 145
subpoenas 36
Sunnyside, Washington 238
Super Bowl 130
Super 8 Motel 18
surveillance 36
suspect 13, 23
suspect-based investigation 17, 279
Sutton, Josiah 135
Swindoll, Charles 221
sympathy 62

Tahan, Annie 71
Tahan, Cheyenne 72
Tahan, Jamie 72
Tahan, Sean 72
tacticians 13
Talbott, William 244
Tapp, Christopher 44, 49, 233, 248
Tardy, Bertha 236
Tardy Furniture 236
technology 24, 25, 93
television 76
tenacity 24, 93
terrorist 12
theme-development 37, 174
USS *Theodore Roosevelt* 124
Thieus, Marshal 22
thin blue line 5
Thompson, William 135
Thousand Oaks, California 64
Three Billboards Outside Ebbing, Missouri 70
Time magazine 64
timelines 166
TNT 47
Todd, Ira 49, 242
toolbox 25
Townsend, Jerry 121
trash pull 36, 149, 152
triangle 54
TrueAllele 145
Twain, Mark 118
23andme 271
Twitter 28

undercover operation 185
unidentified bodies 16
United States 10
U.S. Department of Justice 42
United States Department of Justice Weed and Seed Task Force 20
U.S. Marshall Service 108
U.S. Navy 3
United States Postal Service 155
United States Supreme Court 237
United States Virgin Islands 4, 10, 20
The University of California Newark Center for Science and Society 43
University of Michigan Law School 43
updated crime theory 168
Utrecht Police Department in the Netherlands 11, 22

Vaught, Kimberly Shawn 9, 19, 40
verification 14
Versed 139, 140
vertical blood droplets 29, 88
victim 5, 11, 16, 23, 36, 272
Victim Services Agency 67
victimology 19, 26
Victoria 245
videos 29
Vidocq, Eugene Francois 39

Vidocq Society 39, 40, 42, 259, 313
Virgin Islands 53, 54
Virgin Islands Homicide Task Force 21
Virginia State Police Department 11, 22
Voltaire 50

Walker, Darius 3
Walsh, John 46
Walter, Richard 39, 128, 146
warrant 15
Warren, Marlene 297
Warren, Michael 296, 297
Washington, DC 11
Webber Seavey Award 11, 22
Weigel, Diana 288
Weigel, Dustin 288
Wellman, Ashley 69
Wexler, Chuck 112
white noise 272
Whitley 157
Whitt, John Russell 308
Whitt, Robert "Bobby" Adam 308
Whitt, Young Hwa Cho 308
Whittle, Richard H. 85, 86, 87
whodunit 147
Wicoff, Robert 136
Wiggins, John 5

William Burnham Jr. Death Scene Awareness Project 71, 316
Williams, Matthew 52, 53
Williams, Roger 52, 53
Williamson County Cold Case Unit 281
Willoughby Bay 85
Wilson, Deborah 145
Winona, Mississippi 236
Winston, Salem 289
wire taps 36
witness 30, 36, 70, 88, 93, 108, 218; statements 34
Wolf, Dick 47
Worth, Sam 58
Wrong Man 2, 3, 43, 44, 49, 144, 215, 239, 242

Y-DNA 257
Y-STR 257, 262
Yant Martin 183
Yarborough, Sarah 257, 261
yoga 64
USS *Yorktown* (CG- 48) 20
You Must Remember 268
Young, Donnie Lamon 136
Yusko, Alanda Jean 77

Zamboanga, Phillipines 12, 25

www.ingramcontent.com/pod-product-compliance
Ingram Content Group UK Ltd.
Pitfield, Milton Keynes, MK11 3LW, UK
UKHW041921140426
5217IPUK00014B/264

www.ingramcontent.com/pod-product-compliance
Ingram Content Group UK Ltd.
Pitfield, Milton Keynes, MK11 3LW, UK
UKHW041921140426
5217IPUK00014B/264